NEW PERSPECTIVES IN THE THEOLOGY OF JUDAISM

NEW PERSPECTIVES IN THE THEOLOGY OF JUDAISM

by
Shubert Spero

Boston
2013

Copyright © 2013 Academic Studies Press
All rights reserved
ISBN 978-1-64469-672-9
ISBN 978-1-61811-268-2 (electronic)

Cover design by Ivan Grave

Published by Academic Studies Press in 2013
28 Montfern Avenue
Brighton, MA 02135, USA
press@academicstudiespress.com
www.academicstudiespress.com

Contents

Note From the Publisher
  The Chair, the Incumbent, and the Donors. 7
Introduction 9

PART I
Viewing Judaism as a Whole

Chapter 1
  Is There an Indigenous Jewish Theology?. 24
Chapter 2
  Toward a Philosophy of Modern Orthodoxy. 41
Chapter 3
  Is Judaism an Optimistic Religion?. 55
Chapter 4
  The Meaning of Existentialism for Orthodoxy. 69

PART II
Torah in Depth

Chapter 5
  The Biblical Stories of Creation, the Garden of Eden,
  and the Flood: History or Metaphor? 82
Chapter 6
  Paradise Lost or Outgrown?. 98
Chapter 7
  Multiplicity of Meaning as a Device in Biblical Narrative. . . . 118
Chapter 8
  Torat Hashem/Torat Moshe:
  Exploring their Respective Roles 133

PART III
Reaching for the Heights

Chapter 9
Is God Truly Unknowable? 166

Chapter 10
Love of God. 182

Chapter 11
Selfhood and Godhood in Jewish Thought
and Modern Philosophy 194

Chapter 12
Unity of God as Dynamic of Redemption 208

PART IV
The Analytic in Action

Chapter 13
Toward an Ethical Theory of Judaism 220

Chapter 14
What is Self-theory, and Does Judaism Need One?....... 244

Chapter 15
Judaism and the Aesthetic 275

Chapter 16
Providential History and the Anthropic Principle 299

Chapter 17
The Role of Reason in Jewish Religious Belief 316

PART V
History Come to Life

Chapter 18
The Religious Meaning of the State of Israel 338

Chapter 19
Religious Zionism: What is It?........................ 357

Chapter 20
Does Messianism Imply Inevitability? 368

Acknowledgements 385
Index 386

Note From the Publisher

The Chair, the Incumbent, and the Donors

In January 1983, Bar-Ilan University in Israel, under the presidency of Professor Emanuel Rackman, announced the establishment of the Irving I. Stone Chair in Basic Jewish Thought, with Professor Shubert Spero as its inaugural incumbent. The Chair was chartered to undertake the academic examination of the implications of Judaism, especially Jewish morality and history, for contemporary society, and was designed to serve as a vehicle for teaching, research, and publication in this area. In establishing the Chair's Endowment Fund, Irving Stone (1909-2000) wrote in the charter document:

> ...the main reason for our family's establishment of the Chair was to make it possible for Shubert Spero, who was then retiring after 33 years as our spiritual leader in Cleveland, to bring his important centrist views of Judaism to the attention of the Israeli public.

Each term of his subsequent 29-year academic career at Bar Ilan, the incumbent taught two sections of his signature year-long course entitled *Dat u'Musar,* "Religion and Morality," in which he expounded on the special nature and role of morality in Judaism to the more than 3,000 students who took his course over the years. Under the aegis of the Chair, Spero published innumerable articles in academic journals as well as for the local press, lectured widely in Israel and abroad, and for ten years delivered the annual Irving I. Stone Lecture at the College of Jewish Studies in Cleveland, Ohio. His research during this period resulted in the publication of two works: *Holocaust and Return to Zion: A Study in Jewish Philosophy of History* (2000) and *Aspects of Rabbi Joseph Dov Solovetchick's Philosophy of Judaism* (2009).

Preface. **The Chair, the Incumbent, and the Donors**

The link to the Stone funding has an additional dimension, beyond the academic. This dimension comes through in the warm words of a personal note written by Mr. Morry Weiss, chairman of the Stone Foundation:

> Shubert Spero and his wife Iris have been dear friends for well over 50 years. As my wife and I celebrate our 50 years of marriage, I recall that when I was courting Judy, it was Iris who volunteered to be my character witness. She assured my future in-laws (Irving and Beatrice Stone) that their daughter was choosing her mate wisely. For Iris taking that leap of faith on my behalf, and in honor of our golden anniversary, I am delighted to have the opportunity to show our deep appreciation for two individuals we so greatly admire by making possible the publication of this current volume of the rabbi's most insightful essays.

Introduction

The words "new" and "theology" in the title of this volume may sound ominous to traditionalists. Let me therefore at the very outset set forth the meaning of these terms according to their primary current use and outline the general thrust of this work. The term "theology" has come to mean simply a rational analysis of religious beliefs, or a "philosophy of religion." The reason I use the word "theology" instead of "philosophy" is because it is considered the more appropriate term to use when the analysis is being done by one who stands within the religion being analyzed, in short a believer. The term "philosophy" is best understood as describing an activity in which certain types of questions are directed at almost any subject matter. These are inquiries into the overriding purpose or underlying principles of any discipline or enterprise. That is, they are questions which are the most general in nature, seeking a picture of the whole, or alternatively the most basic, seeking to uncover the ultimate nature of things. In pursuit of these philosophical questions one is expected to use a method of thinking which is at once analytic and critical, rather than speculative, giving priority to the search for meaning before looking for the truth, a method which requires justification for any truth-claims. In this view, which sees philosophy primarily as a method of inquiry, the goal is not, as it has been in the past, to wed or reconcile Judaism with some "outside" existing philosophic system but rather to develop a rational understanding (theology) which is indigenous in the sense that it grows out of the primary sources of Judaism.

It is safe to say that philosophical questions in the sense just described are generally not dealt with in Judaism's primary sources, i.e., the *Tanach*, or Written Torah. Except perhaps for the Book of Job and some isolated verses elsewhere, *Tanach* in its three divisions is essentially a library of "first order" statements about history, law, morality, poetry, exhortations, promises, and visions of the future.[1] It is not reflective. It does not ask questions of itself. It is in rabbinic literature that we first begin to find short excursions into what we might call philosophical inquiry. Chapter 1 discusses in greater detail the role of philosophy in Judaism.

Beginning, however, with Saadia Gaon (882-942) and continuing up to the present, elements of the beliefs and practices of Judaism have been subjected to systematic rational analysis, with the results constituting aspects of the theology of Judaism.

Now this is where the term "perspective" becomes relevant. While anyone claiming to be doing philosophy must abide by the accepted methods, i.e., must be critical, coherent, consistent, and comprehensive, there is an individual subjective element, usually overlooked, that is often present from the very beginning of the process. We may call this the individual's "perspective," that is, certain unexpressed presuppositions or attitudes with which the individual views reality and by which he evaluates the relative importance of things. This explains why different individuals examining the same facts can arrive at different, sometimes mutually exclusive, conclusions. Thus, for example, it is clear that one of the presuppositions of Maimonides, a doctrine that in his day was considered self-evident, was that human reason was capable of attaining knowledge of the metaphysical realm. Today, however, having shown this belief to be largely incorrect, we no longer put any credence in logical proofs for the existence of God, as Maimonides did. Another illustration of "perspective" in Jewish theology is the view that different thinkers had of the importance of the principle of the Creation of the universe "out of nothing" (*creatio ex nihilo*). While Saadia thought it to be a pillar of Jewish belief, in the sense that the very fact of the existence of the world (ourselves included), is clear evidence of the reality and moral nature of God, Maimonides was ready to relinquish the concept

---

[1] Thus in Habakkuk 1:2, 3 and Jeremiah 12:1, the prophets in anguish question God's governance of the world when they see the wicked prosper. The Book of Job in its entirety is devoted to this question, sometimes called "theodicy," understood as the vindication of Divine Providence. Isolated verses such as the following from Ecclesiastes seem to pose theological issues: "Who knows the spirit of man whether it goes upward and the spirit of the beast whether it goes downward to the earth" (Eccles. 3:21).

of *Creatio ex nihilo* if Aristotle had proven the eternity of the universe.[2] Therefore, our endeavor to present "new perspectives" in Jewish theology does not imply suggesting changes in the core beliefs or practices of Judaism but is rather an attempt to look at some of the classical material with different eyes, to focus on elements heretofore ignored, and perhaps to ask questions not considered important in the past.

Viewing Judaism as a Whole

We have said that one of the typical approaches of philosophy is to seek a picture of the whole, to lift oneself above the trees to catch a glimpse of the forest. This is important because philosophically the whole is often greater and more interesting than the brute sum of its parts, so that he who seeks reliable knowledge of any entity must examine it from the overall perspective as well. So it is with Judaism. In early periods, when we were preoccupied with getting to know the "trees," the concept of "forest" rarely arose. However, once the dynamics of history does its work and various changes take place, certain pressures are created that necessitate a knowledge of the "forest." For once we realize that the "forest" of our cultural habitat is not infinite, it becomes important to know its extent, its boundaries, and what is beyond. Once we realize there are other "forests," there is a desire to compare their overall features with our own, the better to appreciate it. So it is with Judaism. As our people were exposed to other cultures and belief systems, it became vital to have a grasp of the overall goals and purposes of Judaism so as to identify its parameters such that comparisons may be made. Also, once Judaism was confronted by home-grown sects which claim to be the "true" Israel, it was necessary to have an understanding of the basic principles of our faith so as to know when one might have strayed beyond its boundaries.

In Chapter 2 we analyze the theological underpinnings and overall features of Modern Orthodoxy to show how it differs from traditional Orthodoxy, and why it claims to be a more authentic version of Judaism than what is known today as *haredi* Judaism.

---

[2] See Saadia Gaon, *The Book of Beliefs and Opinions* (New Haven: Yale University Press, 1948), Treatise I, pp. 36-81; and Moses Maimonides, *Guide for the Perplexed*, trans. M. Friedlander (New York: E. P. Dutton & Co., 1942), I:71, I:113.

Introduction

In recent decades the general mood cultivated by religion has shifted from the naive optimism of progressive Judaism and even from the joyous outlook of hasidism to a more sober view of the human condition. Is the goal of religion to give man "peace of mind" or "peace of soul"? Chapters 3 and 4 deal with these questions and examine the sources in Judaism which deal with the nature of the religious consciousness and its possible connections with a popular school of thought known as Existentialism, as well as the contribution in this regard of the teaching of Rabbi Joseph B. Soloveitchik.

Torah in Depth

The primary source of Judaism is, as we have stated, the written Torah emanating from Divinity and transmitted to man via a process called *nevuah* (prophecy). However, the medium in which these teachings reach man is a particular natural language (called *ivrit*), that is, words formed into sentences which follow rules of syntax and semantics. Unlike some other religions in which the word of the divinity is received in the form of ambiguous oracles or complex codes or obscure expressions which can only be unscrambled by a privileged elite, the primary purpose of the Torah is to have it readily understood by all who use the language. Thus, Moses assures the people, "But the word is very close to you in your mouth and in your heart so that you may do it" (Deut. 30:14). And in writing the words of the Torah on plastered stones upon entering the land of Canaan, Moses is commanded to write *be'eir hetev* (very plainly). In further elaboration of this point, the rabbis maintained that *dibra torah kelashon b'nai adam*, "the Torah speaks in the language of men," which suggests several things: first, that the language of the Torah is not a private language but that the meanings of the words and the ways in which they are used are the same as they are for all native speakers. Also, the sages are saying that the Torah can be expected to use language in all of the many marvelous forms that human beings have developed for their different kinds of communication: as precise description, as dramatic narrative, as poetry, by wedding sound to image in expression of the full range of human emotions. Thus, to truly grasp the Torah text, one must not only comprehend the lexical meaning of the words but be aware of the type of literary product involved. Law, narrative, epic poetry, moral exhortation, metaphor: each requires a different method of interpretation. Of course, in terms of the Halakhah (law), the tradition has preserved various formal rules of exegesis with which to guide the individual in his interpretation of the biblical text.

In recent years, developments in linguistic and literary criticism have made us more sensitive to the possibilities implicit in different types of literature. In Chapters 5 and 6 I offer a fresh approach to the material in the opening chapters of Genesis, based upon an awareness of the nuances implicit in metaphor.

Indeed, we learn much from the rabbinic comparison of the language of the Torah to human language. Nonetheless, in truth human language itself, and the ability of a human being to learn and create in language, remains a marvelous mystery. How do our brains convert the sounds of the words (phonemes) into "meanings"? Where are these "meanings" stored when we are not thinking about them? What is the "connection" between two personalities in meaningful dialogue? If there is mystery in human speech, how much more so in the case of the "word of God," by whose power "the heavens were made," and whose presence in the Torah text mysteriously guides the historical process?[3]

In Chapter 7 we analyze several Torah texts to show how an awareness of the ability of the word of God to bear multiple meanings enables us to appreciate how

> My word which goes forth from My mouth
> shall not return to Me empty
> except it accomplishes that which I please
> and made the thing where I sent it prosper (Isa. 55:10, 11).

Who wrote the Torah, and who is the author of the Torah, are not the same question. This is particularly the case if the questions are being asked within the framework of the Jewish tradition, for then, you will get two different answers. The Torah was written by Moses, whereas the Author, i.e., the originator of the words is God, the Creator. These two principles, one theological and one historical, are included in the response recited by the congregation in the synagogue service when the

---

[3] "By the *word* of God the heavens were made" (Psalms 36:6). For more on how the text of the Torah helps to guide history, see Shubert Spero, *Holocaust and Return to Zion: A Study in Jewish Philosophy of History* (Jersey City, NJ: Ktav Publishing House, 2000), Chapter 7, 251-257.

Torah scroll is held aloft: "And this is the Torah that Moses set before the children of Israel by the mouth of God by the hand of Moses" (Num. 9:23; Deut. 4:44). While some aspects of how this process came about are discussed in rabbinic literature, a more definitive account is offered by Maimonides (Rambam):

> It is our belief that the whole of the Torah came to Moshe from God in a manner which is metaphorically called "speaking." But the real nature of that communication is unknown to all except Moshe to whom it came. In receiving the Torah, Moshe was like a scribe writing from dictation, the whole of it, its chronicles, its narratives and its prescriptions.[4]

While large segments of the Torah, particularly the "statutes and judgments," are indeed presented as "spoken by God to Moses," other historical portions are simply described by an anonymous narrator in third person. At what point did this Divine dictation take place? If, however, the Torah speaks "in the language of men," it should be possible to approach the text objectively, read it analytically from beginning to end in order to learn what we can from *within*, without presuppositions, concerning its composition. I have attempted to do this in Chapter 7, seeking to determine the sense in which the Torah can be called both *Torat Moshe* and *Torat Hashem*.

Reaching for the Heights

The concept of God has always been and remains one of the great challenges to theology. Indeed, the literal meaning of the term "theology" is "the knowledge of God." But for Judaism, there can be no such thing, for there is hardly anything we can know of God since He is transcendent, above and beyond human comprehension. And yet (here is the paradox), for so many believers God is the most alive, the most real, the most vital Presence of all, truly the very ground of our existence! So who needs definitions?

Maimonides, the foremost Jewish theologian of the Middle Ages, was very strict in safeguarding the "otherness" of God. While the Torah reports

---

[4] Commentary on the Mishnah *Perek Helek*, *Sanhedrin*.

many things about God, Maimonides submitted all of its statements to rational analysis and shows that all descriptions of God can be reduced to two categories. First there are "action predicates," that is, words that are not really referring to God Himself but rather to His actions. Thus, to say that God is merciful is to say that God's acts, if done by a person, would be called merciful. However, in regard to what Maimonides calls "essential attributes," for example, that "God lives," and "wills" and possesses "knowledge" and "power," here we *are* talking about God Himself. But at this point we come up against the limits of language. The only meaning that these terms, "life," "knowledge," "power," etc., can have for us comes from our own human experience. How do we know whether these terms are at all appropriate when used to apply to God? Thus was born the popular notion that, at least according to Maimonides, God is completely unknowable, completely beyond human comprehension. The only way man can grow in the knowledge of God is, paradoxically, to increase the number of things that one can say God is not.

However, in spite of the logical rigor of Maimonides's analysis, which seems to shut out completely the experiential aspect of the religious consciousness, I argue in Chapter 9 that his theory, properly understood, nevertheless leaves room to rationally assert what our religious sentiments urge upon us.

Most of the attributes of God called "essential" by Maimonides, such as His existence, wisdom, and power, are inferred from what we are told about God in the Torah. However, there is one particular attribute that is specifically and repeatedly attributed to God, and that is His unity. Emblematic of its importance is that it has been incorporated into the liturgy and is proclaimed twice daily:

Hear O Israel, the Lord our God the Lord is One (Deut. 6:4)

We also read: "The Lord alone did lead him and there was no strange god with Him" (Deut. 32:12). "See now that I even I am He and there is no god with Me" (Deut. 32:39).

In a historical sense this emphasis has been seen as natural, since this was the great announcement of monotheism to a world that had been dominated by polytheism. However, to the theologian, the concept of God's Unity (*achdut hashem*) has always implied more than the arithmetic one-and-not-two, the denial of polytheism. It has always stirred great philosophic interest. Thus, in regard to the question of whether anthropomorphic descriptions of God in the Torah are to be taken as implying that the Deity may have corporeal form, Maimonides rules the possibility out completely, on logical grounds, as incompatible with God's unity. For, he argues, *achdut* implies not only "one and not two," but also simplicity, "one and not composite." Being material in any way would oppose this, as it necessarily means that He was composed of parts and thus not "one" in the sense of simplicity. More importantly, Maimonides defined God as the "First Existant who brought every existing thing into being. All existing things ... exist only through His true existence. If it could be supposed that He did not exist it would follow that nothing else could possibly exist"[5] This important concept states that God is not only the Creator of the universe, who created in an act which took place in the distant past, but is also the abiding ground or support of all being. Maimonides sees this notion as a corollary of *achdut hashem*: "The Lord He is God there is none else beside Him" (Deut. 4:35). That is, God is One in the sense of singularity. He is unique. Only He is truly real and has necessary and absolute existence. In other words, His existence is part of His essence. Everything else in the world, including ourselves, exists but only in a contingent sense, that is, we didn't have to be.

In Chapter 10, I explore a rather neglected aspect of God's unity, which is its implications for the historical process of Redemption. While traces of this connection abound in the tradition, I have not found any serious philosophic treatment of this subject. Our analysis will help to explain the importance of the *Shema* in Jewish life and thought.

However, the Torah itself draws the proper inference for the individual's relationship to God from the absolute nature of His unity. If indeed "there is *nothing else* beside Him," then:

> You shall love the Lord your God with all your heart and with all your soul and with all your might. (Deut. 6:5)

That God's singularity deserves man's exclusive devotion, loyalty and obedience seems true enough. But "love"? How can you love someone you cannot see or really know? Furthermore, can "love" be commanded?

---

[5] Moses Maimonides, *Mishneh Torah, Hilkhot Yesodei Hatorah* 1:1-3.

Chapter 11 subjects Maimonides's interpretation of the commandment to love God to critical analysis and demonstrates how, while maintaining the traditional framework, we can generate a genuine love for God as a response not so much to His wisdom as to His goodness.

One of the enduring themes of theology is the question of God's ongoing relationship with the world. We hear of such terms as General Providence and Special Providence, Open Miracles and Hidden Miracles. At one point Maimonides, in his treatment of this subject, draws a suggestive analogy between the relationship of God to the world and that of man's soul (self, personality) to his body.

> In man there is a certain force which unites the organs of the body, controls them and gives to each of them what it requires. So in the universe there exists a certain force which controls the cosmos, which sets in motion the chief and principal parts and gives them the motive power for governing the rest. That force is God.[6]

Theologians have found this similarity most helpful in elucidating different problems relating to our understanding of God. Man's "soul" is considered to be a non-material, spiritual essence operating within, yet able to impact upon, a material system. So too is God a non-material, spiritual essence in constant relationships with and impacting upon a physical universe.[7] Of course, both are a mystery in the sense that we do not know how it happens. We cannot explain how instructions which originate in the spiritual realm can translate into and impact upon the physical material universe. However, in regard to the soul, man knows of its existence and its activities from the inside. I am my "soul," and I need no proofs of its reality. While the sages were well aware of the pedagogical importance of perceiving God as a model of moral behavior, "As He is compassionate, so be you," we wish to suggest that perhaps in regard to epistemology the line of reasoning might run in the opposite direction. That is, just as we are convinced of the existence of our "soul-self" without "proofs," so we might believe in God, who is the "soul" of the world. In Chapter 12 we examine the validity of this type of reasoning.

---

[6] Maimonides, *Guide*, I:72.

[7] This is clearly the Torah view, as may be inferred from Gen. 1:26 and Gen. 2:7. See my articles in Numbers 675 and 831 of Bar Ilan's Weekly Page, *daf shvui*.

The Analytic in Action

As we indicated earlier, the philosophical approach is marked not only by its seeking a picture of the whole but also by its analytic method, its drive to understand the constituent elements, the underlying structure of a phenomenon. The next five chapters (13-17) exemplify philosophical analysis in action. We have chosen five very broad subjects: morality, the self, history, the aesthetic, and religious belief. Clearly, each of these subjects constitutes the framework for wide areas of Jewish belief and practice.

In Judaism, morality, in the form of codes of behavior, includes the entire area of *mitzvot bein adam le-chaveiro ubein adam le-behamto* (commandments between man and his fellow man and between man and his animals) and, as such, receive attention and elaboration as part of the Halakhah. However, in terms of philosophical analysis, i.e., ethical theory, the subject has failed to elicit adequate attention even from our classical theologians. In Chapter 13 we examine the general role of morality in Judaism and particularly the relationship of God to moral values. The question as to whether there exists a morality "outside" of the Halakhah is also treated.

The *self* is the reflective awareness of that non-material essence which is the basis of our sense of self-identity. Something we tend to locate between our eyes is the arbiter between the urgings of the *yetzer ha-ra* (evil inclination) and the *yetzer tov* (good inclination), the entity we would identify as our *neshama* (soul). Modern Jewish thinkers have not gone much beyond the few hints thrown out by our sages, as the subject straddles the boundary between philosophy and psychology. In Chapter 14 we outline what a Jewish self-theory might look like.

For a human being there can be no more all-embracing concept than that of history—an ongoing process in which we are all embedded and by which we are all affected. For the Jew, however, the subject of history is particularly meaningful.[8] All of the different contents, narratives, laws, poetry are presented to us against the background of world and Jewish history. It is in and through history that the God of Israel manifests Himself, which is why we are commanded to study it: "Remember the days of old, understand the years of many generations" (Deut. 32:7).

---

[8] See Shubert Spero, *Holocaust and Return to Zion: A Jewish Philosophy of History* (New Jersey: Ktav Publishing, 2000).

Introduction

In Chapter 16 we discuss the question as to whether a distinctive philosophy of history can be drawn from the Torah.

The aesthetic in its many forms—music, drama, visual arts, and plastic arts—plays an important and valued role in all of our lives. We particularly appreciate the ways in which it enhances many aspects of our religious experience: the singing and chanting during prayer, the music and dancing at religious celebrations, the literary qualities of Torah narration, the beauty of religious ritual objects. In this area as well, philosophy by its analytic approach may be able to provide a deeper understanding. Is beauty in the eyes of the beholder only? What does the Psalmist mean when he announces, "The voice of God is in beauty"? (Psalms 29:4). What is the significance of the fact that God has provided us with a universe which not only exhibits natural beauty but allows man to create beauty? These are some of the questions we deal with in Chapter 15.

Finally, the most basic subject of all: *religious belief*. Many of us, steeped in our traditions, take our religious beliefs for granted as they seem self-evident. But what should be our response when our child or perhaps an interested stranger asks us, "Why do you believe in God?" or "How do you know there is a God, and that He revealed this Torah to Moshe and the *bnei yisrael*?" We treat these questions in Chapter 17.

It is clear that all of these basic concepts are not subjects that are peculiar to Judaism or even to religion. Indeed, some of these terms (morality, self, aesthetics) as abstract concepts are not found in the Torah as such, although the subject matter they denote certainly is. Each of these concepts has been identified and given systematic thought since the days of Plato and Aristotle. Therefore, our approach has been to consider critically what philosophy in general has discovered regarding these subjects and only then to study the relevant material in Judaism. Our goal, however, in regard to all of these subjects has been to apply the analytic method of the philosophic approach in an attempt to formulate what might be called Judaism's overall view of these basic concepts.

History Come to Life

Questions such as those pertaining to God or to the grounds for the distinction between the moral good and the moral evil can readily be seen to belong to the domain of theology. However, questions regarding the religious significance of the State of Israel strike people as being of a more political or religious or even halakhic nature. In reality, however, given that we are discussing this within the context of Judaism, the question is very much a matter of Jewish theology. In fact, it touches upon a central issue within the Jewish philosophy of history.[9]

It is generally agreed that the biblical God manifests Himself primarily in history, and that the divine plan for man plays itself out within that framework. Over the years, the view that grew into a consensus was that the main components of God's plan were already in place by the time of the destruction of the Second Temple. All that remained was for the people of Israel to acknowledge their waywardness and return to God via Torah observance, and the final redemption would ultimately come. Therefore, the condition of exile and dispersion, thus understood, consigned Israel to a sort of limbo in which its full-time struggle was mainly to maintain its physical survival and Jewish identity. As a result, up to the beginning of the nineteenth century conventional wisdom held that nothing of positive significance was to be expected in history before the occurrence of radical and clearly recognizable events associated with the redemption with all of its restorative and utopian elements. This view remained dominant because nothing came up on the screen of history to challenge it. Beginning, however, with the so-called Emancipation-Enlightenment and more so after the radical changes in the condition of the people of Israel and the land of Israel that took place since then, thoughtful people have felt compelled to reexamine the sources of our philosophy of history, but this time in light of *both* Jewish and world history of the past two millennia. This has led us to a rather different understanding of the reason for Israel's long exilic existence. It should not be seen simply as one long theologically static situation in which the people of Israel tread water, suffering patiently until such time as Divine Providence deems their shortcomings expiated so that they may return home. It was not a situation in which Israel's fate and destiny depended solely on the application of the principle of reward and punishment. The people of Israel may have been driven from their land, and the Temple destroyed, in 70 CE because of their "sins," but their sins alone did not determine the *length* of the exile. Its incredible length (1878, years as compared to 70 after the destruction of the First Temple) was primarily

---

[9] Spero, *Holocaust and Return to Zion*.

due not, as was thought, to "sin" alone but to the need to await essential developments in the education of the messengers (the Jewish people), the elaboration of the message (fuller development of the Halakhah and Jewish theology), and in general conditions in which the message was to be proclaimed (organized world order, secular global economy, realization of the limits of human knowledge, developments in communication, universal access to information). When all of these developments had come to pass and their Divinely-guided interaction bore fruit, a Jewish State in the land of Israel was proclaimed. However, centuries of isolation had dulled the perception and distorted the vision of many of our leaders so that they were unable to realize the positive significance of many elements of "modernity" for the advancement of Torah goals. Furthermore, the deep disillusionment caused by many "false Messiahs" and aborted movements of the "preemption of the End" rendered religious leaders overly cautious to the point of being incapable of recognizing even authentic signs of the redemption.

However, for those willing to take an independent look at the sources of the Jewish philosophy of history and then to analyze the present reality, the following judgment will seem inescapable: the sixty-five-year existence of an economically viable, militarily defensible sovereign Jewish state within the historic boundaries of Eretz Israel, with a population nearing six million Jews from communities world-wide, is unquestionably the handiwork of a Providential God. This is the case not only because of the improbability of the many micro-events combining to make it occur but also because the ultimate ingathering of the Jewish people to their homeland had been foretold from the very beginning by the Hebrew prophets. Close examination of the grounds of these crucial developments will show that in the main they were made possible by conditions produced by the modern age, indicating that the "singularity" we call the re-establishment of the State of Israel could not have happened, at least by non-miraculous means, much earlier or later.

In Chapters 18 and 19 we discuss the religious significance of the modern State of Israel and the special obligations that a recognition of this significance imposes upon the Jew.

One of the key elements in any discussion of the eschatology of Judaism is the concept of Messianism and the effect it has upon believers. Many historians, in portraying the different failed messianic movements, from Bar Kochba to Sabbatai Zvi, emphasize the irrational force and fervor which seem to infect their followers and the harm which these movements bring to their followers and to Judaism as a whole. Israel's victory in the Six Day War, with the attendant liberation of the Temple Mount and the Tomb of the Patriarchs in Hebron awakened in many Jews messianic visions and gave birth to political movements with the aim of settling all parts of Eretz Yisrael. Those opposing Jewish settlement in the disputed territories of Judea, Samaria, and Gaza invoked memories of the damage done in the past by the unbridled enthusiasm of Jewish messianists. Chapter 20 analyzes the role of messianism in Jewish theology and asks whether believing that a particular historic situation has messianic significance implies the further belief that its full messianic realization is inevitable? This question has great relevance to an understanding of the political situation in Israel today.

For the present writer these explorations into the conceptual world of the Torah have constituted the vital core of *chayenu v-orekh yamenu* ("our lives and the length of our days"). We have made them in the humbling awareness that we are dealing ultimately with the "word" of God, but are encouraged by the knowledge that our tool of inquiry was given to us by He who is *chonen le-adam da'at, u-melamed le-enosh binah* ("favors man with knowledge, and teaches mortals understanding").[10]

It is my hope that the perspectives offered here will help to first clarify and then deepen the reader's understanding of various aspects of Judaism, enhance his appreciation for our heritage, and strengthen his faith in He in whose Image we have been formed, as they have mine.

Jerusalem

---

[10] First of the intermediate blessings of the daily *Amidah* prayer.

PART I

VIEWING JUDAISM AS A WHOLE

Chapter One

Is There an Indigenous Jewish Theology?

My purpose in this chapter is to defend the claim that there is an indigenous Jewish theology. Of the several words which comprise this assertion, the one which is most misleading is the two-letter word "is," as in, "There *is* an indigenous Jewish theology." While the words "indigenous" and "Jewish" and "theology" might be vague, the word "is" is systematically ambiguous. No single word has given rise to more confusion and discussion in contemporary philosophy than this simple copula. There are, to name a few, the "is" of predication and the "is" of identity, as well as the "is" of existence, of which our own sentence includes an instance. Bertrand Russell once said that, "It is a disgrace to the human race that it has chosen to employ the same word 'is' for [so many] entirely different ideas."[1]

In what sense, then, am I asserting that there is an indigenous Jewish theology? Consider the question, "Is there a prime number greater than one hundred?" Clearly the answer to this question is not to be found by empirical investigation based on observation but by logical analysis based on the rules for the introduction of new expressions in the system of natural numbers.

Analogously, when I claim that there *is* an indigenous Jewish theology, I do not mean that it necessarily exists as an explicitly-formulated system of propositions, suitably labeled, to be discovered in a book of some sort. What I am asserting is that, given a commitment to the beliefs and practices of Judaism and an acceptance of the Bible and the Talmud, there follows by logical entailment a commitment to certain theological propositions. The individual adherent of Judaism may never have reflected upon the theoretical pre-suppositions of his faith or, if he had, may never have taken the trouble to articulate these propositions in an explicit manner. But that is of no consequence for

---

[1] Bertrand Russell, *Introduction to Mathematical Philosophy*, 2nd ed. (London: Allen and Unwin, 1920), 100.

this question. Jewish theology is there. It is implicit. It is logically entailed by the beliefs and practices of Judaism, by the assertions of the Chumash and the expressions of the Midrash. It is there, waiting to be unpacked, to be drawn out, to be formulated in a systematic way. And, as I will demonstrate later, for many areas of Judaism this has already been done. If an individual Jew, confronted by the articulated implications of his commitment, chooses to ignore them, refuses to recognize them, or rejects them, he does so at the cost of forfeiting his claim to coherence, consistency, and rationality. While the Ravad may have been right in his acerbic stricture against Maimonides, that many greater and better people than he had the same thought, he was right in the sense that perhaps we cannot say of those who believe the one God to have corporeal attributes that they are to be considered heretics, or unworthy of a share in the world to come. On the other hand, Maimonides was undoubtedly correct that logically the unity of God *implies* His incorporeality and that to affirm one and deny the other is a self-contradiction. These others referred to by the Ravad may have been greater and better than Maimonides, but they were certainly less logical.[2]

What is theology? I use the word interchangeably with the phrase religious philosophy. There is perhaps one distinction between the two, as I have said in the Introduction to this work, which is not really relevant for our purposes, and that is that the theologian is one who operates from *within* the faith, from a posture of commitment, while the philosopher of religion may be a professional thinker who is examining religion from the outside, with no personal attachment. However, be it theology or religious philosophy, one is engaged in it as soon as one becomes reflective about one's religious faith and puts into words either for one's own benefit or in order to communicate to others what it is that one believes in or why one is engaged in certain religious practices.

When Rav said that "the *mitzvot* were given only for the purpose of refining mankind," he was laying the groundwork for a philosophy of the *mitzvot*.[3]

---

[2] *Mishneh Torah, Teshuvah* 3:7.
[3] *Bereishit Rabbah* 44.

When Rabbi Akiva said, "Everything is foreseen [by God], but free will is given [to man]," he was highlighting a profound paradox resulting from two opposed religious principles.[4]

When the schools of Hillel and Shammai for two and a half years debated the question of whether the individual would have been better off if he had not been created, they were debating a theological issue with great existential candor.[5]

But even the Bible itself is a mine of Jewish theology. The simple answer to Rashi's opening question, regarding why the Torah did not begin with the words "this month is to you ..." is obviously and precisely, as pointed out by Nachmanides, that the Torah is not merely a halakhic code but is concerned to impart a theology, an anthropology, and a philosophy of history, and that is indeed the material to be found in these early portions. In fact, the case for Jewish theology seems to me to be *so* strong and *so* indubitable that perhaps we should ask why it became a question in the first place. Why should anyone have thought that Judaism does *not* have a theology?

A number of pertinent considerations come to mind:

1) We erroneously learned to equate philosophy and theology with the style of Greek thought, which was systematic, speculative, and formal. Because our people "did" their theology in a different key and with a different style, we sometimes failed to recognize it as theology at all. Jewish theology was enunciated spasmodically, more by impulse, and never, in our primary sources, worked into a formal system.

2) Judaism's emphasis upon deeds, the Halakhah, and external behavior weakened its concern with theology. As Solomon Schechter put it so aptly: "With God as a reality, revelation as a fact, the Torah as a rule of life and the hope of redemption as a most vivid expectation, they felt no need for formulating their dogmas into a creed—which is repeated—not because we *believe* but that we *may* believe."[6] In short, Judaism apparently believed that it is the sign of a healthy religion to have a theology and not to be aware of it.

---

[4] *Avot* 3:16.
[5] *Eruvin* 13b.
[6] Solomon Schechter, *Aspects of Rabbinic Theology* (New York: Schocken Books, 1961), 12.

3) There were some technical objections to the assertion that Judaism had a theology. Strictly speaking, theology means "the science of God." Traditionally, however, Judaism has always had little to say about God other than that He exists, that He is One and His acts are recognized in history, and that He requires certain things of His creatures. Maimonides developed this indigenous Jewish approach in his doctrine of negative differentiation with the well-known paradoxical consequence that the more you assert of God, the less you know about Him. In fact, one recent thinker insists upon regarding the Bible as "God's anthropology" (God's view of man), rather than as man's theology.[7] Another writer who sees the Halakhah as central likes to believe that rather than a theology, what we have is a "Theonomy," a Divine Law.[8] In a current review of Rabbi Joseph B. Soloveitchik's work, his theology is respectfully referred to as a "Misnagid phenomenology."[9] But all of these different names merely help to point up emphases or a particular approach. In the larger sense with which we are concerned, these are all theology.

4) Another reason theology was never encouraged in Judaism is because certain aspects of theology were considered dangerous to Judaism. For example, dogmatics is a part of theology. There were always many who feared the reduction of Judaism to thirteen principles (such as those of Maimonides) or three principles (like those of Rabbi Joseph Albo), with the implication that all else is perhaps not important. This is the same psychology that's behind the warning to be as careful with a minor *mitzvah* as with a major one.[10] It was the same fear which prompted the Chatam Sofer, when asked "How many basic principles does Judaism have?," to answer "613"! Another integral part of Jewish theology has always been an investigation of the reasons for the *mitzvot*. Here, too, tradition has always sensed a danger. King Solomon is held up as the paradigm of one who would use his understanding of the purpose behind the *mitzvah* to reason his way to a personal exemption.[11] In this connection, Maimonides' presentation of the reasons for the *mitzvot* did indeed confirm the fears of the traditionalists. The worst fear of all,

---

[7] A.J. Heschel, *Man is Not Alone* (New York: Farrar, Straus and Young, 1951), 129.
[8] I. Grunfeld, *Horeb* (London: The Soncino Press, 1962), xiv (vol. 1).
[9] E. Borowitz, "The Typological Theology of J.B. Soloveitchik," *Judaism* 15 (1973).
[10] *Avot* 2:1.
[11] *Sanhedrin* 21b.

however, was based on the association of theology with Rationalism as a philosophic school. For many, the inevitable result of theologizing was ending up with religious beliefs based on fickle reason rather than unswerving faith. The proof of the weakness of the former was seen in the large-scale defection of Jews to Christianity in Spain during the massacres of 1391. In France and Germany during the terrible persecutions of the thirteenth and fourteenth centuries, the Ashkenazic communities had stood firm. In Spain at the end of the fourteenth and early fifteenth centuries, a large proportion succumbed. The crucial difference, the verdict of tradition held, was to be found in the weakening of simple faith due to the insidious reasoning of theology and philosophy.[12]

From the historical perspective, it can be granted that there *was* justification to the fears I have just outlined. Some day, some historian of ideas is going to draw a distinction between the value of an idea itself and the use to which the idea is put by certain social groups.

Suffice it to say, then, that there are historical reasons why Judaism never developed a systematic, explicitly formulated theology. The point I wish to make now, however, is that today, when the Jewish community has lost its insularity, when the atmosphere is saturated with the spirit of science, the hallmark of which is skepticism of everything nonempirical, when Orthodoxy must demonstrate its superiority over rival Jewish theologies, one cannot have an intelligent, reflective Judaism either for oneself or for others without developing some kind of theology, some kind of religious philosophy in the broad sense. Once modern man has tasted of the fruit of the tree of philosophic sophistication, he cannot go back to the Eden of simple faith. Once man becomes aware of his epistemological nakedness, God Himself must help him to fashion a conceptual garment. Even in our classic age we were told that we must know what to answer the heretic.[13] The heretic by definition was never interested in mere information. His questions required a justification of Judaism. To answer him one had to know theology. Today the questioning aspect of the heretic has been internalized: the demand for justification is within each of us. And the knowledge of what to answer must be built into our educational agencies if Judaism is to have a future.

---

[12] See Yitzhak Baer, *A sHistory of the Jews in Christian Spain* (Philadelphia: Jewish Publication Society, 1961), vols. 1 & 2, particularly vol. 2.

[13] *Avot* 2:14.

As far as the dangers are concerned, most of those that I have outlined can, I believe, be avoided by the new approach to theology which contemporary philosophy makes possible and whose main characteristics I shall outline later.

What specifically is to be expected from a Jewish theology?

1) Theology is needed to *explicate* various principles of Judaism which are not at all clear from the Bible and Talmud. For example, medieval Jewish philosophy focused upon the concept of God, His Unity, and His attributes, what we can know about God and what we cannot. This was of permanent value and is quite relevant to the crisis in contemporary Jewish thought. An example of something still needed, however, is a clarification of our *eschatological* concepts—Messiah, world to come, and resurrection—not an anthology or relevant passages, but a systematic working-through of these principles showing their meanings and implications.

2) Theology is needed to show the *relationship* between various principles of Judaism. For example, I once attempted to show how the Kabbalistic thinkers alone preserved the dynamic characteristics of the concept of God's Unity and that it is within this concept that one is to find the impulse and the origin of the concept of ultimate and inevitable redemption.[14] *Achdut,* unity, implies *malkhut,* kingship, and, as Rabbi Moses Hayyim Luzzatto points out, there is the notion of an *achdut bishlitah* which is implicit in Rashi's comment on the *Shema*. It happens that neither Saadia Gaon nor Maimonides nor Yehuda Halevi emphasized this point. Why is it important to know this? First, so that when we say the *Shema* we can concentrate on the full meaning of this important principle. Second, so that when we hear a prominent scholar saying that the Jews invented the Messianic vision because they had a lackluster origin, we will be able to supply the correct explanation.[15]

Another illustration of an outstanding relationship with important practical bearing is the problem of ethics and their relationship to God. Is something good because God wants it that way, or does God want it that way because it is good? Our whole understanding of the *Akedah* (the binding of Isaac) depends upon how we resolve this issue.

---

[14] See Chapter 12 in this volume.
[15] J. H. Greenstone, *The Messiah Idea in Jewish History* (Philadelphia: Jewish Publication Society, 1906), 24.

3) A third task for theology is to reconcile apparent conflicts between various principles, such as those between human freedom and divine omniscience, or between God's justice and God's mercy. This task is too well-known to require further elucidation.

I wish to draw the reader's attention to the fact that the three aforementioned tasks are of an *internal* nature, arising out of the *inner needs* of Judaism. None of these functions can be thought of as being motivated by an unholy desire to reconcile Judaism with anything foreign. None of these inquiries comes about through forbidden questions regarding "what is above and what is below, what is before and what is after." They come to the surface simply because a Jew reflects about his Judaism. And that a Jew *may* reflect about his Judaism— nay, *ought* to reflect about his Judaism—was long ago demonstrated by a Saadia, a Maimonides, a Bachya.

The Jew, however, no matter how pious, doesn't simply sit and contemplate his Torah. We live and move in history, and the theoretical principle, clarified or not, sooner or later comes into abrupt confrontation with the jagged and indifferent edge of experience.

There is the problem of evil—the problem of the suffering of the righteous and the good fortune of the wicked—which has vexed and tortured believers from Job onwards. There is conflict with science regarding the origin of species and the age of the earth, with pertinent historical findings, with widely-held psychological theories. Under the pressure of these confrontations, we are sent back both to re-examine our principles and to apply our critical faculties to the findings of science—and out of this intellectual ferment more Jewish theology is born. But how can we neglect to mention the challenge to Jewish thought that is presented by the unique and awesome historic experiences of our own day? Nothing so pointedly illustrates at once *the need for,* and *our lack of* a Jewish theology as our failure to grapple on a theological level with the meaning of Auschwitz or the State of Israel, or the implications of the Space Age[16] and to deduce from them their meaning for our people and a direction for the future.

But over and above all these considerations, there is an even more basic necessity for theology, a fundamental dependence upon philosophy

---

[16] N. Lamm, "The Religious Implications of Extraterrestrial Life," *Tradition* 7, no. 5 (Spring 1966), is a good beginning.

which, it seems to me, no thinking Jew can avoid. One must be able to give a rational answer to the question: why am I an Orthodox Jew? One must be able to give "reasons," not "causes." "Causes" include: "because I was brought up Orthodox," and "because my parents were Orthodox." A "reason" would be: "I am Orthodox because I choose to believe that the Creator of the world revealed Himself to my forefathers at Mt. Sinai." And then one must be able to give reasons justifying that belief. If you reply that your commitment is based upon faith about which you do not reason, you must nevertheless explain why it is that this faith needs no reasons, and why it is that you choose to have faith in Judaism but not in Christianity or in Buddhism. Aristotle once said, "You say one must philosophize, then you must philosophize. You say one should not philosophize. Then, to prove your contention you must philosophize. In any case you must philosophize."

Consider Yehuda Halevi, who in many ways is the most Jewish of our philosophers. He attempted to do away with natural theology to ground Judaism upon its true epistemological basis—historical experience. "We know these things first from personal experience and afterwards through uninterrupted tradition, which is equal to the former."[17] Now, all of this is true, but having taken a position as to the epistemological grounds of our religious belief, we must be prepared to defend them, should someone challenge the veracity of the experience or the authenticity of the tradition. Once again we are in the midst of theology. The same answer has to be given to Samson Raphael Hirsch when he says:

> The basis of your knowledge of God does not rest on belief which can after all allow an element of doubt. It rests solidly on the empirical evidence of your own senses ... on what you have yourselves experienced.... Both the Exodus and the Revelation are completely out of the realm of mere believing or thinking and are irrefutable facts which must serve as the starting points of all our other knowledge with the same certainty as our own experience and the existence of the material world we see about us.[18]

---

[17] Yehuda Halevi, *Kitab Al Khazari*, trans. H. Hirshfeld (New York: Bernard and Richards Co., 1927), 47.

[18] S. R. Hirsch, *Commentary on Ex. 19:4*, translated by I. Levy (London, 1958).

These words are true when directed to the generation of the Exodus. They are not if directed to us. These events *cannot* serve as starting points to be accepted without question. Their acceptance is a matter of believing and thinking, and Hirsch himself attempts elsewhere to justify rationally the acceptance of the Oral Tradition.[19] Once again, we are in the midst of theology.

More recently, Abraham Joshua Heschel has attempted to distinguish between theology and depth theology. According to him, the former deals with the content of believing, while the latter "is a special type of inquiry whose theme is the act of believing; the substratum out of which belief arises."[20] But upon analysis, we find that this is only a confusing way of saying what has been known for a long time: that theology, as such, is never to be equated with the inwardness of faith, the experiential intimacy of the believing heart, the so-called "fact of faith."[21] Indeed, theological theories can never have the sanctity nor the epistemological status of the basic "facts of faith." A few pages later, Heschel himself admits that the "insights of depth theology are vague and often defy formulation and expression and that it is the task of theology to establish the doctrines, bring about coherence and find words compatible with the insights." If so, we are better off to forget this misleading talk of theology and depth theology and speak only of the facts of faith and the attempt to talk about them, which is theology.

Up to this point I have attempted to argue, I hope successfully, 1) that there *is* a Jewish theology, albeit largely implicit, and 2) that in our day, no thinking Jew can escape theologizing.

I now wish to make a few brief remarks about the question of an "indigenous" Jewish theology. Can there be such a thing?

I think it is quite clear that the perennial stumbling block encountered by all who would attempt to develop a Jewish theology has been the invariable intrusion of contemporary philosophical categories or presuppositions in terms of which the theologian would formulate, organize, and interpret his Jewish material. The inevitable result was

---

[19] *Gesammelte Schriften*, vol. 1, edited by N. Frankfort (1908-12), 97.
[20] A.J. Heschel, *The Insecurity of Freedom* (New York: Farrar Straus & Giroux, 1966), 117.
[21] See J. Hick, *Philosophy of Religion* (New Jersey: Prentice Hall, 1963), 76-77.

Chapter One. Is There an Indigenous Jewish Theology?

an Aristotelian Judaism, or a neo-Platonic Judaism, or a neo-Kantian Judaism, or even, as someone recently maintained that he saw in S. R. Hirsch, a "Hegelian" exposition, though I disagree.[22] In the same vein, some traditionalists today might dismiss the work of Rosenzweig and Buber as being an "existential version" of Judaism and, as such, impure and a distortion. This is not to say that every concept so treated necessarily becomes distorted. Quite the contrary, I think that it can be shown in many instances that the employment of foreign philosophical categories can sometimes bring out the truly Jewish content of an idea.

Nevertheless, when this occurs, the theological enterprise in question is at least open to the *charge* of no longer being an "indigenous Jewish theology." Often, these philosophical assumptions are not realized by the thinker himself, who, being a "child of his age," believes his presuppositions to be the very dictates of reason itself and quite "self-evident."[23]

If we are to examine the origins and sources of philosophical categories, it appears doubtful if we ever had, or could have, an "indigenous Jewish theology." Eliezer Berkovits, in a perceptive article, seems willing to accept this condition and suggests that perhaps each generation needs to formulate its own Jewish philosophy in light of the philosophical categories of its day.[24] The criterion of its authenticity as a bona fide Jewish philosophy will be its "acknowledgement of God, Israel and the Torah as historic realities," and the success of its attempt "to provide the metaphysical corollary to the facts and events for which they stand."

I think this criterion is a good one as far as it goes, and it is certainly a necessary condition of any Jewish theology. However, I cannot accept the distinction made by Berkovits that these three—God, Israel, and Torah—are the "constants" of Judaism because they are "events," whereas once we conceptualize regarding these three we are already in the realm of variables. It is clear from philosophical analysis that there

---

[22] Noah H. Rosenbloom, *The "Nineteen Letters of Ben Uziel": A Hegelian Exposition* (New York: Historica Judaica, 1960).

[23] On the role of "pre-suppositions," see R.G. Collinwood, *An Essay in Metaphysics*, Parts I & II (Oxford: Oxford University Press, 1940).

[24] Eliezer Berkovits, "What is Jewish Philosophy?," *Tradition* 3, no. 2 (Spring 1961): 121.

is no absolute distinction between facts and theories, and that facts rarely if ever "speak for themselves." Certainly, it must be granted that "events" such as God, Israel, and Torah, from the very moment they are apprehended by the Jew, are not simple discriminated elements in sense perception, but are already shot through with interpretation and conceptualization. The givenness of Judaism is not merely that an actual communication occurred between the living God and Moses, but that this living God cannot be represented by anything visual, that He is "merciful," and that He is a "jealous God," that He is One. These are already ideas. Torah is not only an event—it has conceptual content. Israel is not merely a people that historically was the recipient of a Divine Revelation—it is a concept in whose givenness there is already an attachment to a land, a Messianic future, a promise of eternity. All of these ideas, vague as they may be, are already part of the *constant* of Judaism, denial of which makes any theology suspect.

I am, however, more optimistic about the possibility of an "indigenous Jewish theology" for two reasons:

1) We are more aware today than ever before of the possibilities of extraneous influences upon our theologizing and of the tentative nature of philosophical systems, and we are not ready to accept any as final. We are much more conscious today of the many-faceted nature of Judaism, of its rationalism as well as its mysticism, of its Halakhah as well as its inwardness, and we will not easily accept a theology which does not, in some serious sense, account for all aspects of historic Judaism.

This awareness, this sophistication, puts us on our guard, makes us highly critical, and enables us to come ever closer to a truly "Jewish theology."

An analogous problem exists in the philosophy of History. It is sometimes claimed that there cannot be an objective writing of history, since each historian brings to his task his biases, his prejudices, and his particular principle of interpretation.[25] For example, does he see economic forces as crucial, or are ideas the causal factor? But here, too, the answer can be that once we are aware of the sources of subjectivity, we can watch for them and work toward a balanced view.

---

[25] See W.H. Walsh, *Philosophy of History* (New York: Harper Torchbooks, 1960), chapter 5.

2) There has been a radical change in our understanding of the task of the philosophic enterprise. Contemporary philosophy in both its empirical and linguistic aspects is suspicious of metaphysical systems. Gone are the ambitious expectations that philosophy through its own royal road to truth can illuminate for us what *ought* to be or tell us about the world of *noumena*. The dominant conception of philosophy today is a sort of anti-philosophy, consisting of a critical examination of the ultimate presuppositions, the notions of explanation, and the logics of belief of the various disciplines. Contemporary philosophy is only concerned with asking what kind of situations theological and religious language talks about and how.[26] Philosophy only supplies the tools of linguistic analysis and the rules of deductive and inductive logic. Thus philosophy itself, employed critically, can help us to detect our prejudgments and purify our theology of extraneous elements. Many of the dangers which Rationalism, in its attempt to prove the existence of God, posed to the faith of Judaism, are not factors in the type of philosophy current today.

In a symposium on the directions of contemporary Jewish philosophy, Michael Wyschogrod—a professional philosopher and an Orthodox Jew—confirms this judgment. "We are living in the post-enlightenment period and Jewish Philosophy can therefore return to its own sources instead of validating itself by criteria foreign to it."[27] This realization has cut across denominational lines, and three years ago at the annual meeting of the Central Conference of American Rabbis, three papers were read urging the attendees, in the words of S. R. Hirsch, "to forget inherited prejudices and opinions concerning Judaism ... to go back to the source ... to know Judaism out of itself." The program of Hirsch, the development of a *"sich selbst begreifendes Judentum,"* can be achieved today. The tools are not Jewish, but they don't have to be. They are universal, as they should be.

How would one recognize an indigenous Jewish theology? What are the conditions of adequacy for such a conceptual structure? In this space we can only present the barest outline. Useful at this point is an analogy to the relationship which exists between scientific theories and

---

[26] I.T. Ramsey, "Contemporary Philosophy and the Christian Faith," *Religious Studies* 1, no. 1 (1965).

[27] *Judaism* 2 (1953): 196.

empirical facts. A scientific theory may be considered confirmed under the following circumstances:
1) It explains or accounts for all the relevant facts in terms of the theory, and
2) When compared to other theories which may do the same thing, it accounts for the facts in the simplest, and ontologically most economical, way.

So it is with our Jewish theology. The "facts" or givenness of our faith are not only God, Israel, and Torah in a general sense, but the specific teachings found in our Torah—our sense of history and God's role within it, our Messianic expectations, our understanding of man as image of God, the role of the nations, the meaning of anti-Semitism, the place of the land of Israel, the power of prophecy, the function of the Halakhah. All must, in some significant sense, be explained and analyzed, and the results shown to correspond with the representative utterances of the Midrash and the *Aggadah* on the subject.

I am fully aware of the imprecision of this word "representative." However, I am convinced that, given sufficient attention, we can develop a set of criteria which will win general agreement. For example, groups of jointly sufficient conditions for calling a saying of our Sages representative can be formulated that might perhaps include location, stature of author, frequency with which the statement is repeated, attention given it by *Rishonim*, and general consistency with other midrashic utterances.

But most significant, a viable Jewish theology must develop the justificatory apparatus showing the sense in which it is reasonable for the Orthodox Jew to make his commitment to God and to tradition on the basis of the evidence available.

I said that Jewish theology must, among other things, account for the Halakhah. In light of the many confused and confusing statements that have been made about the relationship between Halakhah and theology, a few remarks are indicated.

An Orthodox scholar wrote, "The Theology of Judaism is contained largely in the Halakhah ... it is in the Halakhah therefore that the philosophy of Judaism is to be sought."[28] I do not believe this to be true. The main sources of Jewish theology are still the non-halakhic portions of

---

[28] S. Belkin, *In His Image* (London, New York, Toronto: Abelard-Schuman, 1961), 16. A similar view is held by Rabbi Joseph B. Soloveitchik. See Shubert

the Bible and the *Aggadah*. Do not allow our partisan desire to work out a favored position for Orthodox theologizing blind us to the patent facts.

This does not mean that Halakhah is not relevant for the concerns of the theologian. Quite the contrary. As we stated earlier, developing a philosophy of the Halakhah is a necessary condition for an adequate Jewish theology. But what does "Philosophy of the Halakhah" mean? Here we must disentangle several different strands and distinguish several different meanings.

1) An authentic Jewish theology must account for the Halakhah in the sense that it must make a place for it; must show it to be integrally related to the concept of Revelation on the one hand and to the needs of man on the other. Jewish theology must show how the entire structure of the Halakhah is in a sense required by and coherent with the other principles of Judaism. This is the kind of "accounting for" that Gershom Sholem and Alexander Altman claim medieval Jewish philosophy never achieved with the Halakhah, while Kabbalah did.[29]

2) Another task of Jewish theology, and this is another sense of the term "philosophy of the Halakhah," is to subject the Halakhah itself to philosophical analysis. This would give us a philosophy of Halakhah in the same sense in which we have a philosophy of law, a philosophy of history, and a philosophy of science. Its purpose would be to analyze the methods of Halakhah, its special concept of "Truth," its theological and anthropological presuppositions, and the relationship between law and equity, and to extract from the relevant *Halakhot* Judaism's philosophy of society and its relationship to the individual, its philosophy of punishment and responsibility, and so on. It is to be expected that for those aspects of Jewish theology which deal with the law, society, and justice, one is primarily dependent upon the Halakhah. However, our concept of God, for example, does not come from the Halakhah, as such. It comes from the Bible, the Divine record of what is essentially the Jewish historical experience, but to be sure, it is reflected in the Halakhah. Similarly, our concept of man as the bearer of the divine image derives from Genesis 2: 27.

Spero, *Aspects of Rabbi Joseph B. Soloveitchik's Philosophy of Judaism* (New Jersey: Ktav, 2009).

[29] G. Scholem, *Major Trends in Jewish Mysticism* (New York: Shocken Books, 1941), 28.

Once we know what we are looking for we can approach the Halakhah and there find manifestations, reflections, and expressions of these fundamental concepts. However, one cannot expect them to be derived from the Halakhah. Moreover, the details of the Halakhah must be consulted in formulating any philosophy of the *mitzvot*. The classic example of this is the contention of S. R. Hirsch that the purpose of the Sabbath is not merely physical rest. Since an examination of the Halakhah reveals that the Torah forbids *melekhet machshevet* (purposeful work), the purpose of the Sabbath is to teach man that he may not create, that he is only a creature, a "steward of God's estate," and that only God is the creator.

3) There is a third intersection between theology and Halakhah. This is where pure theological principles have become crystallized into Halakhah. So, for example, the Halakhah legislates that if a person does not subscribe to belief in *Torah min Hashamayim* (Divine Revelation of the Torah) he is classified as a heretic, with various halakhic consequences. There are several "duties of the heart" which, once they are prescribed, fall into the area of the Halakhah. Now, these are best described as instances where theology has become part of the content of the Halakhah, and as such these principles are truly authoritative. In fact, one could properly argue that in many of these instances they came to be embodied in the Halakhah because they were principles in Albo's sense—in their absence, Judaism is not viable.

4) Now as a result of doing "philosophy of Halakhah" in the sense of (2), we may come up with certain theological principles which may be called *pre-suppositions of the Halakhah*, which Rabbi Walter S. Wurzburger, in a recent insightful article, calls "meta-halakhic propositions."[30] I cannot agree that all the propositions Rabbi Wurzburger chooses to call meta-halakhic are indeed so. He fails to distinguish, if I read him right, between what I have called "theology crystallized into Halakhah" (my number three), which is merely halakhic propositions, and Halakhah subjected to philosophical analysis, all of whose conclusions can legitimately be called meta-halakhic (my number two). Hence, even if one should hold with Chasdai Crescas that "belief in God" cannot be a *mitzvah* and is thus not Halakhah, nevertheless this principle *can* qualify

---

[30] "Meta-Halakhic Propositions," in *Leo Jung Jubilee Volume* (New York: Jewish Center, 1962).

as a *meta*-halakhic proposition, since it is unquestionably presupposed by the entire structure of Halakhah.

It is not clear to me what significance Rabbi Wurzburger places upon these meta-halakhic propositions. If, as it sometimes appears, he merely wishes to show that the "Halakhah is not devoid of all theological and philosophical presuppositions," and that these are necessary conditions for any authentic Jewish theology, I quite agree. On the other band, if he wishes to claim that "it is feasible to construct a philosophy of Halakhic Judaism [read Orthodox Judaism] out of the Halakhic data available to us,"[31] I cannot agree. It has yet to be demonstrated that a philosophy of the Halakhah is the equivalent of a philosophy of Judaism.

In the latter part of this chapter I have argued for the feasibility today of an indigenous Jewish theology, and the conditions of adequacy which such a theology would be required to meet in order to be so judged. I think it should be clear that on the basis of what I have said there can be more than one indigenous Jewish theology. There are areas where more than one alternate belief may fit the "facts of faith." For example, can a Jew believe that God may reveal another Torah? What does Judaism involve in terms of psychological theory or self theory? Is beauty an objective value in Judaism?

I would also like to suggest that we cease accepting and rejecting theologies as wholes. It is not necessary that we accept or reject Maimonides *in toto*, or Luzzatto *in toto*. Each concept in Judaism must be examined critically and individually. It is by no means obvious that accepting any one part of Maimonides' philosophy necessarily entails a commitment to the whole.

We must also learn to do our theology piecemeal and to build slowly toward a picture of the whole. Instead of first conceiving of an overall grandiose scheme as to the purpose and character of Judaism, and then trying to force the individual concepts into the pattern, we must reverse the process. Before writing treatises on Judaism, we must first write individual monographs. Let us concentrate first upon an analysis of specific concepts, special areas with as few presuppositions as possible. Only after the results of such work are before us can we go on to synthesize our conclusions and join the fragments together.

---

[31] Ibid., 212.

There is today a great need for, and an interest in, Jewish theology. The editors and sponsors of such journals as *Tradition* and *Judaism* are to be commended for providing both a stimulus and an outlet for work in this area. It is true that the word "theology" has had a bad taste and bad associations for traditional Jews in the past. I believe, however, that the term can be reinstated if we remember that "we can admit that religious truth arises in the heart and all that theology asks is that it come out through the head."

Chapter Two
Toward a Philosophy of Modern Orthodoxy

Sociological studies of the American Jewish community have reported the existence of two different camps among the committed Orthodox: the traditional and the modern.[1] In my judgement, these studies, while making correct institutional identifications, have not been sufficiently clear in stating the distinguishing characteristics of the two groups.[2] However, two of the authors of these studies, Charles Liebman and Samuel Heilman, seem to agree that the modern Orthodox lack a halakhic-theologic framework for their position and that their apparent inability to develop an effective ideological justification is responsible for the emergence of the modern Orthodox "as the weaker of the two."[3]

In this chapter, I shall attempt to show (1) that the crucial differences between the modern and the traditional Orthodox are of a special type called "philosophical differences," and that other behavioral or attitudinal differentia may be understood as consequences of this fact, and (2) that what has impeded the development of a valid philosophy of modern Orthodoxy has been the lack of an adequate model.

Concerning any discipline which human thought recognizes as a more or less self-contained entity, there can arise questions which cannot be answered by the rules and procedures of the discipline itself. Thus, the question of the purpose of chess–playing, or how often one

---

[1] Charles S. Liebman, "Orthodoxy in American Jewish Life," *American Jewish Year Book* 66 (1965): 21-98; idem, *The Ambivalent American Jew* (Philadelphia: Jewish Publication Society, 1973); idem, "Orthodox Judaism Today," *Midstream* (August-September 1979): 19-26; Samuel C. Heilman, *Synagogue Life* (Chicago: University of Chicago Press, 1973): idem, "Inner and Outer Identities," *Jewish Social Studies* 39, no. 3 (Summer 1979): 227-240; idem, "The Many Faces of Orthodoxy," *Modern Judaism* 2 no. 1 (February 1982): 23-51; David Singer, "Voices of Orthodoxy," *Commentary* (July 1974): 54-60; William B. Helmreich, "Old Wine in New Bottles," *American Jewish History* 59, no. 2 (December 1979): 234-256.

[2] See my article "Modern Orthodoxy: A Movement in Search of Leaders," published in the R.C.A. Jubilee Volume (Jerusalem: Magnes Press, 1985).

[3] C. Liebman, "Orthodox Judaism Today," 22.

should play chess, cannot be answered by any of the rules of chess. The question of the meaning of "scientific law" or "natural cause" similarly cannot be answered by the procedures of the scientific method, and the question of the aims and priorities of education cannot be answered by examining the principles of pedagogy. Very general and fundamental questions involving meaning and goals and priorities are usually philosophic questions. Therefore, the above questions appropriately belong to the area of philosophy—philosophy of games, philosophy of science, and philosophy of education—and are indeed seriously cultivated by trained philosophers as are the philosophy of law, art and morality.

Similarly, in regard to Orthodox Judaism, there are many general and fundamental questions of meaning and emphasis whose answers cannot be found within the Halakhah or even implied in the Torah. These are legitimate philosophic questions that have always been raised by thoughtful people committed to Orthodox Judaism. Thus, for years the disciples of Hillel and Shammai debated the question of "whether it is better for man to have been created or not."[4] Regardless of the precise meaning of the question, it was evidently clear to that entire generation of great rabbis that neither Halakhah nor the Torah as a whole contained an obvious answer to it. And it is most curious that no party to the debate thought of suggesting that the views of his teacher represented Da'as Torah, and accusing anyone who disagreed with it of fomenting heresy. Consider the teaching of Simon the Just: "Upon three things does the world stand: on Torah, on divine worship, and on acts of kindness (gemilut chasadim)."[5] Where in the Halakhah or in the Torah as a whole did Simon the Just find the sources to conclude that in Judaism acts of kindness, which essentially involve relations with one's fellow man, are to be placed on the same level as Torah and Avodah, which are so all-encompassing and God oriented? In a later period, we find that a recognized rabbinic leader was able to take the position, contrary to Maimonides, that it is proper for a Jew to believe that God may give another Torah to Israel, providing that it is done in the same manner in which the original Torah was given.[6]

---

[4] *Eruvin* 13b.
[5] *Avot* 1:2.
[6] Joseph Albo, *Sefer Ha-Ikarim*, volume 3 (Philadelphia: Jewish Publication Society, 1930), 14.

Chapter Two. Toward a Philosophy of Modern Orthodoxy

The conclusion is inescapable: in regard to such philosophic questions there may be more than one "correct" answer, in the sense that both are consistent and coherent with Orthodox Judaism. This test of coherence and consistency is the only legitimation that a philosophical position within Orthodoxy can receive or requires.

The most important difference between the modern and the traditional Orthodox is the issue of one's relationship to general culture, which is a clear philosophic question regarding the nature and purpose of Torah. The modern Orthodox believe that while the Torah is indeed of unique and supreme value, indispensable to the Jew and to mankind, it (in its narrow sense) was not meant to be a sufficient condition of human fulfillment. The Torah provides directives on how to live, morally and ritually, and basic insights into the nature of God, man, and sacred history. What human culture has to provide are the substantive conditions of life itself and further knowledge of man and the world, both for its insight into the wisdom and goodness of God and because of the power it gives man to better his material and social conditions. The religious obligation of the Jew according to the modern Orthodox is not only to learn and to use what is of value in general culture, but also to help produce it.

The modern Orthodox policy of working together with Reform, Conservative, and secular Jews for shared goals is another instance of a philosophic difference. Involved is a judgement as to whether the value of the shared goals, combined with the love of Israel flowing out of cooperation, transcends the possible negative consequences of recognizing or encouraging the deviant ideologies of these groups through the cooperation. As a question of policy relating to communal bodies this issue has no clear warrant within the Halakhah, although claims have been made by the traditional camp that it has.[7]

On the question of Israel, in which the modern Orthodox tend to follow the line of the religious Zionists, the issues are once again philosophical. Whether to see in the risen State of Israel the beginnings of the much-promised and long-awaited redemption, or a satanic development designed to tempt once again the sorely-tried remnant of Israel, is a function of one's overall view of the meaning of Galut and Geulah, exile

---

[7] See my article, Shubert Spero, "Does Participation Imply Recognition?" *Tradition* 8, no. 4 (Winter 1966): 56-64, and "Modern Orthodoxy."

and redemption, and where they are placed on the activism-passivism continuum.[8]

Most difficult of all is a philosophic explication of the modern Orthodox approach to Halakhah as a whole. To many, what characterizes the modern Orthodox is simply religious weakness, charitably described as laxity or permissiveness. However, I would argue that here too the crucial difference rests on a philosophic question: Does Jewish piety and devotion require that one adopt the most stringent view possible in all areas of the Halakhah? Perhaps one can justify a view of the Halakhah which holds that in ritual areas one may seek out the more lenient view without compromising one's religiosity or *yirat shamaim*.

Assuming that these four issues characterize the distinctive approaches of the modern Orthodox, the question that arises next regards what has to be done to combine these particular positions into a unified philosophy of Orthodox Judaism. To begin with, we must be reminded that our task is not the construction of a new religious philosophy from the ground up. We are talking about a variation of Orthodoxy, so we are starting out with the already fully-developed philosophy of Orthodox Judaism. Now, of the four philosophic positions that characterize modern Orthodoxy, it seems clear that only the first, a perception of Torah that leaves room for general culture, actually involves a structural change in the philosophy of Orthodoxy, i.e., a repositioning of some of its parts. The other concepts, once the modifications have been made, can be inserted into their respective slots. Thus, while the modern Orthodox may have a different concept of the Halakhah, the overall place of the Halakhah within the framework of their Judaism remains pretty much the same. And the same may be said regarding the modern Orthodox understanding of the concept of redemption. Therefore, the problem of developing a philosophy of modern Orthodoxy involves essentially the question of the relationship between Torah and modern culture, or in Hirschean terms the relationship between Torah and *derech eretz*.

Little progress has been made toward solving this problem. I wish to suggest that this may have been because of our fixation on an inadequate model. Usually, proposals to relate the two elements of Torah

---

[8] See chapter 18 in this volume, and my "Is There a Crisis in Religious Zionism?," *Forum* 50 (Winter 1983/84): 49-57.

Chapter Two. Toward a Philosophy of Modern Orthodoxy

and *derech eretz* are given in terms of a Hegelian synthesis. Calls are heard for *interaction* between and *integration* of the two. However, the implications of such an interaction, vaguely suggestive of a sort of chemical mixture, are that the original components are transformed into some third reality. However, this is precisely what Orthodoxy cannot accept—the idea that one's Torah has changed as a result of the influence of general culture. Where the model fails is that within this framework one cannot think of interaction without synthesis, which in turn implies transformation. And yet there must be interaction of some sort. For while as an Orthodox Jew one rejects some aspects of general culture, other aspects are absorbed and shape our attitudes. What model, then, can we use to explicate this kind of relationship between Torah and *derech eretz*?

Instead of thinking in terms of a chemical mixture or mechanical interaction, let us try to conceptualize the relationship between Torah and culture in terms of geological phenomena, which we shall call the *model of sequential strata*—which is to say, successive layers of semi-permeable material laid down in a very particular order, wherein a lower level might act as a filter for the material in the level above.

The clue to this approach lies in the Torah itself. If we take an overall scan of the Genesis account, we perceive the following: in the first stage man is placed in an environment and told to work and to conserve and then is given one negative commandment: to refrain from eating of the Tree of Knowledge of Good and Evil.[9] The command to "work and guard it (the garden)" must be seen in conjunction with the mandate given earlier to man, "to subdue and have dominion" over his environment.[10] The point is that man is given Divine guidance prior to being introduced into a life-situation, with its varied choices and experiences, where man is mandated to interact creatively with his environment in order to fulfill his needs. The explicitly Divine contribution takes the form of guidance—permitting this, prohibiting that (Gen. 2:16).

In his second stage, man finds himself in a much more difficult environment, but again the sequence and proportion of guidance to culture is the same. True, man is given additional instructions, but his essential

---

[9] Gen. 2:15-17.
[10] Gen. 1:28.

and overwhelming preoccupation is meeting the demands of mundane life and his own physical and emotional needs. As man proceeds to live life, he transforms his environment, creating ever more complex cultural forms.[11]

In the post-deluvial state, man enters upon a more benign physical environment which permits the development of various social institutions, but once again the same sequence is repeated: a stratum of instruction followed by a stratum of culture.[12] What is already clear even at this point is that Divine guidance seems to be primarily a response to man's mistakes, preventive or remedial.[13] It also appears that this guidance generally takes the form of moral rules and values and broad philosophical outlooks which might be said to float above general culture and are not rivals of culture.[14] To make this last point more clear, let us analyze the broad constituents of general culture.

First we have the vast area called material culture, which ranges from the clay pots and four-room stone houses adopted by our early ancestors from the Canaanites, to the technological wonders of today. Ever since he was driven from the Garden of Eden, man generally has managed to provide for his basic needs, and has continued beyond function and utility to decoration and recreation, and the entire realm of the arts. More recently in human history, with the development of the scientific method, man has been able to lay claim to theoretical knowledge, public,

---

[11] Gen. 4:2, 6-7, 20-22.

[12] Gen. 8:15-17, 9:1-7.

[13] "The Lord created the evil inclination in man and He created for it the Torah with which to season (temper) it" (*Kiddushin* 30b).

"Every positive or negative precept the reason of which is unknown to thee take as a remedy against some of those diseases with which we are unacquainted at present...."

"Most of the "statutes" (*hukkim*) the reason of which is unknown to us serve as a fence against idolatry" (Moses Maimonides, *Guide for the Perplexed*, trans. M. Friedlander [New York: E. P. Dutton & Co., 1942], III:49).

[14] Mordechai Kaplan's use of the phrase "Judaism as Civilization" is not to be construed as a statement in conflict with my thesis that Judaism today is not in competition with the main elements of general culture. His use of that phrase for the title of his book was intended primarily to emphasize his sociological view of the origins of Judaism, like all religions, as a group affair, and to serve the polemical purpose of minimizing the cognitive aspects of religious belief.

objective, and verifiable, providing an increasingly reliable picture of man and his universe, ranging from understanding the microstructures of the DNA particle to becoming aware of hitherto unsuspected celestial entities such as pulsars and "black-holes."

With regard to all of these three fundamental components of human culture or *derech eretz*—the material or technical, the artistic, and the pure scientific—Torah or Divine guidance, in its essential thrust, has no argument. Torah has never presumed to teach man how to build a house, plant grains, build a bridge, or split an atom. Not only was man permitted by the Torah to benefit from all of these areas of human culture, making for himself a more secure, more pleasant, and healthier life, but he was commanded to participate in the production and creation of culture so as to unlock the mysteries of nature from which we can learn to love and respect its Creator. As Rabbi J. B. Soloveitchik pointed out, since man as a moral agent has been given responsibility to help others, conserve value, preserve life, and eradicate evil, he is morally obliged to seek the power and the knowledge, the means and the instrumentation to achieve all of this. If new sources of energy can eradicate poverty, if knowledge of genetic engineering promises to prevent certain diseases, then man is morally obligated to seek out this knowledge. The doctrine of Imitatio Dei is the operational mode of the concept of man created in the image of God. As God is creative, so man ought to be creative. This brings us to the "triple equation": "Humanity equals dignity equals responsibility equals majesty."[15]

The element of human culture which Torah was designed to contest in direct confrontation was that known variously as the mythological or the religious or the philosophical. Those human conceptual constructs which, beyond the above, presumed to "explain" the origins of the universe, the purpose and destiny of man, and the nature of good and evil, or to unveil the metaphysical mysteries of "what is above and below, before and after," were viewed by the Torah to be largely false and misleading.[16] Of course, it must be remembered that until very recently, many

---

[15] Joseph B. Soloveitchik, "The Lonely Man of Faith," *Tradition* 7, no. 2 (Summer 1965): 5-67.

[16] See Maimonides' account of the rise of idolatry and the struggle by Abraham to preserve the belief in ethical monotheism, leading to the creation of the Jewish people and its covenant with God (*Hilkhot Avodat Kokhavim*, Chap. I).

elements that belong to the three areas of culture mentioned above were also opposed by the Torah because they were associated in various inextricable ways with pagan religion. Thus early Babylonian astronomy was tied in with sorcery and divination, and the Greek Olympic Games had a pagan idolatrous framework. But even more important, the entire fields of literature and the plastic representational arts were quite justifiably viewed with grave suspicion by Judaism, and only recently came to be considered as useful and integral parts of human culture.[17] What we have been witnessing has been the gradual secularization of much of human culture and its disconnection from various mythologies and religious traditions, making it possible for Orthodox Jews to become involved.

This relationship between Divine guidance and human culture did not change with the advent of Israel as a nation.[18] Once again, the basic motivation was remedial. Because man had failed to fulfill his moral potential, Providence was to try again by creating a special people covenanted to God, with all the features of a nation living a full national life in a land of its own. Once again, the sequence of strata was first Divine guidance received in a wilderness, and only afterward the opportunity for a full national life in the Promised Land.[19] Even though Divine

---

[17] See M.B. Bloomfield, "Judaism and the Study of Literature," *Tradition* 13, no. 1 (Fall 1971): 21-37.

[18] This basic continuity of the task of man, both prior to Sinai and after, is thus expressed by S.R. Hirsch:

> Thus every man, as man, is born for justice. In the early history of mankind, however, man has forgotten to respect man as man. It was then that God created Israel as His people amidst the nations, so that Israel might be the standard bearer of human justice and realize it by his example. You, therefore, as man and Israelite (MENSCH-JISSROEL) are doubly called upon to fulfill the image of justice and to be just in all your ways. You cast aside man's and Israel's dignity if you are unjust to any creature about you... (*Horeb*, 222).

[19] There are two problematic items in the Book of Exodus which can be explained in terms of the sequential relationship of culture to Divine guidance. After the miracle of the splitting of the sea, and before the revelation at Sinai, we are told, "There He made for them a statute and an ordinance and there He proved them." (Exod. 15:25). If, as most commentators say, these statutes were given by God, the question arises as to why it was necessary to give Israel "statutes and ordinances" at this point, when the entire Torah was

guidance, now in the form of the Torah, had increased to 613 commandments and in sheer quantity and range seemed to constitute a "civilization" of its own, its essential nature remained the same as before. The Torah, offering a world outlook, a moral code, and a mode of worship, continued to float above culture. However, because the Torah not only addresses the human condition but seeks to create a self-conscious Jew, it actually adds significant cultural elements to the life of the Jew, such as Sabbath and holidays, ritualized rites of passage, welfare institutions, and elements of attire. These heighten Jewish God-consciousness and introduce a quality of *Kedushah*. Nevertheless, the essential function of Torah is not to replace human culture but merely to act as the grid or filter through which human culture is absorbed by the Jew. Thus, some of the more coarse elements of contemporary culture may be prevented from reaching the Jewish consciousness altogether. Others are colored and modified as they pass through the lens of halakhic regulation and Torah world-view. But that is precisely the function of Torah, to enable to Jew to participate more fully in ordinary life and yet not be shaped completely by that life; to share in the great human discoveries and yet to be detached enough to be critical and selective; to be sufficiently in touch with contemporary culture so as to have significant input.

The model we have been trying to develop would seem to do justice to the view of Samson Raphael Hirsch, the modern exponent of "*Torah im derech eretz,*" which has been reliably described as follows:

> For S.R. Hirsch, there is no opposing the secular sphere of study requiring synthesis with the sacred sphere of Torah. There is only general relative knowledge whichafter it is purified by the absolute standard of Torah Truth, widens and deepens our conception

---

soon to follow? But, if we accept the notion that at any point Divine guidance must precede culture, then we might say that since even during this short interval between leaving Egypt and receiving the Law at Sinai the Jewish people would be involved with life, with filling their basic needs for food and for social arbitration, there was a need even before Sinai for some guidance, some Torah. This also explains why Moshe was able to accept the suggestion of Jethro for a system of judges (Exod. 18) representing human culture, since he had already received some "statutes and ordinances," some moral values. (See the discussion in Nachmanides on Exod. 18:1 regarding whether Jethro arrived before or after *matan Torah*.)

of the world in which God has placed us to live according to His Torah ... *derech eretz* is the raw material which is to be fashioned and wrought, found and transformed by the Divine Torah. There must be a *derech eretz* on which the Torah laws can operate and have their effect.[20]

It should be remembered that there did develop among the talmudic sages a point of view which has been called the "Torah only" approach, which saw in the Torah itself, particularly in its study, all of the worthwhile culture needed by a Jew.[21] According to this view, material culture should be kept to its functional minimum, aesthetic values are largely a waste of time, and the theoretical knowledge of the world which has come from science is either to be found in the Torah or is irrelevant. While this point of view is popular today among the traditional Orthodox, and is urged upon us as normative Orthodoxy, the pertinent discussion in the Talmud leaves one with the impression that the "Torah only" approach may legitimately be regarded as a religious ideal only for a small elite.

In applying our model of sequential strata we have left the most important element for the last. We have stated that according to Judaism the human personality, both as individual and as social unit called Israel, is enveloped first by some sort of Divine guidance which acts as a filter or strainer selectively permitting passage to elements of general culture in the layer above. However, we must now ask, does the Divine guidance itself fall upon purely virgin or passive ground? Are the words of prophesy truly the primeval layer of significance in the human consciousness? The answer must be in the negative, for the human personality is not a tabula rasa. Man, as he first emerges into being, already possesses the intelligence to understand and the freedom to obey or disobey the command of God.[22] This is God's gift: "Thou favorest man with knowledge and teachest mortals understanding."[23] At every point and at every turn, Judaism assumes man's exercise of reason to distinguish between truth and falsity, to interpret the Torah properly, and to employ *sevarah* and the hermeneutical rules correctly so as to deduce the implications of the

---

[20] S.E. Danziger, "Clarification of Rabbi Hirsch's Concepts," *Tradition* 6, No. 2 (Spring/Summer 1964): 141-158.
[21] *Berakhot* 35b.
[22] See Rashi and Sforno on Gen. 1:26.
[23] This is the fourth of the 18 blessings contained in the Amidah prayer.

Halakhah.²⁴ Moreover, reason is assumed not only in interpreting the Torah, but in the crucial initial step of embracing it. Again and again the Torah demands of the Jew obedience and a correct response, but the appeal is always to reason. It is the intelligent, the prudential, the moral thing, for Israel to trust and to follow God.²⁵

As I have argued elsewhere, the existence of special sources of knowledge within Judaism, such as revelation or prophesy, does not alleviate our dependence upon reason.²⁶ For even granting the *possibility* of revelation, what is the evidence that it ever took place? Asserting the fact of revelation simply becomes another cognitive "belief-that" statement, which requires justification. Similarly, the emphasis in Judaism upon certain overwhelming historical events, such as the Exodus, or the appeal to uninterrupted tradition which affirms these events, does not constitute an alternative epistemological base, for the question then simply becomes one of the authenticity of the record and the reliability of the tradition, again requiring justification. Even an appeal to a religious experience of a personal nature cannot bypass the need for rational judgement, for religious encounters even of the most unusual kind are always reduceable to psychological statements about feelings and sensations, which cannot warrant any existential deductions.

---

²⁴ By "interpreting the Torah properly," I have in mind basic judgements, such as which non-halakhic passages are to be treated allegorically and which literally (see the comments of Menachem HeMeiri on *Avot* 3:14), and whether some sections of the Torah are more important than others. Already among the Rabbis of the Talmud we find such discussions as: Rabbi Akiva said, "'And thou shalt love they neighbor as thyself, this is a great principle of the Torah.' Ben Zoma said, 'There is an even greater principle than this.'" (*Sifra* on Lev. 19:18). It is clear that these sages were using personal criteria in judging some commandments of the Torah to be more significant than others. Thus Rabbi Abraham ben David (Rabad) of Toledo in his *Emunah Ramah* points out that "not all parts of the Torah are of equal prominence...," and of course Maimonides made a similar judgement (Maimonides, *Guide*, III:51). Regardless of whether the criteria for making such judgements are contributed by the individual or can perhaps be drawn out of the Torah itself in some way, the point remains that it is human reason that must do the work. For a treatment of the use of logic and reason in the development of the Halakha, see chapter 9 of my book *Morality, Halakha and the Jewish Tradition* (New York: Ktav and Yeshiva University Press, 1983).

²⁵ Deut. 4:1, 6, 40; Deut. 6:3, 18,24; Deut. 8:1; Deut. 11:9; Deut. 30:11-20; Deut. 32:6.

²⁶ See Chapter 1 of this volume, and also Shubert Spero, "Faith and its Justification," *Tradition* 12, no. 2 (Fall 1971): 54-69.

Throughout it all, the human being remains preeminently the rational being who must, if he is to retain his rationality, give reasons for the following: why am I committed to Judaism? Why do I accept the Torah version of things rather than some other version?

Religious belief, including a commitment to Orthodox Judaism, cannot produce any special exemption from the demands of rationality, and like any other belief must be accompanied by reasons, evidence, and justification.

This unavoidable dependence upon rationality at every important point in the understanding and acceptance of Divine guidance, and in the interpretation and development of Torah, provides another and decisive intersection between the religious Jew and human culture: namely, the study of philosophy. For while, as we have argued, the Torah at every juncture seems to assume human reason and builds upon it, nowhere (of course other than by stating that man cannot know God Himself)[27] does the Torah give us an explication of the nature and area of competence of human reason; nowhere does it discuss the rules of correct reasoning and the limits of human reason. It is here that all—including Orthodox Jews—have to wait upon the deliverances of philosophy, by which we simply mean the process by which human reason reflects upon itself; a process in which the subject matter and the instrument by which we study the subject matter are one and the same. This pivotal problem of epistemology, our understanding of human rationality, is the one element of general culture which precedes Divine guidance and is the stratum through which the Torah itself must be filtered before it penetrates the human consciousness. Every age's understanding of the nature and limits of human reason, rightly or wrongly, is the premise from which every effort of Jewish theology must begin. Whatever mistakes Maimonides may have made in his philosophy sprang not from an unquestioned acceptance of Aristotle, for in truth Maimonides filtered his Aristotle through the grid of Torah, but rather from a flawed concept of reason, which was one of the presuppositions of the age.[28] Hirsch,

---

[27] Exod. 33:20

[28] See the article by Rabbi A. I. Kook on Maimonides in the back of vol. 12 of *Toldot Yisroel* by Zev Yavetz, and Hermann Cohen, "The Character of Maimonides' Moral Doctrine," in *Selected Essays from 'Judische Schriften' by Hermann Cohen* (Jerusalem: Mosad Bialik, 1977) (in Hebrew).

for all of his criticism of Maimonides, was no less a "rationalist," but he differed from the Sage of Fostat not primarily by his approach to general culture but by his understanding of the term "human reason." By Hirsch's time, the general understanding of the area of competence of human reason had shrunk considerably. The centuries-old controversy between empiricist and rationalist, culminating in the work of Hume and Kant, had decisively shaped a philosophic consensus which in broad

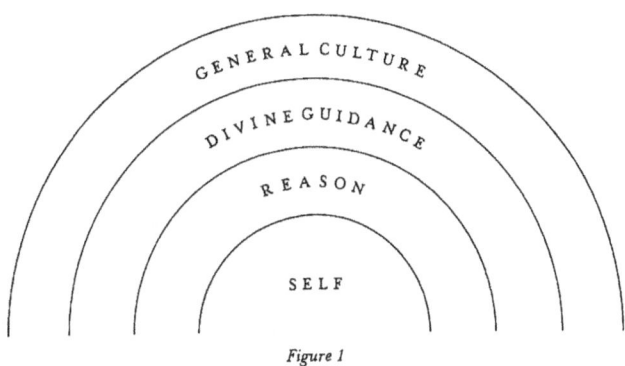

Figure 1

outline perceived human reason essentially as a reliable tool for negotiating the empirical realm rather than as a reservoir of original and certain truths. This achievement in itself has made the study of general philosophy an indispensable requirement for every thinking Jew who wishes to understand the rational underpinnings of his faith.

The schema that emerges from our model can be graphically portrayed as in Figure 1. Human consciousness is "naturally" endowed by God with the marvelous tool of rationality, which enables the self to organize the sense data temporally, spatially, and causally, and to make judgements regarding truth and falsity resulting in man's developing a growing dominion over his environment. Part of this natural endowment includes certain moral intuitions regarding gratitude and promise-keeping.[29]

This layer of rational and moral cognition enables man to "receive" Divine guidance, that is to say to perceive the guidance as divine at every stage of human development, to understand it and to interpret it and to

---

[29] See chapter 3 in my *Morality, Halakhah, and the Jewish Tradition* (New York: Yeshiva University Press, 1983).

decide to obey it. This is the element of *derech eretz* which may be said to be logically prior to Torah. Once the stratum of Torah or Divine guidance has been laid down and absorbed, it becomes the prism through which all subsequent expressions of general culture must be passed and analyzed. Many elements of general culture will easily pass through without any interference; others will be reshaped or modified in passage; still others will find their way irrevocably blocked. What should be kept in mind is that the process by which human culture penetrates to the consciousness of the religious Jew is a function of both the Torah and human reason working together, rather than a mechanical application of halakhic norms.

Viewed in this manner, Torah, for its part, was never then and is not now in competition with general culture. Since there is no confrontation between Torah and *derech eretz*, "synthesis" is neither desired nor desirable, nor even relevant. General culture is the raw material upon which Torah norms can operate and become effective. General culture, in all of its ramifications, is the life which our Torah (which, while it is truly "a desirable instrument," is still only an instrument[30]) comes to regulate and to sanctify.

Thus, the philosophy of modern Orthodoxy is not a cut and patched-up version of Orthodox Judaism, but an original conception flowing out of an authentic understanding of the meaning of Torah and its relationship to general culture. And it is within this modified structure of Torah, culture, and human reason that the modern Orthodox understandings of Halakhah, redemption, and *Klal Yisrael* find their traditional place and full expression.

---

[30] *Avot* 3:18.

Chapter Three

Is Judaism an Optimistic Religion?

Two intellectual currents have been the favorites of riders of the Jewish theological surf in recent years. One is the existentialist wave of pessimism, the sense of human helplessness and the futility of human reason, ridden mainly by estranged intellectuals returning to Judaism. The second is the "know thyself" current of depth psychology and psychiatry ridden mainly by leaders of Liberal and Reform Judaism. Presumably, Orthodoxy can get to the beach under its own motive power and needs the help of neither current. Certain interesting issues, however, have arisen as a result of the conflicting views on Judaism emerging from the two aforementioned groups.

Ever since the publication of *Peace of Mind* in 1946, publicists of liberal Judaism have not tired of pointing out the affinity between the counsels of psychiatry and the insights of Judaism. The secret of happiness, it is asserted, lies completely within the human being and his ability to accept a new morality which will overcome inner anxieties and teach him how to love, accept death with courage, and become a mature, responsible adult. God is to be encountered in a "good friend, a wise father, a loving mother, and in general in the love, sympathy and relationships of the world."[1] Man is a responsible co-worker with God who must persist in his confidence in eternal progress and social victory. Peace of mind, so understood, seemed to have primarily therapeutic value, consisting of the ability to accept life's disappointments, rejections, and death without becoming inwardly tormented or emotionally unhappy, or developing any recognizable neuroses or anxieties.[2] The underlying premise peculiar to this entire tendency is the notion that with the eradication of all mental illness and social evils, life in its "natural healthy state" justifies itself and will generate fulfillment and satisfaction.

---

[1] Joshua Loth Liebman, *Peace of Mind* (New York: Simon & Schuster, 1946), 165, 171.
[2] Ibid., 202.

Related to this view, and indeed presupposed by it, is the oft-repeated notion that Judaism is an optimistic religion. Speaking of the exaggerated pessimism of the existentialists, a leader of Liberal Judaism tells us that "this is diametrically opposed to Judaism, which does not build God's absolutism on man's nothingness. Man can, to a large degree, make it."[3] And again, we are told, "Judaism's faith is suffused with optimism, and therefore reactions against tendencies towards varieties of asceticism among Jews were bound to set in, for they were not at heart native or intrinsically Jewish. The life-loving and optimistic spirit of Judaism was certain to resist it."[4]

It appears to the present writer that much of the discussion on this subject has failed to maintain the distinction between optimism as the quality of metaphysics and optimism as the subjective state of an individual temperament. There can be no question that Judaism as a system of thought is metaphysically optimistic. Our view of the unity of God, the doctrine of creation *ex nihilo*, the perfectibility of man, the relative character of evil, and the promise of a messianic future all reflect an overall view which pronounces "good" upon the world and promises ultimate victory for the forces of divinity. However, it does not necessarily follow from this that the individual Jew, the devout believing Jew, is therefore endowed with a sustained optimistic mental attitude. The very opposite can be shown to be the case.

I disagree with the thesis which holds that historical lapses from "natural Jewish optimism" are to be explained in terms of persecution and suffering which darkened the cheerful Jewish spirit. If persecution and suffering made for pessimism, then it would be more correct to say that by now pessimism has become "natural" for the Jew. Moreover, pessimism has more often been the result of repletion and satiety than the result of want and deprivation. Koheleth was written by Solomon, not by Bar Kochba!

What I wish to assert is that any attempt to take God and Judaism seriously must involve profound, life-long anxieties, and not peace of mind in any usual sense of the term; that metaphysical optimism notwithstanding, the more accurate description of the Jewish religious temperament is probably pessimism; that in spite of the fact that the

---

[3] Abba Hillel Silver, *Where Judaism Differed* (New York: Macmillan, 1957), 179.
[4] Ibid., 210.

Chapter Three. Is Judaism an Optimistic Religion?

Torah does not forbid us to enjoy life, it does not follow that the thinking Jew therefore does enjoy it. The origins of liberal Judaism's bias in the direction of optimism are to be found in a weakness traditionally associated with the liberal position.[5]

It would be futile to attempt to demonstrate the optimistic or pessimistic character of Judaism solely by an appeal to appropriate passages in scripture and in the Talmud. Let us assume that one could amass an impressive collection of references in support of either view. Of course, the very ability to do this would suggest a rather comfortable hypothesis: perhaps Judaism *qua* Judaism is "beyond pessimism and optimism" and is something which lends itself to free will, to the determination of individual temperaments and historical epochs.[6]

Indeed William James, in one of the earliest analyses of the psychology of religion, distinguishes between what he calls "the religion of healthy-mindedness" and "the religion of the sick soul."[7] The former is an expression of a religious sentiment which is happy, optimistic, and usually extroverted. It sees the good in all things, looks upon evil and misfortune as an "accident," and greets the dawn of each new day with cheer and joy. The latter road is the opposite of all this. The religion of the "sick soul" is pessimistic and is given to periods of melancholy and depression. This type of religious sentiment senses the dark side of things, suffering and death, and sees little in life to be cheerful about. As students of the psychology of religion have pointed out, it is doubtful whether the majority of individuals fall into either of the categories represented by the extreme poles of these two approaches. More likely, one is apt to discover a continuum of characteristics.[8] However, if these categories are in any way descriptive of basic human types, than one can maintain that Judaism in its rich modal variety lies before the devotee, and that the "sick soul" opts for those elements conducive to his temperament while the "healthy-minded" appropriates those aspects suitable to his emotional structure.

---

[5] Walter Houston Clark, *The Psychology of Religion* (New York: Macmillan, 1958), 159.
[6] H. Rose, "Beyond Pessimism and Optimism," *Judaism* 6 (1957).
[7] William James, *The Varieties of Religious Experience* (New York: Modern Library, 1994), 66, 77-163.
[8] Clark, *Psychology of Religion*, 155.

While one may find occasional references which appear to support this approach, I nevertheless believe that a careful examination of the sources will reveal a structured view which leans in the direction of pessimism.[9] Of the two broad outlooks on life, pessimism and optimism, the former represents the more realistic and more Jewish view. Elsewhere, James rejects the view that answers the question "Is life worth living?" with the rejoinder "It depends upon the liver!" and casts his vote in favor of pessimism. Says he, "We are bound to say that morbid-mindedness ranges over the wider scale of experience. The method of averting one's attention from evil and living simply in the light of the good is splendid as long as it will work. But it breaks down impotently as soon as "tragedy comes."[10] Of course, asserts James, there are the lucky few who live their years unscathed and appear to escape frustrations and failures, catastrophes and sudden death. However, even the most healthy-minded of men must surely know what life can have in store.

The fact that we can die, that we can be ill at all, is what perplexes us; the fact that we now for a moment live and are well is irrelevant to that perplexity. We need a life not correlated to death, a health not liable to illness, a kind of food that will not perish, a good that flies beyond the goods of nature.[11]

As James astutely observed, "The luster of the present hour is always borrowed from the backgrounds of possibilities it goes with." Once a person's eyes are opened to the radical contingency of human life, the breath of the sepulcher will forever be present. Hence, "they [the morbid experiences of life] may be after all the best key to life's significance and possibly the only openers of our eyes to the deepest levels of truth."[12]

From another direction, Freud too confirms the basic unfriendliness of life to the program of the pleasure-principle. From three pervasive quarters there constantly arise experiences which run counter to happiness as construed in its narrow sense: from our own bodies, where anxiety and pain are danger signals of decay and dissolution; from the outer world with its forces of destruction; and from our relations with

---

[9] William James, *The Will to Believe* (New York: Dover, 1956), 32.
[10] James, *Varieties of Religious Experience*, 160.
[11] Ibid., 137.
[12] Ibid.

other men. Concludes Freud, "the intention that man should be 'happy' is not included in the scheme of 'creation'." [13]

I should like to call this realistic view, which sees much of man's existence as characterized by suffering, anxiety, and frustration, as "first-order pessimism." This type of pessimism has been incorporated in the philosophies of despair cultivated by the Stoics and the Epicureans. As James rightfully observed, Stoics and Epicureans should be considered not merely as historical schools, but as a "typical attitude marking a definite stage in the development of the sick soul."[14] One can clearly see this kind of attitude reflected in the writings of many thinkers today, who adopt the sober position of naturalism. While committed to a transcendent pessimism, they nevertheless advocate a philosophy which possesses at least courage and dignity. Sidney Hook, for example, pointed out that "pragmatism is an attempt to make it possible for men to live in a precarious world of inescapable tragedy ... by the arts of intelligent social control.... It may be a lost cause. I do not know of a better one.[15]

These views represent what James calls "the highest flight of purely natural man."

Let us examine the claims of the advocates of Jewish optimism and the Jewish love of life and attempt to comprehend how this is achieved. The thesis has been suggested that the Jewish way of life, with its Sabbaths, holidays, and ceremonials, gives the Jew a "zest for life" by simply developing his faculty "to get more joy than sorrow out of life."[16] "Although the cup of Jewish suffering was virtually always running over, the cup of Jewish joys was yet fuller."[17] This is a rather strange notion. Does the concept of *simcha shel mitzvah,* and the fact that the Jewish tradition bids us to enjoy life, imply that the resulting joy to the Jew is so intense that he will, to a greater degree than others, affirm life and tenaciously cling to it, "never be gloomy even in the most tragic periods," and "savor life as long as there is breath in one's nostrils"? What shall we

---

[13] Sigmund Freud, *Civilization and Its Discontents* (London: Hogarth Press, 1930), chapter 2.
[14] James, *Varieties of Religious Experience,* 141.
[15] Sidney Hook, "Pragmatism and the Tragic Sense of Life," *Commentary* 14, no. 10 (August 1960).
[16] Ibid.
[17] Trude Weiss-Rosmarin, *Jewish Survival* (New York: Philosophical Library, 1949), 207.

say of Rabbi Judah the Prince, who at his death called upon heaven as witness that he did not enjoy this world, even to the extent of his little finger?[18]

An alternative explanation is one which shifts the grounds of the Jewish will-to-live from an egotistic, subjective hedonism to the concept of a transcendent happiness. That is to say, Judaism as a system of values, irrespective of the joys it may give or not give, is considered meaningful and worthwhile. "Judaism fills the Jew rooted in the traditions of his people with the certainty of significant self-fulfillment before which even the harshest sufferings pale."[19] This is, of course, something entirely different. Such a view of the Jewish affirmation of life simply draws the implications of its metaphysical optimism and assigns to life values and meanings which are beyond the reach of the vicissitudes of our worldly existence. But then, what is unique about this? There are countless philosophies of life, including the classic formulations of ancient Greece, which equate man's happiness with the fulfillment of his particular *telos* or end, each differently conceived. Such abstract happiness, however, does not necessarily entail cheerfulness rather than sadness, joy rather than depression.

Upon consideration, it appears that the initial effect of a religious consciousness upon the outlook and feeling tone of an individual is in the direction of pessimism. James, for example, maintains that pessimism is essentially a religious disease. "It consists in nothing but a religious demand to which there comes no normal religious reply." On the basis of mere animal existence, the expression of first-order pessimism can perhaps be overcome by the resignation and courage of the Stoic approach. Man is a small part of a cosmic process. This is life and there is no more. Let us make the best of it.

But if, as a result of a religious orientation, man encourages attitudes which attribute a supreme worth to the human spirit and to certain values, and which see a Spirit beyond reality and posit intrinsic good, then the sheer contradiction between the religious evaluation of things and the harsh reality of existence plunges him into a nightmarish pessimism of a far deeper nature. Precisely because life is good, intrinsically good, transcendentally good, its negation is bad. To the extent that the

---

[18] *Ketubot* 104a. See commentaries of Rashi and Tosafot.
[19] Rosmarin, *Jewish Survival*, 210

religious outlook invests life with tremendous spiritual opportunities, to that extent must it look upon every frustration of these opportunities with increased horror and a heightened sense of tragedy. Thus we arrive at a "second order of pessimism," which has, as its reflective source, religious sentiment.

Whenever Judaism has been taken seriously, this element of pessimism has been apparent. Perhaps its clearest expression is to be found in the Talmud, wherein is recorded an issue debated for two and a half years between the House of Hillel and the House of Shammai. The House of Hillel maintained, "Better is it for man to have been created than not to have been created." The House of Shammai maintained, "Better would it have been for man not to have been created than to have been created." The issue was called to a decision, and it was concluded, "Better would it have been for man not to have been created, but now that he has been created, let him examine his behavior. [20] What we have here does not contradict the accepted view of the metaphysical optimism of Judaism. "And the Lord saw everything that He had made, and behold, it was very good." Creation gives man an opportunity he would otherwise not have. Nevertheless, looked at existentially, as part of my own individual, personal being, the possibility (no matter how small) of not achieving the goal, the possibility that my fate might be "death and evil" can well engender the reaction "Neither thy sting nor thy honey": better that I not be given this crushing responsibility, better not to have been created!

Indeed, the truly righteous person will constantly question and be critical of his own deeds and behavior, and will be forever anxious about the state of his relationship with God. Does not the Bible itself record that Jacob, in his hour of peril, "was sorely afraid" lest his sins be the cause of a suspension of God's providence? [21] Does not the Talmud stipulate that hints of the esoteric wisdom may be revealed only to him "whose heart worries inside of him?"[22] There can be no question but that the individual who takes the absolute demand of his religion seriously will develop profound anxieties of guilt concerning the quality and validity of his religious response. The modern Musar movement in particular stressed the need for constant vigilance and constant tension on the

---

[20] *Eruvin* 13b.
[21] Gen. 32:8.
[22] *Chagigah* 13a.

part of the God-fearing person. Rabbi Israel Salanter taught: "Man may be compared to the bird. It is within the power of the bird to ascend ever higher on condition that it continues to flap its wings without cessation. If it should stop flapping for a moment, it would fall into the abyss. So is it with man."[23]

Psychologists have observed the conditional quality of even the most ego-bolstering of Jewish concepts. One of them remarks rather perceptively, "The Jews have very often been in situations which have caused them to doubt ... the love of their God.... All their trials and tribulations have been regarded as sent by God as punishment for their sins, but also as special proof of His love, since only through suffering could they be made worthy of a Covenant with Him ... the Jew's self-esteem has none of the serenity of certainty. It is restless and based on doubts."[24] A recent sociological study of the shtetl finds evidence of "intense and unremitting anxiety" in spite of strict observance of the law. The very elements which liberal Judaism sees as making for optimism are seen here as conducive to anxiety:

> The combination of the two concepts, free will and predestination, discourages fatalism and fosters anxiety. God has decreed the circumstances of each man's life but the individual alone is responsible for what he does with them. There are so many opportunities for failure in fulfillment of the commandments, in the amount of effort one expends on earning a livelihood, in all one's activities and relationships. Ignorance of circumstances may be an excuse, but ignorance of the Law is not, and there is no excuse for ignorance due to oversight or negligence. Obligations are so many, opposite God, family, and fellows, that no matter how much one does, it is never really enough. There is always the burden of un-discharged duty.[25]

There is yet another aspect to this issue. The existentialist analysis of man as a creature beset by a natural anxiety stemming from his awareness of his own finitude affords us an opportunity to restate the

---

[23] Dov Katz, *Tenuat ha-Musar* (Tel Aviv: Beita ha-Sefer, 1946), 269.
[24] Rudolph M. Loewenstein, *Christians and Jews* (New York: International Universities Press, 1952), 139.
[25] Mark Zborowski and Elizabeth Herzog, *Life is with People* (New York: International Universities Press, 1952), 411.

authentic Jewish view on a metaphysical level. Existentialist literature abounds with analyses of man's growing anxiety and sense of alienation. To call our time an age of anxiety has become almost a truism. Alienation is a fact. Undoubtedly all of the sociological explanations— the breakdown of the family, the impersonalism of modem industry, the uncontrollability of political events, the element of infinitude in the new cosmological image—are relevant. Alienation is a multidimensional phenomenon. Religious thinkers, however, have asked whether modem man's estrangement is merely "the itch of personal neuroses" to be overcome by the wisdom of the Fromms and Peales, or whether it is perhaps revelatory of human existence as it really is. The latter view holds that there are forms of anxiety which belong to existence as such and are to be distinguished from an abnormal state of mind, as in neurotic anxiety. This notion is already implicit in the account of Genesis, in which man is described as having been created in a condition of freedom—a condition of sheer possibility, in which he can negate as well as affirm, destroy as well as create. This condition of indeterminate potentiality with its awful responsibilities is already a condition of anxiety. Finitude, temporality, selfhood, and sexuality are aspects of the grandeur of creation. But we rarely encounter them in this unspoiled condition. "Sin lieth at the door and its desire is unto thee, but thou canst rule over it."[26]

Kierkegaard and Tillich after him raised the phenomena of guilt, fear, despair, the prospect of one's own death, and the prospect of salvation beyond the sphere of purely psychological considerations into aspects of metaphysical thought, which is what they have always been for traditional Judaism. Kierkegaard maintains that the self is a synthesis of the infinite and the finite, the eternal and the temporal, freedom and necessity.[27] Man is thus not self-sufficient and can achieve true selfhood only by being related aright to God. Whether man is aware of it or not, God is both the criterion and the goal of selfhood. Hence, whoever has no God has no self, and whoever has no self is in despair, which is a specific illness of man as a spiritual being. Despair, to Kierkegaard, is any imbalance in the relationship of the self to itself. Any attempt by man to

---

[26] Gen. 4:7.
[27] Soren Kierkegaard, *The Sickness unto Death* (New York: Doubleday, 1954), 182-207.

separate himself from the power which created him, or to neglect what is eternal in him, or to fight his spiritual nature, will result in despair. Kierkegaard goes on to analyze the different types of despair, such as the "despair of weakness" and the "despair of defiance," which correspond to well-known types in the Jewish gallery of the godless. There is little here that Jewish theology could not agree with. Even Tillich's formulation of the basic types of anxieties[28]—the anxiety of death, the anxiety of meaninglessness, and the anxiety of guilt—is implicit in traditional accounts of repentance.[29]

---

[28] Paul Tillich, *The Courage to Be* (New Haven: Yale University Press, 1952), 35, 27.

[29] Despair of weakness is the unwillingness to be oneself, which results in a life of pure immediacy. In this condition, a person looks at others in order to discover what he himself is and "recognizes himself by his dress." He becomes "an imitation, a number, a cipher in the crowd." He flees reflection, plunges into the outgoing, active life, and takes his cue from external circumstances. If he ever experiences self-reflection, it is thrust into forgetfulness or attributed to the instability of youth. In despair of defiance, man wills to be himself but tries to overcome finitude on his own power. He attempts to create his self to his own specifications by sheer assertion of will. This is "the despairing abuse of the eternal in the self to the point of being despairingly determined to be oneself." In its final desperate form, this defiance turns into demonic rage, in which the despairer wills to be himself with his torment, which he believes constitutes a proof against the goodness of existence, and thus revolts and protests against the whole of existence. He will not hear of any help, because comfort now "would be the destruction of him as an objection against existence and would rid him of his justification for being what he is." From this psychological analysis, Kierkegaard moves forward to theological considerations and asserts that "sin is the potentiation of despair before God."

These analyses apply quite readily to well-known types in our own literature. The despair of weakness may well explain the disciples of Balaam, with their "evil eye, haughty spirit, and excessive desire" (*Avot* 5:22), or even he who "blesses himself in his heart saying, I will have peace" (Deut. 29:18), or the *kesil*, who has all the knowledge but is lost in his "immediacy" (see commentary of Malbim on Prov. 1:22), or those "whose stomachs have become their gods, and their clothing their Torah" (*Chovot ha-Levavot*, Shaar ha-Perishut 2). Those afflicted with the despair of defiance have a recognized niche in Jewish thought. This genre starts with Nimrod, who "knows his Master but deliberately rebels against Him" (see Rashi on Gen. 10:9), continues with the "stiff-necked ones who persist in their ways though there be proof to the contrary" (see Sforno on Deut. 9:6), and concludes with the "wicked ones who refuse to repent even on the threshold of Gehinnom" (*Eruvin* 19a).

Chapter Three. Is Judaism an Optimistic Religion?

Another approach, also not without interest to traditional Jewish thinking, sees as basic in current analyses of the dynamics of anxiety a positive urge that is somehow frustrated. This view maintains that the experience of anxiety has a certain constant structure. Whether described by a Catholic mystic, an agnostic existentialist, or an atheistic psychoanalyst, it exhibits a specific character. "That character is anxious longing. The experience itself is constituted by a polar tension between fear and longing. Anxiety is desire aware of a threat to its fulfillment."[30]

Could we not therefore understand anxiety as the consequence of a genuine desire for God, a longing for the elements of goodness and divinity, and at the same time a reflection of the impediments faced by this finite creature in responding to this call? The anxiety of the sinner is thus his tendency to erect false gods and encounter inevitable

---

According to Tillich, man's ontic self-affirmation as a created being is threatened from three directions by nonbeing. Awareness of this threefold threat is anxiety appearing in three forms: threat of death, threat of emptiness or loss of meaning, and threat of condemnation or guilt. In all of these the anxiety is existential, i.e., it belongs to man's nature. If we accept this analysis, then making man aware of his anxieties and the sources of his anxieties can perhaps bring him to the realization that he can overcome these anxieties only by grounding himself in God.

It is not difficult to see that the rabbis have consistently appealed to these three kinds of anxieties in attempting to bring about the experience of repentance. The entire Book of Koheleth is an appeal to the emptiness of man's existence if it is lived only "under the sun" (see R. Jonah Gerondi, *Shaarei Teshuva* 2: 19-20). Remembrance of the day of one's death is suggested as the most potent stimulus for *teshuva* (Berachot 5), while the constant theme of the prophets is to point to Israel's obligation, both collectively and individually, to God as "liberator from Egypt," as "Father and as Master," as "the Rock that begot thee," and "the God who made thee," and the ingratitude with which Israel has responded. The purpose of all of this is, of course, to generate a sense of guilt and remorse, which is the first step toward repentance (Maimonides, Hilchot Teshuva 2:2).

It is quite plausible that these three anxieties are implied in the dictum of R. Akavya ben Mahalel: "You come from a fetid drop"—your existence, due essentially to egotistic sexuality, is thus meaningless. "You are going to a place of dust and worms"—the anxiety of death. And "Before Whom are you destined to give judgment and reckoning? Before the Almighty"—the anxiety of guilt (*Avot* 3:1).

[30] Fred Berthold, Jr., *Fear of God* (New York: Harper, 1959), 75, 90, 92.

frustration as he seeks to satisfy the soul's thirst for God with imperfect substitutes of things of this world.

Expressions of the soul thirsting after God are found in Psalms[31]. Rabbi Joseph Albo taught, "Everything has a desire for that which is of the same nature as and similar to itself ... so the mind desires to fulfill the will of God because it is natural to do so."[32] Rabbi Nissan ben Reuben adds: "Just as man's sense of touch fears the fire because it is contrary to its nature, so does the mind fear to violate the commands of the Almighty because its very nature requires compliance."[33] It remains for us to draw the implications and with them to formulate a hypothesis in explanation of the empirical phenomena of anxiety and alienation. Indeed, Saadia already saw this as an intimation of the world-to-come:

> I find furthermore that none of God's creatures known to me feel secure and tranquil in this world, even when they have reached the most exalted ruling position and the highest station therein. Now this feeling is not something natural to the soul. It is due, rather, to its consciousness of the fact that there is reserved for it an abode that is superior to all the excellence of its present dwelling. That is why its eyes look forward longingly to it. Were it not so, the soul would have felt secure and have been at rest.[34]

It appears, therefore, that traditional Judaism possesses all the ingredients required for creating a doctrine of human nature which could incorporate the phenomenon of existential anxiety and offer an explanation for man's growing sense of alienation. We stated that the initial effect of the religious outlook is in the direction of pessimism. The religious person is in a position to develop a fuller recognition of the terror and insecurity of ordinary human life, of the blackness of sin, and, as far as one's own strength goes, of the possibility of slipping back into evil and nothingness. Indeed, it has been rightfully said that the religious outlook does not give peace of mind but simply substitutes the right anxieties for the wrong anxieties. This is reflected in a teaching of

---

[31] Psalms 42:2, 3; 63:2.
[32] Joseph Albo, *Sefer Ha-Ikarim*, vol. 3 (Philadelphia: Jewish Publication Society, 1930), 301.
[33] Rabbenu Nissim, *Shneim Assar Derushim* (Jerusalem, 1955), *derash* 10, p. 69.
[34] Saadia Gaon, *The Book of Beliefs and Opinions* (New Haven: Yale University Press, 1948), Treatise IX, chapter 1, p. 324.

Rabbi Nachman of Bratslav: "Man is afraid of things that cannot harm him and he knows it, and he craves things that cannot be of help to him and he knows it; but in truth the one thing man is afraid of is within himself and the one thing he craves is within himself."[35]

Is this, however, the ultimate condition, or can we perhaps find in Judaism some final turn, some higher level of feeling which bespeaks joy? I believe that the key to the teaching of Judaism on this point lies in the phrase "serve the Lord with fear and rejoice in trembling."[36]

Thinkers as diverse as Rabbi Joseph Albo and Rabbi Judah Loew of Prague are one in their understanding of this passage.[37] Both agree in describing man's initial awareness of himself as a creature subject to contingency and temporality in terms of fear and sadness which cause the heart "to tremble and grieve." Rabbi Loew specifically points to what we have called the first-order pessimism of the creature as he faces death, and also the second-order pessimism which takes hold of man as he contemplates the rigors of ultimate judgment. This is the fear of God, which is not only the beginning of wisdom but the ultimate salvation. This state of fear and trembling is prior to any other and constitutes "the fundamental spirit of service." As a more recent thinker has put it,

> All religious reality begins with what biblical religion calls the "fear of God." It comes when our existence between birth and death becomes incomprehensible and uncanny, when all security is shattered through the mystery. This is not the relative mystery of that which is inaccessible only to the present state of human knowledge and is hence in principle discoverable. It is the essential mystery, the inscrutableness of which belongs to its very nature; it is the unknowable.[38]

However, once man reaches the state of fear of God he can, as he contemplates his trembling, find cause for joy, "because he realizes that he fears that which is deserving of fear—an indication of spiritual perfection and health on his part.."[39] This "joy in trembling" is neither the

---

[35] Martin Buber, *The Tales of Rabbi Nachman* (New York: Horizon Press, 1956), 37.
[36] Psalms 2:11.
[37] Albo, *Sefer Ha-Ikarim*, 308; Judah Loewe, *Netivot Olam* (Tel Aviv: Pardes, 1956), Netiv Halizanut, 167. See also discussion in *Berakhot* 30.
[38] Martin Buber, *Eclipse of God* (New York: Harper, 1952), 50.
[39] Albo, *Sefer Ha-Ikarim*.

hedonistic zest of life described above nor the healthy-minded optimism which believes it can, by positive thinking and talking, blind itself to the grim realities of life. This Jewish joy is instead a tempered optimism, a "holy insecurity" which recognizes that existence has meaning under God not in spite of its tragedies and sufferings, but perhaps through its tragedies and sufferings, by means of the trivial and the prosaic. Kierkegaard observed with great sensitivity that Abraham, who attained the level of faith, unlike one who has merely achieved the level of resignation, does not lose the finite but rather regains it.[40] "After passing through the dark gate, the believing man steps forth into the everyday which is henceforth hallowed as the place in which he has to live with mystery."[41] The believing Jew has looked sadness in the face. He knows that wife, family, career, and daily tasks are not the ultimate answer. But precisely because he has accepted their contingency they can have for him freshness and be a source of tempered joy. We can indeed experience the simple joys of life if we know their limitations beforehand. The cry of "vanity of vanities, all is vanity" comes as no surprise, because we did not strain the simple joys with a burden they are not equipped to bear. We did not ask them to justify life for us. "Serve the Lord with fear, and rejoice in trembling."

In summation, Judaism as a metaphysical system is optimistic, yet recognizes fully the tragic character of human existence. On the existential level, it fosters sobriety and shifts the locus of anxieties to the areas that count—concern for the state of one's soul and one's relationship to God. Those who repress their thirst for the spirit expose themselves to futile frustrations and suffer the unmitigated consequences of man's naturally anxious condition. The mature religious personality who fixes his gaze on the infinite can, however, regain the finite in tempered joy.

---

[40] Soren Kierkegaard, *Fear and Trembling* (New York: Doubleday, 1954), 46.
[41] Buber, *Eclipse of God*.

Chapter Four

The Meaning of Existentialism for Orthodoxy

Husserl once wrote that there were two steps in the spread of a new doctrine. In the first stage, everyone cries, "It is absurd!" During the second stage, everyone sneers indignantly, "But everyone knows that!"

In considering the impact the movement known as Existentialism has had on Jewish thinking, one finds both of the above reactions happening at once. However, in our case the reasons for the divergence of the reactions stem from sources much deeper than the psychological vagaries of the human response to the new.

First, what do we mean by Existentialism? This "new thinking" has both a technical, philosophic meaning and a broader, more general connotation, with ramifications in psychology as well as in the arts. Its particular contribution philosophically is the idea that existence is prior to essence. As such, Existentialism is a reaction against the Hegelian world view which moved from pure thought to actuality and existence. Out of pure logic, the existentialist argued, the hard, concrete fact of individual existence could never emerge. The existence which was thus juxtaposed to the ethereal "essences" was not simply uniform sense impressions or even the "big booming buzzing confusion" of William James but the unique, inexpressible concreteness of one's own particular existence. If Kant was correct that existence cannot be represented by a concept, it is not because it is too general and remote to be conceived, but rather because it is too rich and concrete. "The fact that I exist is so compelling and enveloping a reality that it cannot be reproduced thinly in a mental concept."[1]

Given this basic orientation, Existentialism has exhibited certain general characteristics in all of the various forms it has taken. To begin with, it is a protest against all forms of rationalism, which assume that reality can be completely understood and explained by intellectual

---

[1] William Barrett, *Irrational Man* (New York: Anchor, 1962), 144.

means. It opposes the assertion that "the real is rational, and the rational, the real." However, it is absurd to claim that Existentialism is therefore a reversion to "mysticism and superstition" and hence a step backward. Existentialist thinking does not deny the validity or the importance of reason's achievements in the realm of science. It merely maintains that reason has its definite limitations; that the most significant areas of life may have been bypassed by the objective quantitative methods of science.

Secondly, Existentialism is in opposition to all views which regard man as fully explained in terms of chemical reactions and electrical impulses, of social functions and mechanical movements. It upholds the uniqueness of the individual person, the preciousness of his spontaneity and freedom, urging resistance to the influences of mass-mindedness and conformities of an increasingly regulated society. But of greater significance is the fact that Existentialism sees the human predicament as filled with contradictions and tensions. This condition is not something which can be remedied by scientific discovery or by better education because it stems from the very nature of man himself—"a being darkly wise and rudely great ... in doubt to deem himself a god or beast"—finite and moving inevitably towards death, yet free in action and imagination. As such, man is fundamentally ambiguous, torn by doubts and anxieties, inner strife, and feelings of estrangement.

Finally, Existentialism emphasizes the notion of the committed or "impassioned" thinker by sharply distinguishing between objective and subjective truth. Again, while not denying that science and logic can give us genuine, verifiable, objective truth, it nevertheless asserts that for the ultimate issues of life one cannot ignore the concerns and feelings of the individual thinker. The whole man, with the involvement of his entire subjective being, must be "grasped by the truth" to the point where he is ready to commit his life in a really decisive way.

Such a sketchy characterization is of necessity oversimplified and incomplete. However, I believe it catches the more outstanding emphasis of the movement, which for our present purposes should be adequate.[2]

Now then, what can such a philosophy mean to the Jewish thinker? It has already been observed that, on the whole, Reform and Reconstruc-

---

[2] John Passmore, ed., *A Hundred Years of Philosophy* (London: Gerald Duckworth and Co., 1957), chapter 19.

Chapter Four. The Meaning of Existentialism for Orthodoxy

tionist Judaism have rejected Existentialism.³ It must be agreed that the reason for liberal Judaism's lack of sympathy could hardly be because of the "Christian religious origin" of Existentialism, first because, as we shall show, Existentialism does not begin and end with Kierkegaard, and secondly, because liberal Judaism does not necessarily have an aversion to Christian influence. As correctly surmised by Eugene Borowitz, the reason goes deeper than that. For indeed, Reform and Reconstructionism are based upon reason, and therefore oppose a movement which sees reason "humiliated" before the vital realities of life. One can therefore expect disagreement and opposition, but how is one to explain, as Borowitz astutely observes, "the fury of their attack"?

I would like to suggest that the very existence, and certainly the growing acceptance, of Existentialism today invalidates and undermines the entire intellectual justification of liberal Judaism. Ostensibly, Reform was necessary because the modern, enlightened, sophisticated Jew could no longer recite the thirteen *ani maamins* with conviction. A supernatural G-d, Revelation, a personal messiah, prayer in expectation of an answer—these could no longer be accepted in the rational world of the enlightenment.⁴ The changes in practices and rituals that were instituted were the consequences of the prior breakdown of traditional theological principles. Similarly, the entire emphasis of Reconstructionism has been on naturalism and acceptance of the overriding role of intelligence in human affairs as being the application of the scientific method to the social realm. The influence of scientism and Deweyan pragmatism in the thinking of Mordechai Kaplan, the founder of Reconstructionism, is quite apparent.⁵ Here too then, Judaism has been reformed and reformulated to coincide with what an educated Jew steeped in the dominant philosophy of that day could supposedly believe in.

Now what we have in Existentialism is a long-awaited corrective which contraverts the popular assumption that the practical achievements of science validate beyond dispute the views of logical Positivism

---

[3] Eugene Borowitz, "Existentialism's Meaning for Judaism," *Commentary* 28, no. 5 (Nov. 1959).

[4] "Judaism is a Progressive Religion ever Striving to be in Accord with the Postulates of Reason," *Pittsburgh Platform Yearbook* (Pittsburgh: Central Conference of American Rabbis, 1935).

[5] See Jacob Agus, *Modern Philosophies of Judaism* (New York: Behrman, 1970), 296 and 309.

or pragmatism with their denial of everything which cannot fit into the instruments of science. Theological categories which were clearly to be avoided at all costs by any wide-awake apologist for Orthodoxy are today considered quite fashionable and tenable even in the light of modern knowledge. The criteria of a meaningful religious system are no longer the mental stability it may bring or its possibility of social acceptance, the doctrines it shares with other religions or its sweet reasonableness. On the contrary, the very elements of Judaism which but yesterday were in ill repute—the Jewish people's unique chosenness, the reality of evil, the deadly seriousness and unconditional demands of the life of service to God—have today been reinstated. A sign of the times is a very curious review of Herman Wouk's *This is My God*, in which the author is criticized for omitting a glimpse of "the vision of that which exceeds man, of the grandeur which upsets and destroys his stupidity, arrogance, and selfishness," and in general for not treating the basic theological themes of Orthodoxy such as Revelation, election of Israel, etc.[6]

I do not wish to argue at this point that the popularity of Existentialism in any way proves the superiority of Orthodoxy. What I am asserting is that the strictly rational approach to religion seen as decisively compelling because it supposedly carried the exclusive *hechsher* of modern times, and in response to which traditional Judaism had to be refashioned—can today be seen as only one approach among many. Indeed, it appears today that Reform was merely the "product of the simple-minded rationalism of the times."[7]

The reasons for the "fury of the attack" are now clear. Even if Existentialism is only a "possible" approach, liberal Judaism stands condemned of indecent haste in rejecting vital and meaningful aspects of traditional Judaism. Its *teshuva* cannot stop at the adoption of more ceremonials but must involve a thorough re-examination of its motivating fundamentals. Looking back at the road it has taken over the past century, liberal Judaism must ask itself—was this trip necessary?

From the Orthodox point of view, however, the importance of Existentialism is far greater than its merely negative role as a caster of

---

[6] Arthur A. Cohen, "Herman Wouk's Orthodoxy," *Congress Bi-Weekly*, November 2, 1959.

[7] Nathan Glazer, *American Judaism* (Chicago: University of Chicago Press, 1957), 52.

doubts upon Reform and Reconstructionist premises. However, this must be understood in correct perspective. In surveying the Orthodox movement, Eugene Borowitz finds in the person of Rabbi J. B. Soloveitchik a "committed Existentialist" and in his thought, "Orthodox Existentialism." However, Borowitz continues, "most of the leaders (Orthodox) are unprepared for so radical a readjustment."[8] I believe this is an incorrect analysis. If Rabbi Soloveitchik is an Existentialist, so was my teacher, Rabbi Shraga Feivel Mendlowitz,[9] and indeed so was Rabbi Moses Hayyim Luzzatto, and certainly Rabbi Yehuda Halevi. I submit that almost all of the fundamental Existentialist approaches are indigenous to Orthodox Judaism and have been basic to the main stream of authentic Jewish thinking through biblical, Talmudic, and medieval times. The similarity between the biblical approach and Existentialism has been seen by almost every serious student of the subject. As David Roberts observes, "Indeed anyone who takes biblical revelation seriously must approach philosophical problems in a fashion which incorporates certain Existential elements, whether he uses the term or not."[10] And as William Barrett states, "The features of Hebraic man are those which Existential philosophy has attempted to exhume and bring to the reflective consciousness of our time."[11]

What are the features of Hebraic man? Certainly Judaism has always had its rational strain. However, not only has Judaism always maintained that reason could not fathom the ultimate mysteries of reality, but it has also argued that the cultivation of reason itself was not the most important religious virtue. The non-rational element in Judaism has not simply been the inexplicable mystery of the Sinaitic revelation but rather the concept that the religious experience as such and the highest religious quality is not the intellectual knowledge of God but the love for, joy in, and fear of the Lord which permeate the Jew's entire being.[12]

In his *Kuzari*, Halevi states that the category of the Holy represents a level of experience *sui generis* irreducible to intellectual or emotional

---

[8] Borowitz, "Existentialism's Meaning for Judaism."
[9] Dean of Yeshiva and Metifta Torah Vodaath in Brooklyn, New York.
[10] David Roberts, *Existentialism and Religious Belief* (Oxford: Oxford University Press, 1957), 4.
[11] Barrett, "Irrational Man," 69.
[12] Joseph Albo, *Sefer Ha-Ikarim*, vol. 3 (Philadelphia: Jewish Publication Society, 1930).

terms.[13] Thus, not only are certain principles of Judaism beyond rational explication, but what vitally concerns Judaism is the total man inasmuch as "fear of the Lord" involves thought, feeling, and behavior. The concept of the whole person, serving the Lord in fear and joy through the total community, received further expression in the hasidic movement, which explains the movement's popularity with Existential thinkers.[14]

Again, the notion that the inner life of the religious personality is not all "green pastures" and "still waters," but is rather an existence of inner doubts, anguish, struggle, and pain, is an insight open to any serious reader of the Bible. From the Patriarchs through Moses, through the Prophets, through the passionate expressions of David in the Psalms, to the classic experience of Job, it is clear that even to know God and to hear His voice is still to experience fear and doubt, anguish and remorse and black failure. This has always been so. We cannot deny this simply because Karl Barth now appreciates these basic biblical insights. Preoccupation with these themes in Soloveitchik's *Man of Halacha* is probably the reason for designating him an Existentialist.[15]

Furthermore, there have always been in Judaism implicit and explicit basic paradoxes, such as those of free will vs. God's omniscience, time vs. eternity, pride vs. humility, *din* vs. *rachamim*, transcendence vs. immanence, and *keva* vs. *kavana*, which reason has been unable to solve without doing violence to one of the elements involved. Today, under the liberating influence of Existentialism, we tend to approach these problems in terms of polarity or an unblushing acceptance of the paradox. But here again, Existentialism did not contribute the paradoxes, but merely gave us the courage to face up to them and to savor their truth in the full strength of their irrationality.

Another Existential element always present in traditional Jewish thought has been an awareness of the obtrusiveness and reality of evil. The depth of man's evil capacities and the existence of the demonic are reported again and again in the Bible, causing untold embarrassment

---

[13] Judah Halevi, *Kuzari*, Part III, 23. See also chapters on Halevi in Heinneman, *Taamei Ha-Mitzvot b'sifrut Yisrael* (Jerusalem, 1966).
[14] See works of Buber.
[15] Rabbi Joseph B. Soloveitchik, "Man of Halacha," *Talpioth* 1, no. 3-4 (April-Sept., 1944): 653, footnote 4.

to Sunday school teachers. The influence of the "progress" myth on Judaism as well as the "goody-goody" theory of human nature are well known. Yet it was the Jew's intuitive grasp of reality which would not permit him to take seriously a theory which taught that "evil was a negation—simply the absence of good," and which instead caused him to take to heart the Kabbala (and the Zohar), which "did not turn its back upon the primitive side of life, that all-important region where mortals are afraid of life and in fear of death, and derive scant wisdom from rational philosophy. To most Kabbalists the existence of evil is one of the most pressing problems. They have a strong sense of the reality of evil and the dark horror that is about everything living."[16] This preoccupation with man's sinful propensities, and its conscious and subconscious manifestations, have been passed on to the Musar movement and thence to modern Orthodoxy.[17]

The role of the irrational in Judaism was recently subjected to further probing and study thanks to Existentialism. Abraham's offering of Isaac—the Akeda—long ago relegated to the exclusive domain of Rosh Hashana sermon material, has once again come alive in the pages of our serious periodicals. The issue: is Kierkegaard's interpretation of the Akeda, as the teleological suspension of the ethical, a Jewish view? Do we really have in the Akeda an instance wherein the command of the Divine contradicts the ethical norm? Attempts to refute the Kierkegaardian interpretation have been as varied as they have been futile.[18] One can indeed claim that the case is atypical, or that God's refusing the sacrifice reinstates the ethical as higher. Nevertheless, I fail to see how anyone at all familiar with rabbinic thought can deny that from the point of view of Abraham, he was being asked not only to give up his son, but also to sacrifice his entire rational understanding of God's consistency, God's requirements of him in terms of ethical behavior, and his entire historic future through Isaac as promised by

---

[16] Gershom Scholem, *Major Trends in Jewish Mysticism* (New York: Shocken Books, 1941), 35.

[17] See Rabbi Dov Katz, *Tnuat Ha-Musar*, vol. 1 (Jerusalem: Magnes Press, 1982), 54-56.

[18] Joseph H. Gumbiner, "Existentialism and Father Abraham," *Commentary* 5 (Feb. 1948); David Baumgardt, "Man's Morals and God's Will," *Commentary* 9 (Mar. 1950); Marvin Fox, "Kierkegaard and Rabbinic Judaism," *Judaism* 2 (1953).

God.[19] That this profound anguish was part of Abraham's experience is clearly stated by the Midrash:

> Rav Acha said—Abraham asked, "Yesterday you promised: 'For in Isaac will thy seed be called.' Then you changed and commanded me: 'Take your only son and offer as a sacrifice.' And now you change again and declare: 'Do not stretch forth thy hand upon the lad.' I am bewildered."[20]

What this implies in terms of the general nature of "faith" and its relation to the ethical is another matter. Here one need not agree with Kierkegaard. But I am convinced that in his *Fear and Trembling*, insofar as we are accorded insight into the agonizing experience of Abraham, Kierkegaard's approach is truly rabbinic. The only question which remains to be answered is, does this make of Kierkegaard a rabbinite, or of Rav Acha an Existentialist?

Finally, the notion of the "Impassioned Thinker" is clearly identical with the biblical image of the man of faith. Nowhere in the Bible is detached wisdom or abstract thought held up as the path to be followed. Abraham's truth, initially intellectual according to the Midrash, becomes decisive only when he is ready to enter Nimrod's furnace in its defense and commit his entire future on its behalf. Jacob risks even his father's love and respect in his faith in the meaning of the mission of Abraham. Nowhere are correct thoughts alone applauded; only decisive deeds stemming from fateful commitments are viewed with approval: Moses' violent intercession on behalf of the beaten Jewish slave; the plunge of Nachshon Ben Aminadov into the Red Sea; the quick action of Pinchas, the zealot. Indeed, the key to an understanding of Job lies in the transformation of a religious loyalty that is at first formal and impersonal into a shattering experience involving the very core of Job's existence. This is the charge of Eliphaz: "Thy words have upholden him that was falling, and thou hast strengthened the feeble knees. But now it is come unto thee, and thou are weary, it toucheth thee and thou

---

[19] This has been seen by Jacob L. Halevi, "Kierkegaard and the Midrash," *Judaism* 4 (1955). It has also been discussed by I. Epstein, *Faith of Judaism* (London: Soncino Press, 1954), 88.

[20] *Bereshit Rabbah*, 56:12. Compare with Soloveitchik, "Man of Halacha," footnote 5.

are afrighted."²¹ Job is thoroughly familiar with all the rational explanations of "evil" and, in fact, used them in an academic sort of way to console others in their misery. But now the problem of evil has become an "existential" one for Job, a terribly personal matter. And so Eliphaz poses the question: can religion based on rational understanding alone prove adequate for a deeply involved person whose very existence is now imperiled? In the end, of course, Job's relationship to God also moves on to the Existential plane.

In short, then, Rabbi Soloveitchik's thinking is profound biblical insight seen from the special perspective of the Volozhin-Brisk tradition with its emphasis upon Halakhah. I do not believe that it warrants the designation "Existential." What Existentialism has done has been to create the philosophical climate, and to popularize certain categories of thought, wherein classic biblical concepts can again be spoken of and appreciated. It is instructive to note that the same difficulty of "classification" has arisen in connection with another genuinely Jewish thinker—A. J. Heschel. As has been convincingly shown, Heschel remains a biblical thinker writing from the special perspective of hasidic inwardness, rather than an Existentialist.²² The only legitimate meaning that could possibly be accorded the term "Orthodox Existentialist" would be to designate a person who has arrived at Orthodoxy through an awareness of his Existential predicament.

It is perhaps in this last point that we find the chief significance of Existentialism for Orthodoxy. Quite obviously, if we have atheistic Existentialism as well as religious Existentialism, then the philosophy of Existentialism is not a religious philosophy as such. It is, however, "a brilliant statement of the tragic dilemma of man in our time."²³ Therefore, Existentialism is of great benefit to Orthodoxy in describing and analyzing for us the characteristics and symptoms of man's predicament without God. Even Nietzsche's or Sartre's insights are of inestimable value in ripping aside the illusions, the anodynes with which society

---

[21] Job 4:4, 5.
[22] J.J. Petuchowski, "Faith as the Leap of Action," *Commentary* 25, no. 5 (May 1958), Edmond L. Cherbonnier, "A.J. Heschel and the Philosophy of the Bible," *Commentary* 27, no. 1 (Jan. 1959).
[23] Marjorie Grene, *Dreadful Freedom* (Chicago: University of Chicago Press, 1948), 14.

and routine seek to anaesthetize us to the abyss beneath our feet. If, indeed, estrangement and anxiety, finitude and guilt, characterize man's universal condition, then we may ask how he got this way, and what we must do to overcome this estrangement. As Tillich has put it, "The Existentialist raises the question to which the theologian can then give the answer—an answer given not from the human situation itself."[24] There are, of course, many answers—secular, atheistic, and nihilistic. But at the end of the Existentialist road one can indeed opt for the religious commitment, and the life under God. For the religious hypothesis including the meaning of God and the consequences of sin can indeed explain how it is possible that the being of man exhibits such a structure. Without falling into the doctrine of original sin, the philosophic Kabbalists such as Rabbi M. Ch. Luzzatto make much of man's expulsion from Eden as the cause of man's ambiguous situation. Indeed, the dire predictions of the *tochacha* need not be interpreted in the sense of physical persecution only, but may also reflect man's anguish and inner conflict resulting from an existence without God. "The Lord shall give thee there a trembling heart, and a failing of eyes, and sorrow of mind ... so that they will say on that day: Are not these evils come upon us because our God is not among us?"[25]

But how indeed does the traveler of the Existentialist road cross the abyss of nothingness to arrive upon the firm ground of faith? Herberg speaks of a "leap of faith." Heschel advocates a "leap of action." William James once spoke of a "will to believe." And the high priests of reason in the academic halls of American Judaism seem scandalized by all this. And yet how does faith come to a Jew who has not had it before? The rabbis spoke of *kabbalat ol malchut shamayim*—"acceptance of the yoke of the Kingdom of Heaven," which is embodied in the declaration of Shema, and which was recognized as belonging to a class of experience logically prior to the acceptance and performance of the mitzvot.[26] This was identified with the first of the Ten Commandments—"I am the Lord thy God"—and construed by Maimonides as a command to believe in the existence of God. Precisely what is involved in the "ac-

---

[24] Paul Tillich, *Theology of Culture* (New York: Oxford University Press, 1964), 125.
[25] See Deut. 28:65, Deut. 31:17. Compare to Soloveitchik, *Man of Halacha*, footnote 4.
[26] See Mechilta on Exod. 20:3.

Chapter Four. The Meaning of Existentialism for Orthodoxy

ceptance of the yoke of the Kingdom of Heaven"? Surely it must involve one's volition—if not, it could not be the subject of a mitzvah! What difference, then, if a decision to accept the authority of the Lord and His Revelation is called a step, a leap, a skip, or a jump! Is anyone prepared to take the position that there is an official way in which a man arrives at faith in God which precludes the term "leap"?[27]

Abarbanel, for example, states that belief in God involves certain preparations in the form of seeking, examining nature, studying religion, and reading the Bible which are matters of the will. This much a man is commanded to do, for it is within his power. However, the fully developed faith in God as a completed state of mind comes of itself as a consequence of man's preparations.[28] Tradition assures us that the man who sincerely seeks God will be met halfway: "He who comes to purify himself will be aided from Heaven."[29]

Indeed, this may be the very condition necessary for a man to meet in order to grasp the truth of Torah. He must demonstrate the sincerity of his search by being ready to risk commitment in the form of living the life of an observant Jew. This was perhaps the "Divine secret" of "we will do and we will hear," and it is perhaps the allusion of the Psalmist—"Taste and see that the Lord is good." As a perceptive thinker summed it up: "Truth is revealed in religion not just to anybody but only to those who seek and to those who care."[30]

Regardless of what may or may not follow, the experience must be initiated by man himself. He must decide to subject himself to the authority of God and His Torah. It may come suddenly or it may come gradually; it may precede faith, in the hope that the experience will follow, or it may come as a consequence of an "awareness of the unconditional" and the conviction that this is to be identified with the God of Moses. It may be preceded by intellectual considerations, or the experience may come first, as with Rosenzweig, and the "reasoning process afterwards."[31] But at some point, by an act which starts with "will" and ultimately involves

---

[27] Compare the interpretation of "Chatam Sofer," on *acharon shel Pesach* in Torat Moshe.
[28] Isaac Abarbanel, *Rosh Amana*, chapter 11.
[29] *Berakhot* 34.
[30] D. E. Trueblood, *Philosophy of Religion* (Grand Rapids, MI: Baker, 1957), 22.
[31] Nahum N. Glatzer, "F. Rosenzweig: The Story of a Conversion," *Judaism* 10 (Jan. 1952).

his entire being, he passes over from opinion to commitment; to where he can say with conviction—"the Lord *our* God." For many to whom "acceptance of the yoke of Heaven" comes after a life of estrangement from the God of Abraham, Isaac, and Jacob, the act of faith may very well be described as a "leap."

In summation then, Existentialism is important to Orthodoxy because it helps us see the inadequacy of philosophies of reason and, by implication, the tenuous validity of versions of Judaism tailored to fit current philosophic thought.

Secondly, it has revived and made respectable categories of thought which give faithful expression to basic biblical and rabbinic concepts.

Finally, by emphasizing the uneasy and anxious condition of man's natural state, Existentialism makes clear the vital need for deep and serious faith in God, and has thus brought many to drink from the "spring of living waters."

I believe we should ponder the following advice: "Theology has received a tremendous gift from Existentialism. Existentialists themselves need not know that they have given us these great things. But the theologians should know it."[32]

---

[32] Tillich *Theology of Culture*, 126.

PART II

TORAH
IN DEPTH

Chapter Five

The Biblical Stories of Creation, the Garden of Eden, and the Flood: History or Metaphor?

The rabbis long ago endorsed the idea that the written Torah contains more than one level of meaning.[1] This is not surprising, given on the one hand the rich complexity and multidimensional character of human language and on the other the analytic power of the human mind. However, in regard to the Torah, the problem of multiple meanings is different than it is in the case of a poem or novel. In regard to the latter, the reader is expected and even encouraged to exercise his own powers of analysis and imagination in finding all sorts of meanings, even if he may actually be reading some of them "into" the text. Indeed, it has even been suggested that seeking the meanings of works of art, such as painting and literature, by focusing on what the artist had in mind is to commit the "intentional fallacy."[2]

However, the Torah, as its very name indicates, is a document to which the religious reader turns for guidance and instruction. The reader, therefore, wishes first and foremost to learn what it is that the Torah is saying, rather than to learn some individual's reaction to the text, even though the text may have inspired the reaction. Given the possibility of multiple meanings in the Torah, the real problem for the religious reader is deciding when a text is to be read as having literal meaning *only* or metaphorical meaning *only*, and when it has meaning on both levels, with *both* having been intended by the Author.

---

[1] *Sanhedrin* 34a; see also the commentary of Menahem haMeiri on *Avot* 3:14 and Moses Maimonides, *Guide for the Perplexed*, trans. M. Friedlander (New York: E. P. Dutton & Co., 1942), II:25.

[2] See Joseph Margolis, ed., *Philosophy Looks at the Arts*, revised edition (Philadelphia: Temple University Press, 1978), 289-362. Netziv (R. Naftali Tsevi Yehuda Berlin of Volozhin) in his introduction to his commentary (*Ha-Emek Devar*) on Genesis observes that from the fact that the rabbis applied the term *shira*—"song" or "poetry"—to the entire Torah (*Nedarim* 38, *Deuteronomy* 31:30), it may be inferred that the text assumes the form of metaphor.

Chapter Five. The Biblical Stories of Creation, the Garden of Eden, and the Flood

I wish to suggest the following method: before one either rejects a literal meaning entirely or decides that it is incomplete in the sense that it must be complemented by meaning on another level, one must supply reasons or justifications for doing so. For it must be presumed that if "the Torah speaks in the languages of men," in the first instance it employs the language in its most direct and effective form for conveying information and providing practical instruction. In other words, it utilizes words and sentences for their descriptive content, which we call the literal meaning.[3]

Those parts of the Torah, for example, for which understanding the literal meaning of the text seems perfectly adequate are those which embody the laws and commandments, statutes such as "Thou shall not commit adultery" (Exod. 20:13) or "Seven days no leaven shall be found in your houses" (Exod. 12:19). While there may be differences of opinion in explicating the full extent of some of these laws and in arriving at a precise definition of "adultery" and "leaven," it is still only the *literal* meaning of the text that is in question. Should someone propose, for example, that in place of the literal meaning or in addition to it, Exodus 12:19 is to be read in some symbolic way in which "leaven" stands for the "evil urge" in man, we should respond by saying that it is his privilege to so interpret the text. However, since he can provide no plausible reason to believe that it is the intent of the Torah to have the reader, in this particular case, go beyond the literal meaning, we shall classify his interpretation merely as personal *midrash*.

An example of a text where the literal meaning is not acceptable is the following report on conditions in the land of Canaan: "the cities are great and fortified up to the heavens" (Deut. 1:28). The reader's sense of realism precludes the belief that the scouts meant to say that the fortifications actually touched the heavens! We assume that words are being used here in a symbolic or metaphorical fashion. The native speaker is quite aware of the natural tendency of language to develop such usages in everyday speech. Another example of this is Deuteronomy 10:16: "Circumcise therefore the foreskin of your heart…." Although taking the

---

[3] *Berakhot* 31b, *Shabbat* 63a. See also Yeshayahu Maori, "The Approach of Classical Jewish Exegesis to *Peshat* and *Derash*," *Tradition* 21 (Fall 1984). I do not deal here with the view that the Torah may contain a level of meaning called *sod*, esoteric or secret meanings known only to initiates.

form of a command, this prescription, unlike Genesis 17:11, "And ye shall be circumcised in the flesh of your foreskin," is clearly not to be taken literally, but rather interpreted as a metaphor.

The Story of the Garden of Eden

A text which helps to point out the reasons for the occasional insufficiency of the literal meaning is the classic story of Adam and Eve in the Garden of Eden (Gen. 3). The story, naively read, is fascinating, with a didactic plot and a cast of characters that includes a tragic hero, a beguiled woman, a villainous talking serpent, and trees with wondrous powers. But what impels the reader to seek here another level of meaning? What makes him think that here the Torah intended something additional?[4] Once again, the point of departure is the presupposition that the Torah is a book of instruction. Therefore, any text which, if taken literally, does not instruct but mystifies and obfuscates signifies that one should look beyond the literal. A "tree" whose fruit bestows "knowledge of good and evil" or eternal life cannot be a "real" tree in the sense in which we know it. A "garden" in which the snake has an agenda and speaks persuasively cannot be our kind of garden. Also, the nature of the "knowledge of good and evil" that man acquires after eating of the forbidden fruit is not immediately apparent.[5] It certainly cannot be the ability to distinguish between good and evil, because when God commanded Adam earlier the Torah assumed that man would realize that obedience to God is good and disobedience evil. A clue seems to be given in the words, "And the eyes of both were opened and they knew that they were naked." But what does this tell us about the nature of the change that man underwent?[6] In short, the failure of the language to instruct, if taken literally, leads us to think of the possibility of metaphor. The characters and events are to be interpreted in a symbolic way. This story seems to be dealing with the origin and nature of evil in man and seeks to explain how it is that man and woman, the special creations of a moral and benevolent God, soon find themselves in a hostile environment with vital needs unprovided

---

[4] See the discussion in the commentary of Isaac Abarbanel on this chapter.
[5] See the interpretation of Malbim on this chapter.
[6] See the illuminating comments of Martin Buber, *Good and Evil* (New York: Charles Scribner's Sons, 1953), 67-80.

for. In a pre-philosophical age, the solution to such an extremely difficult theological problem could only be suggested and alluded to by means of this literary device called metaphor.[7]

Note here an important difference between the story of the Garden of Eden and the sentence in Deuteronomy 1:28. In the case of the latter, should a reader believe the text to be saying that the fortifications of the cities of Canaan did indeed touch the heavens, he is simply wrong. However, in the text of the Garden an entire *story* in the form of a metaphor is involved. This means that the story and what it stands for resemble each other in certain ways. Thus, even if a reader believes that these were real trees or, believing them to be symbols, does not know *what* they symbolize, he may still be said to have learned something positive. He now understands that some kind of disobedience on the part of early man brought him to his present predicament. Regarding this type of metaphor, therefore, the literal meaning, although not complete, is not misleading, and the full intended meaning may be partially deciphered and grasped in degrees.

The Story of Creation

Let us now consider the Creation story as it appears in the opening 31 verses of Genesis. Here we are informed not only that God brought the world into existence, apparently out of nothing, but also *how* He did it: the time it took, the different stages, the particular sequence. From a theological point of view, it is quite clear that the doctrine of Creation *ex nihilo*, i.e., that God is the Maker of heaven and earth and all that is in it; that God is the Ground of all being; that He is the only necessary existant while all else is dependent upon Him, is central to Judaism and is what distinguished it from the paganistic beliefs that had preceded it.[8] However, this crucial doctrine is already clearly proclaimed in

---

[7] The philosophic age may be said to have started with Plato and Aristotle, when abstract philosophical questions began to be analyzed in a rational and critical manner, separating out the empirical, logical, and metaphysical elements.

[8] See Joseph Albo, *Sefer Ha-Ikarim* (Philadelphia: Jewish Publication Society, 1930), 112; Yehezkel Kaufmann, "The Biblical Age," in *Great Ages and Ideas of the Jewish People,* ed. Leo W. Schwarz (New York: Random House, 1956), 8-14. "For all the gods of the people are things of naught; but the Lord made the heavens" (Psalms 96:5).

the very first verse. Why did the Torah continue to go into detail as to *how* the world was created?[9] Of what relevance to man is this account of natural history? After all, the process by which this universe came into being, whatever it may have been, was a *singularity*, a never-to-be repeated event which, as such, is outside the scope of science. Thus, while the "whys and wherefores" of the Big Bang itself is a legitimate part of *religious* explanation, everything *after that* has already been preempted by the fast-developing branch of science known as cosmology or cosmonogy.[10] Should we therefore conclude from the plethora of detail in Genesis 1:2 to Genesis 1:31 that the Torah wishes to teach us science, and thereby run the risk that its account may someday be in competition with that of a later science?[11]

Let us examine more closely the language of the story of Creation. We have before us a straightforward description whose language seems intended to be taken literally. We are told how God puts into execution what seems to be an orderly plan to bring the visible universe into existence. In the course of sequential stages over time, a proper environment for life-forms is fashioned in which life develops, beginning with the simple and proceeding to the complex, culminating in man. The words used to describe what is created are all readily understood, concrete terms referring to phenomena well-known from human experience: water, light, earth, dry land, sun, moon, stars, grass, herbs, trees, fruit, birds, reptiles, morning, evening, etc. The verbs used to describe how God produces these things are also familiar, but in this particular context not very illuminating: "God *created*...," "God *made*...," and "God *said*, let there be ... and there *was* ..." In terms of *human* creativity we are interested not only in the objects created but in *how* it was done, the techniques used. In the case of Genesis 1:1-31, we do not, for all of its detail, really learn anything about the actual mechanics of how God produced our world except that He is the final and efficient cause

---

[9] The rabbis had already raised this question: "With ten Sayings the world was created. Could it not have been created with one Saying? What does this teach us?" (*Avot* 5:1).

[10] See Steven Weinberg, *The First Three Minutes: A Modern View of the Origin of the Universe* (New York: Basic Books, Inc., 1977).

[11] There is a lucid discussion of the interesting views of Rav Kook on science and creation in Sholom Rosenberg, "Introduction to the Thought of Rav Kook," in *The World of Rav Kook's Thought* (New York: Avi Chai, 1991), 88-97.

Chapter Five. The Biblical Stories of Creation, the Garden of Eden, and the Flood

and is alone responsible for all. If this is so, we remain with our original question: would it not have been sufficient for the Torah to have limited its account to the first sentence, which clearly teaches that it is God and God alone who brought the universe into existence? Why was it necessary for us to be told about the *how* of creation?

Let us consider the problem in more general terms. For reasons we shall shortly discuss, the Torah indeed wished man to know something about the methods used by God in creating the universe. Assuming that the Author knew precisely how the entire cosmos—the meta-galaxies, the galaxies, the Milky Way, the solar system, the planet Earth and all the different life-forms—emerged out of the Big Bang and was able to describe it in correct mathematical and scientific terms, in what language was He to express this to people in a pre-scientific age? Obviously, He could not tell it all, nor use terms that were not intelligible to them. On the other hand, what was written had to be of such a nature that later generations, coming after the advent of science, would not think themselves misled as they read the biblical account.

The Torah intended the story of Creation to be taken literally, but with one reservation: that it be understood that the terms had "stretchability," i.e., that while all of the nouns would retain their common-sense meanings, in the event that future scientific discoveries should broaden our knowledge of such phenomena as light, time, water, sun, stars, heavens, and firmament (*rakia*), we should be prepared to "stretch" their primary meanings to cover and include these new phenomena, with the overall account remaining essentially "true."

What gives us the right to believe that this is the intention of the Torah? The same test of "reality" or "coherence" used earlier to alert us to the metaphorical nature of "fortifications that reach the heavens" or "trees whose fruit bestows the knowledge of good and evil," applies here as well. If on the first day of Creation, before there was any sun or moon, we are told, "And there was light," and we are puzzled as to the source of this light, this constitutes a signal to leave room for a meaning that may come in the future. What are considered textual anomalies to one generation are hints that, in time, may become the entrance to another level of meaning. Indeed, recent works by Torah-knowledgeable scientists point out that the "light" mentioned in Genesis 1:2 may be referring to the radiation which suffused the early universe, and whose detection in 1964 was hailed as evidence of the occurrence of the Big

Bang. They seek to demonstrate that the Torah account in its simple, concrete, common-sense terminology is quite close to the latest findings of cosmology.[12] But, however true, why does the Torah want us to know *how* God created the world? What does it teach us?

The answer may be related to Moshe's urgent plea to the Lord, to which he received a positive, albeit partial, reply: "Now, therefore, I pray thee, if I have found grace in Thy sight, make known to me Thy ways" (Exod. 33:13). This implies (1) that to an extent man *can* learn something about the "ways of God," the methods employed by Divine Providence in nature and history, and (2) that such knowledge is useful to man.[13]

The action used most frequently by God in bringing the world into existence is speech: "And the Lord said 'Let there be light,' and there was light" (Gen. 1:3), "He spoke and it was..." (Psalms 33:9). Later in the process God's speech is directed to that which has already been created. "And the Lord said, let the *waters* swarm with living creatures ... let the *earth* bring forth" (Gen. 1:20, 24). Unlike the initial creation "out of nothing," this can be understood as a consequence of the fact that God had encoded already existing elements with the ability to unfold or *evolve* into higher, more complex levels of life. Yet at other times in the creation process, God is described as acting directly. For example, in the case of the sun and the moon we are told: "And God *made* the two great lights and *set them* in the firmament of the heavens" (Gen. 1:16, 17). Taken together, the unfolding and the direct action seem to suggest a method which might be called *guided punctuated evolution*.

To call a process evolutionary is to imply that it contains the following elements.

> 1) Conservative: Older features that have proven useful are retained.
>
> 2) Innovative: There are possibilities of new elements appearing.

---

[12] Gerald L. Schroeder, *Genesis and the Big Bang* (New York: Bantam Books, 1990), Nathan Aviezer, *In the Beginning: Biblical Creation and Science* (Hoboken, NJ: Ktav Publishing, 1990).

[13] The "ways of God" (*derekh Hashem* or *darkei Hashem*) has three different meanings in the Bible. Sometimes it refers specifically to the moral ways of God, as in Deut. 10:12 and Gen. 18:19, sometimes to God's way in nature and history, as in Exod. 33:13, and sometimes to the way in which God wishes man to walk, as in Exod. 18:20.

3) Selective: In the course of this process certain possibilities are never realized, others come into existence but disappear, and still others endure.[14]

In the beginning God, in His infinite wisdom and power, creates a single, infinitesimal bit of energy. This energy is encoded so that by a process of self-development it responds to rapidly changing conditions of space and temperature which are themselves self-developing, evolving in the direction of the variegated and complex universe we experience today. However, it is not the case that man as he contemplates himself and his condition can conclude that the universe is the predictable result of the unfolding of certain general principles implanted in nature at the beginning of creation. The Torah instructs the reader that the process was not all automatic or inevitable. At various crucial points in the development of all aspects of the cosmos, galactic clusters, our solar system, and life on planet Earth, God's guidance or intervention was necessary in order to arrive at the desired goal. Seen from the scientists' vantage point, of course, these "interventions" are perceived as "dumb luck" or as fortunate "accidents."[15]

Originally the theory of evolution was applied to the area of biology to answer the question of the origin of species because Darwin believed he had discovered the mechanism by which these changes could be explained. However, the fossil record, uncovered since Darwin, does not support the theory. It shows that for millions of years certain species persist without change and suddenly disappear. Then new species appear, most of them fully formed, and disappear unchanged. Why certain species vanish and others come into being cannot be explained by any principle in nature. And when we do find a cause, such as drastic climate change or the impact of a meteor, the result, while fortunate from a human point of view, seems to be a matter of "sheer accident."

---

[14] See Timothy Ferris, *The Whole Shebang* (New York: Simon & Schuster, 1997). For differing views on the compatibility between Judaism and evolution, see A. Carmell and Cyril Domb, eds., *Challenge: Torah Views on Science and its Problems* (New York: Feldheim, 1976), Section II, "Creation and Evolution," and Lawrence Kaplan, "Torah V'Madda in the Thought of Rabbi Samson Raphael Hirsch," *BDD* 5 (Summer 1997).

[15] See Schroeder, *Genesis and the Big Bang*, chapters 7 and 8, and Aviezer, *In the Beginning*, 72-74.

The knowledge that *guided punctuated evolution* is one of the "ways of God" is of particular help in the sensitive area of the creation of man. By use of mutational and environmental changes, God unobtrusively guides the evolutionary process in the direction of the physical development of *homo sapiens*. This is the meaning of "Then the Lord God formed man of the dust of the earth" (Gen. 2:7). Then, at the crucial moment, when the form is ready to receive, God once again creates *ex nihilo* in what the Torah describes as "...and [God] breathed into his nostrils the breath of life and man became a living soul" (Gen. 2:7).[16]

Further evidence of the consistency of the Creator in His "work methods" is the growing consensus among cosmologists that the processes being observed in outer space can best be described as *evolutionary*, even though we have no idea as yet of the mechanism.

> The process that hoisted the universe from the relative uniformity of the Big Bang to the incredible variety and diversity we see today in the sky seems more properly to be described as evolutionary.... Not only do galaxies evolve chemically, their stars brewing hydrogen and helium into heavier elements so that old galaxies are more chemically complicated and varied than young ones, but galactic evolution results from processes operating across entire clusters of galaxies. Molecules are built within the interstellar thunderheads known as giant molecular clouds and in planets.... The very laws of nature seem to have evolved from simpler original laws....[17]

Since these heavier elements are necessary for the appearance of life, in the absence of any mechanism to explain why galactic evolution took this direction we might attribute it to Divine Guidance. And if our present laws of nature evolved from simpler original laws, then here too we

---

[16] Science has no explanation for the sudden appearance of modern man. See Aviezer, *In the Beginning*, 92-93. An article in the journal *Cell* reported an experiment by a Dr. S. Paabo of the University of Munich in which a DNA strand from a Neanderthal skeleton was compared to that of modern human DNA. The differences were found to be vast, suggesting that *homo sapiens* and Neanderthal, although they were for a while contemporaneous, did not interbreed. Thus *homo sapiens* most certainly did not gradually "descend" from the Neanderthal.

[17] Ferris, *The Whole Shebang*, 173 and 199.

Chapter Five. The Biblical Stories of Creation, the Garden of Eden, and the Flood

might ask how it is that the laws that have evolved are just those that make possible the appearance and development of intelligent life?

But probably the most significant implication of the insight that *guided punctuated evolution* is one of the ways of God is its usefulness in the understanding of history. After all, God in the Torah is active not only in nature but also in human affairs. One of the most important emphases of the Bible is on man's obligation to perceive and celebrate the mighty acts of God in our national history: the Exodus from Egypt, the wandering in the wilderness, the conquest of Canaan, the destruction of the Temples. These individual historical events ascribed to Divine agency are effectively linked together and tell an interconnected story of God's plan for, subsequent disappointment with, and punishment of the people called Israel. However, at the point where the biblical narrative breaks off (*circa* 450 BCE) we are left without a story-line! True, the believer is left with the promise of an ultimate messianic redemption, but he has no criteria, no map by which to judge the significance and direction of the events during the long stretch of about 2,500 years that has elapsed since then. Of course, God is active behind the scenes, but what method is He using? What is His strategy? Will the Redemption, when it comes, have any connection with the events that preceded it?

Operating almost exclusively with the principle of reward and punishment, most traditional Jewish thinkers were prevented from discerning any pattern in Jewish post-exilic history or from discovering any line of growth or development. The believer is simply to fear the Lord, keep His commandments, and hope that when enough people are deserving God will send His Messiah to redeem Israel and the world. These were the only parameters of significance by which to view and evaluate what was happening in the world.

Perhaps, however, the teaching of Genesis that guided evolution is one of the ways of God should be applied to our understanding of human history as a whole. Perhaps our focus has been too narrow, concentrating exclusively on what was happening to the Jewish people. We forget that while the Jewish people were in a sort of political limbo, driven or wandering from country to country and continent to continent, the victims of anti-Semitism in all of its virulent forms, there were evolving painfully and gradually the political institutions of democracy and the methodology of modern science and technology, which together are the positive elements in the culture we call modernity.[18] It is precisely these conditions that made possible today the development and dissemination of Torah in all of its different aspects, and the return of the Jewish people to its land as a sovereign state.[19]

The Story of the Flood

While in terms of language the story of the Creation, according to our interpretation, turned out to be closer to the literal, and the story of the Garden closer to the metaphorical, the story of Noah and the Flood at first glance seems rather equivocal. Its location prior to the stories of the Patriarchs, where one might say real history begins, would appear to suggest that the story of the Flood belongs to those early developments in the history of man which are at best only hinted at. For example, the story of the Tower of Babel, which appears after the story of the Flood but before the story of Abraham, while presumably about a particular tower in a particular valley called Shinar, has all of the signs of being essentially a metaphor about a certain type of civilization with which God seems displeased. Also, the first four verses of Chapter 7, which have so far eluded credible interpretation and which speak of strange human types, seem to comprise an introduction to the story of the Flood.[20] Terms such as "sons of God," "daughters of men," *nefilim* (who may be giants), and "mighty men" suggest a prehistoric setting, and may refer to earlier forms of hominids who, it is currently believed, coexisted with man. Yet the story of the Flood opens with God commanding Noah to build a seaworthy craft, giving specifications as to size, material, and waterproofing. Similarly, the many details as to dates, how long it rained, and the specific incident of the raven and the dove seem to be descriptions of a historical event. However, as we have indicated earlier,

---

[18] "The concept of 'historical explanation' as explaining an event only after it has happened but not being able to predict it causes us to think of God's reply to Moses when he asks that "I be made to know Thy ways." The Lord answers "... And thou shalt see My back but My face shall not be seen'" (Exod. 33:23). See Stephen Jay Gould, *Wonderful Life* (New York: W.W. Norton & Co., 1989), 278-289.

[19] See Shubert Spero, *Holocaust and Return to Zion: A Study in Jewish Philosophy of History* (New Jersey: Ktav Publishing House, 2000).

[20] See the interpretation of Malbim on Gen. 7:1-4.

Chapter Five. The Biblical Stories of Creation, the Garden of Eden, and the Flood

the presence of unrealistic elements in the story should alert us to the possibility of metaphor. As Nahmanides has pointed out, the logistics of fitting all the animals into the Ark and the task of caring for them, let alone their converging on their own and marching into the Ark in the desired numbers seems to invoke the miraculous. The judgment, therefore, has to be made as to whether to adopt a historical interpretation in many ways miraculous or, as I shall argue, to see it as metaphor. Involved here is the difficult question of whether we can deduce from the Torah criteria as to when and under what circumstances Providence resorts to miracles.[21]

But if the tale is a metaphor, what is it a metaphor of? What is the intention of the Torah in telling us the story of the Flood? We wish to suggest that this type of metaphor is designed to call our attention to that which is universal in the story; that aspect of the event that makes it an example of the kind of thing that has happened many times before.[22] Scientific research has revealed that the development of life forms on this planet was not an even, gradual process, but one punctuated by several violent mass extinctions, in which over ninety percent of once-existing plant, marine, and animal genera were wiped out. The last such mass extinction is said to have taken place 65 million years ago and included the dinosaurs, as well as forty percent of marine genera. The causes of these destructions were sharp changes in sea levels and climate, volcanic eruptions, and the impacts of asteroids. The last Ice Age took place about 10,000 years ago, well within the orbit of human memory, and may have registered on the collective human subconscious.

Perhaps, therefore, the story of Noah and the Flood is to be understood not as a historical description of a particular world-wide deluge that took place somewhere between 4000 and 5000 BCE but as a metaphor to give the Torah's view of all the destructions and mass extinctions which took place on our planet from the very beginning. And the teaching is that it has been Divine Guidance that has ensured the evolution and survival over vast stretches of time of just those plants,

---

[21] See Rambam, *Hilkhot Yesodei haTorah*, Chapter 7, and the comments of Gersonides on Josh. 10:12-14.
[22] See Northrop Frye, *The Great Code: The Bible and Literature* (New York: Harcourt Brace Jovanovich, 1981), 46.

marine genera, and animals that do not block the appearance of man and those that are useful, and that strain of man in whom a moral spark had taken hold.

However, it has remained for modern science to bring to light some interesting facts about the origins and developments of different human societies which may give us some insight into some further implications of the Flood story. In his fascinating *Guns, Germs, and Steel*, Jared Diamond sets out to explain why it is that history proceeded so very differently for peoples in different parts of the world.[23] Why is it that today certain societies enjoy all the benefits of what we call "civilization," while others still have non-literate farming societies, and still others have remained hunter-gatherers who use stone tools? Diamond's research shows that "history followed different courses for different peoples because of differences among people's environments (geography, climate and the flora and fauna) and not because of biological differences among people themselves."[24] A comparative survey of the history of the different continents and geographic areas in the world reveals that what has been called the Fertile Crescent (the land of Israel, Mesopotamia, and part of Anatolia) was the earliest locale for a whole string of developments in the history of civilization: the building of cities, the invention of writing, the formation of empires. Diamond explains this by the fact that the people in this area had a "head start" in that they were the first to experience two basic developments, two giant steps in the human economy:

> 1) The transition from being dependent on food secured by a system of "hunting and gathering" (hunting wild game or scavenging and gathering wild fruits and grains) to actual food production (the cultivation of food plants on a regular crop basis).
>
> 2) The domestication of animals for food, traction, and transportation.[25]

Diamond goes on to demonstrate that once a society has achieved these two fundamental developments, it rapidly goes on to the next

---

[23] Jared Diamond, *Guns, Germs, and Steel: The Fates of Human Societies* (New York: W.W. Norton & Co., 1997).
[24] Ibid., 25.
[25] Ibid., Part 2, 83-176.

stages, developing a sedentary population, cities, a ruling class, a bureaucracy, and professional craftsmen and soldiers—all that we associate with civilization.[26]

Now let us take the question back one step and ask what it was about the Fertile Crescent that enabled its people to be the first to develop food production and domestication of animals? Scientific research shows the following: in the Fertile Crescent and only in the Fertile Crescent were the wild ancestors of all of the eight most important plants of the modern world to be found in abundance. These were: emmer wheat, einkorn wheat, barley, lentils, peas, chickpeas, bitter vetch, and flax. These crops, many of which are self-pollinators and high in protein, were discovered, gathered, and later cultivated by farmers. Also in the Fertile Crescent were the wild ancestors of today's goats, sheep, cows, and pigs, the most valuable and easily domesticable mammals. These were already domesticated in this area by 6000 BCE; the horse and the camel came much later. What this means is that "the crops and animals of the Fertile Crescent's first farmers were able to meet humanity's basic economic needs: carbohydrates, protein, fat, clothing, traction and transport," giving the area a head start in the development of the later stages of civilization.[27]

What is the relevance of all this to the story of the Flood? Let us point out two aspects of the story that we have not yet mentioned:

> 1) Noah in his ark was carrying not only animals of all sorts but also selected grains, plants, shoots, and seedlings, as food for himself and the animals and also to transplant them into the soil of the post-diluvian world.[28]
>
> 2) The Torah finds it important to mention where the Ark came to rest: "And the Ark rested upon the mountains of Ararat" (Gen. 8:4). That is to say, those in the Ark disembarked and its contents were unloaded in the area of the Fertile Crescent.

If we factor in the findings of modern science as to the role of the land of the Bible in the development of civilization, and the reasons for it, we

---

[26] The Torah seems to emphasize the importance of food production and animal domestication by associating them with the beginnings of human history: "Abel was a keeper of sheep and Cain was a tiller of the earth" (Gen. 4:2).
[27] Diamond, *Guns, Germs, and Steel*, 142.
[28] See Gen. 6:21 and Rashi on Gen. 9:20.

arrive at a better understanding of what the story of the Flood comes to teach us. It is to be understood as a kind of metaphor in which the relationship between the story and what it stands for is analogical. Was there really a world-wide destruction? Not once but many times! And every time it happened, certain life forms, plants, and animals survived, *thanks to man*. That is to say, those which were inimical to the evolution of man became extinct; those useful to man survived. But in the midst of these general teachings about Divine Guidance during the world's many destructions there emerges a truth about a particular geographic area which was also a consequence of Divine Guidance. At the conclusion of these upheavals and disruptions, drastic climate changes, floods and ice ages, and the redistributions of plant and animal life, it appears that a certain corner of Asia Minor received the best of what had been selected to endure. "And the Ark rested on the mountains of Ararat." While ultimately all of mankind benefited from who and what survived, a particular geographic area was especially favored. This explains why it is in this area that the story of civilization first begins, where it first fails, and where Divine wisdom initiates the process of amelioration: "And the Lord said to Abram: Get thee out of thy country ... unto the land that I will show thee" (Gen. 12:1).

In summary, then, how is the believer to understand the literary character of these three pivotal stories in Genesis whose texts continue to engage us as we reread them in the light of scientific discoveries and philosophic refinement?

The story of Creation as contained in the first 31 verses of Genesis is a historical description, in common-sense language, of what happened during the singularity. However, in view of the unique nature of the event and the fact that some of the findings of science are counter-intuitive, the terms used must be "stretched" considerably so that the text may accommodate the discoveries of cosmology. We are given this description of how God created the world in order that we may learn "His way" in nature and history, which is a way of *guided evolution*. Once we know this, we can discern and appreciate His kindnesses in the past and try to detect the direction toward which He beckons in the future.

The story of the Garden of Eden is a metaphor in which object-language is being used to express a content for which language as such is really inadequate. It is an attempt to say something about the nature of man and the origin of evil, and to explain the difficult conditions of man on earth. Thinkers continue to wrestle with the story and search the text for insights into these perplexing theological questions.

The story of the Flood is a metaphor structured as an analogy that tells us about all the destructions and extinctions which occurred in the prehistoric past. It is a story about the survival of the deserving and of those aspects of the universe (the climate, stability, and flora and fauna) which are prerequisites for man's development on earth, materially, socially, and culturally. It also explains why the rest of the biblical story takes place in the Fertile Crescent. Most important, it tells of a divine covenant with man, in which the stability and regularity of nature is guaranteed.

Chapter Six

Paradise Lost or Outgrown?

I

The account of Adam and Eve in the Garden of Eden is certainly the best known story in the Bible, and probably the least understood. Unfortunately, for many of us our first encounter with this story as children was also our last. Our sages from early on believed that this story was a metaphor representing certain profound truths and should not be interpreted literally.[1] How is the modern reader to understand these second and third chapters in Genesis and what is he to learn therefrom?[2]

The key to it all, I believe, lies in the perception that this story serves as a bridge between what went before in the text and what comes after. That is to say, chapter one, with its most concise account of the creation including the human species, concludes with the pronouncement, "And God saw everything that he had made and behold it was very good" (Gen. 1:31). Soon after chapters four and five take place, within a setting that reflects the human condition as we know it today— people are born and die, there is strife and misery, and men work hard to sustain themselves and often fail. In short, things do not appear to be "very good"! What happened in the interim? Surely it was to be expected that a good and wise God would have provided His human creatures with a much kinder and user-friendly environment than that in which, according to the anthropologists, early man actually found himself. Indeed, was that not implied in the pronouncement that all was "very good"? It is to bridge this gap that we are given in chapters two and three, the story of Adam and Eve in Gan Eden.

---

[1] See Moses Maimonides, *Guide for the Perplexed,* trans. M. Friedlander (New York: E.P. Dutton and Co., 1942), II:30.
[2] For a brief scholarly and balanced approach, see Yechezkel Kaufman, *The Religion of Israel* (Chicago: University of Chicago Press, 1960), 292-294. For a truly contemporary comprehensive analysis see Leon R. Kass, *The Beginning of Wisdom* (New York: Free Press, 2003), 54-122.

Chapter Six. Paradise Lost or Outgrown?

This begins with man having been placed in a "good" place indeed, a veritable paradise that can provide for all his needs, but at the end of the story the human species finds itself out in the real world, exposed to tough and hostile surroundings not at all amenable to human needs and concerns.

How and why did this transformation take place?[3] The suggestion of the text is that the answer is to be found in the story of man in Gan Eden. However, the answer is clearest if the story is read as a metaphor rather than literally. Of course, if and when a particular text should be seen as metaphor has been and remains a sensitive issue in biblical exegesis. Used indiscriminately as a general approach, allegory can reduce a practical commandment or a historical account to a mere literary device designed to convey an idea. On the other hand, refusal to recognize the metaphoric nature of certain texts such as the Gan Eden story is to deprive oneself of one of the main sources of the wisdom of the Torah.

As I suggested in an earlier study,[4] the first clue of the possibility of metaphor is that the text, if taken literally, does not inform or illuminate but instead mystifies and obfuscates, and seems to border on the fanciful. On its face, the Gan Eden story seems to be dealing with the important issues of "knowledge" and "immortality." Surely the Torah cannot mean to suggest that these come about as the result of someone eating the fruit of a particular tree! Therefore, metaphor is indicated. However, as a coherent story containing action, drama, and a cast of characters, it is rather complex as metaphors go. By comparison, for example, to say that the sentence "The fortification walls reached the heavens" (Deut. 1:28) is a metaphor means that the walls did not really touch the heavens but only that they were unusually high. In the case of a complex story it is not a particular term or phrase that must be interpreted differently—the entire action, to whom the action is attributed, and the relationship between the characters carry a meaning on an altogether different level than the immediately apparent. Thus, I shall

---

[3] The basic elements in my approach are derived from the interpretations of Isaac Abarbanel on Gen. 3:1-5; Rabbi Meir Leibush Malbum on Gen. 2:16, 17; Gen. 3:3-7; and comments of Martin Buber, *Good and Evil* (New York: Charles Scribners' Sons, 1958), 67-80.

[4] See Chapter 5 of the present volume. Also see note 18 in this chapter.

argue that the crucial element in this story that brings about the radical change in the human condition is not *what* is eaten but the very act of disobedience and the psychological process that brings it about. And while the story focuses on the actions of two individuals, as metaphor it represents changes that took place in the psyche as it evolved over generations in the pre-*homo sapiens* period.

Why would the Torah (which term means literally "teaching" or "instruction") choose to use metaphor in describing this phase in the creation of man? After all, metaphor does not inform directly or univocally, but only gives hints and suggestions. Indeed, it is entirely possible to misinterpret the metaphor, or even to find it completely mystifying! However, when dealing with a particularly abstruse philosophical and theological subject such as the nature of the human self and the dynamics of free will there are precious few options. One can follow the advice of Ludwig Wittgenstein: "Whereof one cannot speak, thereof one must be silent." However, an apt metaphor can indicate a direction and close out various false alternatives. Its very amenability to different interpretations gives metaphor the flexibility to keep pace with advances in our understandings of ourselves and make sense in different ages. The Gan Eden story is constructed so artfully that even if earlier generations understood it literally they were not learning an untruth!

In chronological terms, this story is a flashback to an earlier phase designed to describe events that occurred before our world had started to function on its own, and before the creation of the human species had been completed. In terms of the biblical time-frame humanity's creation came late in the sixth day, before the Shabbat. This means that the human is still a "work in progress," so that every act performed by or for this creature is helping to define his ultimate nature. And while man was already experiencing elements in his consciousness which would later be identified as reason, will, sense of self, emotions, and imagination, the precise extent and nature of the interaction between them were as yet undetermined. These early events could be crucial because the slightest untoward impact would leave a lasting impression, like a leaf landing on wet cement.

According to the story, God places the as-yet-incomplete man in a Garden of His planting, filled will all sorts of fruit trees which are "desirable to the sight and good for food" with a mysterious qualification: "But of the tree of knowledge of good and evil you shall not eat; for in the day you shall eat of it you will surely die" (Gen. 2:17).[5] Within the context of the story taken literally, the warning is quite clear (certainly this is the way man and the serpent understand it)— to eat of the fruit of this particular tree is to incur death! But what is the meaning of "knowledge of good and evil"? This could not have been very intelligible to Adam and Eve. Nor is it very clear whether or not "knowledge of good and evil" was to be considered something desirable. On the one hand, "knowledge" sounds attractive to the human mind. However, the presence of the term "evil" is off-putting. The implication is that one eats of the fruit of this tree and acquires some kind of knowledge. Yet from Genesis 3:6 it does not appear that the gaining of this knowledge was the primary motive in Eve's eating of the fruit. The only thing that is clear is that God has forbidden man to eat of its fruit. In terms of the metaphor this is the important element.

This very vagueness suggests a story composed as metaphor. What manner of tree is this which finds its place among regular fruit trees but whose fruit provides "knowledge" of some kind? The text does not ascribe any magical or supernatural powers to this tree in order to explain its unusual effect. Furthermore, the text makes no effort to describe the appearance of this tree or its exact location so that future men could steer clear of it. Later, I will suggest that the name given the tree at the very beginning—*Etz Ha-Da'at Tov V'Ra*, the Tree of Knowledge of Good

---

[5] While in fact Adam and Eve do not die on the day they eat of the tree, they lose their chance to eat of the tree of life and so become subject to death (Nachmanides). Since the Tree of Eternal Life never actually comes into play and the Tree of Knowledge is prohibited, one cannot but be struck by the incongruity of these two mythic "trees" being placed, as it were, inconspicuously in the midst of a garden of "real" fruit trees, "pleasant to the sight and good for food" (Gen. 2:9). In the popular mythology of Mesopotamia, the images of a Tree of Eternal Life and a Tree of Knowledge were probably well known. Since life-eternal and knowledge were much valued and sought after by man, and since life-eternal and knowledge were possessed by the gods, it was useful to think of them as natural products growing on special trees, so that all that one had to do to acquire either of them was to locate the trees! The ploy of placing the Tree of Life and the Tree of Knowledge in the midst of the primeval garden, when they serve only as stage props for the main drama of man's disobedience, was perhaps intended to de-sacralize the concept and show its irrelevance. The point is that elements such as Eternal Life and Knowledge do not grow on trees and cannot be acquired simply by taking a suitable "pill."

and Evil was given *al shem sofo*, on account of its end, to reflect the change that took place in the human perception of moral value after primal man "disobeyed God." In short, the name given to the tree is appropriately ambiguous, which enables it to be understood by those inside the story or reading it literally, and at the same time to be understood quite differently by those who think they have deciphered the metaphor.

In the meantime, man develops his cognitive faculties and learns the habits and natures of the garden's wildlife, and is able to "name" and categorize the different types of fauna, which is to note similarities and differences. As man becomes aware of his social needs and desire for suitable companionship, God provides him with "woman," a human female counterpart, a suitable "helpmeet."[6] Presumably, man conveys to woman all that God has instructed him as to life in the Garden.

Up to this point matters seem to have proceeded as planned. Enter the "serpent," however, and matters take an unexpected turn. Of course, there never was and probably never will be a "talking serpent"! We should see the "words" of the serpent as a "voice within the woman."[7] That is to say, a "silent conversation" takes place within her consciousness between her curiosity, her awakened desires, and her reason. Let us imaginatively reconstruct how all this might have happened.

The woman is strolling in the Garden wondering which of the fruits she should have today for lunch, permitting the exotic shapes, the attractive colors, and the familiar aromas to sharpen her appetite. Having already tasted many of them, she is looking for something new when her eyes come to rest on what she has been told was "forbidden." As she contemplates its tantalizing possibilities her hunger grows and she falls into a reverie. Talking to herself, her musings take on a dialogical form:

> So let us see, why is it again we are not supposed to eat of this tree? M-m-m, as I recall, I was told that should we even touch it we

---

[6] The manner in which woman is formed and presented to man has been seen as a mother lode of hints and insights regarding the proper relationship between the sexes from the Talmudic sages up through modern commentators. See Leon Kass, *The Beginning of Wisdom*, 98-151, and Joseph B. Soloveitchik, *Family Redeemed* (Hoboken, NJ: Me-Otzar HaRav, 2000), 3-31.

[7] According to Abarbanel (Gen. 3:1), the woman repeatedly saw the serpent coiled around the tree's branches and eating of its fruits with no apparent ill effects. This triggered her "conversation" with the serpent.

would die! (Gen. 3:3)[8] Yet yesterday I accidentally brushed against it and nothing happened! Adam said something about the tree being a "tree of knowledge," but why would God wish to keep us from knowledge of any kind? Surely "knowledge" is a good thing! Could it be because we would then become as powerful as God?

The woman by now holds the forbidden fruit in her hands, enjoying its fragrance and texture as she fantasizes how it will taste.

> And when the woman saw that the tree was good for food, that it was a delight to the eyes, and that the tree was to be desired to make one wise, she ate and gave also to her husband and he did eat. (Gen. 3:6)

How are we to judge this act, and why did it have the dire consequences attributed to it? It should be noted that the text does not use the usual Hebrew word for "sin," *ḥet* (חטא), in condemning the act.[9] But it was, of course, an act of disobedience. The human couple contravened the command of God and did what they had been explicitly told not to do! While this was not a moral transgression in the sense that Cain's act of fratricide was, obedience is generally considered a virtue and disobedience a vice. However, this is only when the particular command one is to obey is itself morally compelling, or when the one issuing the command is in a position which morally obligates. In our case, God's relationship to man is one of benefactor, a relationship which, according to the story, man was surely aware of, since God had communicated directly with him. This could be seen in the verse, "And the Lord God took (*vayikach*) the man and put him into the Garden of Eden…" (Gen. 2:15). In explaining the verbosity, Rashi comments: "'*Took* him' with pleasant words and persuaded him to enter."[10] Undoubtedly man was thus made aware of the bounty and special care he was being given by his Creator, and a sense of gratitude must have followed. With all of his needs provided for it would have been sheer churlishness for him to have felt a need to eat from the single tree whose fruit he was forbidden to eat by a beneficent

---

[8] Of course, the original prohibition spoke only of "eating" and not of "touching." From this the rabbis derive the teaching that whoever adds to the command of God ends up reducing it (see Rashi on Gen. 3:3).

[9] In connection with Cain's act of fratricide, the word *ḥet* is used. See Gen. 4:7.

[10] Rashi on Gen. 2:8.

God. Furthermore, man had been given a perfectly good reason not to eat of that particular tree: "for in the day you will eat you will surely die." Thus, supporting man's obedience was both the moral sentiment of gratitude and a purely pragmatic consideration. In this regard, however, woman's position was quite different. She never had a direct encounter with God, so for her, God is an abstraction whose command and goodness were only hearsay. Also, for the woman, who came into existence in the Garden, her entire situation, including the ease of living there was a given and taken for granted. She could hardly have known that the Garden was especially planted for them by a caring God.

What were the psychological levers that were brought into play as the woman stood musing before the Tree of Knowledge? Both man and woman already possessed the power of free choice by virtue of their having been created in the "image of God," which included the ability to reason, make judgements and trace out means-ends relationships.

At the moment under consideration, woman was experiencing a complex of emotions of growing intensity, compounded of hunger, desire, and curiosity. Feeding this desire was a fertile imagination which enabled her to fantasize as to how this fruit might taste and what new powers this "knowledge" might unlock. What caused her to hesitate, however, was her reason, which reminded her that the tree was not even to be touched lest she "die," which she presumed was a bad thing! But experience had shown this prediction to be inaccurate, since earlier contact with the tree had resulted in no such thing. In addition, she speculated that God had only wished to frighten them with a false threat to keep them from eating of the tree so that He could keep those powers exclusively for Himself. And so she hesitated no longer.

Unknowingly, woman had successfully neutralized her faculty of reason, which alone stood in the way of her powerful desire, by discovering and exercising the ability to "rationalize." This is a process which occurs when raw desire influences the will to enter the rational process and offer a rational but specious explanation. God had never said that the day one *touches* the tree, one will die, so her earlier experience actually signifies nothing. Thus, the biblical story reveals the Achilles' heel of the rational process. Although the reasoning may be correct, the premise may be false, and so the conclusion will be false.

Of course, this sort of thing happens all the time even today. The reason it had such fateful consequences in our story is because at that time

Chapter Six. Paradise Lost or Outgrown?

human nature was to an extent raw, unfixed, and malleable. Because of the nature of the human psyche and its essential freedom, faculties such as reason, emotion, imagination, and sense of self could not have been brought into existence fully formed in sharply demarcated compartments. The outer limits of these components, and the precise modes of their interactions, would take shape gradually under the impact of living experience. Had the precise line of development hinted at in the metaphor not taken place when it did, perhaps man's rational faculty would have developed in ways that made it more resistant to manipulation by rationalization and man's emotions less responsive to his imagination. However, because it occurred when it did ("late on the sixth day before Shabbat"), at that crucial juncture in human evolution when man's proto-faculties were already sufficiently developed to be in use but still raw enough that improper moves now become permanent possibilities for all generations, this event takes on tragic dimensions. It signifies that much more work would have to be done, much more history would have to ensue, before a culture could be developed in which a balance of influences playing upon man would enable reason, desire, and the moral impulse to work together so that man in freedom and with responsibility could choose the good and reject the evil.

II

In order to hint at what happened as a result of eating of the Tree of Knowledge, the description of the event is juxtaposed between two statements, one immediately before it and the other immediately after:

> And they were both naked, the man and his wife and they were not ashamed. (Gen. 2:25)
>
> And the eyes of both were opened and they knew (וידעו) that they were naked and they sewed fig leaves and made for themselves girdles. (Gen. 3:7)

While in Genesis 2:25 the text sums up their indifference to their nakedness by simply saying "they were not ashamed," the description of the change in Genesis 3:7 does not refer to "shame" but instead says, "they *knew* that they were naked." This implies that the emotion of shame was seen merely as a symptom of sensitivity to nakedness, which itself, however, involves a far more complex cognitive process ("they *knew* that they were naked"). Animals and small children are not embarrassed by their nakedness, nor by many other things that might embarrass an adult human. This is because they lack self-consciousness and a self-image. However, in the account of the couple's hiding from God after their act of disobedience and their ensuing conversation, there are traces of guilt and embarrassment, so it would appear that they had now developed a self-image and a capacity for self-consciousness.[11] Thus, the statement in Genesis 3:7 must be read as saying that whereas prior to the event exposure of the erogenous parts of their bodies did not bother them, now it did. But why? Does our analysis of the Tree of Knowledge metaphor provide a credible explanation for this change?

It should be noted that the two biological drives involved in the story are those for food ("good to be eaten…") and for sex ("naked"), two of the strongest in human experience. In the case of animals both of these vital needs are controlled by hormones and gastric juices, and are limited, in the case of sex, to mating seasons and, in the case of food, to hunger pangs. The text implies that as a consequence of their act of "disobedience" (which was an exercise of free choice in response to a fantasy-driven appetite) the desires for food and sex in humans became permanently disconnected from any biological limitations and if fueled by imagination and fantasy ("and their eyes were opened…") could overwhelm reason.

The text emphasizes the role of perception: "And when the woman *saw*…" "that it was a delight to the *eyes*…" (Gen. 3:16), implying that under the effects of a powerful imagination one sees things differently than before.[12] Thus, "*seeing* themselves naked" now triggered in their consciousnesses a number of possibilities. "And the *eyes* of them both were *opened*" (Gen. 3:7). What they now "saw" in their minds' eyes shocked and embarrassed them. Their effort to cover themselves suggests the societal awareness that continual exposure to sexual stimuli is distracting in everyday interaction between the sexes. Generally, the particular situation that may arouse shame is culturally determined and

---

[11] See Genesis Rabbah 17:5. After naming the various animals, God asks man "and what is your name?" To which he replies, "It is proper that I be called Adam for I have been created from the *adamah* [earth]." "And what is My name?" asks God. Man answered, "It is proper that You be called *adonai* for you are the master [*adon*] of all of Your creatures."

[12] See Rashi on Num. 15:39.

Chapter Six. Paradise Lost or Outgrown?

depends upon one's self-image. The analysis we have offered here suggests that sometimes the experience of discomfort or embarrassment may be occasioned by our own thoughts, aroused by circumstances which may conflict with our self-image.

How does God view His creatures' eating of the forbidden fruit? In terms of the metaphor, of course, God is displeased. However, because Adam and Eve here represent emerging *homo sapiens*, we must not judge their action in conventional terms of "sin" or God's reaction as "punishment," or look to them for "repentance."[13] As stated earlier, this story is designed to explain why human development has had to take such a long and difficult road. A metaphor has been employed to explain how the human being got to be the way he is.

Man's answer to God, "The woman whom You gave to be with me, she gave me of the tree..." (Gen. 3:12), is not mere evasion of responsibility but an attempt to point out that he had some reason to assume that the woman, designed by God to be a "helpmeet," could be trusted. Similarly, woman's references to a "serpent," "The serpent beguiled me and I did eat..." (Gen. 3:13), is really an argument to the effect that since she had never had an experience of this sort before, the persuasive "voice" she heard in her consciousness sounded "authoritative" and its message convincing. These should be read not as lame excuses but as honest descriptions of their thinking at the time. Indeed, something tragic had happened, but since we are not talking "sin" there is no "blame" to be apportioned.

In His response, God addresses the three principle players in reverse order: "And the Lord said to the *serpent*..." (Gen. 3:14), "Unto *woman* He said..." (Gen. 3:16), and unto *man* He said..." (Gen. 3:17). However, there is no real sense of anger or retribution in His words but rather

---

[13] The Christian view as set forth by Augustine is that Adam was created good and intelligent. Since he was endowed with free will and could have chosen not to sin, his and Eve's eating of the forbidden fruit was committed in willfulness and pride. After this "fall," they and all of their descendants have been in a state of "original sin" from which no one can escape by his own efforts and are dependent upon God's love and grace in order to be redeemed. Judaism must reject such a view in terms of both theology and biblical exegesis. Judaism believes that every living human being has the freedom to resist and overcome sin, and will be judged by his own merit rather than be burdened by the sins of others. See Deut. 30:15, 19 and Gen. 4:7. Nowhere in the biblical story is man, as such, "cursed" for what happened. Even if Adam "sinned" it would not be just to punish the children for the sins of the parents.

a sad enumeration of the necessary changes in the human condition now to take place as a consequence of their action.[14] Because of the new alignment of reason, emotion, and imagination in man's psyche, a new order in the relationship between man and nature was now required if the human was to become what he was meant to be. The old order in a garden paradise, where man's basic needs, as it were, "grow on trees" will no longer serve the purpose. Man is no longer "innocent," and too much time on his hands spells trouble. The only way man can truly learn about himself is to be confronted by existential challenges and choices so that he can on his own gradually discern his potential and learn to distinguish between significant opportunities and roads that go nowhere.

In contrast to a life of leisure where the "living comes easy," man will now face a life of toil and struggle in order to provide the necessities. "By the sweat of your brow will you eat bread" (Gen. 3:19). Cast out into an indifferent world, he will ruefully remember the blessing to be "Great Lord of all things," but will now be "prey to all."[15] And if the human sex drive, grown powerful and constant under the stimulation of an active imagination, seems to defy restraint, it was now to be complicated by associating it with child-bearing, which by being painful to the woman might encourage restraint and a sense of responsibility. Also, relations between men and women can no longer be expected to be wholly rational, based on equality, but will be marked by tension and a struggle for dominance. Finally, man in this kind of world can no longer dream of a Tree of Life and must come to terms with his own mortality. "Dust you are and to dust you will return" (Gen. 3:19).[16] And if until now he was "in

---

[14] In the story God "curses" the snake and the earth because of man. However, God does not curse Adam or Eve.

[15] Alexander Pope, *Essay on Man*, Epistle II.

[16] Before expelling man from the Garden the text has God saying the following: "Behold the man has become *k'echad mimenu, as one of us*, to know good and evil and now lest ... he take also from the Tree of Life and eat and live forever..." (Gen 3:22). This passage as translated above presents many difficulties. For creative translations and interpretations, see Rashi, Malbim, and David Tzvi Hoffmann on Gen. 3:22. Perhaps it can be read as follows: "Behold man has become unique in his class of earthly creatures [by virtue of his freedom of choice] as I [God] am above, but since good and evil have become so intertwined that men have difficulty choosing the good, they cannot be permitted to live forever lest they delude themselves into thinking they are gods!"

Chapter Six. Paradise Lost or Outgrown?

doubt to deem himself a god or beast,"[17] he is to know that in truth he is neither but only man who, having been created in the *image* of God, tselem, can by his own efforts become *like* Him, demut.

God's words to the serpent make sense only in a literal interpretation of the story. The creature did a deceitful thing and therefore is "cursed" by henceforth having to slither about "on its belly" (Gen. 3:14). In order to retain the inner logic of the story, the text must include God's response to the serpent as well as to the others. But the purpose of this part of the story seems primarily aetiological, that is, to explain in a popular mode a natural fact that must have appeared most strange: why the snake, of all creatures, has no feet of any kind and for locomotion must slither around on its belly.[18] The "answer" supplied by the story in the metaphor is that the snake was "cursed" for its role in man's act of disobedience.

---

[17] Pope, *Essay on Man*.

[18] While there can be no doubt that the Torah intended later generations to interpret the Gan Eden story in light of their growing understanding of the human psyche, the story even taken literally imparts a coherent message. It is clear from the discoveries of the cultures of the Middle East that in the cases of the Garden of Eden and the Flood, the Torah used material from Mesopotamian legends, images familiar to the people, and by recasting them and infusing the product with the prophetic spirit turned it into an instrument for Torah teaching.

Parables that are invented *de nova* for a particular occasion can be stripped of all irrelevant material so that they emphasize only those features which the *mashal* and the *nimshal* share, such as Isaiah's parable of the vineyard or the "steaming pot" of Jeremiah. In our case, however, where one starts with an already existing plot and cast of characters, one may not be able to find a right application for every one of the minor elements in the parable. Thus I argued in the previous chapter that in its broad outlines the Bible Flood story may be generalized to represent the many destructions and extinctions that took place on this planet up to and including the Ice Ages. However, I could not generalize certain details in the story, such as the sending out of the raven and dove to see if the waters had receded. (Interestingly, these details appear in the Babylonian Flood story, only in reverse order.) I would answer that these also served an aetiological purpose in "explaining" certain observed characteristics of these birds. However, the fact that these details have been retained in the Torah text might signify that *natnu le-chadash*, each generation is to find therein meaningful homiletical interpretation. A sort of precedent for this approach might be seen in the insight of the sages that, although a dream may in the main have

III

We suggested earlier that when at the beginning of the story the text refers to an *Etz Ha-Da'at Tov V'Ra*, usually translated "the tree of knowledge of good and evil," this name should be seen as reflecting not what eating its fruit can produce, but rather the reality of what happened after man's "disobedience."[19] How is this to be understood? First, what sort of "knowledge" is involved here? Actually the Hebrew term *da'at* is sometimes used to refer to "acquaintanceship" (similar to the French *savoir*), that is, an intersubjective relationship based on experience rather than "knowledge" as cognition (similar to the French *connaitre*). So, by da'at tov v'ra we are referring to the human experience of those moral opposites, Good and Evil. Some have interpreted this to mean "the knowledge to *distinguish between* the words good and evil." However, this knowledge was already in man's possession as a consequence of his having been created in the "image of God."[20] Indeed, we are told that God had forbidden man to eat of that tree and that then, when he did, God held him morally responsible. This clearly implies that man already knew that to obey is morally right and to disobey morally wrong or evil.

What then is the meaning of da'at tov v'ra? It is the "experience of moral good *and* evil," conjoined by complex circumstances and mixed motives so that it is difficult to extricate one from the other. As we said

---

prophetic significance, some details may resist the overall interpretation and remain non-prophetic or even *devarim betelim*. See Rashi on Gen. 36:10.

We find the Trees of Life and the snake playing prominent roles in the mythology of ancient Mesopotamia. The snake is usually cast as clever, powerful, and malicious, and is a symbol of male superiority. Jeremy Black and Anthony Green, *Gods, Demons and Symbols of Ancient Mesopotamia* (British Museum Press, 1992).

In line with our interpretation that the snake in the story represents the "evil inclination," the "curse" it receives seems appropriate: once the evil inclination is recognized for what it is, it must go about its business by "slithering about," camouflaged, striking by surprise by injecting the poison of desire.

[19] *Al Shem Sofo*. See David Tzvi Hoffmann on Gen. 2:17.

[20] See Genesis Rabbah 16:9 on Gen. 2:16, 17: "And the Lord God *commanded* [Vayitzav] the man saying ... but of the Tree of the Knowledge of Good and Evil you shall not eat..." Here the sages found an indication that in this, God's first "command," *mitzvah*, to man there were included six of the seven Noahide laws. That is to say, from this point on man was already endowed with a moral sense.

earlier, the misuse of reason to rationalize immoral courses of action in early human development resulted in the permanent blurring of man's moral perception and the loss of sensitivity on the part of his moral sense. Whereas before the event in Gan Eden man experienced Good and Evil as clearly demarcated and open to decisive judgement, now Good and Evil have become inextricably intertwined. Therefore, the "tree" of the Gan Eden story metaphor, so centrally involved in this fateful event, is referred to as *Etz Ha-Da'at Tov V'Ra*, the tree which symbolizes man's moral experience, which is generally a mixture of good and evil.[21]

IV

But what would have happened if the humans had not disobeyed, had not eaten from the forbidden fruit? Were they to have remained in Gan Eden forever? What was God's original plan for man? These questions involve several familiar theological issues. Did not God foresee man's disobedience? Does not defeat of God's plan reflect upon His Omnipotence? Of course we have a similar problem later, in connection with the corruption in the days of Noah, which brings God to explicitly admit, "I regret having made them ..." (Gen. 6:7) and to decide to erase man from the face of the earth.

There are those who maintain that the conditions for human existence that have developed on our planet during the last 10,000 years support the proposition that ours "is the best of all possible worlds." That is to say, from the point of view of the Creator who wishes to provide man with an environment which effectively preserves his freedom in moral matters, our world, with its bewildering mixture of good and evil, joy and sadness, faith and doubt, strikes the proper balance in which free and responsible choices can be made. Accordingly, it would seem that the world that emerged after the Flood was what was anticipated by God, who foresaw all that ultimately happened. On this view, texts that imply otherwise, that speak of a God who seems surprised, "regrets" having made man, and is "upset" by his actions, are designed for the casual reader in the spirit of the rabbinic saying, "the Torah speaks in the language of men." However, the Garden of Eden story does suggest that God intended a far more friendly and manageable environment for man

---

[21] See commentary of the Malbim on Gen. 2:16, 17 and Gen. 3:3-7.

than what, in the short term, actually came about. Indeed, we are compelled to say that the Garden of Eden would have been "the best of all possible worlds" had man's nature developed in the intended direction, i.e., with the faculties of man's consciousness more compartmentalized so that intellect, emotion, and imagination would interact along more fixed paths and be less subject to the vagaries of impulse and fancy.

So who or what was it that thwarted God's plan? While Judaism knows of a Satan, a *yetzer harah* (evil inclination), and an "Angel of Death," it knows of no independent powers of evil that are operative in the affairs of men. The "serpent," as we have already indicated, was nothing more than a metaphor for the woman's imagination. This brings us back to the elusive "freedom of choice," that most precious gift from God to man which actually constitutes the human being. The human sense of self is essentially that of a freely-choosing entity. By giving man something of Himself, an element of "spirit," God was knowingly endowing His creature with a certain autonomy and in some sense restricting His own.[22]

---

[22] Two ideas we have elaborated in this essay have their analogues in the mystical literature of the Kabbala:

1) In the first we stated that the creation of man did not eventuate as originally planned. Somehow while evolving into *homo sapiens*, man exercising his will made the choice which upset the delicate balance between reason, emotion, and imagination. Because of this, history took the chaotic course we are familiar with. In Lurianic Kabbala there is the complex doctrine called "Breaking of the Vessels" (*shvirat hakelim*). It seems that the cosmic process required that the Divine Light which flowed into the primordial space differentiate into individual beams of the Sephirot, which required bowls or vessels to hold them. For reasons that are in dispute, there was an "accident" in which the vessels of some of the Sephirot could not contain the powerful light and so were broken or shattered and the light scattered. According to this theory, this event was "the cause of that inner deficiency which is inherent in everything that exists and of the power that evil enjoys and will persist as long as the damage is not mended (*tikkun*)" (Gershom Scholem, *Major Trends in Jewish Mysticism* [New York: Schocken Books, 1941], 265-268).

2) We have stated that by allowing man freedom of will, God placed certain limitations on His own power. The analogue in Kabbalah is the concept of *tsimtsum*, which means "concentration" or "contraction" or "withdrawal." If God is everywhere, where is there room for the world? How can there be things that are not God? Thus, God had to withdraw into Himself, abandon a region within Himself, and leave a primordial space in which the world could appear. Scholem calls this "one of the most amazing and far-reaching conceptions ever

Chapter Six. Paradise Lost or Outgrown?

It is man alone who can stand up to God and bring about changes, detours, and delays in the Divine plan for history. This is reflected in the early stories in Genesis and later, for example, in the negative response of Israel to the report of spies-scouts which delayed their entrance into the Promised Land for decades.[23] However, in this primeval setting, the consequences were much more fateful. For this was the inaugural human exercise of free choice, in its very "breaking-in" period during which it was to be integrated with the other human faculties. The tragic element here is that as his very first act of free choice the human chose to act disobediently, violating God's command. This had an unbalancing and permanent effect upon man's still-developing psyche, giving an edge to his imaginative faculty and enhancing the power of the pleasure principle.

In terms of the metaphor, all of this comes about as the result of a single act of Adam and Eve in Gan Eden. However, we must understand that in reality this event refers to some drawn-out evolutionary process from hominid to *homo sapiens* whose precise circumstances and mechanisms we may never learn.

According to the rabbinic timetable, the story of Adam and Eve in Gan Eden took place late in the afternoon of the sixth day of creation before Shabbat, before the formal completion of the cosmos. Thus God's pronouncement, "And God saw everything that He had made and behold it was very good" (Gen. 1:31) comes afterward, and encompasses the changes that came about in man's nature and in his relationship to the environment. That is to say, even after man's expulsion from the Garden, mankind will still be able to achieve its Divinely appointed destiny. It will, however, be much more difficult and more costly, and will take much longer. Can we therefore say that from the biblical point of view ours is still "the best of all possible worlds"? Well, "best" perhaps from God's perspective, and "possible" taking into consideration the limitations of the post-paradisiacal reality of the human psyche. This is clear from the biblical narrative itself. After all of His earlier regrets, God is prepared to try again with the Noahide survivors of the Flood, and promises "Neither

---

put forward in the whole history of Kabbalism" (Scholem, *Major Trends*, 260-261). Kabbala placed the "blame" for an imperfect universe on some technical flaw in the cosmos. We have located it in a misuse by man of his freedom of will.

[23] Num. 14:28-35.

will I smite any more every living thing as I have done…" (Gen 8:21). For all intents and purposes, then, history is back on track and God's plan proceeds to go forward. So much for biblical exegesis.

V

In our day, however, questions as to the worthwhileness of life (is it truly "very good"?) have been reopened and upgraded to the more serious level of "existential." That is to say, this issue is not seen simply as an intellectual puzzle to be solved by some nice theory or lofty philosophy. The individual lives his life every minute of every day, and his subjective experience cannot be ignored. After all, whether something is to be designated "good" is a value judgement and cannot be objectively considered unless some specific criteria can be agreed upon in advance.

In its own development, Judaism has not been content to leave the matter with the "very good" pronouncement of Gen. 1:31. Thus, for example, included in the canon of holy scripture is Kohelet, whose question "what remains to a man from all of his toil which he toils under the sun?" (1:3) remains largely unanswered. The Talmudic-period debate, regarding whether it is better for an individual to have been created or not to have been created, discussed earlier in this volume is said to have lasted for two and a half years.[24]

But surely if the Bible states that *all* that God made, including the human being, was "very good," how could the rabbis even raise the question of whether it would have been better for man not to have been created? Perhaps by this time Jewish thought had become analytic enough to legitimize a distinction between a view of things as seen from the view of God (as found in the Pentateuch) and a view of things as seen by autonomous man. For it can be acknowledged that God's purposes can indeed by achieved under existing conditions, but one can still ask whether it is in the interests of the individual human being to be part of what we call "life"?[25]

---

[24] *Eruvin* 13b.
[25] I would think that most individuals in developed countries, if asked this question at middle age, would answer that they are happy to have been born. Clearly from the individual subjective viewpoint much depends on the particular slice of life one has been apportioned.

Chapter Six. Paradise Lost or Outgrown?

In terms of Judaism, man is a free and responsible human being who may or may not fulfill his destiny as a human being and/or as a Jew. In either case he will be held accountable for what he does with his life. The stakes are enormous, with the consequences of either success or failure touching upon the very meaning of one's life. The question, therefore, is: given this particular person's chances for success or failure, would it perhaps have been better for him never to have been created and therefore never to have had to run the risk of failure? But then he would never have had the opportunity to achieve whatever it is that Judaism holds out as the supreme reward.

How one answers this question would appear to depend upon one's assumptions regarding the following: (1) The probabilities of the "average" person succeeding or failing; (2) The positive value to be assigned to success and the negative value to failure. The fact that the issue was debated for so long indicates that rabbinic opinion was divided over these basic assumptions, and that both views were considered acceptable within the framework of the Jewish world view. That a majority could have been found in favor of the more pessimistic view should not surprise us, as many of the rabbis tended to see this approach as having didactic value.[26]

VI

However, if the rabbis were not all that convinced that existence is an unmixed blessing for man, why did a "good" God persist in creating him? Indeed, the rabbis remained quite sensitive to this question and found an opportunity early in Genesis to express their unease.

In describing the creation of man, there is this very problematic text: "And God said, *'Let us* make a man in Our image and in Our likeness...'" (Gen. 1:26). To whom was God speaking? Indeed, early critics would point to this verse as evidence that the Israelite God presided over a pantheon.[27] In Aggadic literature, however, there are at least three different

---

[26] See *Avot* 4:30, 3:1. See also Chapter 3 in the present volume. In discussing the possible outcomes of Pascal's Wager, William James points out that the individual has little to lose and much to gain in making the "leap of faith."

[27] See Rashi on Gen. 1:26, where he states that God was willing to take the risk of being misunderstood as long as He could teach a moral lesson that it is proper for even those recognized as superior to take counsel with those on the lower rung of authority.

midrashim in which the rabbis interpret this verse to mean that God took counsel with His ministering angels as to whether He should create man. After inquiring as to the nature of this proposed creature and his deeds, the angels unanimously advised against it. God's particular response in each midrash is different. What they have in common, however, is that God finds a way to ignore their advice and proceeds to create this problematic creature on His own.[28]

Whatever the original reason for the use of the collective in the passage "*let* us make man," the rabbis, with their ear for the finer nuances in the biblical text, sensed here a suggestion of hesitancy on the part of God. After all, why the need for any advance announcement on the part of an omniscient Creator who needs neither assistance nor a second opinion? And so the rabbis employed the textual anomaly to voice a nagging concern. Is it good even from the point of view of the values espoused by God, such as justice, righteousness, and loving-kindness, for man to have been created? After all, look at all the evil men introduce into the world, even against their own kind!

The angels in the midrashim represent the voice of reason and common sense. Given the early record of man's destructive use of the Divine gift of freedom of choice, the creation of man will mean, at least initially, violence, human pain and anguish, and continuous interference with God's goals in history. Who needs this *tzarah* (trouble)?

The issue is never explicitly argued, as God does not respond substantively even when confronted by the angels with irrefutable evidence of man's evil. However, the most poignant of the midrashim ends with God citing the following cryptic passage from Isaiah:

ועד זקנה אני הוא	Even to old age I am He
ועד שיבה אני אסבל	And even to grey hair will I carry you
אני עשיתי ואני אשא	I have made and I will bear
ואני אסבל ואמלט	Yes, I will carry and I will redeem (Isa. 46:4)

---

[28] In a *midrash* in which the angels representing moral values come up with a tie vote, God hurls one of the opposing angels down to earth so that the vote is now in favor of creation. In another *midrash*, after the angels present God with a unanimous negative vote, God replies: "[Sorry folks] you are too late; I have already created him." Both *midrashim* can be found in Genesis Rabba 8:5.

Chapter Six. Paradise Lost or Outgrown?

The words echo with a certain sadness, and one can detect a note of resignation. But there is at the same time a sort of reassurance: God accepts responsibility for what He has done ("I have made and I will bear [with patience]") no matter how long it takes ("Even to old age … and to grey hair"). The six-fold repetition of the personal pronoun, the Divine "I," implies that this entire conundrum defies our understanding because it emanates from the unique unknowable subjectivity, the "I" which is God, He who is beyond space and time and paradoxically incorporates both justice and mercy, rationality and love. In the end, however, He who created man against all counsel has faith in His creatures and He will yet redeem.

Here the sages are saying more than that this problem is beyond rational explication. They are suggesting that because creation, in the ways we have examined, is not perfect, God, the Creator, may be viewed as a tragic figure. "My soul shall weep in secret [*mistarim*]…" (Jeremiah 13:17). Say the rabbis, "the Holy One, Blessed be He, has a place called *mistarim* where He goes to weep."[29] God, it would seem at this point, will do no more. However, here it is man who *can* and ought to. "They brought matters to a vote and concluded: 'It would have been better for man not to have been created, but now that he is here, let him look to his deeds.'"[30]

---

[29] *Chagigah* 5b.
[30] Ibid.

Chapter Seven

Multiplicity of Meaning as a Device in Biblical Narrative

Throughout biblical literature, God acts in the world by means of what is called His "voice" (*kol*) or His "word" (*davar*). Sometimes God is described as bringing about His ends by the use of various intermediaries, but, when He acts directly, His instrumentality seems to be the word. In connection with the creation of the world, we are told: "By the word of the Lord were the heavens made" (Psalms 33:6). The ongoing forces of nature are described thus: "Fire and hail, snow and vapour, stormy wind fulfilling His word." But, above all, in communicating with man, in revealing His will through prophecy, it is the voice of God (Exod. 19:19) which translates itself into visions (Isa. 2:1), commands (Jer. 1:4), and meaningful concepts (Ezek. 3:16). For the *word* implies dialogue. The *word* is spoken *to* someone.

The voice of God, however, is not only power that can "hew out flames of fire" and "break into pieces the cedars of Lebanon" (Psalms 29), but is a creative force that can bring things into existence: "He spoke and it was" (Psalms 33:9). Most important, however, is the aspect of *kol* as the *word*: as a vehicle of meaning and intelligence. This concept shaped the essential character of Jewish thought. As Gershom Scholem observed in speaking of the Kabbalists:

> Language in its purest form, that is Hebrew, reflects the fundamental spiritual nature of the world. Speech reaches God because it comes from God.... All that lives is an expression of God's Language.[1]

It does not appear that the rabbis of the Talmud perceived of God's *word* or *voice* as an intermediary or ontological entity, as Philo did, nor that they saw in the unfolding of the elements of divine speech a symbol of the hidden world of the Sefirot or divine manifestations, as we find in

---

[1] Gershom Scholem, *Major Trends in Jewish Mysticism* (New York: Schocken Books, 1941), 17.

Chapter Seven. Multiplicity of Meaning as a Device in Biblical Narrative

the Zohar.² However, basing themselves upon biblical texts such as "God thundereth marvelously with His voice," (Job 37:5) the rabbis did attribute wondrous and unusual powers to the voice and word of God. Thus, in response to the discrepancy between the two versions of the fourth commandment of the Decalogue (Exodus reads "Remember [*zakhor*] the Sabbath day to keep it holy," while Deuteronomy reads "Keep [*shamor*] the Sabbath day..."³) the Rabbis commented, "*Zakhor* and *shamor* were spoken in one utterance." And when the people of Israel, listening to the voice of God at Sinai, perceived the sound coming from different directions (Exod. 20:15), the rabbis taught that there was a sense in which the people could actually *see* what was heard!⁴

Most significant of the "marvels" of God's *word* is its ability to impart multiple meanings either to the same person at different times or to different people at the same time. Thus, for example, Rabbi Yohanan noted that, at Sinai, the *kol* of God issued forth and then split into seventy voices, each in a different language, so that the message might be understood by all the nations of the world. He also noted that each person who stood at Sinai received the message according to his own individual level of comprehension,⁵ reflecting the basic rabbinic concept that the Torah text contains an infinity of meanings, a plurality of interpretations.⁶ Interpretation, therefore, is not separate from the text but an extension of it. On this view, language is essentially a metaphor which leads us to see resemblances within differences, to trace relationships between dissimilars.⁷ In the realm of the Halakhah, this leads to the astonishing concept applied to opposing rulings, "[Both] these and those are the words of the living God,"⁸ and, in the more fluid Aggadah, to the concept that "One biblical verse is susceptible to many different

---

² H.A. Wolfson, *Philo*, volume 1 (Cambridge, MA: Harvard University Press, 1947), 286; Scholem, *Major Trends in Jewish Mysticism*, 215-216.
³ Exod. 20:8; Deut. 5:12.
⁴ *Shemot Rabbah* 5:9.
⁵ *Midrash Tanhuma* on Exod. 4:27.
⁶ It is important to bear in mind this point made by Max Kadushin: "From the idea that God revealed the Torah it does not necessarily follow that the words of the Torah are susceptible of many interpretations" *The Rabbinic Mind* (New York: Bloch Pub. Co., 1972), 106.
⁷ See the discussion in Susan A. Handelman, *The Slayers of Moses* (Albany: State University of New York Press, 1982).
⁸ *Eruvin* 14.

interpretations." The much-quoted passage in Jeremiah 23:29: "Is not my word like as fire saith the Lord, like a hammer that breaketh the rock?" is commented upon by the rabbis with the following thought: "Just as the hammer breaks up a rock into many sparks, so, too, may one passage give rise to several meanings."[9]

In a more particular instance, the *Tanhumah* tells us that when God wanted Moses to return to Egypt from Midian, He issued a single utterance which split into "two facets," one heard by Moses in Midian, saying: "Go (*lekh*) return unto Egypt" (Exod. 4:19), and the other heard by Aaron in Egypt saying, "Go (*lekh*) into the wilderness to meet Moses" (Exod. 4:27). This would appear to be a concrete instance of the verse, "God has spoken once; two things have we heard" (Psalms 62:11). Of course, if we focus on the referential meanings of these two statements, then they are, indeed, not only different but in opposition. Moses and Aaron are being told to go in opposite directions: Moses from the wilderness to Egypt, Aaron from Egypt to the wilderness. However, the intention in both cases is identical: to bring about a meeting between the brothers. Conceivably, therefore, assuming that they knew each other's locations, one statement could have sufficed, "Go towards your brother." The midrash, therefore, is really not so fanciful as it may first appear. In emanating from God, the utterance expressing the intentional meaning is a single one. (Both statements actually begin with the worl *lekh*— "go.") However, the proposition then "marvelously" transposes itself into two distinct sentences with different referential meanings, so as to inform both Moses and Aaron where they are to go.

It has been noted that this rabbinic understanding of the special properties of the word of God has further important implications for our approach to the word of man. As Susan Handelman has pointed out, "If, for the Rabbis, the primary reality is linguistic and true being is a God who speaks and creates texts then *imitatio deus* is not silent suffering but speaking and interpreting."[10] More particularly, however, when God inspires man to speak His word, when the voice of God issues forth from the "throats of His prophets," then that *word*, as well, shares to some degree the special properties of the *dvar Hashem* and becomes a vehicle for multiple meanings.

---

[9] *Sanhedrin* 34b.
[10] See Susan Handelman, *The Slayers of Moses*, 4.

Chapter Seven. Multiplicity of Meaning as a Device in Biblical Narrative

While the rabbinical approach to the possibility of multiple meanings has been well noted, its use by the Bible itself has not received adequate recognition. The aim of this paper is to show that, in several instances in the Bible, multiplicity of meaning is consciously employed as a literary device. That is to say, the dialogue in certain situations is so constructed as to be understood one way by the speaker, in a different way by the person spoken to, and in a third way by the reader. It is clear from the context that the words which occasion the multiple meanings, while uttered by human beings, are inspired by God. In all of these cases, it is the multiple meaning which makes it possible for the speaker to achieve his immediate purpose and for the reader to grasp the overall intent of the biblical author. We shall argue that, in these particular cases, only if the dialogue is so interpreted can these narratives be clearly understood.

In order to perceive the theoretical background for this, we must wed the concept of multiple meanings to the concept of the word as "creative force." That is to say, just as God can, through the instrumentality of the word, bring worlds into existence—"Let there be light" becomes as it were, the empirical laws of physics—so, too, does the word of God, as a vehicle for multiple meanings, enter into the world of men to carry out God's purposes in history. But since men are creatures endowed with freedom and intelligence, the *word* of God must restrain its power and work within the matrix of human will and desire. The *word* in this context can achieve its goals only by appealing, stimulating, or convincing. This applies to the original utterances within the framework of the biblical narrative as well as to the now-canonical words of the Torah, which again and again may be expected to evoke responses that carry forward the divine purpose.[11] In the words of Isaiah:

> For as the rain cometh down and the snow from heaven,
> And returneth not thither,
> Except it water the earth,
> And make it bring forth and bud,
> And give seed to the sower and bread to the eater:
> So shall My word be that goeth forth from out of My mouth;
> It shall not return unto Me void.

---

[11] According to Josephus, Cyrus the Persian was inspired to permit the Jews to return to Jerusalem to rebuild their Temple after he was shown the relevant prophecies in the Book of Isaiah.

Except it accomplish that which I please
And make the thing whereto I sent it prosper. (55:10-11)

In comparing God's word to the fruitful effect of rain upon the earth. Isaiah seems to be saying that the word can have a pragmatic meaning as well as a referential meaning: the word itself, by its effect upon people, can bring about God's purpose.

The three portions of biblical narrative that I wish to deal with all involve a dialogue with or between idolaters: the servant of Abraham's interactions with Laban and Bethuel, Moses and Aaron's interactions with Pharaoh, and Balaam's interactions with Balak. In each case, the word inspired by God and relayed by the biblical protagonist operates on two distinct levels and assumes three different meanings.

The first level takes place within the biblical narrative, with different meanings assumed by the speaker and the one spoken to. The second level operates outside of the biblical narrative, where the reader, aided by his perspective of the narrative as a whole, is able to grasp the implied meaning of the dialogue.

The speaker, operating within the context of the story, is given a certain task, is promised divine aid, or is specifically instructed by God, and proceeds to say the sort of thing which seems quite reasonable under the circumstances.

For the idolater, with his pagan presuppositions and unfamiliarity with the God of Israel, the words within the context of the narrative are perceived in such a way as to induce him to act in the required manner to realize the inadequacy of his own beliefs, and to impress upon him the power of the God of Israel. On the other hand, the reader, who stands outside of the biblical narrative and responds to these words and Torah, derives therefrom, in addition, much broader truths which are not perceived within the narrative.

Case I

Abraham dispatches his "servant" (presumably Eliezer of Damascus) upon a most significant and difficult task: to find a wife for his son, Isaac, the same Isaac in whom Abraham's "seed will be called" and who has been charged to "do justice and righteousness," who was dedicated as a living offering upon the altar, and in whom the momentous future of a

Chapter Seven. Multiplicity of Meaning as a Device in Biblical Narrative

new people rests. Obviously, a wife for such a one must have a character appropriate for her special role.

But Abraham, apparently, gives no guidance regarding this wife, merely instructing the servant on the geographic area whence the woman is to come: "... from my land and my birthplace" (Gen. 24:4). It is not clear whether the geographic requirement is a substantive one or merely an aid for locating a woman with character. The servant accepts the mission but asks what he is to do if the woman refuses to come to Canaan. To this Abraham responds with faith and the promise of divine aid: "The Lord, God of the heavens ... who spoke to me ... He will send *His messenger* before you..." (Gen. 24:7).

The servant's formidable task as he sets out for Aram Naharaim is threefold:

> 1) He has to find a woman with the substantive qualities appropriate for a wife for Isaac.
>
> 2) This woman must fulfill the formal requirements stipulated by Abraham. She must be from "my land and my birthplace." It is not clear whether this means Abraham's original country, town, tribe, or family.[12]
>
> 3) The woman has to want to marry Isaac, move to Canaan and her parents have to consent.

Having arrived at the main watering spot of the city of Haran, the servant addresses God and in effect, sets up a formal framework in which to receive divine aid, which is, at the same time, a substantive criterion by which to determine the appropriate wife for Isaac: "And it shall be that the maiden to whom I will say, 'incline your jug that I may drink,' and she will say, 'drink and also for your camels will I give to drink,' she have you chosen for your servant Isaac" (24:14).

We must pause to ask the following: what if the woman who passes the character test is not of the family of Abraham but from some other family in the city (Abraham's "land and birthplace")? Would she be acceptable? Would the servant consider his prayers answered? On the basis of the text we would have to answer in the affirmative.

---

[12] See *Rashi* on Gen. 24:4.

But behold, the very first maiden to whom the servant directs his request responds positively and turns out to be none other than Rebecca, the daughter of Bethuel, son of Nahor, brother of Abraham! Thus, divine providence has confirmed the servant's criterion and has helped him to achieve his first two goals in a most spectacular way. He has discovered a woman of character who is not only from Abraham's city and birthplace but from Abraham's family. But the remaining task is the most difficult of all: what if her parents will not permit her to leave home, or if Rebecca herself refuses to go?

In order to accomplish this last task, the servant of the man to whom God has spoken now decides to perform a speech-act, to describe in words what has happened. He tells Rebecca's astonished family that he will not take food "until I have spoken my words" (24:33). For the third time we hear the entire episode in all its detail, beginning with Abraham's charging of the servant up to the appearance of Rebecca. The rabbis wondered about all of this repetition, which seemed inconsistent with the Torah's verbal economy elsewhere.[13]

But suddenly, we realize what is happening. The servant does not merely repeat the story the way he understood it before. This is what his master Abraham had intended from the very beginning—a maiden from his own family! The servant now retells the story in such a way as to convince his listeners that "the thing *(davar)* has issued forth from the Lord..." (Gen. 24:50). This match was "made in heaven." In this version, the servant makes it explicit that from the outset Abraham wanted a maiden from his own family. The servant remembers Abraham as saying or meaning, "unto *my father's house* and my *family* shalt thou go" (Gen. 24:38). When the first maiden to respond with the proper words turns out to have been, indeed, from Abraham's own family, the providential aspect is stunning and overwhelming. The "thing" *(davar)* has truly issued forth from the Lord! (The reader may be inclined to interpret *davar* here as "word" instead of "thing".)

Indeed, it seems plausible to suggest that the "words" referred to by the servant in his ". . . until I have spoken my *words*," may be the "messenger" of God promised by Abraham.[14] For these verbal "messengers"

---

[13] See Rashi on Gen. 24:42.

[14] See Rashi's comment on Num. 20:16: Perhaps all of this is implied in the lesson that the rabbis gleaned from this repetition: "The conversations of the servants

achieve their goal: they move Laban and Bethuel to give their consent for Rebecca to return with the servant.

In this instance, it is easy to see the multiple meanings involved because the servant deliberately retells the story with a different emphasis. For Bethuel and Laban and perhaps Rebecca, we have here a miraculous answer to a prayer! A sign was asked for and a sign was immediately given; there is overwhelming evidence of divine selection and favor. What was important for Laban to know was not what Rebecca said (showing her kindly character) but that it was the required sign. The words of the servant, merely by being uttered, "accomplish that which God pleases." Rebecca's family agrees to the marriage.

But, of course, for the readers of the Torah the faith of an Abraham and the wisdom of his servant are but the occasions for reminding us of the most important single value in building the House of Israel: the attribute of *hesed,* "lovingkindness," as exemplified by a woman who will say to a travel-weary stranger, "Drink, and also to your camels will I give to drink" (Gen. 24: 14) and, as the servant concludes his prayer: "And with this will I know that you have done a kindness *(hesed)* with my master," meaning that with a daughter-in-law such as this, a continuation of the Abrahamic tradition of *hesed* will be assured.[15]

Case II

The second instance has to do with the words used by Moses in presenting his demands to Pharaoh that he release the Israelites from Egypt. Here it is clear that Moses is speaking the word of God, for he has been promised: "I will be with your mouth and I will teach you that which you are to speak" (Exod. 4:16). He repeatedly demands of Pharaoh: "Send forth My people so that they may serve Me." (Exod. 7:26) Four words in Hebrew: *"shelah et ami veya-avdooni."* Initially, Pharaoh is so shocked by the brazenness of the first three words that he tends to ignore the last one, i.e., the purpose for which the Israelites are to be sent forth: "so that

---

of the Patriarchs are more valued by God than the Torah of the sons." That is to say, the apparent repetitions of the servant are as important as Torah. Indeed, they are Torah, because they are words which by their effects on the hearer achieve God's purpose.

[15] See comments on *Malbim* on Gen. 24:14.

they may serve Me." It is only after the fourth plague that he realizes he must take the demand seriously and begins to consider whether the demand "to serve God" can be satisfied and he yet retains the Israelites as slaves. Therefore, he throws out his first compromise proposal:

(A) "Go sacrifice to your God in the land" (Exod. 8:21).

In line with the religious assumptions of the age, Pharaoh equates "service" or worship of God with "animal sacrifices." Thus, if the purpose of sending forth the Israelites is solely to "serve God" then it is quite reasonable to propose that they perform the sacrifice right there in Egypt. No need to go elsewhere!

Moses replies that the animal (lamb?) which they would sacrifice is venerated by the Egyptians, so it would be dangerous and disruptive to perform this "service" in their land. Israel must be permitted to go into the wilderness to sacrifice.

Two other attempts are made by Pharaoh to accommodate Moses' demand that the Israelites "serve God" and yet to somehow retain his hold upon them, once after the seventh plague and again after the ninth (Exod. 10:8, 24).

Here again we seem to have an instance wherein the same words of God are simultaneously directed at two different audiences with different effects. To Pharaoh, Moses' responses to his proposals appears transparently evasive, obviously duplicitous, and designed simply as a clumsy pretense to effectuate a total release of the Israelites. To those around Pharaoh, the divine King of Egypt is being made a fool of, is being mocked and held up for ridicule by someone who claims to speak for some unfamiliar but powerful God.[16]

To the reader, however, these three exchanges reveal the profound innovative and radical nature of the new "service" demanded by the God of the Hebrews. As we shall show, all of the three replies of Moses are to be seen not simply as ploys to counter the self-serving schemes of Pharaoh but as deep insights and prophetic anticipations of the nature and consequences of the revolutionary worship demanded by the God of Israel.

In the first exchange, Moses points out that the Israelites' method of worship is considered an abomination in Egypt and it would be dangerous, therefore, to perform it in that land. It is easy, with historic

---

[16] See Rashi on Exod. 10:2.

hindsight, to broaden this observation and to see it as a general observation about an abiding and recurring effect of the practice of Judaism upon surrounding people. It seems to have been the historic fate of the Jewish religion to evoke hostility and suspicion in the peoples among whom its adherents lived. In the pagan world, Jewish monotheism, by virtue of its implicit claim of the falsity of all other gods, was considered an "abomination." In ancient Rome, observance of the Jewish Sabbath was ridiculed as an encouragement of idleness. In the Christian world, Judaism was for centuries certainly perceived as an "abomination." Israel was often seen as "sacrificing" that which the Christian world "venerated," with disastrous consequences for Jewish communities. In the Nazi view, Judaism deserved extirpation because it taught inhuman doctrines and polluted the human race, and Marxists saw it as an excrescence of capitalism.

In even broader terms, Pharaoh's suggestion that Israel serve God in Egypt can be seen as an invitation to reject the territorial dimension of Judaism. The reader will hear in Pharaoh's call the perennial temptation to reconstruct Judaism as a universal diaspora phenomenon, and to see therein its ultimate fulfillment. Moses' rejection says, in effect, that there is no future for Israel except in the land promised to the forefathers.

(B) In the second exchange, Pharaoh looks more carefully at the request to "serve God," and offers to let the men, and only the men, go. Moses, however, insists that "with our young people and with our old people we will go, with our sons and with our daughters, with our flocks and with our herds we will go; for we must hold a celebration unto the Lord" (Exod. 10:8).

Justifiably angry, Pharaoh drives Moses and Aaron out of his presence, for, on the premise that "serving God" meant "sacrificing," it was reasonable to assume that children have no place there.[17] The demand that infants be permitted to accompany the pilgrimage is clear evidence that this talk of a divine service is just so much pretense to effectuate a total exodus.

Within the context of the narrative as a whole, Moses is clearly "playing" with Pharaoh! And yet, from the perspective of his revelational experience, Moses' reply is a very accurate and faithful expression of his

---

[17] See Rashi on Exod. 10:11.

understanding of what God is, indeed, requiring of Israel. He has been told not only of an exodus from Egypt but also of being brought into a land, and of a unique and open-ended relationship between God and this entire people: "And I will take you unto Me for a people and I will be unto you for a God" (Exod. 6:7). Moses perceives that he is dealing here not merely with a one-time religious festival, a limited set of ritual observances, but with a radically new concept in divine-human relationship. The God of heaven and earth is about to adopt a particular people who are to become His "first-born." Thus, there can be no question of men only, or women only, or senior-citizens only. Every man, woman, and child of Israel must participate in the covenant. Indeed, any human being, who heeds this call and perceives its truth and beauty (like the "mixed-multitude") must be permitted to go.[18] Moses' demand may be interpreted as "send forth" those who wish to become "my people" so that "they may serve Me"—as a people.

(C) In the final exchange, Pharaoh picks up the discussion at the point where it had been left and proposes that the children may indeed go, but that the sheep and cattle must remain in Egypt. He seems to be arguing along the following lines: "If, indeed, Moses, it is as you say that we are dealing here with a new concept in which 'worship' involves the entire people, then 'sacrifices' seem no longer relevant. In that case, take the infants but leave the cattle!"

Moses replies that matters are not so clear-cut. Sacrifices have not become irrelevant. Indeed, Pharaoh himself is invited to contribute offerings to the service.[19] As for the Israelites, all of their livestock must go with them as a pool from which the offerings will be selected.

And then Moses makes a most revealing statement which is nothing but the truth but which is perceived by Pharaoh as the most disingenuous ploy of all: "For we will not know how to serve God until we get there" (Exod. 10:26). Knowing that priests are the creators of their religion (especially of new ones!), Pharaoh is infuriated by this sudden bold-faced retreat by Moses into ignorance, and forbids Moses and Aaron to come before him on pain of death.

---

[18] Exod. 12:38.
[19] At the end, Pharaoh does indeed ask Moses and Aaron for their "blessing" (Exod. 12:32).

Chapter Seven. Multiplicity of Meaning as a Device in Biblical Narrative

And yet, from the reader's perspective, isn't that the truth? God had said to Moses: "When you take this people out of Egypt you shall serve God on this mountain" (Exod. 3:12). The service, the reader knows, will include an unprecedented theophany in which a unique covenant-community will be established and a Torah, whose emphasis is morality, will be received. Of course, sacrifices are still brought (Exod. 23:5-8), but the essential "service" is new, non-cultic, and unexpected.

Alas, poor Pharaoh, Moses was not trying to obfuscate or to be clever. In truth, he really did not know what God would require of them until they got there! "One thing has God spoken; two things have we heard."

Case III

The third example is the story of Balaam, the Mesopotamian magician and soothsayer. As the Bible tells it, a delegation of the rulers of Moab and Midian, fearful of the approaching Israelites, appeal to Balaam, well known as a diviner with great oracular and imprecatory power, to come and curse Israel. After hearing their request, he promises them a reply in the morning: "I will bring you back word as God will speak with me" (Num. 22:8).

When God actually comes to Balaam in the night and says, "Do not go with them," no one is more surprised than Balaam himself. We cannot assume that Balaam was on a regular speaking basis with God, and his pious remark to the delegation was merely a diviner's way of saying, "I have to think it over." When in the morning Balaam (we must imagine him white-faced and shaken) reports God's instructions to his guests, they are not at all surprised. Dutifully they return to Moab and simply report, "Balaam does not wish to come with us" (Num. 22: 14). There is no mention at all of God, of His visitation to Balaam, or of God's refusal to have Balaam go with them. Clearly, the delegation does not for one moment believe that Balaam was serious when he told them to wait until "God will speak with me." [20] They probably winked and nodded to each other knowingly, realizing such "God talk" was only a facade behind which Balaam deliberated as to whether the price was right, for to be a sorcerer and a diviner in that environment was precisely to have

---

[20] See comments of Netziv, *Ha-Emek Davar*, on this passage.

the knowledge by which to manipulate the gods and influence their decrees.[21] Balaam's reputation was set before him: "he whom thou blessest is blessed and he whom thou cursest is cursed" (Num. 22:6).

Naturally Balak, king of Moab, sends a more distinguished delegation, with the promises of more honors and a larger fee. Once again, Balaam solemnly assures them that his decision has nothing to do with gold and silver but that he must consult with God: "I simply cannot go beyond the word of the Lord my God" (Num. 22:18). When, in the morning, a bewildered Balaam reports that God has now consented for him to go, his visitors (unlike the biblical commentators) are not at all surprised at such capriciousness. Of course, they assume, God is not talking to Balaam. This is simply Balaam's way of saying, "the price is right"!

What is the purpose of this entire narrative, which the tradition identifies as a self-contained entity called *Parshat Balaam* or *Sefer Balaam*? Considered simply as one of the many dangers which Israel overcame in its journey through the wilderness, it would have been enough, and in a sense even more dramatic, for God to have let an unsuspecting Balaam agree to "curse" Israel and then when expectations were at their highest, either to silence him or to turn his curses into blessings. Why all of these confusing appearances of God, the talking-ass, and the four actual orations of Balaam![22]

It would seem that we have here an attempt to transform Balaam in his own eyes and in the eyes of his contemporaries from a willing manipulator of divine decrees to an unwilling spokesman of the word of God, and in the process to debunk the false notions of the age and to poke fun at the pretenses of the self-serving men who deceitfully claim to have the power to "hear the words of God," "to see the visions of the Almighty," and "to know the knowledge of the most high" (Num. 23:14,16). God is mocking and playing with Balaam, the idolater, even as He mocked and played with Pharaoh, the idolater.

Balaam speaks the word of God in a straightforward way. Yet the meaning that these words carry for the men of Moab and Midian is altogether different. The irony is exquisite. Balaam, the buffoon, is the

---

[21] See Y. Kaufmann, *The Religion of Israel* (Chicago: University of Chicago Press, 1960).

[22] See *Rashi* on Num. 22:29.

Chapter Seven. Multiplicity of Meaning as a Device in Biblical Narrative

prisoner of his own lies. Try as he may to convince his clients that God has truly appeared to him and instructed him, he cannot break through to them because the religious vocabulary ("God," "speak," "vision") has been corrupted of its original meanings and pressed into the service of a false set of beliefs.

The same word of God uttered by Balaam achieves different things with two different audiences. For Balaam and his friends, within the context of the narrative, God's word effectuates a devastating expose of the falsity of the prevailing concept of the sorcerer, and a brief but revelational glimpse of what it is to be a prophet of the living God. For the reader of the Torah, these same words describe how it was that "The Lord thy God turned the curse into a blessing unto thee because the Lord thy God loved thee" (Deut. 23:6). They have also given us some of the most lofty prophetic utterances about Israel to be found in the Torah.

The episode of the talking ass further humbles and humiliates Balaam. The one who claims to be able to "see the visions of the Almighty" cannot see the angel blocking the road, even though the ass can! The one whose curses are considered deadly blurts out helplessly, "If I had a sword in my hand I would have killed you!" (Num. 22:29).[23]

Finally Balaam, who has been placed under tight rein to speak only that which God permits him to, finds himself listening to his ass, who is freely jabbering away without restraint!

In the final portion of the story, when Balaam comes before Balak, four separate attempts are made to curse Israel, but each time only blessings come forth. In disgust, Balak orders Balaam back to where he came from. What happens during these four attempts is the gradual realization by Balak and his people that Balaam has been speaking the literal truth all along. From his first appearance Balaam had declared, "Have I now any power at all to speak anything? The word that God putteth in my mouth, that shall I speak" (Num. 22:38). Initially, Balak sees this only as a pious platitude, false modesty, the powerful magician hiding behind the God whom he claims to manipulate. But when, again and again, Balaam's words form blessings, it becomes clear that Balaam is indeed in the grip of a more powerful force—that man cannot manipulate the divine.

---

[23] Num. 24:1, 2.

And Balaam himself senses his own metamorphosis. The first two orations are consciously prepared as divination with God forcing the words of blessing upon Balaam. In the last two, Balaam yields to the spirit of the Lord and truly becomes a prophet of the living God.[24]

The foregoing analysis of the major biblical encounters is an attempt to demonstrate the usefulness of perceiving multiplicity of meaning as an effective literary device consciously resorted to by the biblical narrator. An approach based on this assumption enables one to better appreciate what is being said, why it is being said, how the dialogue serves the action, and how the intended effects are achieved, both upon the characters within the narrative and upon the reader.

---

[24] Nahmanides on Num. 24:1.

Chapter Eight

Torat Hashem / Torat Moshe: Exploring their Respective Roles

I

An analysis of the respective roles of God and Moshe in the composition of the Torah serves to clarify the sense in which the Torah can simultaneously and justifiably be called *Torat Hashem* and *Torat Moshe*. Maimonides asserts that the Torah came to Moshe through a process of prophetic communication called "speaking." Moshe, acting as a "scribe taking dictation," writes it all down as commanded by God. Was this a continuous process, or was there an interval between God's speaking to Moshe and the writing process? This chapter attempts to bring Maimonides' formulation into dialogue with the biblical text. It will be argued that what imparts canonical status as word of God to all of the contents of the *Chumash*, also known as the Five Books of Moses or Pentateuch, regardless of origin, is their having been written by Moshe while in a state of prophetic inspiration.

Discussions in Judaism as to the relative importance of theory to practice, doctrine to deeds, and study to action are ancient.[1] However, that all are necessary components of Judaism was never doubted, at least not in our biblical and rabbinic sources. In the Bible, doctrine is mainly assumed rather than explicitly stated. Nevertheless, doubts about the *practices* of Judaism, first about particular practices and later about ritual in general, were soon heard from sectarians such as the Sadducees, the followers of Pauline Christianity, and the Karaites.[2] But it was in the age of rationalism that *doctrine* first came under critical

---

[1] *Avot* 3:12, 23; *Megila* 26a.
[2] It would seem that as early as among Alexandrian Jewry in the days of Philo (c. 40 CE) there were some who believed that once they had attained philosophic understanding of the inner meanings of the laws, such as Sabbath, the festivals, and circumcision, they no longer needed to observe these laws in practice. (See H. A. Wolfson, *Philo*, vol. 1 [Cambridge, MA: Harvard University Press, 1947], 67, 78.)

scrutiny, leading ultimately to Mendelssohn's supposed assertion that "Judaism has no dogmas."[3] However, I imagine all would agree that, regardless of the roles we might assign to these components, doctrine certainly *affects* practice in important ways and vice versa.

Here is one difference that doctrine could make:

> Political economy, hygiene, statistics are very fine things. But no sane man would for them make those sacrifices which Judaism requires from us. It is only for God's sake, to fulfill His commands and to accomplish His purpose, that religion becomes worth living and dying for. And this can only be possible with a religion which possesses dogmas.[4]

Indeed, one of the most crucial and consequential doctrines underlying the Jewish religion is the one that speaks to the nature of the source of authority of the Jewish scripture, principally the Five Books of Moses. For it is in these Books that one finds Judaism's legislative core, prescriptions, and moral teachings that guide behavior. But, as these mainly take the form of commandments, the important questions are who is doing the commanding, and why should we obey?

Anyone who has attended synagogue services run according to the Ashkenazi tradition has probably, at a particular point, found himself proclaiming what appears to be some sort of Torah doctrine: when the Torah reading has been completed, the scroll is held aloft (*hagbaha*) and turned so that the writing is visible to the congregation.[5] The members of the congregation rise and, pointing to the scroll, chant in unison:

וזאת התורה אשר שם משה לפני בני ישראל, על פי ד' ביד משה.
And this is the Torah that Moshe set before the Children of Israel, by the mouth of God by the hand of Moshe.[6]

---

[3] Solomon Schechter, "The Dogmas of Judaism," *Studies in Judaism* (First Series) (Philadelphia: Jewish Publication Society, 1945).

[4] Ibid., 181.

[5] In the Ashkenazi tradition the lifting of the scroll (*hagbaha*) is done *after* the reading and the composite verses are recited. In the Sephardi tradition it is done *before* the reading, and only the verse from Deuteronomy is recited. (See I. Jacobson, *Netiv Bina*, Vol. II [Tel Aviv: Sinai Publishing, 1968], 221-223 [Hebrew].)

[6] Deut. 4:44; Num. 9:23.

Chapter Eight. Torat Hashem/Torat Moshe:Exploring their Respective Roles

This statement is composed of parts of two different biblical verses which in combination are held to express the traditional belief as to the origins of the Torah. However, the language is vague enough that it does not immediately challenge the congregant's theological beliefs, whatever they may be.[7] The first part of the declaration expresses belief that the text of the Torah (the phonemes, not the script) is the same as what was given by Moshe to Israel (Deut. 31:8). It would appear that for most of Jewish history this, the reliability of the transmission, was the element that was most vulnerable. Even accepting the fact that God revealed a Torah to Moshe as described, how do we know that this is it? After all, involved is a time interval of well over 3,000 years under the most trying circumstances, during which the original work was supposed to have been preserved intact.[8] It is precisely the centrality, albeit also the fragility, of this belief that prompted Maimonides to include it in the eighth of his Thirteen Principles of Judaism.[9]

However, the modern temper has caused a shift in focus. Whereas, in the past, we were happy to leave the last five words of the *hagbaha* declaration nice and vague, today we are pressured to spell out precisely what we mean. What was the role of God in the formation of the Torah, how was it manifested, and what was the role of Moshe? Philosophical positivism has questioned the meaningfulness of "God-talk" in general, as well as the precise sense in which a particular text can be called "the word of God,"[10] while, from the very beginning of historical criticism, doubts have been raised concerning the Mosaic authorship of the Pentateuch, leading to the formulation of the Documentary Hypothesis.[11]

---

[7] Taken literally, *al pi* could mean "spoken by God" and *b'yad Moshe* "written by Moshe." Alternatively, the two phrases can be translated as "by the order of God," and "transmitted by Moshe."

[8] See D.H. Halivni, *Revelation Restored* (Boulder, CO: Westview Press, 1997).

[9] See Menachem Kellner, *Dogma in Medieval Jewish Thought* (Oxford: Oxford University Press, 1986).

[10] See *Talk of God*, Royal Institute of Philosophy Lectures, Vol. 2 (London: Macmillan, 1969) and Ronald E. Santoni, ed., *Religious Language and the Problem of Religious Knowledge* (Bloomington, IN: Indiana University Press, 1968).

[11] For a brief sketch of the "doubts" concerning Mosaic authorship of the Pentateuch, see Jakob V. Petuchowski, *Ever Since Sinai* (New York: Scribe Publications, 1961), 1-25. The primary alternative to the theory of Mosaic authorship

In this paper I shall explore both the theological question regarding the nature of the divine input to the Torah and the historical-literary problem of Mosaic authorship within the context of the traditional approach, which is thus described by Maimonides:

> It is our belief that the whole of the Torah found in our hands today is the Torah that was given to Moshe and that it is all of Divine origin. That is to say, the whole of the Torah came to him from God in a manner which is metaphorically called "speaking." But the real nature of that communication is unknown to all except Moshe to whom it came. In receiving the Torah, Moshe was like a scribe writing from dictation the whole of it, its chronicles, its narratives and its prescriptions.[12]

Finding sources in the Torah itself, Maimonides states that the prophetic communication experienced by Moshe differed from the prophecy of the other prophets in ways which made his revelation unique and of the highest authority.[13]

From the above it might be thought that the prophetic process by which God "speaks" to Moshe, and Moshe writes as "a scribe receiving dictation," was always a single uninterrupted action: Moshe writes as God speaks to him, and what is written constitutes our Torah. However, as we read different portions of the text, it does not appear to have happened that way. Consider, for example, an early and prime example of the singular nature of Moshe's prophetic experience, the extended dialogue between God and Moshe at the vision of the burning bush.

---

was known as the Documentary Hypothesis. For a critical treatment, see U. Cassuto, *The Documentary Hypothesis and the Composition of the Pentateuch* (Jerusalem: Magnes Press, 1959) (Hebrew). See also Mordechai Breuer, "The Study of Bible and the Primacy of the Fear of Heaven," and Shnayer Z. Leiman, "Response to Rabbi Breuer," in *Modern Scholarship in the Study of Torah*, ed. Shalom Carmy (Northdale, NJ: Jason Aronson Inc., 1996), 159-189.

[12] Commentary on the Mishnah, *Perek Helek, Sanhedrin.*

[13] This is Maimonides' Seventh Principle. Moshe's level of prophecy was unique in four ways: (1) Moshe's prophecy reached him directly, without intermediaries; (2) Moshe's prophecy reached him while he was awake and conscious, not in a dream or vision; (3) while experiencing prophecy, Moshe did not tremble or suffer physical agitation; and (4) Moshe could initiate prophetic communication at any time of his choosing.

Chapter Eight. Torat Hashem/Torat Moshe: Exploring their Respective Roles

There is not even a hint of anything being written at the time. We must therefore assume that the process described as Moshe "writing like a scribe receiving dictation" was a separate and later event.

There is another consideration which leads us to distinguish between the "writing" of the Torah by Moshe as a "scribe receiving dictation" and the events which are being described in the writing. The analogy of a "scribe receiving dictation" implies a mechanical process in which the function of the scribe is to accurately record the specific words, but not necessarily to fully comprehend the sense of the material. This is contrary to the role of Moshe which emerges from even a cursory reading of the text. When we read that God "speaks" to Moshe (*peh el peh*), telling him to speak to the Israelites concerning the different laws (*torot, chukim, mishpatim*), it is clear that Moshe's task is to *teach* these rules and injunctions with the emphasis on meaning and understanding. This implies that the initial communication of prescriptive material from God to Moshe is primarily a cognitive experience. Here Moshe is not a writer or recorder, but a man whose intellect is being filled with the concepts of Divine Law which he struggles to comprehend.[14] Again, the special writing process in which Moshe functions as a scribe is separate, and seems to come at the end of Moshe's career.

I wish to suggest that an awareness of the temporal gap between the final writing of the Torah and the occurrence of the events described in that writing is crucial for an understanding and appreciation of the distinctive literary structure and variety of styles that the Torah exhibits.

The first question raised by this awareness is in relation to the legislation, the many *mitzvot* that God communicates to Moshe during his ministry. How were these preserved until the time of the final writing of the Torah?[15] Considering the importance of the material, it is rea-

---

[14] This is the source of the concepts of *halakhah l'Moshe mi-Sinai* and of *Torah she-b'al peh*. The revelation that Moshe received, it is believed, was much richer, and imparted far more content than was actually written down by Moshe. This further material became the core of the material handed down orally, and was the basis for *Torah she-b'al peh*.

[15] The Talmud (Gittin 60a) records two different views as to how the Torah was "given." One view claims that: (1) *Torah megilla megilla nitnah* "The Torah was given a *megilla* (scroll) at a time." The other view asserts: (2) *Torah Chatumah nitnah* "The Torah was given as a single entity." Rashi explains the two views as follows: according to (1), as each *parsha* (biblical section) was spoken to Moshe,

sonable to assume that each "code," after it was received, was written down in separate scrolls (*megillot*). Thus, the final prophetic writing of the Torah (in which Moshe is like a scribe taking dictation), which takes place toward the end of Moshe's life on the plains of Moab, should not be seen as a revelation of entirely new material but rather as a gathering together, a selection and often a reformulation of already existing material whose sources range from *megillot* containing primary prophetic revelations of *mitzvot* from God to Moshe to tribal archives of various censuses taken during the travels in the wilderness.

In the study that follows I shall attempt to show the significance of the above in helping to alleviate certain difficulties which often beset the conscientious student of the Torah.

I wish, however, to adopt a somewhat unconventional approach. Let us accept, as a working hypothesis, the view that in the Pentateuch we have before us a unitary work, purporting to be a veridical description of certain realities. In addition, let us as far as possible put aside conventional presuppositions and permit this composition to present itself in its own terms. At the same time, we will bear in mind that the more-than-3,000-year divide that separates us from the alleged time of the Pentateuch's writing has affected literary conventions and the use of language, including the meanings of basic terms.

---

it was written down as a separate *megilla*. At the end of 40 years, after all the *parshiot* had been received, Moshe sewed the *megillot* together, and that was the Torah. According to the second view, the Torah was not written until all the *parshiot* had been received at the very end of the 40 years. Those *parshiot* received by Moshe during the first and second years were preserved in his memory until they were written. Both views, as thus interpreted, are difficult. It does make sense to say that Moshe wrote each revelation of *mitzvot* down as a separate *megilla*. But what about the historical portions, the narrative of which the revelation is a part? There is no hint at all in the Torah, for example, of Moshe writing down the events of the Exodus or any part thereof. As for the second view, it is hard to believe that Moshe would have relied simply on memory to preserve the content of the early revelations.

Naturally, there is a sense in which both views can be true! *God gave the Torah to Moshe*, piecemeal, and this was the way he wrote it down. But this writing did not yet make it the Torah! Only at the end of 40 years did Moshe, under prophetic inspiration as we shall explain, write the entire Torah as a unitary *sefer* and give it to Israel. The word "*sefer*" in this context means a "written entity," a "document," a "letter," a "scroll."

Chapter Eight. Torat Hashem/Torat Moshe: Exploring their Respective Roles

What does the Torah wish the reader to believe about its authorship? What can we glean from the text itself as to how it is to be regarded? Let us begin by examining the opening sentences of this work, which I have always found puzzling: "In the beginning, God created the heavens and the earth. And the earth was unformed and void...." What is remarkable is the absence of any superscriptive introductions, such as appear elsewhere in the Bible:[16]

> These are the words which Moshe spoke to all Israel beyond the Jordan (Deut. 1: 1).
>
> And the Lord spoke to Moshe in the wilderness of Sinai ... saying ... (Num. 1:1).
>
> And the Lord called unto Moshe and spoke to him out of the tent of meeting ... saying ... (Lev. 1:1).

And in the works of the later prophets:

> The vision of Isaiah, son of Amoz ... (Isa. 1:1).
>
> The words of Jeremiah, son of Hilkiah ... (Jer. 1: 1).
>
> The words of the Lord that came to Hosea, the son of Beeri... (Hos. 1:1).

In the case of the Book of Genesis, in contrast, the reader is immediately plunged into the narrative without any idea of who is speaking. Who is writing this? Why was the text arranged this way? What was the intention? I will deal with this question later on. But as of now, it seems to me that it says: Dear Reader, first read the work with an open mind and later consider questions of origin!

I

Let us examine some sample types of Torah material and consider what they may disclose as to their source and provenance.

1) There are several collections of laws variously called *mitzvot, chukim,* and *mishpatim* in the books of Exodus, Leviticus, and Numbers pertaining to civil, moral, and ritual matters which are introduced by

---

[16] The Ramban asks this question in his introduction to the Book of Genesis.

variations on the words: "And the Lord *spoke* to Moshe saying: "*Speak* to the children of Israel and *say* to them...."[17] These sections, which constitute the legislative and prescriptive core of the Torah, clearly describe the material as having been spoken by God to Moshe, and are to be transmitted verbally by him to the others. These revelations came to Moshe at different times and at different locations. [18]

When these revelations come in regard to specific situations, as for example the Passover preparations (Exod. 12:1-20), the text follows up by relating how Moshe did indeed convey the message to the people (12:21-28) and, sometimes, how the people reacted (12:29). When the revelation involves a particular stated subject, such as the *moadim* ("appointed seasons") (Lev. 23:1), we are subsequently told, "And Moshe declared the appointed seasons of the Lord to the Children of Israel" (Lev. 23:44).

The first extensive code, called *mishpatim* (judgments), is given while at Sinai. This code covers three chapters (21-23), and is a continuation of the material which begins, "And the Lord said to Moshe, 'So shall you say to the Children of Israel'" (Exod. 20:19). However, it ends abruptly and we are not told immediately if and when Moshe conveyed this to the people (Exod. 23:33). There is, however, a sort of summary statement much later that would seem to cover these commandments as well:

> And Moshe called them and Aaron and all the leaders [*nesiim*] of the congregation returned to him and Moshe spoke to them. And afterwards all the Children of Israel drew close and he commanded them regarding all that the Lord has spoken to him at Mount Sinai. (Exod. 34:31, 32)

The rabbis deduced from this an entire system of oral transmission by which Moshe taught the revealed material to the people.[19] Indeed,

---

[17] Exod. 21-23:19; Lev. 19, 20; Num. 15, 28, 29. Sometimes the Word of God is said to come to Moshe and Aaron, as in Num. 2:1 and 4:1, and sometimes to Aaron, as in Num. 18:8.

[18] In Egypt (as, for example, Exod. 12:13), at Sinai (Exod. 20; Lev. 25); in the Tent of Meeting (Lev. 16; Num. 9:1-14), on the plains of Moab (Num. 5-6:21, 33:50-56, 35, 36; Deut. 2:17, 2:31, 31: 14, 32:48) over a period of some 40 years.

[19] See Rashi on Exod. 34:3 1, 32. "Our Rabbis taught: What was the order of study? Moshe would learn from the mouth of God, Aaron then entered and Moshe taught him his *perek*. Aaron rose and sat to the left of Moshe. Aaron's

it is noted that the unusual expression "And these are the judgments (*mishpatim*) you shall *set before them*" (Exod. 21:1) implies that Moshe was mandated to employ more sophisticated teaching methods than mere oral repetition.[20]

It is, however, important to note that all the codes in these books are embedded in a third-person, narrative framework, as are all of the other types of material contained in the Torah. This imparts a sense of unity to the entire *Chumash*, the unity of a single continuous story related by the same narrator who, in some sense, stands above the events being described. At this stage, one might of course assume that Moshe himself is the narrator. But, if so, why adopt a third-person voice? Also, how do we account for the fact that this continuous story includes events that happened in pre-history (Gen. 1-3), or after the death of Moshe? (Deut. 34:5-12).[21] As we have already indicated, however, in regard to these extensive codes, it seems reasonable to suppose that either God commanded Moshe to commit each code to writing as he received it, or Moshe did this on his own rather than leave it to memory.[22] In any event, we have here an indication of the existence of already revealed material in written form long before the final prophetic composition of the complete Torah was undertaken.

2) The Book of Deuteronomy, unlike the others, is presented as a series of first-person addresses delivered by Moshe to the Israelites on the plains of Moab shortly before he died. Much of the material is a review of the laws and events contained in the earlier books, with an awareness that this generation is about to enter the Promised Land. However, some

---

sons entered and Moshe taught it to them. They rose and Elazar sat to the right of Moshe and Itamar to the left of Aaron. The Elders entered and Moshe taught it to them. The Elders arose and sat to their sides. Then all the people entered and Moshe taught it to them. Thus, all the people heard it once, the Elders twice, the sons of Aaron three times, and Aaron, four times" (*Erubin* 54(.

[20] See Rashi on Exod. 21:1.

[21] For a full survey of the views of the talmudic rabbis on the question of the writing of the Torah, see Abraham Joshua Heschel, *Torah Min ha-Shamayim b-Aspeklaria, Sefer Sheni* (London and New York: Soncino Press, 1965), 344-357.

[22] According to Rambam, Exod. 24 occurred after *matan torah*. Therefore, verse 24:4: "and Moshe wrote all the words of the Lord...," refers to the laws given in chapters 21-23. This then would have been one of the earlier *megillot* in existence, prior to the prophetic writing of the entire Torah.

commandments and nuances appear here for the first time.[23] Although the words are attributed to Moshe, it is again the narrator who frames the citations: "These are the words which Moshe spoke to all Israel..." (Deut. 1: 1-4). There is also a third-person account of Moshe's last moments, of his death, and an appreciation of his role as leader (Deut. 34). What is clear is that the narrator is dealing here with words already spoken by Moshe, which he is incorporating into this fifth book of the Torah. Deuteronomy, however, presents an additional problem: how are we to view the canonical authority of the laws contained in this book as compared to the prescriptions in the other books which are presented as the word of God? After all, these are the words of Moshe, spoken on his own initiative.

3) Another section in the Torah which raises questions as to its provenance is the story of Balak and Balaam (Num. 22-24), discussed earlier in another context in this volume. This section is a self-contained literary gem. It portrays the apprehension aroused by the approaching Israelites among the neighboring kingdoms, holds up to ridicule the pagan beliefs in divination and soothsaying, and preserves some of the most beautiful prophetic utterances of the Bible. However, how did this entire narrative, which takes place strictly within the lives of Balak and Balaam. and in which Moshe does not figure, come to be included in the Torah? How did this material, with its long quotations of what Balaam recited, become available? And if it is answered that this story was received verbatim by Moshe in a prophetic revelation, then it should have been so noted. The fact that this section (Num. 22-24) appears without a break immediately after the narration of certain other events (20-21) directly experienced by Israel in its journeyings seems to suggest that the provenance and prophetic authority of this section is the same as those of the material that preceded it, i.e., related by the narrator. We shall return to this point later.

It thus appears that while the actual commandments are said to come directly from God to Moshe, there is considerable material containing

---

[23] Some commandments which appear in Deuteronomy for the first time are the laws of one who brings up an evil name (Deut. 22:14); the law of Bill of Divorcement (*Gerushin*) (Deut. 24:1); and the law of Levirate Marriage (Deut. 25:5). See commentary on Pentateuch of Naphtali Tzvi Yehuda Berlin, *Ha'amek Davar*, introduction to the Book of Deuteronomy.

Chapter Eight. Torat Hashem / Torat Moshe: Exploring their Respective Roles

descriptions of events and conversations that are not presented as divine revelations. Thus, before the Ten Commandments are pronounced, we read: "And the Lord came down upon Mt. Sinai at the top of the mount and the Lord called Moshe to the top of the mount and Moshe went up" (Exod. 19:20). Who wrote this? Who composed the entire story of the Israelites' sojourn in Egypt, from the coming of Jacob through the birth of Moshe, up to the Exodus and including the laws given by God to Moshe while he was still in Egypt?

But most intriguing of all is the question of who composed the Book of Genesis which, as we have noted, has no superscription and which contains material vital to the theological and moral-historical outlook of Judaism: the story of the Creation, the early history of man, and the stories of the Patriarchs. We will come back to these questions.

4) Most of the last fifteen chapters of the Book of Exodus (chapters 25-40) are taken up with the construction of the Tabernacle (*mishkan*). Here we have a most detailed and seemingly repetitious account of: (a) the instructions and specifications concerning its materials, furniture and vessels, priestly vestments, and induction ceremony, as received from God by Moshe and as "shown" to Moshe (Exod. 25-31:12); (b) the instructions and specifications as relayed by Moshe to the Israelites and how they responded (Exod. 35:4-38:20); and (c) a final accounting of the materials contributed and objects constructed, and how they were placed in the completed Tabernacle (Exod. 38:21-40). All aspects of the *mishkan* are presented as part of a third-person narrative.

The unusual amount of detail and repetition contained in these chapters requires explanation. Undoubtedly, the *mishkan* or *mikdash* (sanctuary) was considered extremely significant. Some say it was an attempt to reproduce the exalted experience of Sinai by institutionalizing the indwelling Presence of God (*shechina*) in what was called the "tent of meeting" (*ohel moed*). Others argue that it was an *ad hoc* measure adopted only after the sin of the "golden calf" revealed the need of the people for physical symbols of the invisible God. Regardless, this method of treatment has all the signs of being a contemporary account maintained by a leadership concerned to record all phases of a project undertaken in order to unify a shocked and disillusioned people. The construction of the *mishkan* required the combined, organized efforts of the entire group. All were urged to participate by contributing material possessions, artistic talents, time, and effort to create a portable sanctuary for the indwelling

Presence of God (*shechina*) embodied in the *aron habrit*, which would lead the Israelites in their journeying and from which Moshe would continue to hear the voice of God. Throughout the account we hear a tone of pride and satisfaction that this people, so recently disgraced by a grievous sin, were able to respond generously and enthusiastically: "And Moshe saw all the work and behold they had done it as the Lord had commanded.... And Moshe blessed them" (Exod. 39:43).

If our surmise is correct, we have here another instance suggesting that there probably existed written records of the entire project of the building of the *mishkan* from the original divine command through the final accounting, and a description of its being put into actual operation. The account fittingly ends with the confirming appearance of the glory of God (Exod. 40:34-38).

Our brief examination of representative types of Torah material reveals the following: an all-pervasive narrative framework employing a third-person voice unifies the diverse types of literary material that comprise the five Books of Moses, including legal codes, epic poetry, historical events, dramatic narratives. Many of these existed as oral traditions or written documents prior to the construction of the overall narrative framework.

The overall narrative framework is the result of the later prophetic writing process, which produced the Torah in our possession today.

II

Let us consider the matter of the *writing* of the Torah. The Torah in our possession is a *written* document. Yet the text is quite clear that, except for the Ten Commandments, which after having been publicly proclaimed were received inscribed on stone tablets, the word of God comes to Moshe as something which he *hears* and which he, in turn, is commanded to "speak" or "say" to the people. Are there any clues in the Torah itself as to how, when, and by whom the Torah material came to be *written*?

First, the text seems to assume a basic literacy on the part of at least some elements of the population.[24] A popular commandment directed

---

[24] From the third millennium BCE on, there existed in the Middle East two complex writing systems. From Mesopotamia we have the wedge-shaped linear

at all house-dwellers requires writing: "And you shall write them upon the doorposts of your house and upon your gates" (Deut. 6:9). On another occasion, Moshe is told: "And now write down this song and teach it to the children of Israel" (Deut. 31:19). Then there are certain events in connection with which Moshe is commanded to write: "And the Lord said to Moshe '*write* this down for a memorial in a book and rehearse it in the ears of Joshua'..." (Exod. 17:14). In regard to the stations where Israel camped during their journeyings in the wilderness, we are told: "... and Moshe *wrote* their goings forth, stage by stage, by the command of the Lord and these are their stages by their goings forth..." (Num. 33:2).[25]

The prevalence of writing suggests that over the course of years there surely must have been all sorts of items which, for purely practical and administrative reasons, were committed to writing even when their writing had not been directly commanded by God. These would have included the population figures of the tribes after each census, the amount and kind of material donated for the Tabernacle, the tribal formations for journeying, and the geographical boundaries of *Eretz Yisrael*. When first written down, these records would not have had any

---

signs (over 1,500 different signs), impressed on wet clay, called cuneiform. From Egypt we have the pictographic-syllabic system called hieroglyphs, which also involved a huge number of different signs. The Israelites were certainly acquainted with both forms of writing. The Patriarchs, who came from Mesopotamia, undoubtedly knew cuneiform and their descendants, during their long stay in Egypt, would have picked up hieroglyphics. Moshe, having been brought up at court, was certainly acquainted with both. However, there is reason to believe that the script in which the Ten Commandments and the other writing done by Moshe and his scribes was written, was in the new alphabetic script which appeared in the world at just about that time. This was providential, as an alphabetic script (which is defined as a system with a limited number of signs [20-30] which have a fixed order) facilitates universal literacy is presupposed by the Torah. See Shubert Spero, "And the Writing was the Writing of God," *Jewish Bible Quarterly* 25: 1 (1997).

[25] The commentators are divided over whether the words "... by the command of the Lord..." "refer to the stations or to the "writing." If we accept the view of Ibn Ezra that the verse refers to the stations, then it means that the decision to write, to record the list of the wilderness journeyings and stations, was Moshe's own, which strengthens the view that Moshe on his own is doing a good deal of primary recording.

sacred character and would merely have formed part of the Israelites' tribal archives.

But when and how did the process of writing the Torah, *as Torah*, take place? Here are two "givens" that clearly emerge from the text which have to be taken into account by any theory:

1) The prescriptive parts of the Torah are given *by God to Moshe orally* in separate collections, at different times and at different places (see page 000, note 1, above).

2) The Torah is given *by Moshe to Israel in written form* as a *sefer*, a complete single entity.[26]

"And Moshe wrote this Torah and gave it to the priests, the sons of Levi that carried the Ark of the Covenant of the Lord, and to all the elders of Israel" (Deut. 31:9).

"And it came to pass when Moshe had made an end of writing the words of the Torah in a book [*sefer*] until they were completed" (Deut. 31:24).

Thus, our text attributes to Moshe the writing and completion of a work called "the Torah" in the form of a *sefer*. Some have argued that the term "Torah" here may be referring to the Book of Deuteronomy only. However, that book is explicitly presented as the freely-initiated addresses of Moshe who is reviewing the *chukim* and *mishpatim* which were given in the past (Deut. 4:13, 14). Surely, then, if we are told that Moshe, before his death, "writes *the* Torah" and completes it, it must refer to the original revelations rather than to Moshe's later recollections.[27]

The idea that Moshe wrote the Torah sounds plausible enough when you realize that from the second chapter of Exodus on, all that occurs takes place during his lifetime and involves Moshe in one way or another. Who else but Moshe would know what God said to him at the "burning bush," or the particulars of the conversations he had with Pharaoh, or about his dialogue with God when he went up to receive the second tablets of the Covenant? But if Moshe wrote the Torah, why did

---

[26] This is supported by the following verses, in which Moshe, warning the people of impending punishment, points to an existing *sefer hatorah hazeh*: Deut. 28:61, 29:20, 30:10. Also, in the law of the King, there is a reference to "this Torah" (Deut. 17:19).

[27] David Zvi Hoffman, *Decisive Evidence against Wellhausen* (Berlin, 1904), 44.

he write it in third person, and how could he write of his own demise and praise himself?[28]

These difficulties notwithstanding, the existing evidence still points toward Moshe as the writer of the Torah.

III

At this time we must return to the question of the role of God. What do we mean when we declare the entire Torah to be *al pi hashem*? True, all the commandments are said in the text to be given by God, and it is God who is the dominant figure in all that happens. But we know all this only because it is so related in the Torah, which brings us back to the question of the role of the writer-narrator.

The view I wish to support is that Moshe did indeed write the entire Pentateuch that is in our possession today. However, as Maimonides states, this very act of writing, undertaken by divine command, was a most singular phenomenon of prophetic inspiration,[29] in which the consciousness of Moshe is taken over by the Divine Will, which exerts control over both the content and the writing, down to the choice of words. While the will of Moshe is bypassed, he is by no means a mere channel or writing-machine. God, as it were, dips into the layers of Moshe's stored memory in order to reconstruct a prophetic account of the events in question.[30] Also, for example, in writing of the building of the *mishkan* (Tabernacle), Moshe may have been directed to selectively incorporate already existing administrative lists of the contributors as well as information from other written records and oral traditions. Regardless of the source, be they the words of Pharaoh or Balak, Jethro or Korach, or the Song of the Sea itself, all are melted down in the fires of prophecy, reformulated, and "downloaded" as our Torah text. It is this, *the writing of the Torah,* that constitutes the defining event in the transformation of the material selected from diverse sources into the "word of God" or *al pi hashem*, and which confers the authority of scripture upon the text. This

---

[28] See Rashi on Deut. 34:5.
[29] Isaac Abarbanel (introduction to his commentary on the Book of Deuteronomy) proposes this interpretation in regard to the Book of Deuteronomy. It is the command of God to Moshe to incorporate his own farewell address into a written *sefer* which enables this book to be included in the Pentateuch.
[30] See A. J. Heschel, *The Prophets* (New York: Harper & Row, 1962), 443, 446.

is perhaps the deeper meaning of the phrase *Torah sheʾbʾchtav* ("the written Torah"), by which we designate the Pentateuch, i.e., *this has become Torah only as a consequence of its having been written.*

What we have said may be understood in the light of the rabbinic dictum, "The Torah speaks in human language."[31] That is to say, no matter how original, profound, and eternal are the teachings of God, they can only be expressed in terms which respect contemporary intellectual horizons, so that they may be intelligible to those who receive them. That is why Divine Revelation may employ the language and concepts found in the consciousness of the prophet, or even adopt images found in the epics and myths of contemporary culture, to be reworked into articulating the divine message.[32]

Equipped with our new thesis, let us, by briefly reexamining each book, see if our understanding is enhanced and some old problems resolved.

Deuteronomy

We have now identified our narrator, who, writing in the third person, opens the book with the words: "These are the words which Moshe spoke..." (Deut. 1:1), and then later intersperses these addresses with segments of history, such as "Then Moshe separated three cities beyond the Jordan..." (Deut. 4:41), and finally closes with an account of the death and burial of Moshe (Deut. 34). Although the writer-narrator is Moshe himself, he is now functioning under prophetic inspiration and is not conscious of what he is writing.

We therefore have here a rather curious situation. The bulk of the book consists of words spoken by Moshe on various occasions, on his own initiative, expressing his own thoughts. These include his three farewell addresses,[33] the "blessings and curses" (*tochecha*) (Deut. 28), the epic

---

[31] Berachot 31b.

[32] What we say here should not be taken as an attempt to reduce religious mystery to the banality of ordinary discourse. Of course, how the Divine Mind coalesces with the human will forever remain beyond human comprehension. However, this does not exempt us from the obligation to attempt to locate the point of divine input. Not to do this is to invite perpetual confusion.

[33] According to D.T. Hoffman, the three main addresses are Deut. 1:16 to 4:40, Deut. 4:44 to 26:19, and Deut. 27:9 to 30:20.

Chapter Eight. Torat Hashem / Torat Moshe: Exploring their Respective Roles

ha'azinu poem (Deut. 32), and the "blessings" of the tribes (Deut. 33). It was not Moshe's choice to include these in the Torah but that of God, who thereby confirms their timeless significance.[34]

Our thesis explains the appearance in our text of certain apparently parenthetic explanatory expressions which, in all likelihood, were not part of the original spoken address but were added later by the writer to be helpful to later generations.[35]

The emphasis on the writing alleviates the problem of the canonical authority of the Book of Deuteronomy. We can now understand why, in the eyes of the rabbis, the content of this book was considered to be the "word of God" on a par with the other books, each word to be explicated in accordance with the interpretive rules of *midrash halakhah* and *midrash aggadah*. Since the decisive divine influence was manifested during the process of writing, the precise source of the material was irrelevant. The diverse sources of the material are neutralized by the prophetic selection and reformulation. Therefore, in respect to authority, all five books have a common property—all were written by Moshe under the influence of prophetic inspiration. The adoption of a third-person style of presentation should be seen as a literary device designed to signal that a power other than Moshe has taken over.[36]

---

[34] See the interpretation of the Netziv on Deut. 31:19 and Deut. 31:22, which points out that the *shirat ha'azinu* was unusual in that it was committed to writing at the express command of God and taught to the Israelites in that form (Deut. 31:19). It was later incorporated into the complete Torah (Deut. 31:24).

[35] For example: "And we took the land at that time out of the hand of the two kings of the Amorites that were beyond the Jordan, from the valley of the Arnon unto Mount Hermon, *which Hermon the Sidonians call Sirion and the Amorites call it Senir*, all the cities of the plain..." (Deut. 31:8-10). Certainly the italicized words would not have been part of a public address. This was an explanatory note to identify the mountain, which was known by different names (see Hoffman's commentary on Deuteronomy). See also Deut. 2:10-12.

[36] There is a statement which appears frequently in rabbinical discussions of Deuteronomy: "*Shekhinah medaberet mitoch g'rono shel Moshe*", "The Divine Presence speaks from the throat of Moshe." This is used in various ways to justify the acceptance of Deuteronomy as Holy Writ. This statement does not appear in the Talmud or Midrash; its source seems to be the Zohar. In line with our thesis, we would take it to mean that the spirit of prophecy selected the addresses of Moshe to be included in the written Torah because it recognized divine elements which informed the original addresses.

Numbers

Proceeding in reverse, let us consider the Book of Numbers. Here, too, the overall framework is a third-person narrative, this time of the *mitzvot* received by Moshe in the completed Tabernacle called the "tent of meeting" (*ohel moed*) and of the events that occurred during the journeys of the Israelites. Chronologically, the book is sharply divided into two periods. The first 20 chapters relate the history of the first two years after the Exodus, with particular reference to those subjects dealt with in the last part of the Book of Exodus.[37] The latter part of the book deals with events occurring in the fortieth year, to the generation about to enter the Promised Land.[38]

As with the Book of Deuteronomy, the prophetic writing process had to do here with an assortment of material that already existed in written and/or oral form:

- The many *chukim* and *mishpatim* received by Moshe during this period, which as we have discussed were preserved either by oral traditions or in separate scrolls (*megillot*).
- The memory of crucial events in which Moshe has been involved, such as the rebellion of Korach and the report of the *meraglim* (spies or scouts).
- Written lists of census figures, tribal leaders, and genealogies.

There are two unusual references in this book, one to an unknown *sefer milchamot ha-shem* (book of the wars of God) and the other to "a song from those who speak in parables" (*moshlim*) (Num. 21:27-30). The former was evidently an independently written chronicle of the wars engaged in by the Israelites during this period. The latter was a local folk-saying which the prophetic writing process drew upon to confirm information about earlier conquests of Heshbon, an important city in Transjordan. This is clear evidence of the availability to the narrator of

---

[37] Matters such as the Tabernacle, the census, the tribal marching order.
[38] This underscores the highly selective character of the Pentateuch as history. We are told nothing about what may have happened to the Israelites during a stretch of 38 years. From the list of stations, it would appear that the tribes were centered around the oasis of Kadesh Barnea during this period.

independent outside sources and of his readiness to draw upon them and even to cite them.

Earlier, we referred to the special problem posed by the story of Balak and Balaam (Num. 22-24). How did the Israelites learn of this story, given that it took place within the geographical and cultural orbit of another people? The rabbis, evidently aware of this problem, chose it for special mention. In speaking of the authorship of the different biblical books, they said, "Moshe wrote his book [Pentateuch] and the portion of Balaam."[39] Since the portion of Balaam is part of the "book of Moshe," what point were the rabbis trying to make? But perhaps, rather than solving the problem of Balaam, the rabbis were trying to elucidate how Moshe "wrote *his* book." That is to say, just as the "story of Balaam" existed independently but was reworked and incorporated into the Torah, so too there were other records and oral traditions which were reworked by the prophetic process in the writing of Moshe's book.[40]

Leviticus

The Book of Leviticus) poses no problem for our thesis, for it consists mainly of a series of verbatim commands from God to Moshe and Aaron on a number of subjects. There are, in addition, a few narrative portions told in the third person.[41] Thus, in the writing of this book, the prophetic process had mainly to work with the records, oral or written, of earlier revelations.

---

[39] Bava Batra 14b. The wording in the Jerusalem Talmud is even more curious:
משה כתב חמשה ספרי תורה וחזר וכתב פרשת בלק ובלעם (ירושלמי סוטה פרק ה' בסוף

[40] I would like to conjecture that as a result of the battles in the area (Num. 31) there came into Moshe's possession a written record from the royal archives of Moab describing the entire event, including the prophecies of Balaam. Again it was the prophetic writing process, "at the hand of Moshe," that transformed a Moabite archive into a part of the Torah. A few years ago there was a remarkable archaeological find in Jordan where an inscription dated to the seventh century BCE consisted of fragments of a hymn which clearly mentioned the name of "Baalam son of B'Or" (*Biblical Archaeological Review* [Sept./Oct. 1985], Vol. 11, No. 5).

[41] These are, for example, the ceremonies attending the dedication of the *mishkan*, the investiture of the *kohanim*, the death of the two sons of Aaron, the incident of the man who blasphemed.

The simplicity of the narrative frame of Leviticus can be appreciated by examining the opening and closing verses of the book:

> "And He called to Moshe and the Lord spoke to him out of the tent of meeting saying: 'Speak to the children of Israel and say to them.'" (Lev. 1: 1, 2)

> "These are the commandments which the Lord commanded Moshe for the children of Israel on Mount Sinai." (Lev. 27:34)

The rabbis called this book *torat kohanim*, the "law of the priests," thereby recognizing the specialized nature of the material, which gives a heightened sense of unity to the book, for all of its laws pertain to the *kohanim* in one way or another. Either they apply to the *kohanim* only[42] or, while they apply to all Israelites, they are laws that are administered by the *kohanim*,[43] or reflect values that are to be exemplified by the *kohanim*.[44] This special focus is supported by the fact that God is often described in this book as speaking to Moshe and Aaron (the High Priest) together (Lev. 11:1, 13:1, 14:34), and even to Aaron alone[45] (Lev. 10:8).

---

[42] For example, all of the laws pertaining to the various sacrifices (*korbonot*) which were performed by the *kohanim* (chapters 1 to 7), as well as other rules that applied only to *kohanim* (Lev. 9:8-11; Lev. 21).

[43] For example, the laws of ritual impurity (*tzoraat*) that may infect clothing, the walls of a house, or one's skin had to be diagnosed and treated by the *kohanim* (Lev. 12-15).

[44] This refers to the entire concept of *kedusha* (holiness or sanctity) which, while a special obligation of the *kohanim* (Lev. 21:6), was also demanded from all Israelites (Lev. 19:2), who were called upon to become a "kingdom of *kohanim* and a *holy* nation" (Exod. 19:6). The Holiness Code, which applied to *kohanim* and Israelites alike, included dietary laws (Lev. 11), sexual mores (Lev. 17, 18), and the rules of festivals and holidays (Lev. 25), as well as the entire range of the moral commandments (Lev. 19).

[45] Some of the rabbis interpreted the phrase "And God spoke to Moshe and Aaron" as meaning "Moshe, for the sake of Aaron," probably because to interpret it as it stands might put into question the principle of the uniqueness of Moshe's level of prophecy. However, if the text states that God spoke to Aaron (alone), one can simply say that the level of prophecy was commensurate with the recipient. In light of our thesis that the prophetic writing process was what gave canonical authority to the Torah, the precise prophetic level of the revelational sources from which the written Torah was composed is irrelevant.

Indeed, as *torat kohanim,* there is more reason to believe that as soon as these revelations were received they were written down, perhaps by Aaron himself.[46] As a group known for their conscientiousness,[47] *kohanim* could be expected to have appreciated the importance of a written text in educating their cadres.

Exodus

The Book of Genesis had brought the stories of the Patriarchs to a close, with the offspring of Jacob (Israel) comfortably settled in the lush delta region of Egypt. The Book of Exodus is a seamless continuation of the narrative, picking up the story at that point. Its essential purpose is to describe how this clan grew into a "people" (*am*) (Exod. 1:9), and all that happens to enable them to become the "people of God" (Exod. 6:7). Like the book before it, Exodus is a straightforward third-person narrative, beginning "And these are the names of the sons of Israel who came into Egypt with Jacob..." (Exod. 1:1), and continuing in this manner for the remainder of the book. Within this framework, the narrative becomes increasingly punctuated with complete texts of various sorts: the laws pertaining to Pesach (Exod. 12, 13), the Song of the Sea (Exod. 15), the Ten Commandments and various laws and statutes (Exod. 21), and others. However, all of these are integrated into the account of the events which are being described, and flow smoothly as part of the narrative.

In the book are two remarkable dialogues between God and Moshe which have long been regarded as being of great religious and literary significance. The first centers around the vision of the burning bush (Exod. 3, 4—a total of 39 verses), in which God invites Moshe to accept

---

[46] There is a verse in Psalms that equates Moshe, Aaron, and Samuel, among other ways, in their all having received from God a "statute" (*chok*): "Moshe and Aaron among His priests and Samuel that call upon His name ... and He answered them. In a pillar of cloud did He speak to them; they kept His testimonies and *a statute did He give them*" (Psalms 99:6, 7).

We know, of course, that Moshe received and wrote the Torah. Concerning Samuel, we are told, "Then Samuel told the people the manner of the monarchy (*mishpat hamalkah*) and wrote it in a book" (I Sam. 10:25). We might then surmise that Aaron, too, upon receiving his *torat kohanim,* wrote it down.

[47] *Shabbat* 20.

the task of speaking to Pharaoh to ask that he release the Israelites from servitude. In the course of five rounds of conversation, in which Moshe demurs and God presses, we learn much about Moshe's personality and about the purposes and methods of God. In this gem of religious literature, every rejoinder and counterproposal is revealing; every phrase is nuanced and balanced. The second text relates to the aftermath of the worship of the golden calf (Exod. 33:12-23, 34:1-11), when Moshe beseeches God to forgive the people, and reascends the mountain to receive a replacement for the broken tablets of the Covenant. Here the dialogue is interspersed with snatches of third-person narrative (Exod. 34:5, 6). The sequence is not always clear and some of the verses are obscure. The underlying tension is palpable. In this close encounter with Divinity, Moshe is pleading for the life of his people and, at the same time, seeking a deeper understanding of the God before Whom he stands. This text, like the first, has been a mine of information and inspiration for students of the Bible over the years, revealing much about the moral nature of God.[48]

I draw your attention to these texts in order to make the following point: the only *human* source of information as to what happened, what was said and in what sequence, would be Moshe himself. And yet, under these unusual circumstances, can it be expected that Moshe would have remembered so much, and would have been able to articulate it in this manner? But it is precisely this kind of situation that is best explained by the theory we have proposed. When Moshe is writing the Torah, the prophetic process takes over his consciousness and, in order to give us a sense of the encounter as experienced by Moshe, makes selective use of his memory. What posterity receives in the end is an account of two unique encounters between the man Moshe and the God of Abraham, Isaac, and Jacob, written by the hand of the man who experienced it all—but controlled by the Divinity on the other side of the encounter and told in words which reveal only that which He wishes to reveal.

---

[48] Included in this revelation are the "thirteen attributes of mercy" which constitute the heart of the *selichot* service. Compare this text to Moshe's entreaty after the sin of the *meraglim* (Num. 14:11-20).

Genesis

The question of who wrote the Book of Genesis is, of course, the most intriguing and the most challenging to our theory, for here, Moshe is not the obvious choice. The events described here are not within Moshe's experience, nor is there anything in the text that pertains to Moshe. Moreover, nowhere in the text is there anything that hints at how or by whom the book was written.

Let us note that the material in Genesis is of two kinds. The later portion (Gen. 12-50) appears to be historical and deals with the stories of the men and women who were the ancestors of the Israelites.[49] Since, as we have shown, the Book of Exodus is a continuation of Genesis, the relevance of this material to the overall purpose of the Torah is clear. Was this information known before it appeared as part of the Torah? It is well known that tribal societies tend to preserve knowledge of their past in the form of epic poems, songs, and stories that are passed down through the generations. The rabbis report that the Israelites in Egypt had in their possession various scrolls (*megillot*) pertaining to their past which they read and related to their children.[50] Indeed, it may be assumed that during the time Yocheved helped raise her son Moshe in the Egyptian court, she may have revealed to him his identity as a Hebrew and told him the stories of the Patriarchs.

The first eleven chapters of Genesis deal with "pre-history" going back to the Creation, the early history of man, the development of civilization, and the dispersion of the nations. The decision to include this in the Torah is indicative of the universal breadth of the conception of Israel's vocation. Hanging on the success of Israel's implementation of the Covenant is the fate of all mankind, indeed of Creation itself! But where did this information come from? The stories of the Creation, the Garden of Eden, Noah and the Flood, the Tower of Babel, the Table

---

[49] While there is no archaeological evidence of the actual existence of Abraham, Isaac, and Jacob, the language, customs, place-names, and general conditions found in the Bible stories of the Patriarchs fit in well with what archaeology has discovered about those times and places. "The Bible's narrative accurately reflects the times to which it refers" (John Bright, *A History of Israel* [Philadelphia: Westminster Press, 1981], 93).

[50] See *Shemot Rabbah* 5:18; U. Cassuto, *The Documentary Hypothesis* (Jerusalem: Magnes Press, 1959), 83 (Hebrew).

of the Nations?—these were undoubtedly all part of the culture of the time, but not in the form in which they appear in the Torah. I would think that Moshe was probably aware of the various myths and legends prevalent in his time concerning the origin of the world, the origin of evil, the history of man and culture. Moshe had learned these things growing up as a prince in the court of Pharaoh and in the course of his travels in Pharaoh's foreign service, as well as from the traditions of the Hebrews who had preserved elements of culture from Mesopotamia, the original home of the Patriarchs.[51]

Thus, once it was decided to include in the Torah an account of the "beginnings," the writing method of the prophetic process was the same as with the other books. The raw material is the conventional wisdom as reflected in the stored memory of Moshe and in oral and written traditions. Here, too, the Divine Will directing Moshe's writing hand works with these raw materials to select, add, and delete, modify and amend, in words which best express the divine teachings relative to the conceptual level of the times.

Are there any hints in the Torah as to when and why the Book of Genesis might have been composed? After the account of the epiphany at Sinai (Exod. 20), and after the chapters dealing with the judgments (*mishpatim*) which Moshe set before the people (chapters 21, 22, 23), we read the following:

> And Moshe came and told the people all the words of the Lord and all the ordinances and all the people answered with one voice and said: 'All the words which the Lord has spoken we will do.' And Moshe wrote all the words of the Lord...." (Exod. 24:3, 4)

> And he took the *book of the covenant* and read in the hearing of the people and they said: 'All that the Lord has spoken, we will do and obey.' (Exod. 24:7)

---

[51] The Midrash preserves a tradition that Moshe traveled extensively in the land of Cush (*Yalkut Shimoni*, Exod. 168). This is entirely credible, as we must account for the long span of years from the time Moshe flees Egypt, as a young man, until he appears before Pharaoh at the age of 80 (Exod. 7:7). The travels of Sinuhe, a gem of Egyptian literature of the Twelfth Dynasty, long before Moshe's time, testifies to the fascinating possibilities of travel by a single Egyptian dignitary in the region.

Chapter Eight. Torat Hashem/Torat Moshe: Exploring their Respective Roles

What "words of the Lord" did Moshe here report to the people? And what was this "book of the covenant"? The response of the people is identical to their response before the giving of the Torah as described earlier: "And all the people answered together and said, 'All that the Lord has spoken we will do'" (Exod. 19:8).

Therefore, in spite of its irregular location, the general opinion is that this text (Exod. 24:7) is a "flashback" to the events prior to the public promulgation of the Ten Commandments. As such, we are here being given new information as to what happened during the fateful hours in which Israel was being readied to enter into a covenant with the Creator-God. Since in verse 4 we are told that Moshe "wrote the words of the Lord," and verse 7 speaks of a "book of the covenant," it is fair to assume that the "book" is the product of Moshe's writing. But what could Moshe have written, given that this is taking place prior to the giving of the Torah? The key may be in the ringing response of the people: "All that the Lord has spoken we will do," which, as we have shown, first occurs in Exod. 19:8. Now what was it that preceded *that* response? Most of chapter 19 deals with the ritual preparations required of the people and the prohibition to approach too close to the mountain. However, there was a pressing need to give the anxious people some understanding of what was about to take place! What does it mean to enter into a covenant with the omnipotent God who has led them from slavery to freedom? And so Moshe is instructed to tell the following to the people in the name of God:[52]

"You have seen what I did to the Egyptians and that I bore you on eagles' wings and brought you unto Myself. And so if you will hearken to My voice and keep my covenant, then you shall be My own treasure from among all the peoples [*segula mikol ha'amim*] for all the earth is Mine. And you shall be to Me a kingdom of priests and a holy nation" (Exod. 19:4-6).

It is after hearing this that the people respond with their wholehearted commitment (19:8). From this we see that the surprisingly positive and evidently unanimous commitment of the people was not in response to some specific list of "do's" and "don'ts" but rather to an

---

[52] "I know no other text which expresses so clearly and effectually the theo-political idea of Moses: the conception of the relationship between God and Israel," Martin Buber, *Moses* (Oxford: East and West Library, 1946), 101.

exciting *conception,* a lofty *vision* of what a covenant such as this would imply. If Chapter 24 is a more detailed account of the same event, then the purpose of the reading of the "book of the covenant" which preceded the people's unanimous response of *naaseh venishma,* we will do and we will hear, must have been the same as that of the "upon eagles' wings" declaration. That is to say, the purpose of both was to provide the "why," "wherefore," and consequences of such a covenant, why God wanted it and what it would mean for Israel, and thereby to generate appreciation and enthusiasm on the part of the people.

With this as background, we are perhaps in a better position to consider the view that identifies the "book of the covenant" as the Book of Genesis that had recently been written by Moshe at God's command.[53] Just as the "upon eagles' wings" declaration gave the people a sense of what it would mean to become a people covenanted to God, so too reading to them the Book of Genesis would show the people why God needed a "kingdom of priests and a holy nation."[54] It is conceivable, therefore, that Moshe wrote the *sefer habrit,* which was the proto-book of Genesis, on his own initiative. Years later, when the completed Torah was being written under prophetic inspiration, this *sefer habrit* was incorporated after suitable emendations, even as Moshe's farewell address became part of the Book of Deuteronomy.[55]

---

[53] See Rashi on Exod. 24:7 and the introduction of Nachmanides to Genesis.

[54] See Shubert Spero, "We Will Do and We Will Hearken," *The Jewish Bible Quarterly* 92 (Oct.-Dec. 1995): 229.

[55] There is a very obscure but suggestive verse that occurs toward the end of Moshe's second stay on Mt. Sinai, where he had been summoned to receive the replacement set of the stone tablets of the Covenant:

> And the Lord said to Moshe: "Write you these words, for it is according to these words that I have made a covenant with you and with Israel." (Exod. 34:27)

Although the next verse reads, "and he wrote upon the tablets the words of the covenant, the ten words" (Exod. 34:28), this cannot be the follow-up to God's command to Moshe to "write" because, although it is indeed Moshe who this time supplies the stone tablets (Deut. 9:4), it is God Himself who, as on the original tablets, does the writing! (Exod. 34:1). According to Rashi, the stress in verse 34:27 is on *"these* words," i.e., in the future when you, Moshe, commit the Torah to writing, be advised that you must limit your writing to the words you hear directly in this revelation. Other material which you have learned is to be considered part of the *oral tradition* and is *not* to be written.

Chapter Eight. Torat Hashem / Torat Moshe: Exploring their Respective Roles

Let us return to the question posed earlier: why does the Book of Genesis open without any superscription? Actually, the circumstances of its composition being as we have outlined, it is difficult to think of a proper introduction. We could not, for example, say "these are the words which Moshe wrote," because the present text of Genesis is the reworking of the material by prophecy and therefore not properly attributable to Moshe. On the other hand, to introduce the Book of Genesis by saying: "These are the words which Moshe wrote as commanded by God" would be puzzling to the casual reader as he would not have been introduced either to Moshe or to God!

Perhaps there is no alternative except to permit the Torah to address the individual without presuppositions, to let the Torah speak for itself, tell its own story, and let the reader decide who it is that calls us.

CONCLUSION

The foregoing has been an analysis of the respective roles of God and Moshe in the composition of the Torah in order to clarify the precise sense in which this work can simultaneously and justifiably be called *Torat Hashem* and *Torat Moshe*. I believe our theory satisfies both the evidence contained in the text itself and the doctrinal requirements of Judaism. We have argued that the decisive event of revelation, which determined the canonical status of the Torah as "word of God," was the act of its being written as a unitary work by Moshe while in a state of prophetic inspiration. In this state, the Divine Will takes over

---

Abarbanel, likewise, sees the emphasis as being on "*these* words": although Israel has sinned grievously, says the Lord, I do not intend to add new conditions to the covenant. It is still according to *these words* only that I established My covenant with them. There is, however, a suggestion in the Ramban and Malbim that the writing being alluded to here is the *sefer habrit* of Exod. 24:3, 4, 7 (see above), which Moshe read to the people prior to the proclamation of the Ten Commandments. Perhaps, even as the first Tablets were broken as a sign of the violated covenant, so too the original *sefer habrit* was also voided or destroyed! Hence God commands Moshe to rewrite the *sefer habrit* so that it can again be ratified by the people. Although we are not sure what it is exactly that Moshe is being commanded to write, the fact that it does not refer to the tablets provides us with a source for Moshe being *commanded* by God to *write* some part of the Torah as a *sefer*.

Moshe's consciousness and dictates what is to be written. However, while the prophetic writing is revelationally final, in the sense that it alone establishes what is the "word of God," it is derivative in terms of the material it contains. For much of that material, such as the commandments or the dialogues between God and Moshe, are the results of earlier revelations to Moshe and of historical experiences. Other components of the Torah, not considered "word of God" at the time, such as the Song of the Sea, *shirat ha'azinu*, the population figures of the tribes, and stories of the Patriarchs, were also more or less previously known to the people.

One of the strengths of our theory is that it accounts for the similarities noted between some of the Torah forms of worship, certain legal formulations,[56] and stories of pre-history and corresponding products of neighboring cultures. For, as we have emphasized, the Torah wishes to convey its unique teachings in terms of the concepts and vocabulary of the times. This is in accordance with the principle that "the Torah speaks in the language of human beings." Hence, the prophetic writing process deliberately starts out using known and familiar elements.

Another advantage of our theory is that by linking the final prophetic input to the writing process, we are implying:

1) that the Torah, for all its variety of content and style, is to be viewed as a unitary work "given from one shepherd" (Eccles. 12:11) and

2) that the choice of words, the repetitions, and the apparent contradictions are not accidental, so that the rabbinical method of *midrash halakhah* thus receives theoretical justification.

CONCLUDING EPISTEMOLOGICAL POSTSCRIPT

Our discussion so far has been largely analytic, attempting to explicate the Maimonidean formulation of *Torah min hashamayim* and bring it into dialogue with the actual text.

I wish now to direct some concluding remarks to the question of whether it is rational for a person today to accept this doctrine as true.

---

[56] See Moshe Greenberg, "Foundations of Criminal Law in the Bible," in *Torah Nidreshet* (Tel Aviv: Am Oved, 1984).

Chapter Eight. Torat Hashem/Torat Moshe: Exploring their Respective Roles

Clearly, this question deserves a broader treatment than is possible here. However, having broached this general subject, I feel it incumbent on me to conclude with some general observations on this aspect of cognitive belief.[57]

It is important to note that the question of whether Moshe wrote the Torah is a historical one similar to other inquiries concerning past events. However, the question of what canons of judgment to apply and what amount of evidence is sufficient in deciding whether to accept such a belief is a complex philosophical one about which there is no consensus.[58]

The fact is that the assertion: "Moshe wrote the Torah" presupposes the truth of two other propositions:

1) At a particular time and place there actually existed a person answering the description of the biblical Moshe ben Amram; and

2) the Torah (Pentateuch) is the kind of work that plausibly might be attributed to a single author, and have been written around the time of the biblical Moshe.

Let us briefly examine these two propositions.

1) After examining the history of the Israelite religion and the unique ideas and revolutionary beliefs that suddenly appeared, Kaufmann concludes that these testify to the working of a creative genius and leader of men. For, if history records that a particular people undergoes a religious revolution, at the heart of which is a new concept of worldwide significance, we must seek out the initiator of that revolution. "Following the Biblical saga, we call this pioneer creative spirit by the name of Moses."[59] According to Kaufmann, "the historicity of Moses is vouched for by trustworthy historical facts."

Similarly, Buber claims to have shown in his book the "historical work" of Moshe and to have provided a description of him as a "concrete

---

[57] See Shubert Spero, "Faith and its Justification," *Tradition* 13:1 (Fall 1971).
[58] Ibid.
[59] Yehezkel Kaufmann, *The Religion of Israel*, translated and abridged by Moshe Greenberg (Chicago: University of Chicago Press, 1960), 224. Kaufmann refers to one of these unique ideas as "apostolic prophecy." "For the first time in history a prophet is commissioned by a god to redeem men … the first prophet with a mission to a people was Moses" (Greenberg, 224).

individuality." After listing the unique qualities and activities of the God of Moses, Buber concludes, "That Moses experiences Him in this fashion and serves Him accordingly is what has set that man apart as a living and effective force at all times."[60]

2) On the question of the unitary character of the Pentateuch as a literary work, Segal states:

> I wish to dwell on the synthetic aspect of the Torah, upon its unity as a complete creation that integrates its rich and varied content into one structure according to a preconceived plan and for a clear and known purpose. The entire work (which governs what is included and what is deleted) may be understood as the history of a single event that occurred during the time of Moshe: the covenant *(brit)* between Israel and its God by which Israel becomes the people of God and the land of Canaan becomes the land of Israel. The focus of the entire Pentateuch is upon the generation that stands ready to enter the Promised Land: to relate to them the story of their origins, the significance of their mission and the difficulties in the task that lies ahead.[61]

As a literary work, the Pentateuch is an epic poem or a divine drama in five acts.[62] The five books are united by logical continuity and constitute five consecutive stages in the development of a common theme: the dedication and preparation of Israel for the service of God as a Holy nation in the Holy land. This is the unitary creation of one Creator and not a collection of bits and pieces of different compositions from different times. The entire Torah (Pentateuch) is a work that belongs to the

---

[60] See Buber, *Moses*, 6-8.

[61] See Moshe Tzvi Segal, *Masoret Ubakoret* (Jerusalem: Kiryat Sefer, 1957), introduction, 1. "It is impossible to assign the composition of the Book of Deuteronomy except to the last days of Moshe" (106). See also evidence from the Book of Leviticus that the material was given in the time of Moshe, as discussed by David Tzvi Hoffman in his introduction to his commentary on *Sefer Vayikra* (Jerusalem: Mosad Harav Kuk, 1966), 11. (Hebrew)

[62] Genesis relates the long process of the selection of Israel from among the nations. Exodus deals with the actual event of the making of the Covenant. Leviticus contains the laws and statutes by which the Covenant is to be actualized. Numbers relates the journey to the land in which the Covenant is to be realized. Deuteronomy prepares the young nation for the covenanted life in the land of the Covenant.

Chapter Eight. Torat Hashem/Torat Moshe:Exploring their Respective Roles

generation of Moshe. "Informed opinion dictates *(hadaat notenet)* that in its original form the Torah was written in the days of Moshe by the hand of Moshe."[63]

Can a synagogue-going Jew today who prides himself on his open-mindedness, his critical intelligence, and his non-obscurantism, feel comfortable reciting the *vezote hatorah* as the Torah scroll is held aloft? This, in face of the largely negative scholarship on this question over the last two centuries?

On the historical question of Mosaic authorship, I believe the answer to be in the affirmative. I have cited people like Kaufmann, Buber, and Segal by name not as "authorities" to be accepted as such but as scholars who have defended their views in written works and have attempted to address the arguments of their opponents. The reader is invited to consult their works and decide for himself.

Of course, one does not have to *prove* that Moshe wrote the Torah. The text supports the likelihood that he did, and that presumption holds until there is evidence that indicates otherwise. Once the counterarguments to this thesis have been neutralized, one may legitimately bring to bear extraneous considerations, exercise one's "will to believe," and opt in favor of the view that provides religious satisfaction. [64]

While the above addresses the historical aspect of the *vezot hatorah* declaration, which is the portion that speaks of *by the hand of Moshe,* the theological element, the *by the mouth of God,* remains to be examined. We have explained this as prophetic inspiration which directs Moshe's writing hand. Belief such as this is a matter of religious faith and can be neither proven nor disproven. Nevertheless, even religious faith ultimately should have some basis in rationality. Although we may speak of a "leap of faith," one should have some idea *into what* one is leaping, in which direction, and why now? Thus, in the case of the Torah, one might seek out elements in the text which become more understandable once they are seen as the product of divine prophetic inspiration.[65] However,

---

[63] Segal, *Masoret Ubakoret*, 9.
[64] See William James, *The Will to Believe* (New York: Dover Publications, 1956).
[65] The real signs of divine inspiration in the Bible are seen in its moral teachings and institutions, such as the observance of *Shabbat*. However, there are certain puzzling features which invite speculation. For example, the Torah stipulates that animals must have two signs in order to be considered fit for eating: they must have cloven hooves and chew their cuds. Then it continues, "Of these you

there are others who hold that faith by the individual in the Torah as the "word of God" rests not upon argument but upon the individual's ability to directly sense the Presence of God within and behind the words of the text.[66] To do this is to gain an immediate "knowledge of God," knowledge by acquaintance, to feel that one is being personally addressed by a Being with the attributes of "mind" and "person." Experiences of this kind may be taken as striking evidence of the doctrine that ours is indeed *Torat Hashem*.

---

shall *not* eat, that *only* chew the cud or that have *only* cloven hooves, the camel … the rock badger, the hare … and the swine" (Lev. 11:4-7). Surely, for all practical purposes it was enough to give the general rule. What was to be gained by listing four species that have only one sign and, of course, may not be eaten? Perhaps it was to exhibit a most surprising knowledge of nature, for the fact is that to this day no additional species have been discovered which have only one of these signs! Divine inspiration or coincidence?

Until very recently, one of the thorniest problems for students reading the Bible was the verse "And the Lord said, Let there be light and there was light" (Gen. 1:3). What sort of a light could this have been when the sun and the moon were first created on the fourth day? (Gen. 1:14). However, today, after the most recent cosmological discoveries, we know that, as a result of the "big bang," the first matter that appeared was composed of photons—light—traces of which have in recent decades been discovered as background radiation. Coincidence or divine inspiration? See chapter 5 in this volume.

[66] "… And how do we know that even one who sits and immerses himself in the Torah, the Divine Presence rests upon him?" (*Avot* 3:7). It seems that Rabbi Joseph B. Soloveitchik followed this approach. See Shubert Spero, *Aspects of Rabbi Joseph B. Soloveitchik's Philosophy of Judaism* (New Jersey: Ktav, 2009).

PART III

REACHING
FOR
THE HEIGHTS

Chapter Nine

Is God Truly Unknowable?

Generally, a person's motivations in developing a particular theory are irrelevant to our judgment of the validity of that theory. The psychologist, of course, may be interested in discovering relationships between an individual's temperament and the kind of beliefs he espouses. The historian, too, is concerned, among other things, with tracing the influence of earlier thinkers upon the thought of contemporaries. The philosopher, however, is persuaded by his logic that whatever may have brought a person to make a particular statement does not affect the truth content of that statement. And since the philosopher qua philosopher is primarily engaged in the pursuit of truth, he is usually not given to motivational analysis. Consider, however, a situation where the precise meaning of the theory itself is in question, so that we have before us two possible interpretations. Were we to have an insight into the author's intentions or what considerations brought him to adopt this theory, we might have some guidance as to the proper exegesis. As the problem of meaning is logically prior to the question of truth and presupposed by it, understanding a thinker's motivations can thus have heuristic value in assisting the philosopher toward his ultimate goal.

The above observations seem to me to have a useful application in the case of Maimonides' theory of our knowledge of God and the way it has figured in recent discussion. Norbert Samuelson introduces the reader to a discussion of Maimonides' views of our knowledge of God by posing the problem of theodicy.[1] He points out that the presence of evil in the world seems to contradict God's omniscience, omnipotence, or goodness. In order to overcome the problem, the believer may take refuge in the claim that these predicates, when applied to God, mean something else than when they are applied to man: "What is good in the eyes of God is not what is good in the eyes of man."[2] The implication of

---

[1] Norbert Samuelson, "On Knowing God: Maimonides, Gersonides, and the Philosophy of Religion," *Judaism* 18, no. 1 (Winter 1969): 64-77.
[2] Ibid., 65.

Samuelson's presentation seems to be that Maimonides' theory of the divine attributes is in some sense a proposed solution to the problem of theodicy. Such an implication is misleading. Maimonides never offers his theory as such, and for good reason. He acknowledges that the moral attributes of God describe His actions and His relations to human beings, but God's relations to His creatures have always served as a model and inspiration for human beings in their relationship to each other: "Abba Shaul says, 'Be like unto Him, as He is merciful and gracious, so shall you be merciful and gracious.'"[3] Therefore, when we are told that, "All His ways are just," the predicate "just," of necessity, means the same as it does when it is applied to inter-human relationships throughout the Bible. "For it has been told to thee, O man, what is good." And if what is good in the eyes of God is not good in the eyes of man, then the entire point of a moral God and the rabbinic teaching of Imitato Dei collapses![4] Whatever solutions may be offered for the problem of theodicy, an equivocal use of ethical predicates cannot be one of them. (And, to my knowledge, the idea was never proposed by Jewish theologians.)

In another recent article, Fred Sommers uses as his springboard into a discussion of Maimonides' concept of God the Aristotelian theory that no term can be univocally predicated of things that belong to two different categories.[5] Although Sommers ultimately shows the Aristotelean theory to be fallacious and introduces other, more cogent grounds for Maimonides' teaching, he concludes that "medieval theologians were too hasty in their effort to remove from God all traces of materiality" and may have paid too high a price.[6]

I wish to argue that Maimonides' theory of negative theology need not be given the agnostic interpretation attributed to it by the aforementioned writers. By "negative theology" we refer to the doctrine which states that descriptions of God are positive in their grammatical

---

[3] Shabbat 133b.
[4] In this spirit, Maimonides interprets the conclusion of Moses' prayer in Exod. 33:16: "That I may know Thee, that I may find grace in Thy sight and consider that this nation is Thy people." Says Maimonides, "That is to say, the people whom I have to rule by certain acts in the performance of which I must be guided by Thy own acts in governing them" (Moses Maimonides, *Guide for the Perplexed,* trans. M. Friedlander [New York: E. P. Dutton & Co., 1942], I:54).
[5] Fred Sommers, "What We Can Say About God," *Judaism* 15 (1966): 61-73.
[6] Ibid., 72.

form only. In reality, they tell us what God is not. Thus, the proposition "God is wise" means only that He is not what in man we call foolish. The more we learn to negate of God, the more we grow in our real knowledge of Him. While according to Maimonides we cannot know the essence of God, there is nevertheless a good deal we can say about God which is illuminating and which is adequate to support the Jewish religious enterprise. I shall attempt to demonstrate the incorrectness of Sommers' assertion "that there is no middle ground between univocity and equivocity." Contrary to Samuelson, I wish to assert that, for Maimonides, the God of the philosophers is the God of Abraham, Isaac, and Jacob, successfully, consistently, and truly. I shall try to show that understanding the pressures which led Maimonides to his theory tends to support the thesis that Maimonides intended to use his theory of negative attributes as a means for expressing a positive content in our knowledge of God.

The popular image of Maimonides as one who reconciled Judaism and Greek thought conceives of him as a philosopher overwhelmed by the truth of metaphysical speculation who proceeds to "adjust" biblical theology accordingly.[7] Whatever merit this image may have for Maimonides' philosophy generally, which will not be discussed in depth here, I wish to suggest that it is profoundly misleading if applied to his concept of God. Here, I believe it can be shown, Maimonides did not distort theology to fit philosophy, but simply utilized philosophical methods to sharpen and refine a theological concept.[8] And to submit a religious idea to philosophical analysis was, in itself, seen as a genuine religious demand. Nothing could be clearer than the biblical insistence upon the unity of God, the prohibitions against picturing Him, and His uniqueness.[9] Not quite as explicit, but no less central in biblical and rabbinic thought, is the concept of God as the everlasting and totally independent ground of all being which later comes to be called *absolute existence* or *necessary existence*.[10] It is here, and no place else, that we must locate the source

---

[7] For a spirited defense of the "Jewishness" of Maimonides' theology, see the essay of Rabbi A. I. Kook in Zev Yavetz, *Toldot Yisroel*, vol. 12 (Tel Aviv, 1934).

[8] See Izhak Guttmann, *Dat Umadah* (Jerusalem, 1954), 104.

[9] Deut. 4:12; Deut. 6:4; Isa., 45:5-7; Isa., 40:25.

[10] Exod. 3:14; *Midrash Tehillim* on Psalm XC:1; Joseph Albo, *Sefer Ha-Ikarim*, volume 2 (Philadelphia: Jewish Publication Society, 1930), 27.

Chapter Nine. Is God Truly Unknowable?

and pressure point which leads to Maimonides' concept of negative attributes. The impulse does not emerge from Aristotle's theory of the categories or from the problem of evil in the world. The primary motivation stems from basic and profound religious principles—God's unity and absolute existence—and their implications.[11]

Let us briefly trace the unfolding of the problem as perceived by Maimonides. The Bible, in proclaiming "The Lord is one," teaches that God's nature is simple and incomposite, which, in the language of Maimonides' time, means that God's existence is identical with His essence. Now there is no predicate which does not signify either an essential attribute or an accidental attribute. By the former, we mean any quality which defines the primary nature of something or which makes a thing what it is. By the latter, we mean qualities which can be altered without affecting a thing's real nature. For example, having a seat is an essential attribute of a chair, for without a seat an object could not function as a chair. But being a particular color, such as brown, is not essential to being a chair and so for chairs color is an accidental attribute.

The use of essential attributes in reference to God would appear to be innocuous, since they turn out to be either tautologies or mere explanations of a name. But even as such they prove inadmissible because God is not a member of any class or genus. Hence, a conventional definition in terms of genus and difference similar to "Man is a rational animal" is impossible in reference to God. But accidental attributes certainly cannot be ascribed to God, for to make God the subject of predicates is to imply that He consists of an essence bearing qualities, which is already composite and not simple. It would therefore follow that it is logically impossible to predicate any sort of attributes of God.

Does this mean that God is totally unknowable or completely beyond human comprehension and description? In the sense that man cannot know anything about the essence of God, the answer is in the affirmative. Clearly, therefore, any predication that is nevertheless made of God cannot mean what the term ordinarily means in human discourse. But this is not to say that these sentences are unintelligible and just so much gibberish. As a professing Jew, Maimonides had to account for the biblical descriptions of God as possessing aspects of personality, as well as descriptions of Him as a source of ethical value, creator of the

---
[11] Maimonides, *Guide*.

world a living reality in the lives of individuals, and the guiding factor in the affairs of nations. It was in answer to this need that Maimonides offered his doctrine of negative theology, which consists of two aspects: the attributes of action and the negative attributes. These two aspects of our knowledge of God must be considered separately, as well as in interaction with each other, in order to be fully understood.

In view of the setting of the problem, what we should expect to find in this doctrine is not unrelieved agnosticism but a device which, while respecting the logical implications of God's otherness, will enable us to meaningfully assert of God what our religious sentiments urge upon us. Let us now examine the doctrine itself and see whether Maimonides was successful in his program.

The essence of the Torah's teaching on the subject of our knowledge of God, according to Maimonides, is contained in the Book of Exodus in the dialogue between Moses and God. Moses makes two requests of God: (1) "Show me Thy ways," and (2) "Show me Thy glory."[12] The first is a request for the knowledge of God's attributes, the second is a request for the knowledge of God's essence. In response to the latter, Moses is told, "Man cannot see Me and live," which means that the essence of God is unknowable for man as man. However, Moses does receive a favorable reply to his first question, namely, "I will cause all my goodness to pass before thee." This in effect means, as is borne out by the remainder of that section in the Torah, that God can be known by His qualities (*middot*), which are nothing more than a knowledge of the works or actions of God.[13] Maimonides makes it clear that to describe God by attributing to Him certain actions or works is an appropriate form of description because it does not imply anything as to how these actions are produced or what elements must be contained in the agent in order to produce the actions.[14] Thus, in response to the question, "Who is God?," it is perfectly legitimate to reply, "God is the creator of the world, the giver of the Torah, the liberator of our people from Egyptian bondage."

Furthermore, attributions of certain qualities to God, such as "graciousness" or "mercy," are to be reduced to, or analyzed as, attributes of action. When we say that "A is merciful," where A is a human being, we

---

[12] Exod. 33:13, 18.
[13] Maimonides, *Guide*, I:54.
[14] Ibid., I:52.

imply two things: (1) that A performs certain kinds of actions of beneficial consequence to others, particularly the weak and helpless; and (2) that A is subject to certain emotions or psychical dispositions. When we say that "God is merciful" we must reject (2) since nothing may be added to God's essence, but we retain (1).

If attributes of action are admissible as descriptions of God, relational attributes are as well, for the former can be transposed into the latter. Thus, if God can be described as the creator of the world, then my relationship to God is that of creature to creator. If God is the giver of the Torah and legislates for man, then there is a sense in which I can relate to God as obedient subject or as rebel. At one point, Maimonides clearly identifies the two by saying, "There is no difference whether these various attributes refer to His actions or to relations between Him and His works."[15]

What has been found confusing, however, is the fact that Maimonides seems to reject the attribution of the quality of relation to God, which would deny that there can be any relation between God and His creatures. A careful review of the relevant passages, however, leads to the conclusion that Maimonides distinguished between a strong and weak sense of relational attributes. Maimonides was convinced that in a *strict and literal sense*, for two things to be related or correlated they must belong to the same category, which implies some degree of similarity. Although he acknowledges that "relations are not the essence of a thing nor are they so intimately connected with it as qualities,"[16] nevertheless Maimonides contends that logically, were we to attribute relations to God, the concept of God's unity would be impaired, as "God would be subject to the accident of relation." However, the nicety of the logical

---

[15] Ibid., I:53.

[16] This does not appear convincing to us today. Maimonides says, "There is no relation between two things that have no similarity to each other" (p. 79) and "It is impossible to imagine a relation between intellect and sight" (p. 71). But why not? Could it not be said that intellect is partially dependent upon sight for the perceptions which it tries to understand? Maimonides seems to have felt that to say that two things are related in the strict sense is to assume certain knowledge about both terms in the relationship and a real interaction between them. Maimonides does seem to find acceptable a use of the term relation in reference to God wherein "these relations exist only in the thoughts of men" (p. 74).

point must be waived in the light of Maimonides' conclusion that, "these (relational attributes) are the most appropriate of all attributes to be employed, *in a less strict sense,* in reference to God because they do not imply that a plurality of eternal things exist or that any change takes place in the essence of God when those things change to which God is in relation."[17]

We see that Maimonides insists upon the admissibility of assertions about God which are necessary to describe the religious experience of the Jew. God, whatever His essence may be, impinges upon the life of man through His activities. Man, in becoming aware of God's agency in these works, acknowledges the relationship which is thus seen to obtain between himself and God.[18]

In order to perceive how all of this is related to the theory of negative attributes, we must take another look at the attributes of action. What do we mean when we say that God created the world or that He liberated Israel from bondage? Are we saying merely that God is the mechanical cause of the universe, the antecedent factor that produced the universe, or do we have something more in mind? The biblical account of the relationship between God and the universe and between God and man quite clearly includes the notion of *purposive* action. God is not only cause but agent. The universe as it comes into being, the Bible suggests, possesses certain features in consequence of a plan or objective intended by God. The Jewish people are brought forth from Egypt in order to assume a certain role in history so that God's goals may be realized. In order to describe fully the actions of God, therefore, we are compelled to speak of a purposive element which suggests that God possesses something which corresponds to the will in man, in virtue of which He gives to things existence in accordance with His desire. Furthermore, purposive creation, in the sense described, combined with the biblical concept of providence, implies that God knows, or has knowledge, at least in the sense that He is aware of what He is doing. Finally, to create implies the power to create. It follows, therefore, that God possesses something which corresponds to power in human experience. But note what has

---

[17] Maimonides, *Guide*, I:52.
[18] For the importance of relational predicates see Eliezer Berkovits, *God, Men and History* (New York: Jonathan David, 1959), 55-59, and Martin Buber, *Eclipse of God* (New York: Harper and Brothers, 1952), 126-127.

happened in the course of our discussion. We are no longer describing God's actions but have been led into an attempt to express something about God Himself. We thus arrive at the so-called "essential attributes": God's "life," power, wisdom, and will.[19] But the principle of God's unity precludes the addition of any element to His essence. Hence, to express ourselves correctly, we must say, "God lives without possessing the attribute of life; knows without possessing the attribute of knowledge; is omnipotent without possessing the attribute of omnipotence."[20] Maimonides argues that the assertion that one simple substance can cause different actions is not unintelligible. However, since there is no similarity between God and man, the term "knows" must be predicated equivocally. Granting, therefore, all that has been said, we have still not solved the problem of what is meant by the word "knows" in the sentence, "God knows without possessing the attribute of knowledge."

It is at this point that Maimonides introduces his theory of the negative. In recent discussions on the intelligibility of "God-talk" in philosophical literature, there has been a good deal of analysis of analogical predication, the method favored by Aquinas, but very little about the *via negativa*.[21] Even when negative theology is mentioned for the sake of completeness, it is soon dismissed with the judgment that it has never been clearly formulated or that it is obviously inadequate.[22] Thus, for example, it has been argued that, according to the theory of negative attributes, the assertion, "God is wise," is to be translated as, "God is not ignorant." But "ignorance" is the absence of wisdom or "not-wise." Therefore, to assert "God is not ignorant" is the equivalent of saying that "God is not not-wise" which, by the meaning of double negation, is "God is wise." What, therefore, has been gained by using the locution, "God is not ignorant?"

However, in so construing Maimonides' theory of negative attributes, a twofold injustice has been done to the sage of Fostat. He has

---

[19] Maimonides, *Guide*, I:53.
[20] Ibid., I:57.
[21] The following two works do not treat negative theology at all, while giving full treatment to the theory of analogy: Frederick Ferre, *Language, Logic and God* (New York: Harper and Row, 1961), 67-78, and William T. Blackstone, *The Problem of Religious Knowledge* (Englewood Cliffs, NJ: Prentice-Hall, 1963), 62-70.
[22] Frank Dilley, *Metaphysics and Religious Language* (New York: Columbia University Press, 1964), 86; Joseph M. Bochenski, *The Logic of Religion* (New York: New York University Press, 1965), 111.

been criticized for what he did not teach, and his actual contribution has gone generally unrecognized.[23]

To begin with, he meant his theory to apply only to the so-called essential attributes like knowledge, power, wisdom, and life. Other predicates function differently when ascribed to God. Secondly, Maimonides spoke of privation instead of negation. When we say God is one, we are not saying He is not many, but that He is non-many, i.e., the terms of quantity cannot at all be predicated of Him. The difference between the negative and the privative depends on the object of the negation. In the negative proposition, the negative attacks the copula. Thus, to say, "The enterprise is not making profit," is to deny the assertion, "The enterprise *is* making profit." In the privative proposition, the negative attacks the predicate. Therefore, to say, "The enterprise is non profit-making," is to deny that the *predicate* "making profit" applies at all to this particular enterprise. The privative proposition may also be called infinite because it eliminates from the infinite number of possible predicates only one, so that the infinity remains untouched. In its developed form, Maimonides construes the attribution of the essential attributes to God as a privation of a privation. Thus, to say "God is wise" is to say "God is non-ignorant" or "non non-wise." It is a positive infinite proposition.

In our case, this proposition, "God is non-non-wise," amounts to the statement "Whatever we may exclude from being predicated about God, wisdom must remain." As Diesendruck points out, such an analysis is both less and more than a positive attribute. It is less, because the predicate remains at a certain distance from the subject in the field of possible predicates. It is more, because it asserts a necessary connection instead of a factual one. We are saying, "Of God one *must* be able to say that He is wise." The end result is something highly positive. We have removed the possibility of eliminating wisdom from God.

This theory of double privation is to be regarded only as the logical framework which makes it technically possible for these essential attributes to be predicated of God. Through its means, we are able to express, in the form of a necessary proposition, the concept that these essential attributes must remain possible predicates.

---

[23] In my interpretation of Maimonides' theory of negative attributes I follow the analysis of Zevi Diesendruck, "Maimonides' Theory of the Negation of Privation," *Proceedings of the American Academy for Jewish Research* VI (1934-1935): 141.

Chapter Nine. Is God Truly Unknowable?

This positive interpretation of Maimonides is shared by Julius Guttmann, who writes, "Maimonides' doctrine of the negation of privations enables us to say that the simple essence of God includes within itself perfections which correspond in one way or another to the qualities of knowledge, will and power but whose essence remains undetermined."[24]

This interpretation is supported by the several instances in which Maimonides, in responding to a problem, is not satisfied simply to state that the attribute involved is applied to God and man equivocally, but insists on trying to provide some intelligibility to the distinction. Thus, he distinguishes between the knowledge that an outsider has of an object by observation and the knowledge that the producer has of the object from within, as it were, because he built it in a certain way. "God," says Maimonides, "knows fully His unchangeable essence and thus has a knowledge of all that results from any of His acts."[25]

Similarly, in discussing the concept of will, Maimonides argues that if we can imagine the will of an absolutely spiritual being which does not depend on external causes, it would be unchangeable even if it desires "one thing one day and another thing another day."[26]

These efforts on the part of Maimonides to discuss the attributes of will and knowledge as they *might* apply to God, while at the same time upholding the equivocity of these predicates if positively affirmed of God, seems to suggest that these attributions, correctly construed as analyzed above, contain some intelligibility nevertheless.[27] Although qualitatively different, there is some perfection in God's essence which corresponds to knowledge. To use a spatial metaphor, Divine knowledge grounded in the Godhead is shrouded in mystery, but by virtue of God's relations to a universe which He has created and which He governs, we can reliably affirm that we are somehow known to God. In short, whatever content is to be given to these attributes emanates from the human side and is directed at God's works, i.e., the points at which He relates to man and the world.

Perhaps we can best do justice to Maimonides' theory by exploring what we might call the "allusive use of language." By this we do not mean

---

[24] Julius Guttmann, *Philosophies of Judaism* (New York: Holt, Rinehart and Winston, 1964), 164.
[25] Maimonides, *Guide,* III:21.
[26] Ibid., II:18.
[27] Guttmann, *Dat Umadah,* 110-111.

to say that whatever corresponds to knowledge in God has properties in common with human knowledge, or that they are analogates which bear resemblance to each other. We do mean to suggest that perhaps language can be used in such a way as to give an impression of what is beyond experience, hint at God, suggest what we are to expect or, at least, "face us in a determinate direction."[28]

Let us consider two examples of this type of language-use. The first involves the use of the word "spirit," by which we intend to designate God as transcendent or meta-empirical. Can we give any kind of intelligible content to this notion? We wish to answer in the affirmative and claim that the word is taken from our own human experience and deliberately pressed into theological service, where it is given a frankly extraordinary use in the hope that it enables us to convey an allusion or hint of what we mean by God. Although God lies outside the range of possible conception, the human experience in which the word "spirit" arises points us in a "determinate direction."

The experience we are referring to is the standpoint of agent, from which we can describe what is going on in us. As agents, we utilize a set of concepts which are different from, and not reducible to, physicalist or sense data or behavioristic language. When we regard ourselves as agents, we cannot accept with complete satisfaction the idea that we are spatial-temporal objects. For certain aspects of human experience—loving, hoping, feeling—have a relative independence of space. It is here that the notion of man as spirit is born. The experience of our own subjectivity gives us the idea of something which can transcend the spatial-temporal realm.[29]

Of course, the words "spirit" and "spiritual" occur in our language in connection with subjectivity only in relation to characteristics and activities of people, and are always correlated to physical and behavioristic activities. However, when we draft the word for theological use and describe God as pure spirit, we deliberately commit a category mistake and assert (1) that "spirit" retains specific meaning by connection with

---

[28] I.M. Crombie, "The Possibility of Theological Statements," in *Religious Language and the Problem of Religious Knowledge,* ed. Ronald E. Santoni (Bloomington, IN: Indiana University Press, 1968), 108.

[29] Ian T. Ramsey, "On Understanding Mystery," in *Philosophy and Religion,* ed. J. A. Gill (Minneapolis, MN: Burgess Pub. Co., 1968). 298.

Chapter Nine. Is God Truly Unknowable?

spirituality as the name of a human aspect, but (2) that it is to be governed by a rule declaring that this noun is not to be taken as an abstract noun like "smile" but as a concrete noun like "man."

I wish to make it clear that I am not arguing that we now have a perfectly clear concept of disembodied spirit or pure spirit or of a being that is beyond space and time. I am claiming that, by abstraction from ordinary experience, we can gain some hint of a reality where "what is imperfectly realized in us is fully and perfectly realized." We are referred out of experience but in a specific direction.

A second instance of the allusive use of language is the use of the terms "infinite" and "unconditioned" as applied to God. Here, too, as we noticed in connection with the term "spirit," the word does not acquire its sense by reference to God's properties, but rather from some human experience which, far from being a model, nevertheless suggests, in some sense, a direction in which to look and hints at what sort of thing to expect. The experience I have reference to is what has been called "the sense of contingency." This can start with the feeling, often noted in religious literature, of the transiency of all things, of the tenuous and precarious character of our existence, of the uncertainty and gratuitousness of all things. From here it is but a step to the insight that our universe is, in some sense, a derivative one, dependent upon something else, both from an explanatory and from an ontological point of view. But here, again, I am not concerned with reviving the cosmological argument for the existence of God or arguing from contingency to the existence of a necessary being. All I wish to claim is that the sense of contingency gives some meaning to the notion of infinite or unconditioned being. Many writers who reject the cosmological proof as such nevertheless acknowledge its authenticity as an expression of certain general features of our experience—wonderment and anxiety from which we can go on "to imagine a mode of being that is instead stable and invulnerable."

In the words of Crombie,

> From the fact that this universe is something about which one is prompted to ask where it comes from, there emerges the corollary that there might be something about which one was not prompted to ask this question.[30]

---

[30] Crombie, "The Possibility of Theological Statements," 113.

From our awareness of a sense that this is a derivative universe, that it is not its own origin, can spring the corollary that a non-derivative being might exist, a being concerning whom there would not arise the sort of "intellectual dissatisfaction" which we sometimes experience with the notion that this universe is a complete self-subsistent system.

Here, again, theology must plead guilty to deliberate distortion of language. The words "contingent" and "necessary," which are traditionally employed in this context, are ordinarily used to apply to statements only. A necessary statement is one whose denial involves a breach of the laws of logic. By this criterion, all existential statements are contingent, so that the phrase "necessary existent" is a self-contradiction. But, as in the previous example, we are induced to strain and distort our language in order to respond to the intellectual pressures of religious insight and give expression to them. Thus,

> the expression "God" is to refer to that object whatever it is, and if there be one, which is such that the knowledge of it would be to us knowledge of the unfamiliar term in the contrast between finite and infinite.[31]

This ability on our part to use our notion of limited and deficient perfection as a springboard to point the mind beyond the limits of its experience is likewise seen by W. N. Clarke as the solution to our dilemma of intelligibility. He says,

> The meaningfulness of our language and thought about the infinite finds its support in the profound human experience of discerning within our world the latter's intrinsic character of radical limitation, deficiency, and inability to satisfy our deepest exigencies of intellect and will. This notion ... is a highly dynamic one ... which points beyond itself to a mysterious plenitude in the same line, affirmable though not representable.[32]

---

[31] I.M. Crombie, "Theology and Falsification," in *New Essays in Philosophical Theology*, ed. Anthony Flew and Alasdair MacIntyre (New York: The Macmillan Co., 1955), 124.

[32] W. Norris Clarke, "On Professors Ziff, Niebuhr, and Tillich," in *Religious Experience and Truth*, ed. Sidney Hook (New York: New York University Press, 1961), 229.

Chapter Nine. Is God Truly Unknowable?

We do not properly look away from the finite to find the infinite; "we find it by looking more deeply into the finite itself."

It is important to see how this approach differs from the theory of analogical predication favored by Thomas Aquinas. In this type of usage, the word, in its analogical application, is not identical in meaning with its ordinary usage, but is similar in some sense. For example, if I say, "The lion is king of the beasts," I do not mean that the lion is a king in exactly the same way as Haile Selassie is king. But it might mean that the lion is regal in its bearing, or that the other beasts fear it. In the view of its supporters, this doctrine of analogical predication, when applied to God, is supposed to avoid effectively both univocal and equivocal predication while retaining the meaningfulness of religious sentences. This they attempt to do by appealing to the notion of proportionality. Thus, while both cabbages and men may be said to be alive, each possesses life in the mode proper to its kind. Therefore, we might assert that God's goodness is to God as man's goodness is to man. However, it has been argued, that whereas our non-analogical knowledge of cabbages enables us to form some idea as to the sense in which cabbages may be said to be alive, we have no other knowledge of God in connection with which we can understand His goodness.

In any event, analogical predication constitutes a positive attribution, with the burden of intelligibility resting on the side of God. It is, therefore, to be seriously doubted whether this approach gives us any knowledge of God. In the case of Maimonides, however, using his logical framework, I maintain that these essential attributes are not being predicated of God. To say, "God knows" is to use the term "knows" in a sense that is equivocal with its use in ordinary discourse. That sentence may be uttered meaningfully only if it is translated as negation of privation. The conceptual content that we now give it, by means of allusion, comes from the human side. Whatever God's knowledge consists of, it must eventuate in that kind of relationship with His creatures in which it is not absurd to say, "We are known by God."

It has been suggested that when we apply a predicate to God in this sense, we are using it as a "floor concept" rather than as a "ceiling concept." That is to say that whatever this predicate may turn out to be in God, it cannot fall below this sort of possibility.[33]

---

[33] Ibid., 230.

A somewhat different analysis holds for the moral attributes "merciful, gracious, kind," and the like. I certainly do not wish to say that there is something in God which corresponds to the emotion of mercy. I have already stated that to say that, "God is merciful," is to say that the actions which we attribute to God are of the same type as the actions of a person whom we would call merciful. But this is to relate God to moral predicates in a manner which appears to be at once both more and less intimate than the essential attributes. It is less intimate in the sense already indicated, in that, while we wish to say that there is some perfection in God which corresponds to knowledge, we cannot say that there is something in God which corresponds to mercy. This is because, insofar as this quality exists in man, it is associated with an emotion which Maimonides sees as a defect and which, therefore, may not be attributed to God.[34] On the other hand, there is a sense in which God's relation to moral predicates is more intimate than the essential attributes. For when we affirm that we can expect from God merciful actions and never unjust actions, we are committing God to an ethical course which behaviorally is identical to that which we would expect from humans. Although we thereby expose ourselves to the problem of evil in the world in all its unmitigated force, this is the price we must be prepared to pay, for it is our conception of the merciful and righteous God which is the basis of the important doctrine of Imitato Dei and is the source of Judaism's moral passion and earnestness. There can, therefore, be no equivocation in the essential meaning of moral predicates.

These moral predicates have been called "regulative ideas" of God, in the sense that they do not tell us what God is within Himself but how He wills that we should think of Him in order to guide our behavior. However, even here, language functions in an allusive sense to provide some conceptual content, the way God wants you to think of Him. In the words of Henry Mansel,

> If we could know the life of God, we should see in it something which human love really resembles, so that to call it love would be the best way of saying what it is in human language. Thus, conduct which flows from the belief that God is love is not only the best kind of conduct, judged by the scales of human ethical values, but is also the kind of conduct which corresponds best with reality.

---

[34] Maimonides, *Guide*, I:54.

> If you are unable to imagine what the reality is, you can know at any rate that it is of such a character that the right reaction to it in conduct and feeling is the reaction which follows upon your thinking of the ground of the universe as a loving God.[35]

So conceived, Maimonides' theory of negative attributes emerges not as a doctrine which exudes a cloud of agnosticism over the Jewish concept of God but as a logical device which safeguards concepts of God's unity and uniqueness while providing a framework into which the content of biblical and rabbinic religious experiences could be poured. Therefore, in reply to the assertion of Professor Sommers that "there is no middle ground between univocity and equivocity," I wish to say the following: True, there is no *middle* ground; however, there may be the *high ground* of allusive language which may rewardingly be trod.

To the problems raised by Norbert Samuelson I submit, first, that the interpretation of Maimonides' theory of negative attributes given above escapes the criticism of Gersonides referred to by him. Secondly, identifying the God of Abraham, Isaac, and Jacob with the God of the philosophers was no mistake for Maimonides. For him they are not rivals, but entries in different systems of bookkeeping for the same reality. For Maimonides, philosophy liberated the theological mind from the bewitchment of language. And that is not an inconsiderable contribution.

---

[35] Quoted by Edwyn R. Bevan, *Symbolism and Belief* (New York: Macmillan, 1938), 332-333.

Chapter Ten

Love of God

The Torah calls upon man to bring himself to two loves: love for his fellow man and love for God. In both cases the Torah breaks new moral and religious ground in calling for a love of unusual quality and surprising intensity: in the case of man, "And you shall love your fellow man as yourself"; and in the case of God, "And you shall love the Lord your God with all your heart and with all your soul and with all your might."[1]

Clearly, both of these injunctions would appear to constitute fundamental principles of Judaism inasmuch as they prescribe one of the most profound and powerful of the positive emotions as the underlying component of the entire relationship to man and to God. For "love is strong as death; many waters cannot extinguish love; a very flame of the Lord."[2]

The difficulty, of course, is regarding how the Torah can presume to legislate love, to command emotions as if love were something over which the individual exercises control and which he can turn on or off at will.[3] Also, how can one learn to love someone like God, who cannot be seen?

In regard to the command to love man, most commentators do not interpret the passage as referring to the actual emotion. They point out that there is a difference in the grammatical form, so that *veahavtah le raiakhha* can be translated as, "You shall be loving toward your fellowman," with the focus on deeds and behavior rather than on feelings.[4] Secondly, on moral grounds it is questionable whether all of our fellow men are worthy of such an intense personal emotional attachment. But even in the absence of these considerations, could the Torah realistically believe that it could get us to love our fellow men as we love ourselves?

---

[1] Lev. 19:18; Deut. 6:5.
[2] Songs 8:6-7.
[3] See Ibn Ezra on Exod. 20:14.
[4] See commentaries of Nachmanides and Malbim on Lev. 19:18.

Chapter Ten. Love of God

However, when we turn to the command to love God, it seems that we have no alternative but to interpret the imperative as referring in its basic meaning to the actual human emotion of love. This is the case because, first, neither the grammatical nor the moral considerations which apply to the love of man hold here, but more important, because the teaching to love God appears repeatedly in the Torah, together with the commands to "fear God" and, particularly, to "cleave unto Him," and these two commands form the highest reaches of religious experience.[5] While each of them undoubtedly generates many particular behavioral consequences, they are all, in the first and primary instance, felt inner experiences of a complex affective and conative nature. When we speak of love of God, we are talking about one of the ways through which man can commune with God and draw closer to Him. In the words of Rabbi Joseph Albo, "For love is the union and complete mental identification of lover and the loved."[6]

It is for these reasons, then, that when we speak of the obligation to love God we must understand "love" to be the elemental human emotion which we are familiar with from our own experience, although to be sure when it is applied to God it is of the highest and purest form. Here is Maimonides' description of love for God, given apparently in human terms:

> What is the right kind of love? One is to entertain towards the Lord an exceedingly great and mighty love so that his very soul shall be bound by the love of God; being ever enraptured by it, as is the mind of one who being lovesick does not cease to languish after his beloved on whom he ever dotes whether sitting or rising, eating or drinking: nay, greater than this should be the love for the Lord in the hearts of His lovers who are ever to be enraptured with this love as He commanded us. That is what Solomon said by way of allegory: "For I am lovesick,." The whole book of Canticles is an allegory of man's love for God.[7]

If so, then we remain with the original difficulty: how is it possible for the Torah to command us to love God?

---

[5] Deut. 13:4, 5 and 11:22.
[6] Joseph Albo, *Sefer Ha-Ikarim*, III:36.
[7] Maimonides, *Mishneh Torah, Hilkhot Teshuvah,* 10:3.

Maimonides seems to suggest that while "love" is, indeed, the ultimate goal of the commandment, man is called upon to perform certain acts which are under his control and which are causally related to the love for God. Once these acts are performed, the love of God is sure to follow:

> And what is the way that will lead to the love of Him and the fear of Him? When a person contemplates His great and wondrous works and creatures and from them perceives His wisdom which is incomparable and infinite, he will straightaway love Him, praise Him, glorify Him and long with an exceeding longing to know His great Name; even as David said, "My soul thirsteth for God, for the living God." And when he ponders these same matters he will recoil, frightened, and realize that he is a small creature.[8]

In the process outlined by Maimonides, the following steps can be distinguished:

1) Contemplation of God's works and creatures, i.e., the natural world.
2) Realization of the wisdom of the Maker of the natural world, i.e., God.
3) Experience of a love for God (which follows immediately and necessarily from #2).
4) Development of a desire and a passion to know about God, to come closer to Him. (The more knowledge that man has, the greater his love.)

The immediate difficulty that we have with this account lies in the connection between steps 2 and 3. Even though we may accept the claim that man, by examining the macro- and micro-phenomena of nature—by peering into the intricacies of the genetic code, by grasping the wondrous ways in which our planet is a self-correcting ecosystem, by understanding the life-history of the galaxies from "big-bang" to "black-holes"—might see all of this as the work of God and come to appreciate His greatness, he might still, in his appreciation, be limited to an understanding of God's wisdom. Certainly, "He who spoke and the world came into existence," must surely be a most intelligent, most knowledgeable

---

[8] Maimonides, *Mishneh Torah, Hilkhot Yesodai Hatorah*, 2:1-2.

and most wise Being in addition to possessing unimaginable power. But does this necessarily lead to love? Does the recognition of wisdom in someone imply that I will love that person?

But perhaps Maimonides means something else: When I recognize the great wisdom with which the world was put together and realize that all of that wisdom is aimed at providing man with a rich, beautiful, and challenging life in a cooperative environment, then I am filled with a great rush of love. But in this case, what I experience is primarily a feeling of gratitude for services rendered. While thankfulness is a proper moral response, its source is egoism (I am happy over what you did for *me*), and is far from the ideal of *amor Dei*, which should be altruistic and disinterested. Indeed, in a traditional commentary on the Code, we are told that what Maimonides seems to be referring to is precisely the kind of feeling that is developed for something *not* because one may personally benefit or have some practical use from it. The language is significant:

> The love that attaches to all things beloved can come about in one of two ways. The first results from the good, the pleasure, or the kindness which the lover experiences as a result of the beloved. Such is the nature of the love of a man for a woman or of a servant to his King. The second type of love comes about when a person notices a beautiful thing and approves of it. Then he will love and desire it and when he attains it he will experience joy. As when a person sees a precious stone or a beautiful and stately house, immediately his soul will desire to reach it and cleave to it.[9]

This is, of course, the rabbinic distinction between *ahavah sheteluyah bedavar* and *ahavah she-ainah teluyah bedavar*—love which is intrinsic and disinterested, versus love which is extrinsic and tied to self-interest. What prompts the commentator to identify the love that man must bear for God with *ahavah sheainah teluyah bedavar* is, first, that this is the only lasting love, since it does not depend upon anything transient; second, that this love is purely motivated by the thought of the beloved alone; and third, that this love alone answers to the Torah demand to love God exclusively "with all thy heart and with all thy soul ..." with no room left for self-love of any kind. But if the love required by the *mitzvah*

---

[9] "*Peirush*" on *Hilkhot Yesodei Hatorah,* 2:2 in most standard editions. Author is unknown.

is a disinterested one then we are back to the question: How does an awareness of God's wisdom lead to this kind of love for God?

When we consider the teachings of Maimonides historically, against the background of Greek thought, we come up with quite a different interpretation which, while answering the original question, unfortunately proves unsatisfactory for other reasons. Influenced as he was by Aristotle, Maimonides' philosophy seems, in many key respects, to fit the type of religion which Guttmann calls "intellectualistic" and describes thus:

> This type of religion regards God as Truth, as objective reality, as the supreme intellect. The ultimate in human perfection is for man to possess adequate knowledge which originates in the intellect itself. But the true source of man's knowledge is in God since the human intellect is based on the divine intellect. If man, therefore, achieves adequate knowledge, this in itself proves his contact with the divine. His greatest felicity comes from God; therefore, he loves God. This is the intellectual love of God—*amor Dei intellectualis*.[10]

Guttmann cites Aristotle and Spinoza as examples of this type of philosophy of religion. What is curious is that a system of thought which emphasizes knowledge and the intellect should end up by speaking of love of God which is an emotion that in ordinary life is not usually associated with the intellect. Yet it was Aristotle who, in trying to explain the force by which the prime mover whom he called God set in motion the entire universe, did not think in terms of mechanical push or pull but said that "all things desire God" and in their "love" are drawn toward Him. Used in this context, the term "love" does not refer to a conscious affection but rather means an inherent functioning, a sort of non-mechanical attraction, a movement toward something. Even in terms of man, Aristotle believed that learning and acquiring knowledge was a pleasurable experience which brought in its wake a felt joy. However, on a philosophical level, he maintained that the activity of contemplation in which man exercises his intellect, and thus fulfills his *telos*, results inevitably in a unique kind of satisfaction which is an essential element in the totality which we call happiness.

---

[10] Y.J. Guttmann, *On the Philosophy of Religion* (Jerusalem: Magnes Press, 1976), 98.

There are indications that Maimonides may have had this same thing in mind. For example, we find in the *Guide*:

> "And thou shalt love the Lord thy God with all thy heart": the sense of the entire passage is: make the knowledge of God the aim of all thy actions…. We have already shown in the *Mishneh Torah* that this love is only possible when we comprehend the real nature of things and understand the divine wisdom displayed therein.
>
> The true worship of God (and highest human perfection) is possible only when correct notions of Him have previously been conceived … the intellect is the link that joins you to Him…. For it is said: "To love the Lord your God and to serve Him with all your heart and with all your soul" and as we have shown several times, man's love of God is identical with his knowledge of Him.[11]

It is clear that the knowledge which Maimonides is referring to, and which encompasses "a comprehension of all existence as it really is and God's wisdom contained therein," is really a philosophical knowledge. Also, the love that Maimonides speaks of is not the naive love of the average man but a philosophical, intellectual one.[12]

In this view, the passage in the Code in which Maimonides is explaining the *mitzvah* of *veahavtah* must be interpreted quite differently. We no longer have here a process consisting of distinct stages in which one goes from contemplation to understanding to love. We no longer have a suggestion by Maimonides as to how to generate love for God. What before us appers to be simply Maimonides' definition of the term "love of God." By stating that the "love" comes "immediately" and "necessarily," and by stating that "love is only possible if…," he is saying, in effect, that this "knowledge of God" is the necessary and sufficient condition for "love of God." Indeed, this is exactly what he is saying when he tells us: "Love of God is identical with knowledge of Him." If we accept this interpretation, then Maimonides' comparison of the Love of God to the human love described in *The Song of Songs* must be seen as analogical in a very strict sense, i.e., two very different things are called by the same name because of the resemblance of some secondary features.

---

[11] Moses Maimonides, *Guide for the Perplexed,* trans. M. Friedlander (New York: E. P. Dutton & Co., 1942), I:39; III:28; III:51.

[12] Simon Rawidowicz, *Studies in Jewish Thought* (Philadelphia: Jewish Publication Society, 1974), 291.

Of course, the original problem is now solved. The Torah, according to this view, is not legislating love; it is simply commanding that one acquires the knowledge of God, which *is* love of God. But can we accept this intellectualistic interpretation as the authentic explication of such a fundamental of Judaism as *veahavtah*?

In Maimonides' favor we should point out that certain key terms of the Torah do lend themselves to an intellectualistic interpretation. The prophetic literature abounds with urgings to acquire *da'at ha-Shem*, which is translated "knowledge of God." It is also true that the word *lev*, translated as "heart," can sometimes mean "understanding" so that the command "to love God with all your heart" can be taken to mean to have a love of God that comes through the intellect, which can be equated with knowledge of God.[13] The fact that Maimonides believed the intellect to link man with God encouraged the use of the love analogy, which implied union, Here, again, is *de'vaikut*! Moreover, as Rawidowicz points out, the link of the *ratio* is not something stable, but is capable of growing and diminishing, and the one who determines the growth or diminishment is man.[14] It follows, therefore, that man, in order to maintain and strengthen the link with God (upon which Special Providence depends), must aspire to a "persistent contemplation" of God's wisdom, an "absolute concentration of the thought on God." This emphasis on constancy fits in well with the religious sentiment "I place the Lord before me always," and can easily be expressed in emotional terms as "longing for God," "lovesickness," "passion for God," or "my soul thirsts for the Lord, for the living God."[15]

In spite of these points of resemblance, however, this approach, in its basic conception of the centrality of the intellect, does not seem compatible with the rest of Judaism. Many objective readings of Judaism, attentive to all aspects of the primary sources, suggest that we are dealing here not with an intellectualistic religion but with one in which morality is the major value.[16] Carrying through Guttmann's typology, it follows that with such a religion certain other characteristics are usually associ-

---

[13] Maimonides, *Guide*, I:39.
[14] Simon Rawidowicz, *Studies in Jewish Thought*, 279.
[15] Psalms 42:3.
[16] See S. Spero, *Morality, Halakha and the Jewish Tradition* (New York: Ktav and Yeshiva University Press, 1983).

ated: morality will be the way to achieve proximity to God; the divinity is necessarily a personal one (morality operates only between personal entities); the concept of love of God remains in the category of personal love even where the object of that love is infinite. What, then, are we to make of Maimonides' love of God?

Rabbi Joseph B. Soloveitchik gives voice to this difficulty in one of his articles, arguing that Maimonides is actually proposing an original doctrine in which the intellect and emotions fuse to produce an experience which is a combination of both. "Knowledge feeds the emotions but is also nourished by them." This love of God is not a synonym for a cold cognition. It is, rather, an experience which possesses the rich affective tones of feeling but, at the same time, partakes of the free-willed activity of the conscious intellect. Rabbi Soloveitchik remains faithful, nonetheless, to Maimonides' "intellectualistic" emphasis by concluding that what we have in Maimonides' teaching of *amor Dei* is not so much the *logic de coeur* (reasons or logic of the heart) as the emotionalization of the intellect: "intellectual awareness giving forth sparks of active bubbling emotion."[17]

I wish to propose a somewhat different interpretation of the *mitzvah* of *ahavat ha-Shem*, love of God, as suggested by Maimonides. I am not asserting that what I am about to say can be reconciled with the passages in the *Guide*. However, I do believe that it fits the words in the *Sefer ha-Mitzvot* and, possibly, the passage in the Code. But, independent of Maimonides, my account can explain how one can achieve love of God in a way which does justice to the requirements of the Torah as well as to our present-day understanding of reality.

The basis of my interpretation lies in a point underscored by Rabbi Soloveitchik and made by Guttmann and Rawidowicz which is that, contrary to Aristotle, the Torah is clear that God loves man.[18] Not only *ahavah* (love) but *heshek* (passion); not only *ahavah rabbah* but *ahavat olam*. As with the other attributes of God, the only real meaning we can give to the emotion "love" is in terms of action predicates. When one human being loves another, it follows that he will want to do good and give pleasure

---

[17] Rabbi Joseph B. Soloveitchik, "But From Thence Ye Will Seek...," *Hadarom* 47 (Tishrei 5739): 67-69, footnote 2.

[18] Y.J. Guttmann, *On the Philosophy of Religion*, 94; Rawidowicz, *Studies in Jewish Thought*, 293.

to his beloved, regardless of any question of the beloved being deserving. Similarly, therefore, if God loves man, it can be expected that the world will reflect that love; that God will endow human existence with "plus" factors which are not strictly necessary for His purposes but which give man pleasure; and that God will impart to the world values which man can naturally apprehend, derive pleasure from, and approve of.

This is, perhaps, the meaning of "And the Lord saw everything that He made and behold it was very good."[19] If the individual parts of the universe were simply "good" (as indicated by God's pronouncement at the end of each day's work), how can they all together be pronounced "very good"? Can there be more in the sum than the totality of the parts? The answer is yes, for while the word "good," which appears at the close of the description of most individual days of creation, signifies "good" in the sense of practical, useful, and workable, the expression "very good," when pronounced over the completed world seen as an integrated unity, is the "good" of aesthetic value in a very broad sense. When the universe was all put together, God "saw" (indicating a phenomenon accessible to sensual perception) that in His love He had created a world that was not only useful but beautiful, a world endowed with the values of moral goodness, aesthetic beauty, and cognitive truth which could be apprehended by man.[20]

When man is asked, therefore, to contemplate the world, what do we expect him to find? Scattered references to nature as pointing to God, such as Isaiah's "Lift up your eyes heavenward and see—who created these?" and "The heavens declare the glories of God" are usually interpreted as the scriptural version of the teleological argument for the existence of God, in which we proceed from a recognition of the feature of design in the world to the existence of a designer. But Maimonides' call to a contemplation of nature was, as we have seen, to lead us to a love of God! In the light of our new appreciation of the world as a place suffused with value because of the love of God for man, let us look carefully at Maimonides' teaching in *Sefer ha-Mitzvot*.

> The third commandment is that wherein He has commanded us concerning our love of Him, praised be He; that is to say, we are to dwell upon and contemplate His commandments, His statements

---

[19] Gen. 1:3.
[20] There is a reciprocal relationship between love and value. While the apprehension of value leads to love, love leads to the production of value.

and His deeds so that we may apprehend Him and thereby attain great pleasure, this constituting the love of Him with which we are charged.... We have thus explained to you that through this act of contemplation you will come to apprehend Him and reach that pleasure where love of Him will necessarily follow.

We notice immediately certain differences between the account in *Sefer ha-Mitzvot* and the account that we examined earlier from the Code. While in the latter we are asked to contemplate "His deeds and creatures both wondrous and great," in the *Sefer ha-Mitzvot* we are asked to contemplate "His commandments, His statements and His deeds."[21] In addition, Maimonides here seems to describe a somewhat different process leading to the love of God: (1) contemplation; (2) apprehension of God; (3) experience of pleasure; and (4) love of God (which follows necessarily from 3.)

What is important here is the reference to pleasure, which is not mentioned in the account in the *Mishneh Torah*, and the reference to "apprehension" or "understanding of God" *(hasagah)* which in the *Mishneh Torah* is referred to as God's "wisdom."

By "contemplation" we understand a procedure different from an examination undertaken, let us say, by a physician looking for abnormalities or traces of a specific disease. Contemplation consists of a riveting of attention and interest upon an object. One loses oneself in the object as in aesthetic contemplation, and becomes a clear mirror of the object. This is not to suggest that contemplation is a purely passive experience. Contemplation has been described as a complex of activity—consciousness charged with time and change, a veritable silent

---

[21] The only explanation that I can offer why, in *Mishneh Torah*, Maimonides spoke only of the contemplation of nature and did not mention the commandments as a way to develop love for God, is that perhaps there he was attempting to explain not only love of God but also fear of God, and wished to demonstrate that both can be generated by contemplating the very same things, Thus, he says, ".. pondering upon these very things themselves, he immediately recoils in fear and dread realizing he is but a minute, wretched mortal...." The only thing that could generate in a person fear or awe as well as love is something which contains not only value which produces love but great and wondrous phenomena of overwhelming magnitude which can produce a sense of the sublime, a sense of awe. This could not easily be achieved by the commandments but only by "His deeds and creatures wondrous and great."

whirlpool. Contemplation is attentive, concentrated, and alert, looking for meanings and relations but "bounded and made complete by an interest fulfilled within its borders."[22] That is to say, one does not engage in this sort of activity for the sake of some practical need whose ends lie outside of this experience. Through contemplation we open ourselves to the object, in our case "His commandments, His statements, and His deeds." But what we expect to find are intimations of value: in His commandments moral rightness and goodness; in His statements ("With Ten Statements the world was created") cognitive truth ultimately based on order and simplicity; in His deeds, the beauty, design, and sublimity found in the natural world.

But to experience any of these values is to apprehend God, because God *is* goodness and beauty and truth and the source of all such value experiences. This, then, can be taken as the meaning of Maimonides' point that in contemplating God's commandments, statements, and deeds we can arrive at an apprehension of God which is experienced as pleasure.

Indeed, the feeling of pleasure is the immediate awareness of value. But this pleasure, like aesthetic appreciation, is enjoyed for its own intrinsic value. We enjoy a work of art as an end and we are motivated to look or to listen solely for the experience contained in that act. If you recall the description of pure disinterested love cited earlier in the commentary on the Code, the example was precisely one of aesthetic appreciation of intrinsic value.

The objectivity of this kind of appreciation extends not only to the object, i.e., the commandments, but also to the emotion occasioned by the object, i.e., the pleasure of the value experience. Although it is obviously *my* pleasure, it is experienced in a disinterested or distanced fashion, not as my property. Neither the object nor the emotion is considered in relation to the self but objectively, as intrinsic worth which I associate with God.

This apprehension of value feeling, which is experienced as preferring, as desired and desirable, is already a form of loving. One wishes to get closer to the object of value, to remain in its presence, and what follows when this is associated with God is the desire, the passion, the love for God that is described in human terms in *The Song of Songs*.

---

[22] Arthur Berndtson, *Art Expression and Beauty* (New York: Holt, Rinehart and Winston, Inc., 1969), 89.

Chapter Ten. Love of God

There have been several ethicists, like G.E. Moore, Max Scheler, and N. Hartmann, who have defended the *a priori* nature of value feeling,[23] arguing that values belong to an absolute value realm, that they are given to us only in feeling but are independent of the feelings and transcend the attitudes that we have towards them. What is relevant to our problem is that all of these writers understand the apprehension of value to be a sort of cognition—a getting to know something significant about Being which would explain the constant conjunction which we seem to detect between knowledge of God and love of God. If love of God is based upon the discovery and apprehension of value in the world, then that is itself a form of knowing, inasmuch as value feelings are always directional and intentional. A value feeling that rejects and accepts, condemns and justifies, is a cognitive, emotional act and is to be distinguished from "feeling states such as being tired or elated or nauseated, which are essentially passive physiological states of affairs."

This, then, is how we can go about observing the important *mitzvah* of *ahavat ha-Shem* as suggested by the comments of Maimonides. God, in His love for man, has impregnated His creation with values which are a very real dimension of our world and which man can apprehend as an immediate pleasurable feeling of approval. .Man need only open himself to a disinterested contemplation of these values of moral rightness or, perhaps, holiness in the Torah, and to an aesthetic appreciation of nature, and it will result in love for the God who is Himself these values growing into a passionate longing to draw closer to Him.[24]

---

[23] W.H. Werkmeister, *Theories of Ethics* (Lincoln, NE: Johnsen Pub. Co., 1961), Part II, Section I, Chapter 7.

[24] This approach ties in with the notion of God as artist and the world as His work of art. Tolstoy wrote that art is the great medium through which human beings can communicate their emotions. God, then, in His love for man, has expressed His love through His creative work—this beautiful world—which man can contemplate aesthetically, receive the message of love from, and respond, in turn, with great pleasure and love to the artist.

Chapter Eleven

Selfhood and Godhood in Jewish Thought and Modern Philosophy

Similarities between man's understanding of himself and the personalistic concept of the biblical God are striking and have been noted frequently. The Bible itself teaches that man was created "in the image of God," implying that in some significant respects man resembles God. Some people, less sympathetic to religion and following a reductionist approach, have attempted to explain the similarities by suggesting that on the contrary, man, for a variety of conceptual and psychological reasons, fashioned the idea of God in his (man's) own image. In Jewish thought, the relationship between the concept of self and the concept of God has generally been developed in the direction of the latter to the former. That is, what was known about God was applied to man. This is as expected, since one usually proceeds from the known to the unknown. And what the Bible enabled us to affirm about God was more clear and specific than what we could say with any assurance about man. The point of resemblance between man and God that was most fruitfully developed by the rabbis was in regard to the moral nature and moral capacity of man. Nothing is more central to the Bible than the essentially moral nature of God. Ascribed to the Almighty are a series of moral acts of benevolence such as feeding the hungry, clothing the naked, providing for the lonely, and burying the dead, as well as performing acts of justice such as punishing the wicked, saving the righteous, and fulfilling His promises.[1] More important, in response to a request by Moses to be shown God's "glory" and His "ways," there follows a revelation of God's "goodness," in which He is described as "Lord, who is merciful and compassionate, long-suffering and abundant in kindness and truth...."[2] Since these moral predicates are expressed

---

[1] Gen. 2:16, 3:21, 2:21; Deut. 34:6; Gen. 18; Exod. 3.
[2] Exod. 34:6.

in the form of generalized dispositional attributes, they reveal a more profound and more essential relationship between God and morality than the ascription of individual moral acts. An individual may perform sporadic moral acts and yet not possess a moral character. To be "merciful" is to have developed a resident moral character to the point that one can confidently expect only moral acts.

But man is commanded to "walk after the Lord your God" and to "walk in His ways."[3] This is interpreted to mean, "I must make myself like unto Him. As He is compassionate and gracious, be also compassionate and gracious."

Actually, two principles flow from this concept of *imitatio Dei*. One is that man has the moral capacity, the insight, to know the right and the good, and the freedom to choose the right and the good. Second, man has the obligation to seek out and walk the moral path, which is the *derech Hashem*. What emerges is that man's resemblance to God has a static as well as dynamic aspect. Man, by virtue of what he is, is already a moral agent—free and responsible. But man has yet to develop a moral personality. It was in this sense that the rabbis noted the different terms mentioned in the biblical passage announcing the creation of man. "Let us make man in our image *(tselem)* after our likeness *(demut)*."[4] While God does create man in His image and confers irreducible value upon him, the "likeness," which is the process of *"becoming like,"* lies in the hands of man.[5] He has yet to fulfill this destiny by living a moral life and exercising his divine "image." Man must therefore look to God to learn who he (man) is and to discover what he (man) has yet to do.

In rabbinic literature we do not find any serious effort to cultivate the relationship between selfhood and Godhood in the opposite direction (i.e., to utilize our knowledge of selfhood as a means of enhancing our understanding of the nature of Godhood). As already indicated, there was no real reason to do so, as the intellectual climate and condition of belief were such as to place knowledge of self lower on the cognitive

---

[3] Deut. 10:12.
[4] Gen. 1:26.
[5] This is why in describing the actual act of creation in Gen. 1:27, the Bible states only that God created man in his *tselem*, but does not mention *demut*.

scale than knowledge of God. Furthermore, whatever problems these early thinkers may have had with the concept of God, they were not of the kind that could be elucidated by our knowledge of self.

However, we do find a talmudic teaching in the name of R. Shimi Ben Ukba that draws some interesting parallels between the soul or the self and God, but apparently only for a homiletical purpose:

> Five times did David say, "Bless the lord, O my soul." In reference to what was it said? He said it in reference to the Holy One, blessed be He (God) and in reference to the soul. Just as God fills the entire world, so does the soul fill the entire body. Just as God sees but cannot be seen, so does the soul see but cannot be seen. Just as God nourishes the entire world, so does the soul nourish the entire body. Just as God is pure so is the soul pure. Just as God dwells in an innermost place, so does the soul dwell in an innermost place. Therefore, let the soul which possesses these five attributes come and praise Him to whom these five attributes belong.[6]

Although the wording in this passage is from God to the soul, some of the parallels listed suggested a possible reverse approach to Rabbi Gamaliel, who was once asked by a skeptic, "Where is your God located?"

Rabbi Gamaliel replied, "I do not know."

The other said to him, "Is this your wisdom that you daily offer prayers to Him without knowing where He is?"

Rabbi Gamaliel answered him, "You have questioned me concerning One who is remote from me ... let me question you about something which is with you day and night. Tell me, where is your soul?" The man said, "I do not know."[7]

Here Rabbi Gamaliel points to a familiar and accepted concept—a nonspatial entity called the "soul"—as a possible model for forming a conception about an invisible and incorporeal God. Once we have a situation in which our concept of God has become unintelligible or unconvincing, whereas the notion of selfhood remains a common experience accessible to introspection, the balance has shifted so cognitive illumination can flow from selfhood to Godhood. Indicative of this fact is the

---

[6] *Berakhot* 10a.
[7] Midrash on Psalms 103.

changed sequence of these elements at the conclusion of the midrash: "In the same manner that nobody knows the place of the soul, so does nobody know the place of the Holy One, blessed be He."[8]

Maimonides, whose theological situation was also one of guiding the religiously perplexed, made extensive use of the analogy between God and the universe on one hand and the individual soul and body on the other. In a long chapter, Maimonides develops the notion, already familiar to the rabbis, of man as microcosm, and points out in great detail the structural and organic similarities between man as an individual and the universe as a whole.[9] The crucial element of the parallel, however, lies in the fact that

> in man there is a certain force which unites the members of the body, controls them and gives to each of them what it requires.... It is man's intellectual faculties which enable him to think, consider and act and which governs all the forces of the body.
>
> There also exists in the universe a certain force which controls the whole, which sets in motion the chief and principal parts and gives them the motivepower for governing the rest.... It is the source of the existence of the Universe in all parts. That force is God, blessed be His name.[10]

---

[8] This direction from "soul" to "God" is also seen in another version of the Talmudic teaching found in *Vayikira Rabbah* IV:8.

> What reason did David see for praising the Holy One, blessed be He (God) with his soul? He said: the soul fills the body and *God* fills the universe, as it is written ... let the soul which fills the body come and praise God who fills all the universe. The soul carries (sustains or supports) the body and God carries His universe ... let the soul.... The soul outlasts the body and God outlives the world, let.... The soul is the only one in the body and God is the only one in the universe .... The soul within the body does not eat and as for God there is no eating with Him.... The soul sees but is not seen and God sees but is not seen.... The soul is a pure element in the body and God is the pure one in the universe.... The soul in the body is never asleep and as for God there is no sleep with Him.... let the soul.... (Soncino English Edition)

[9] Moses Maimonides, *Guide for the Perplexed,* trans. M. Friedlander (New York: E. P. Dutton & Co., 1942), chapter I:72.

[10] Maimonides, *Guide*, I:72.

Maimonides is quick to point out that the analogy between man and the universe does not hold in all respects and that there are discrepancies in regard to three points. One is that while man's rational faculty "is a force inherent in the body and not separate from it, God is not a force inherent in the body of the universe but is separate from all of its parts."[11]

What is Maimonides' purpose in drawing the parallel between man and the universe, between the soul and God? It does not seem to be the case that Maimonides is merely indulging in the medievalists' penchant to exhibit the Divine aesthetic by pointing to similar forms and patterns that are repeated in various parts of the creation, for the aesthetic aspect is surely spoiled by the three points in respect to which the analogy breaks down. I suggest that Maimonides realized that there was no way in which he could rationally explicate the manner in which God rules the universe. In his own words:

> How God rules the universe and provides for it is a complete mystery; man is unable to solve it. For on the one hand it can be proven that God is separate from the universe and in no contact whatever with it; but on the other hand, His rule and providence can be proven to exist in all parts of the universe, even in the smallest.[12]

If, however, we go back to the case of man and try to comprehend how the self relates to the body and how the intellect functions as it does, we are confronted by a similar mystery: "The intellect is the highest of all faculties of living creatures; it is very difficult to comprehend and its true character cannot be understood as easily as man's other faculties."

What this analogy tries to generate is a sort of intellectual humility or agnostic consistency. All of us, through introspection, are directly aware of our subjectivity as an abiding continuant, as a unitary self that is most clearly felt in the active role of deciding or willing and which is causally efficacious in the world. "*I deliberate; I act; I remember. Therefore, I am.*"

---

[11] Ibid.
[12] Ibid.

Chapter Eleven. Selfhood and Godhood in Jewish Thought and Modern Philosophy

But neither philosophy nor science has been able to provide an account of the self that would do justice to the introspective evidence of a spirit-like entity and, at the same time, explain its connection with the physical processes of the body. Yet our inability to comprehend the interaction between body and consciousness causes few people to give up their common sense notion of the self as agent. So, too, the fact that we cannot explain how God rules the universe can perhaps be seen as an acceptable measure of mystery within what to Maimonides, at least, must have seemed to be a generally rational scheme of religious belief. Similarly, Rabbi Gamaliel's reply to the skeptic shames him into silence by pointing out that his own self is nonspatial and yet pretty "real" and "alive."

Surely, therefore, the fact that we cannot pinpoint God's location should not deter us from His worship.

In recent years much of the thrust of philosophy of religion has been in the area of meaning rather than truth. That is, the critical apparatus of analytic thought has questioned not whether the basic assertions of religion are true, but whether they make sense. Terms and concepts such as "God," "God's existence," "God's love," "God as Lord of history," and "God as creator of the world" have all been judged as resistant to the ordinary meaning of these terms and therefore empty of sense.

One attempt to fix the reference range of words such as God and to show that the concept of God is not an empty notion makes use of what has been called the allusive function of language.[13] Thus, when we speak of God as a transcendent being or as a spirit, we are using words designed to give us an *impression* of the Divine, *hint* at Him, *suggest* Him. There is no suggestion here of having properties in common or of analogates bearing resemblances to each other.

One of the examples found in current discussions is the use of the word "spirit," by which we designate God as transcendent or metaempirical. Can we give any intelligible content to this notion? What do we have in mind when we talk of a God who is a being outside of space and time and on whom the spatio-temporal universe is in some sense dependent?

Several writers suggest that our willingness to entertain such a notion stems from the self-awareness that we all experience, which is the ground for the intuitive conviction that we ourselves are not simply

---

[13] See the discussion in chapter 9 beginning p. 175.

spatio-temporal objects.¹⁴ Much of what goes on within us can be described from the point of view of the observer using physicalist or behaviorist language. However, when we regard ourselves from within as agents, we find that certain portions of our experience, such as loving, feeling, and hoping, are adequately described only when we use nonphysical concepts. There is something nonspatial about these experiences. It is argued that each of us has a direct awareness of our own subjectivity, a sense of identity that goes beyond the most exhaustive description of distinguishing traits.

> There is a subjectivity which each of us realizes for himself which is not and logically could not be exhausted by any number of third person designates, however far they went and however various they were. Here then is fact—my own existence as I know it in its full subjectivity which eludes any exhaustive direct description.¹⁵

Ramsey calls this a "paradigm of mystery."

To be sure, these writers are not presenting this as evidence for the existence of a "soul," not claiming that because we experience something like *spirit*, there *exists* something like *spirit*. Nor do they claim that we have a perfectly clear concept of "pure being" or "disembodied spirit." Their point is simply that we are able to have some concept of a being independent of space, that by abstraction from ordinary experience we can gain some hint of a reality where "what is imperfectly realized in us is fully and perfectly realized." What we are therefore doing when we draft a word for theological use and describe God as a pure spirit is deliberately to commit a "category mistake." We are asserting first that "spirit" retains specific meaning by connection with spirituality as the name of a human aspect, and second that it is to be governed by a rule that declares that the norm is not to be taken as an abstract noun such as "smile" but as a concrete noun such as "man."¹⁶

---

[14] I.M. Crombie, "The Possibility of Theological Statements," in *Religious Language and the Problem of Religious Knowledge,* ed. Ronald E. Santoni (Bloomington and London: Indiana University Press, 1968); Ian T. Ramsey, "On Understanding Mystery," in *Philosophy and Religion,* ed. J.A. Gill (Minneapolis: Burgess, 1968).

[15] Ramsey, "On Understanding Mystery," 298.

[16] Crombie, "The Possibility of Theological Statements," 110.

Chapter Eleven. Selfhood and Godhood in Jewish Thought and Modern Philosophy

Let us paraphrase the midrash in light of this: "In the same manner as we experience our own subjectivity—as a conscious, nonspatial active agent or spirit—so too may we conceive of the Holy One, blessed be He, as pure or perfect spirit." Here selfhood is used to help us to achieve a conception of the Divine.

A second instance of interaction between selfhood and Godhood is one where the level rises from facilitating conception to perceiving a real possibility. This involves the traditional metaphysical problem of freedom of the will. What has kept this problem alive in contemporary philosophy is the pressure that emanates from two areas of human experience. First, the entire concept of moral responsibility and the juridical apparatus and social sanctions based on it seem to assume the possibility of moral acts that are freely chosen by the self and express the purposes of the self. Thus we are not free and therefore not responsible when (1) our limbs are set in motion by some external physical agency, (2) we act in ignorance of the special circumstances in the situation, or (3) our action is the result of some uncontrollable emotion or the effects of drugs or alcohol or "brain-washing." Moreover, the language of moral judgment expressed in sentences such as, "You ought not to have done X" implies that "You could have refrained from doing X." "Ought" implies "can." The "freedom of will" required by the concept of moral responsibility includes the possibility that the agent could have done other than what he did. This implies what has been called "contracausal" freedom (i.e., that the self, in a moral struggle between his strongest desire flowing from his character as so far formed and his sense of duty, is able to adopt either alternative). This he can do by an exertion of what we call "willpower," which suggests the opening of new sources of energy. What this means in effect is that in a moral situation, the decision that is made by the agent is essentially unpredictable. Assuming a complete and perfect knowledge of the heredity, environment, and character of the agent, it would nevertheless have been impossible to foretell his decision.[17]

---

[17] Those who uphold the doctrine of freedom of the will can agree that there are wide areas of human conduct involving practical interests where contracausal freedom does not operate because there is no need for it. Here "will" and decision conform to "strongest desire." In these areas, therefore, prediction is possible and, indeed, often does take place.

The second source of support for the doctrine of moral freedom is our own immediate experience. There is no doubt that we all feel ourselves to be free in the sense just described. There are many decisions we make in life after prolonged deliberation where we just "know" we could have chosen otherwise. From the standpoint of our practical self-consciousness, from the internal standpoint of living experience, we are "certain that it lies with ourselves to decide whether we shall let our character as so far formed dictate our action or whether we shall by effort oppose its dictates and rise to duty." In short, immediate experience makes us certain that our act is not determined by the totality of our past, and yet we are equally certain that the act is determined by our *self*.[18]

In spite of the best efforts of many thinkers to show that the freedom-of-will issue is a pseudo-problem and that ordinary notions of moral responsibility can be reconciled with a deterministic picture of the universe as revealed by modern science, the issue remains alive, with the philosophical edge, in my judgment, remaining in favor of the Libertarians.[19]

Religious Jews obviously have a vital stake in the outcome of this philosophical controversy. Human beings could hardly be the recipients of moral and ritual *mitzvot* and be held responsible for their observance if they did not possess contracausal freedom. The specific biblical texts are equally clear. "Sin croucheth by the door ... and unto thee is its desire but thou mayest rule over it,"[20] and "I have set before thee, the blessing and the curse; therefore choose life."[21] And Maimonides points out that man's freedom to be righteous or wicked is "the pillar of the Torah" and "the principle upon which all the words of the Prophets rest."[22]

---

[18] Charles A. Campbell, "In Defence of Free Will," in *A Modern Introduction to Ethics*, ed. Milton K. Munitz (Glencoe, IL: Free Press, 1958).

[19] Recent attempts by the Skinner school of psychology to argue that man is *beyond freedom and dignity* were given a devastating critique by Noam Chomsky in the December 30, 1971, issue of the *New York Review of Books*.

[20] Gen. 4:7.

[21] Deut. 30:19.

[22] *Rambam, Hilkhot Tshuva*, Chap. 5. See Isaac Abarbanel in his *Rosh Amana*, Ch. 16, where he explains why Maimonides did not list freedom of will among his 13 principles of faith.

Chapter Eleven. Selfhood and Godhood in Jewish Thought and Modern Philosophy

Aside from the intrinsic importance of this principle, freedom of the will can be viewed as another instance of how selfhood can point us in the direction of Godhood. If, indeed, man has contracausal freedom, what does this imply about the nature of the universe in which we live? It would mean that there is at least one small area of which we are clearly aware wherein the iron laws of determinism do not apply; one exception to the tightly woven network of cause and effect that grips the rest of nature; one chink in the causal nexus through which the self is able to introduce new spiritual energy and moral power. But this would be dramatic evidence of the biblical teaching that the human being transcends nature by virtue of the selfhood implanted in him by God. While in all other respects man is part of nature *(takhtonim)*, his soul or self is an endowment from another order *(elyonim)*, so that he alone is *responsible* (i.e., capable of freely responding to a Divine command, of overruling his strongest desire). It is perhaps in this sense that a נסיון *(nissayon)*, test, is related to a נס *(ness)*, miracle.[23] In a moral test (נסיון), man, if he is successful, exerts his freedom and transcends his own nature. In a "miracle," God exerts His freedom and contravenes the course of nature. A person who passes a moral test has actually performed a "miracle," has overcome his nature as so far formed. Maimonides points to the passage "Behold man has become as one of us to know good and evil" as referring to the fact that man is unique in possessing the power of free choice.[24] This is a capacity that makes man akin to God.

Indeed, if we follow the reasoning of those who maintain that the moral decisions of the individual are in principle unpredictable, we come upon another interesting insight. It is argued that in order to predict a person's conduct one would have to have a complete knowledge of his character and circumstances. But you could not possibly have this sort of knowledge of a person until the end of his life. "Character" is not a fixed quality given once and for all at a certain period and henceforth constant. It is in the making throughout life.[25] Developing

---

[23] See Sefat Emet, Part 1, *Yayera* (New York), 78.
[24] Gen. 3:22. This may be the meaning of the similarity pointed to in *Vayikra Rabbah*, "As the soul is one in the body so God is one in the universe."
[25] Alfred Edward Taylor, *Elements of Metaphysics* (London: University Paperbacks, 1903), 375.

moral experience is possibly the only truly creative activity open to man, the only avenue through which he can introduce true novelty into the world.

If man is free and creative in this sense, we do not live in a closed "block" universe. We therefore have another example of moving from selfhood to an understanding of Godhood. If man can act in contra-causal freedom and thus weave new and unexpected additions to the unhemmed fringes of his personality, it surely is easier to accept the notion of a God who is the uncaused cause and who mysteriously has input into nature and history and is the creator *par excellence*.[26] In the same manner as we know ourselves to be free, to act responsibly, and to create new dimensions of character and personality, so too might there exist a God who is the source of our freedom and creativity and possesses these qualities to a perfect degree. Obadiah S'forno comments on the passage "And God created man in His own image," saying: "In part man is similar to the Almighty who also acts in freedom. However, God always freely chooses the good, which is not the case with man."[27]

A third area where knowledge of self can lead to knowledge of God involves not the knowledge of self but knowledge of other selves. This is an old and familiar epistemological puzzle known as the problem of other minds; it has been discussed for a long time by the philosophers. Each of us believes that we are not alone in the world. There are other beings who think and reason, have sensations and feelings just as we do. However, while a person can observe in others behavior and circumstance, he cannot directly perceive their mental states. We cannot observe the thoughts and feelings of other humans. How then do we know, for example, that a friend, B, is in pain? What is our evidence?

The most plausible answer to this question is the analogical approach, first suggested by Descartes and Locke and since endorsed by a number of modern thinkers. I start with my own case, where I associate certain external pain-behavior (facial grimaces, sighs and groans, clutching of

---

[26] See Meir Simcha of D'vinsk, *Meshekh Hokhma, Parashat Shelach* (Jerusalem), 220-221 that *tzitzit*, or ritual fringes, symbolizes the unfinished state of the universe that it is man's obligation to complete.

[27] Sforno on Genesis 1:27.

certain parts of the body, etc.) with the internal feeling of pain. From there, I proceed to infer from the pain-behavior of others that they must also be experiencing a feeling of pain similar to my own. This analogical approach, which is based on an inductive argument, may schematically be represented as follows:

> 1) Every case of pain-behavior that I have determined by observation, whether or not it was accompanied by pain in the body displaying it (i.e., my own case), was accompanied by pain in that body.
>
> 2) Probably every case of pain-behavior is accompanied by pain in the body displaying it.
>
> 3) B over there is displaying pain behavior.
>
> 4) Probably B feels a pain.

This inductive argument is strikingly similar in form to the traditional teleological argument for the existence of God (generally considered to be the most persuasive of the arguments in the repertoire of natural theology), which can be expressed as follows:

> 1) Everything that exhibits curious adaptation of means to ends and is such that we know whether or not it was the product of intelligent design, was in fact the product of intelligent design.
>
> 2) The universe exhibits curious adaptation of means to ends.
>
> 3) Therefore, the universe is probably the product of intelligent design.

Alvin Plantinga, in a detailed and complex analysis, convincingly demonstrates that both arguments fall victim to similar objections.[28] While much of what he writes is too technical to reproduce here, his conclusion is based on the fact that in both cases the specific evidence on hand supports only one or two of a number of propositions, all of which would have to be upheld in order to arrive at the desired conclusion. Thus, in the case of the teleological argument, to conclude that God exists one would have to maintain not only that the universe is

---

[28] Alvin Plantinga, *God and Other Minds* (Ithaca, NY: Cornell University Press, 1967).

designed (which the evidence *does* support), but also that the following propositions for which the evidence is ambiguous are true:

> 1) The universe is designed by exactly one being.
>
> 2) The universe was created *ex nihilo*.
>
> 3) The universe was created by the being who designed it.
>
> 4) The creator of the universe is omniscient, omnipotent, and perfectly good.
>
> 5) The creator of the universe is an eternal spirit without bodily attributes.

In regard to the analogical argument for the existence of other minds there is likewise a set of additional propositions, the conjunction of which is not rendered more probable by the evidence at hand. These are:

> 1) I am not the only being that feels pain.
>
> 2) There are some pains that I do not feel.
>
> 3) Sometimes certain areas of my body are free from pain.
>
> 4) There are some pains that are not in my body.
>
> 5) There are some cases of pain that are not accompanied by pain-behavior on the part of my body.
>
> 6) I am the only person who feels pain in my body.
>
> 7) Sometimes someone feels pain when I do not.

It seems that the conjunction of the propositions of the teleological argument are as probable on the evidence as is the analogical argument on its evidence. Therefore Plantinga concludes, "If my belief in other minds is rational, so is my belief in God. But obviously the former is rational, so therefore is the latter."[29]

Whether or not Plantinga's conclusion is beyond question is irrelevant for our present purposes. I refer to his thesis only to show that here we have another instance in modern philosophy where selfhood is seen to serve as a guide to Godhood.

---

[29] Plantinga, *God and Other Minds*, 271.

There is a rabbinic teaching that says: "Know what is above (from) you, an eye sees and an ear hears, and all of your deeds are recorded in a book."[30] Some commentators interpreted this in a novel way: "Know what is above?" Do you wish to gain insight into the One above? "(From) You." Think about yourself. Analyze your own selfhood. From your own introspection learn about God. For, as we have seen, awareness of the mystery of self can give us somewhat of a conception of the eternal spirit that is God; the immediate experience of our own freedom makes it easier to believe in the Holy One who is truly free, and, just as we are rationally unembarrassed by our belief in other minds though the evidence and reasons are incomplete, so too we need not shrink from taking the "leap of faith" even though the rational support for that move is not conclusive.

---

[30] *Avot* 2:1.

Chapter Twelve

Unity of God as Dynamic of Redemption

Happy are we! How good is our destiny, how pleasant our lot, how beautiful our heritage ... who early and late, morning and evening, twice every day proclaim: Hear O Israel, the Lord our God, the Lord is One.

—*Morning Prayer*

Recent popular expositions of Judaism. have been equally rhapsodic in describing the centrality and terminal quality of these six words of scripture, known as the *Shema*, and the theological principle they proclaim—the unity of G-d. Quite correctly, this utterance has been variously characterized as "the fundamental thought in Judaism,"[1] "the historic battle cry of Israel,"[2] "the kernel of Jewish prayer,"[3] and "the essence of our Law,"[4] and it is rightfully pointed out that these are the first words of prayer taught to a child, the last conscious words uttered at the death bed, and the words "heroically proclaimed by countless martyrs in their agony." However, in none of these works is the evaluation substantiated or the importance of the principle adequately explained. As a creedal affirmation for the martyr, the reader might more readily appreciate Job's "I know that my redeemer liveth," a confession of faith in God's existence and in His reality rather than in His oneness. To proclaim that G-d is one and not two would seem to the modern mind to be quite irrelevant. The battle against polytheism has long been over. True, we have contributed to the world the notion of monotheism, but why gloat over a contribution that has long ago passed into the mainstream of western civilization?

Should the reader in his quest for enlightenment repair to our philosophers of the middle ages, he would receive little comfort. True, his

---

[1] Meyer Waxman, *Judaism: Religion and Ethics* (New York: T. Yoseloff, 1958), 139.
[2] Beryl D. Cohon, *Judaism in Theory and Practice* (New York: Bloch, 1954), 65.
[3] David DeSola Pool, *Why I Am a Jew* (Nashville, TN: Thomas Nelson and Sons, 1957), 99.
[4] Herman Wouk, *This Is My God* (New York: Doubleday, 1978), 115.

Chapter Twelve. Unity of God as Dynamic of Redemption

understanding of the word "one" would deepen. He would learn that G-d is one not only in a numerical sense of one and not two but also in the sense of simplicity—that is to say that God is not a composite, contains no multiplicity of parts or any element superadded to His essence. Even essential attributes such as God's will, intelligence, and existence must be understood as identical with His essence.

One would further discover that "one" also means unique, i.e., that there is no other unity like God's unity. God is not a member of any class and hence is indescribable and ineffable.

Finally, if our diligent student perseveres, he will be introduced to the subtle distinction between absolute existence and contingent existence. God is unique in that He is the only true and necessary existent. God is one and only because He is the form and final purpose of the entire universe, or, if you wish, the ontological grounds of all and therefore the only truly real.

Armed with his philosophic gleanings, our reader returns to the *Shema* prayer. Does he now understand why this is the phrase uttered by the Jew on his deathbed? Does he now appreciate the relevance of these words on the lips of the martyr in his agony? I submit that he does not. It is rather curious that our systematic thinkers, such as Saadia Gaon, Maimonides, Albo, and Crescas completely overlooked the implication of God's unity for ethics and history. They transformed a religious dynamic into an academic abstraction. Yet the philosophically less-sophisticated representatives of traditional Judaism in the times of the Midrash had intuitively perceived what is clearly the sense of scripture's understanding of the unity and oneness of God. It is first in the Kabbalistic tradition and in those Jewish thinkers touched by it that we find the midrashic insights appreciated and reinstated.

Bachya ibn Pakuda was almost alone among the medieval rationalist philosophers in perceiving the ethical connotations of the doctrine of the unity of G-d. His inquiry into the duties of the heart provided him with that particular orientation which does a maximum of justice to biblical fundamentals, enabling him to see their "practical" implications.

Bachya concludes his philosophic analysis of the concept of the unity of God with the words, "The unity of God requires that the heart and the tongue should be alike in acknowledging the onlyness of God."[5]

---

[5] Bachya ibn Pakuda, *Duties of the Heart*, Sha'ar Hayikhud, Chap. 1.

Therefore, says Bachya, the following would constitute violations of the unity of God: worshipping other gods; serving idols, fetishes, or spirits; holding up any human being for deification; placing reliance in false doctrines; becoming a slave to his own passions and desires, as it is written; "There shall not be *in you* a strange G-d."[6]

What emerges clearly from this approach is first the notion that the unity of G-d is a *mitzvah* and not merely an academic philosophic principle. This is obviously the sense of the biblical injunction, "And ye shall know this day and consider it in thine heart, that the Lord, He is God in heaven above and upon the earth beneath: there is none else."[7] But more important (and here we part company with Maimonides, who, while considering Unity a mitzvah, saw it only as a command to believe[8]), this mitzvah has ethical and behavioural implications. The Jew who seriously believes in "the Lord is One" must experience his conscious life and act in real life as if there is no other power, human or superhuman, doctrinal or passional, which can be independently effective outside of God. Therefore, there shall be no power, human or superhuman, doctrinal or passional which we shall serve or pledge allegiance to or permit to influence our lives outside of God.

Hence Bachya follows his analysis of *Yichud Elokim* with a chapter later on entitled *Yichud Hamaaseh*, which indicates that the "One and Only" G-d must be served exclusively.

It is quite apparent that the rabbis who wrote the Midrash saw in the *Shema* the same ethical implications. They write that when Jacob on his deathbed summoned his children and questioned their faith in G-d, he was answered, "Hear O Israel (Jacob), the Lord our God, the Lord is One—as there is only one in your heart so is there only *one* in our hearts." To this Jacob in his joy responded, "blessed be the name of the glory of His kingdom forever and ever."[9]

Already in the Midrash, therefore, the general principle that the Lord is One becomes transformed at least in one of its senses, into a personal affirmation that the Lord reigns exclusively in one's heart.

---

[6] Ibid., end of Chap. 10.
[7] Deut. 5:39.
[8] Maimonides, *Sefer Hamitzvot,* Positive Command 2.
[9] *Bereishit Rabbah*. 98:4.

Chapter Twelve. Unity of God as Dynamic of Redemption

In reality, this ethical corollary of the *Shema* is implied quite clearly in the Bible. Directly following "the Lord is One," we read, "And you shall love the Lord your God with *all* your heart and with *all* your soul and with *all* your might."[10] If the Lord is one and there is no other, then no part of our personality may remain uncommitted to Him. The themes of love and unity are thus combined in the benediction immediately preceding the *Shema* in the daily prayer service: "And unite out hearts to love ... and to acknowledge your unity in love."

There is however, an additional point to be made in connection with the ethical implications of God's unity. What we are saying is not simply that human acknowledgement of the unity of G-d involves certain ethical corollaries, for the unity of God, unlike His other attributes, does not remain detached from and unaffected by human actions and reactions. Note the consistent use of the transitive form of the verb in such expressions as "a people who unify His name."[11] This is not a question of merely *recognizing* the unity of God but is a matter of actually sustaining it in fact. The rabbis remark in the Midrash: "As I have not associated another god with Thee in heaven so upon earth too, I have not associated with Thee any other God—but I daily enter the synagogue and testify concerning Thee that there is no other god but Thou and I exclaim: Hear O Israel, the Lord our God, the Lord is One."[12]

As God exists alone in the heavens, there being no other gods aside from Him, so too if God is one, He must reign alone on earth in the regard and loyalty of men. If men create other gods, serve other interests, or give allegiance to other factors in life, then they have in fact raised other powers in the world to the point where they are influential and are affecting reality in a manner not ordained by God. God's unity, God's "aloneness," has been compromised.

What distinguishes the rabbinic insight into the unity of God from the analysis of the philosophers is that the former garnered a rich conceptual harvest from the "superficial" numerical sense of God being one and not two. The reason they went further with this negation than their medieval colleagues did was because they saw as the principle adversary of God not other gods, but man in his overweening pride and arrogance.

---

[10] Deut. 6:5.
[11] Kedusha, Sabbath Musaf Service.
[12] *Devarim Rabbah*, 2:23.

Indeed, from the very beginning man in his disobedience was seen as G-d's "competitor."[13] In Isaiah too it is quite clear that it is man and his constructs who stands in opposition to G-d and His unity: "The loftiness of man shall be lowered down, and the haughtiness of men shall be brought low; and the Lord alone shall be exalted in that day."[14]

We are now in a position to comprehend the significance of the unity of God as the underlying dynamic in the Jewish concept of history. We read in the prophet the oft-quoted "On that day, the Lord will be One and His name will be One."[15] Most commentators interpret this to mean that in the end of days—in the Messianic era—God will be recognized as the One and only. However, the text is clearly suggesting something else, namely that so long as there are segments of humanity that recognize other forces as operating independently in history, God's unity is *in actual fact* being compromised and violated. In short, first *on that day* will God truly be One. What we have here therefore is the ethical implication of God's unity for the individual, transposed to the historical level.

In his commentary of the Shema, Rashi gives the following interpretation:

> "The Lord our God, the Lord is One."
> "The Lord" who is "Our God" now, and not the God of the nations, He will be in the future "One Lord," as it is stated. "For then will I turn to the peoples a pure language that they may all call upon the Lord." And it is stated "in that day shall the Lord be One and His name one."

Although basing himself on a Sifre, Rashi upon first *examination seems to* have departed unnecessarily from the plain meaning of the text.[16] While the Zachariah passage is in the future tense and therefore carries a Messianic connotation, the *Shema* simply states that the "Lord is One" now. The final line in our progression of ideas is drawn by the Maharal, who after noting the apparent difficulty in Rashi states:

---

[13] Gen. 3:22.
[14] Isa. 2: 17.
[15] Zech. 14:9.
[16] See the supercommentary of Rabbi Elijah Mizrachi on this passage.

Chapter Twelve. Unity of God as Dynamic of Redemption

> This is the principle sense of the unity of the Almighty ... that He is One now becomes most apparent when we realize that in the end He alone will reign.
>
> From this we understand that all power and influence exercised by kings and princes today is only temporary and borrowed, for in the end He alone will reign.[17]

The concept is now complete: "the Lord, He is God and there is none else beside Him." Thus every individual Jew must serve God alone and not raise up any other "powers" beside Him. When in the course of history we see entire nations and cultures populating the world with the thousand and one gods of their own making which appear to be propelling history in a direction counter to the plan of God then to know that God *is* One is to know that the Kingdom of evil will be crushed on the historical plane and God alone will reign in the regard and worship of His creatures. And, so, ultimate redemption or the Messianic vision becomes an inescapable conclusion flowing from the concept of God's unity.

This was graphically taught by Rabbi Isaac of Corbeil, who questions the justice of the Talmudic teaching that one of the questions asked of a man on the day of judgement will be "Did you hope for the redemption?"[18] Where, asks Rabbi Isaac, were we ever commanded to hope for a redemption, so that we should be held accountable for doing so? In reality, however, concludes the rabbi, in the very first commandment, "I am the Lord your God who brought you forth out of Egypt," we are taught that acknowledgement of the one God has meant redemption in the past and will ensure redemption in the future.[19]

It is strange that many historians should have missed this very basic connection between G-d's unity and the vision of redemption.[20]

To see the Messianic hope as generated by an awareness of G-d's justice is to account only for an expectation of redemption based upon Israel's worth or repentance. It leaves unexplained, however, the Jewish conviction of a necessary, inevitable end to history.

Other psychological explanations are equally unconvincing: "the people of Israel did not have a glorious past hence it was forced to direct

---

[17] Rabbi Judah Loew of Prague, *Gur Aryeh* on Deut. 6:4.
[18] *Shabbat* 31.
[19] Rabbi Isaac of Corbeil, *Sefer Mitzvot Katan*.
[20] A notable exception was the philosopher Hermann Cohen.

its gaze toward a glorious future,"[21] or "it is perfectly natural that a people with such a past would long for a happier future."[22] Such explanations leave us to wonder by what strange alchemy the Jewish people was able to transform wishful thinking into a unique national vision of such strength and intensity as the Messianic expectation.

If we examine the Bible, we find that from the beginning God appears as a redeemer to individuals in specific immediate situations. Noah is saved, Abraham is rescued, Jacob is redeemed. With respect to the Egyptian bondage, God appears as redeemer in fulfillment of a specific promise made to Abraham. However, already here Moses declares that the purpose of the redemption is "in order that ye may know there is none as the Lord, our God,"[23] and "in order that ye may know that there is none like unto me in all the world."[24] The fact that all the wise men of Egypt and their manifold deities cannot prevent the fulfillment of God's promise demonstrates that God in His power and freedom to act is unique—God is One.

In all of the other books of the Pentateuch where the text speaks of exile and suffering and promises redemption, it is always held out on condition: "If you will walk in my statutes ... a blessing, if you obey ... and thou shalt return unto the Lord ... then the Lord thy God will turn thy captivity."

There is, however, one exception. In the last Song of Moses we are told of the downfall of Israel's enemies, of the recognition of the nations, and of forgiveness for Israel.[25] Here, as Nachmanides has noted, there are no conditions and no prerequisites in terms of either repentance or special service.[26] Introducing this prophecy are the significant words, "See now that I, even I, am He, and there are no gods with Me."[27]

Again, God's unity will necessitate ultimate redemption, irrespective of what course human history may seem to take.

---

[21] J.H. Greenstone, *Messiah Idea in Jewish History* (Westport, CT: Greenwood, 1972), 24.
[22] Joseph Klausner, *The Messianic Idea in Israel* (New York: The Macmillan Company, 1955), 15.
[23] Exod. 8:6.
[24] Exod. 9:14.
[25] Deut. 32:43.
[26] Commentary of Nachmanides on Deut. 32:43.
[27] Deut. 32:39.

Chapter Twelve. Unity of God as Dynamic of Redemption

Here we have Judaism's most profound paradox. The human will is free, the kingdom of evil waxes powerful, and yet it is impossible for God not to be victorious in His universe. History is a constant invention in which innumerable free wills strive, clash, and ultimately cooperate: the creative action of God and the co-creative action of man. In spite of, or perhaps because of, the vagaries of human choices and decisions history must inevitably reach the goal set for it by the one God. And so the concept of *malkhut* (kingdom) becomes associated with the concept of God's *akhdut* (unity). As Isaac Abarbanel astutely noted, "'One' also implies completion and perfection ... the realization of God's kingdom is the perfection of His rule and sovereignty. Hence *malkhut* and *akhdut* are in reality the same.... It is for this reason that the passage 'Hear O Israel, the Lord our God, the Lord is One' was included in the benediction of *Malkhuyot* in the New Year liturgy."[28]

This is undoubtedly the source of the rabbinic teaching of the *kaitz* (end), an awareness that history must have a divinely appointed end independent of humanity's deserving of it.[29]

The general approach of historians has been to search for explicit texts of an eschatological nature, and in the absence of these in the early books to conclude that "they know nothing of such a predetermined final resolution of history,"[30] and that the "universalism of the early religion is historical but not eschatologicaL"

It would appear, however, to the present writer that these theories based upon "evidence of silence" overlook a very cogent consideration. Although, much has been said about the nonspeculative nature of the Hebrew mind when compared to the Greek genius, it should be borne in mind that the ancient Hebrews were not philosophically naive. Kaufmann himself has made it abundantly clear that "Israel moved in a world of high and ancient civilization."[31] The Bible in its utterances and narratives presents a world view which is the reflection of certain basic metaphysical principles. This was recently underscored by a Christian scholar who writes "It is true ... Hebrew thought is unspeculative ...

---

[28] Commentary of Rabbi Isaac Abarbanel on Deut. 6: 4.
[29] *Sanhedrin* 98a.
[30] Yehezkel Kaufmann, *The Religion of Israel*, translated and abridged by Moshe Greenberg (Chicago: University of Chicago Press, 1960), 165.
[31] L.W. Schwartz, ed., *Great Ages and Ideas of the Jewish People*, 24.

still it is not devoid of metaphysical foundations nor could it be, for no man, not even the primitive, can look at and interpret the world without some basic metaphysical concepts."[32] Because of the historic nature and function of the Pentateuch, not all of the theological inferences of its metaphysics were explicitly drawn or emphasized. However, we should not assume that inferences were not made or relationships not seen merely because fundamental concepts such as creation, revelation, unity of God, and the nature of good and evil are never presented as a related systematic philosophy.

An illustration of this can be seen in the development of a concept closely related to the idea of a predetermined, necessary end to history. We have spoken of the necessity of redemption for the notion of God's unity. Looked at from the aspect of human acknowledgement, this same principle can be expressed in terms of a concern for the state of God's name in the world. So long as God's unity or His plan is affected by human actions, the state of God's name becomes a principle, operative in the divine direction of history, independent of Israel's moral worth. Nowhere in the Pentateuch is this principle emphasized as such. Yet when God threatens to destroy Israel, Moses argues, "Why should the Egyptians say—for evil did He bring them out, to slay them in the mountains and to destroy them from the face of the earth."[33] And again in another connection, Moses pleads, "Now if thou shalt kill all this people as one man, then the nations which have heard thy fame will speak saying—because the Lord was not able to bring this people into the land which He swore unto them, therefore hath He slain them in the wilderness."[34]

Here we have a very clear inference made by Moses, which is the very earliest form of the concept of God acting "for His name's sake," which is so greatly emphasized by the prophet Ezekiel. Taken to its logical conclusion, this means that redemption cannot be indefinitely postponed by a lack of repentance and must ultimately come because the Lord cannot permit His holy name to be profaned among the nations, "in that men say of them, these are the people of the Lord and out of his land

---

[32] Claude Tresmontant, *A Study of Hebrew Thought* (New York: Desclee Co., 1960), foreword by J. Ostereicher.
[33] Exod. 32:12.
[34] Num. 14: 13-17.

have they gone forth."[35] What to Moses is an argument in a specific situation becomes for Ezekiel the assurance of a Messianic future. What is crucial, however, is that while in Ezekiel this concept is presented as a teaching newly revealed in the name of the Lord, in Exodus the essence of the idea is inferred by Moses from the metaphysical principles already known to him. This would seem to indicate not only that biblical man could reason philosophically, but also that theological principles known were employed only as the historical situation called for them.

Similarly, the implication of God's unity for ultimate redemption may likewise have been recognized quite early, but was not explicitly emphasized because the historic situation did not require it.

This was incisively discussed by Nachmanides, who in explaining the general absence of unconditional visions of redemption in the Pentateuch states that "Moses our teacher was uniquely the prophet of the commandments ... and therefore the burden of his words are not simply to foretell the future but to present the suffering which will come, as a warning, and the good and blessings, as an .inducement to observe the commandments. Hence almost all are in the form of a condition—life and the good if we serve; death and evil, if we rebel...."[36]

An additional insight into the idea of God's unity as the underlying dynamic of the Jewish concept of history is to be found in the writings of that unusual combination of mystic and philosopher, Rabbi Moses Hayyim Luzzatto. He goes so far as to maintain that temporal history as a whole, as a maelstrom of good and evil, is necessitated by the need to demonstrate the truth of God's unity.[37] All of God's other attributes, says Luzzatto, insofar as we can comprehend them, can be understood in a positive manner involving only the good. Once a degree of comprehension is reached, there is little reason to expect new advances with the passage of time. However, in respect to God's unity, we are dealing with something whose essential significance lies in what it negates rather than in what it affirms. One's understanding of "the Lord is God and there is none beside Him" is directly proportional to the number of deities, tyrants, and economic and political doctrines one can perceive as being of "no salvation."

---

[35] Ezek. 36:20-21.
[36] Nachmanides, *Sefer Hageulah*, Shaar Rishon.
[37] Luzzatto, *Daat Tevunot*, 14 and 15.

Hence, in order for men to truly become convinced of God's unity in this sense, it is necessary for the rich tapestry of history, with its opportunities for perversity as well as saintliness, to be unrolled, and for man to discover for himself in the harsh reality of his repeated failures and disillusionments the awful truth of his own insufficiency. Again and again, man is destined to be carried aloft on a wave of enthusiasm and expectation, seeing in some new discovery, in some new "ism," a value worthy of absolute devotion, only to have these hopes, too, carried into the abyss. In the fullness of time man will look out over the debris of his shattered gods and having eliminated all else will realize that "the Lord, He is God ... there is none else." This, then, is the purpose of human history: to unmask all pretenders to the divine throne so that "on that day, God will be One and His name will be One."

So understood, as the expression of the ethical and historical dynamic of Judaism, the *Shema* takes on a new dimension.

The Jew on his deathbed, who has perhaps permitted other considerations and other allegiances to direct his life, confronted by his own finitude and the bankruptcy of his limited values, proclaims now his total commitment to the only reality.

The martyr, in his agony, surrounded by the overwhelming evidence of the power of the "no gods," himself a victim of forces arrayed against divinity, proclaims his faith that this too must pass, that evil is doomed, that in spite of appearances there is none else beside Him; that "the Lord our God, the Lord is One."

PART IV

THE ANALYTIC IN ACTION

Chapter Thirteen

Toward an Ethical Theory of Judaism

Judaism, conceived as a religion whose primary sources are the Bible and the Talmud, contains many ideas that are considered today to be moral teachings. This article analyzes the understanding that the biblical writers and the rabbis might have had of these teachings, and concludes that there is reason to believe that their view is commensurate with the conventional view of morality.[1]

While these sources imply the centrality of moral teachings, no medieval Jewish thinker developed an "ethical theory" indicating the special role of morality. This chapter attempts to explain why this is so, and concludes with an outline of a possible ethical theory of Judaism.

I suppose that the only noncontroversial observation one can make about the ethical theory of Judaism is that there isn't any. This is rather surprising, in that Judaism has been around and studied for some time, and is generally considered to be quite sensitive to the moral dimension. One would expect that at least some of its major thinkers, writing from within the tradition, would have thought it necessary to analyze the special nature and significance of morality and its place within the Jewish religion.

But what is an *ethical theory* and how does it differ from a *moral code*? The latter has an "overtly regulative character," and includes rules enjoining or forbidding selected types of actions, selected character traits, and particular patterns of ends and means. That Judaism contains a moral code in this sense seems indisputable. Ethical theories, on the other hand,

---

In my book *Morality, Halakha and the Jewish Tradition* (New York: Ktav and Yeshiva University Press, 1983), I attempted a philosophical analysis of the moral tradition in Judaism in light of modern ethical theory. (See in particular Chapter Two.) In this essay I attempt some further steps toward the development of an ethical theory of Judaism.

[1] "Morality: Concerned with goodness and badness; of human character or behavior; or with the distinction between right and wrong" (*Concise Oxford Dictionary of Correct English* [Oxford: Clarendon Press, 1990]).

are more reflective and attempt to understand questions such as "What is morality?" An ethical theory "provides an analysis of the basic concepts and methods of morality and an explanation of the relations of morality to the fuller context of human life: to man, to God, and to the world."[2]

Why is it that Jewish thinkers have not explored this seemingly important area? Before we can attempt an answer, we must ask an even more fundamental question: is it possible to enter into a dialogue with a 3,500-year-old cultural tradition over a concept which is not completely clear even to modern people, and which may have been completely unintelligible to our ancestors? To put the question more precisely, what is *our* conception of morality as we ask this question, and what might have been the biblical writers' understandings of those rules and principles that we consider to be a part of its moral code? Was their understanding of these rules and principles in any way commensurate with our own?

Let us propose a definition of morality which is limited to its verbal expression and considered as a subspecies of natural languages, which has its own vocabulary, function, and logic.[3] As such, it is neutral to the major issues in philosophical ethics, such as the nature of values, the subjective/ objective and the absolute/ relativistic dichotomies.

Judgments using approval or disapproval terms such as "good" and "evil," "right" and "wrong," "ought" and "ought not," are to be deemed "moral" when they are thought to be judging individuals not as citizens (bound by certain laws), residents of a certain locality (bound by certain customs), or participants in a particular activity (bound by rules of a game or professional etiquette), but simply as human beings *qua* human beings.

---

[2] Abraham Edel, *Science and the Structure of Ethics: Foundations of the Unity of Science* (Chicago: University of Chicago Press, 1961), 10, 18.

[3] Before anything else, morality "exists" as a collection of words which are a subset of a modern language used to perform a special function in human communication. Just as the work of science is carried on with the help of its special language, and the work of art is facilitated by its "jargon," so can we identify a group of terms which are used by people when they wish to make moral judgements or describe moral aspects of our experience. This linguistic sub-group, like each of the others, has its own function, vocabulary, and even logic. An analysis of these features can reveal the understanding its users have of morality. See Shubert Spero, "Analytic Philosophy and the Morality of Judaism," in *Sefer Higayon: Studies in Rabbinic Logic*, ed. M. Koppel & E. Merzbach (Alon Shevut: Zomet Institute, 1995), 61-70.

Thus, moral codes may differ in substance, i.e., as to what actually is a moral good and moral evil. However, they may be considered to be dealing with the same subject matter, i.e., they are *moral* codes in that they recognize the special nature of morality, i.e., behavior and character traits appropriate to human beings as human beings.

Can we say that the Bible recognizes certain of its teachings as "morality" in this sense? I would answer in the affirmative, and in support offer several arguments.

In its account of the first twenty generations of human history, the Bible describes God as judging the behavior of human beings and holding them responsible for their actions in areas we would call "morality."[4] Yet during this entire period there is no condemnation of idolatry, although it is clear from what occurs later that idolatry was rampant. The implication is that while idolatry is a "great mistake"[5] and a tragedy, in that it consigns man to a life without God, it is not something for which, in those particular circumstances, men are to be punished. Nor was it the reason why God "grieved and had regrets" about His creation.[6] Also, while the Bible is tolerant of certain practices of the Patriarchs which are later prohibited by Sinaitic legislation,[7] it holds all human beings from the beginning of history responsible for observing the principles of justice and righteousness. If, therefore, it is primarily the violation of these principles that engenders God's "regret" and disappointment with Creation, does this not suggest that the Bible believes justice and righteousness to impinge upon the very nature of the human being and, therefore, to qualify for what we would call "morality"?

MORAL AGENCY AND THE IMAGE OF GOD

If, according to our definition, morality deals with principled behavior which is "appropriate to a human being as such," then it might be instructive to ask what Judaism's view of man is. The view is, of course, encompassed in the well-known statement: "And God created man in

---

[4] Gen. 4:9, 10; 6:1, 2; 6:11, 13; 9:22, 11:6. "Murder, violence, corruption."
[5] Moses Maimoides, *Mishneh Torah, Hilkhot Avoda Zara* I:1.
[6] Gen. 6:6.
[7] Jacob married two sisters and the Patriarchs worshipped God by means of a standing stone or pillar *(matzevah)*, both of which were later prohibited (Lev. 18:18; Deut. 16:22).

Chapter Thirteen. Toward an Ethical Theory of Judaism

His own image (*ketzalmo*), in the image of God did He create Him; male and female He created them."[8]

There is nothing explicit in the Bible as to the precise meaning of "image of God." However, from the general context a number of inferences are legitimate. Coming after a detailed account of the Creation, starting with the simpler orders of life—vegetation, marine life, reptiles, flying creatures, and animals—the designation of "man" as a creature formed in the "image of God" implies that it is this which constitutes man as a unique creature different from all the others that preceded him. If so, then by empirical examination we might subtract "animal" from "man" and consider the "remainder" to be the contribution of the "image of God."[9] In thus asking what makes man "different" (really "superior") from the beast, we may arrive at a minimal but probably consensual list of attributes: use of language and conceptual thinking, self-consciousness, sense of identity, free will, superior intelligence, and a moral sense (since the fact that I am a "human being" with the above attributes obligates me to a special kind of behavior). But these are precisely the necessary and sufficient conditions to make one a candidate for moral experience. Thus, to say that every human being is created "in the image of God" is to say that every human being is a potential moral agent which implies that (1) all human beings have and intuit a natural *obligation* to behave morally; and (2) all human beings, by that fact alone, *deserve* moral treatment.

Textual evidence of the connection between morality and the "image of God" is to be found in God's instructions to Noah: "Whoso sheds man's blood by man shall his blood be shed; for in the image of God made He man."[10] The latter part of the verse "explains" the first part. The fact that

---

[8] Gen. 1:27.

[9] Aristotle seems to follow the same line of reasoning in Chapter 7 of the *Nicomachean Ethics*.

[10] Gen. 9:6. It is interesting that Rabbi Akiva uses this proof-text in his important teaching: "He used to say, Beloved is man for he was created in the image of God; but it was by a special love that it was made known to him that he was created in the image of God, as it is said, 'For in the image of God made He man [Gen. 9:6]" (*Avot* 3:18). 1 would suggest that Rabbi Akiva refers to this particular verse, rather than to earlier references to "image of God," because his point is that it was made known to man that he was created in the image of God not because it is so stated in the Torah but because, once man begins to become aware of his moral sense, he begins to realize his connection to the Creator. As we indicate in the text, this verse occurs in connection with a moral precept.

man is created in the "image of God" makes him a moral agent, *capable* of acting morally, *obligated* to act morally, and if he doesn't, *accountable* for his deeds. Hence, "he who sheds man's blood ... shall his blood be shed."

But for a person to be a moral agent and to be held responsible for his actions, it is necessary that he not only have a vague sense that as a human being in certain situations, there are some kinds of actions, some character traits that are appropriate (morally right) and others that are inappropriate (morally wrong), but also that he know in a rather specific way what these actions are. Thus, if God condemns Cain for having murdered his brother and the generation of the Deluge for their "violence" and "corruption," then we must assume that these people had the requisite moral knowledge, i.e., that they knew that those actions were wrong.

But when and how, according to the Torah, did human beings acquire this knowledge? From Genesis 3:22, it appears that whatever happened in the Garden of Eden is relevant to this question.[11] However, as the entire story seems to be a metaphor for some metaphysical teaching, we would do well to pick up the story after man emerges from Eden, i.e., with the historical *homo sapiens*. From that point on, the Bible simply assumes that people know what is morally right and wrong, and have the ability to choose the right, and therefore are held accountable for their choices. Genesis 9:6, quoted earlier, can be seen as a direct prophetic imperative to Noah, and was included by the rabbis among the Seven Noahide Laws.[12] However, this entire concept of the Seven Noahide Laws itself is best understood within an ethical theory which sees the Bible as teaching an intuitive morality, i.e., one that believes that human beings are naturally endowed with certain moral sentiments which enable them to distinguish between that which is morally approvable and that which is not, and to experience the reprehensibleness of murder, stealing, incest, causing unnecessary pain to people and animals, and the obligatoriness of establishing law and order, of meting out justice and righteousness.[13]

What supports this is the fact that nowhere in the Bible, either before or after Sinai, are we given a definition of these important principles

---

[11] "And the Lord God said: Behold the man is become as one of us, to know good and evil..." (Gen. 3:22).

[12] *Sanhedrin* 56.

[13] See the discussion in Shubert Spero, *Morality, Halakha and the Jewish Tradition* (New York: Ktav and Yeshiva University Press, 1983), 64-90, and Chapter 6 in this volume for an analysis of the Garden of Eden.

"justice and righteousness" (*tsedek u-mishpat*), and how they differ, if at all! There seems to be the assumption that the mere mention of these terms will be sufficient for their meanings to be grasped by the reader. The teachings of the Bible clearly presuppose an intuitionist ethical theory, but not only on textual evidence. For what alternative is there? Surely mankind could not wait for the Sinai revelation to discover how to behave! Besides, the Ten Commandments, designed to express the covenant between God and a particular people, does not seem to have been directed toward mankind as a whole, at least not in the first instance. Nor is there anywhere in the Bible the suggestion that the rules and principles of morality were invented by men or discovered on the basis of their social utility.

This conclusion, that the primary elements with which the "image of God" endows man are those making for moral agency, directly confirms another principle of Judaism: that God is a moral God not only in the sense that His actions are always in accordance with the principles of justice and righteousness but also in the more radical sense that moral values, in a form appropriate to God, are resident aspects of God's "personality."[14] This is seen in the revelation to Moshe on Mt. Sinai after the tragedy of the Golden Calf and the smashing of the first Tablets: "And the Lord passed before him and [the Lord] proclaimed: The Lord, the Lord, God merciful and gracious (*rahum v-hanun*), long suffering, abundant in kindness and truth...."[15]

---

[14] The importance of this distinction can be grasped once it is applied on the human level. Case A: All we know is that he has performed certain particular acts of charity. Case B: After a prolonged process of psychological testing and analysis, we are told that he has a deeply-rooted generous character. In regard to future expectations there is an important difference between A and B. Since A's acts of charity in the past might have been motivated by any number of extraneous considerations, we are not sure about his behavior in the future. Since, however, B's generosity has been discovered to be part of his very "nature" or "character," we can have more confidence as to the future. And so it is with God. Also, if moral values can be viewed as, in some sense, aspects of God's very "essence," then to love God is to love the Good and to do the Good out of love for God is to do the Good out of intrinsic love for the Good, thus preserving the autonomy of morality.

[15] Exod. 34:6, 7. The statement "God is merciful" is, strictly speaking, a description of God Himself. That God performs acts of mercy was known before. That mercy is a resident quality of God's personality was not known before. This is why this new information is given in a direct, dramatic, mystical revelation to Moshe.

IMITATIO DEI AND THE MORAL CONNECTION

It is this moral connection between man and God that now becomes the basis for that unique and sublime teaching in Judaism of *Imitatio Dei*.[16] The image (*tselem*) has given man the possibility to become *like* unto (*demut*) the moral God. "As he is merciful so shall you be merciful (virtue morality). As He buried the dead, so shall you bury the dead (act morality). As He is holy, so shall you be holy." Once it has been disclosed that the "way of the Lord" is to do righteousness and justice, then it becomes appropriate for man to be commanded "to walk in His ways."[17]

If the Bible's concept of man focuses primarily on his being a creature capable of moral action, then it follows that morality is indeed behavior appropriate to human beings as such. But going beyond that, the Bible provides a theological explanation as to why man happens to be the way he is. This means that in Judaism, morality is ultimately grounded in God and possesses religious significance.[18]

But if our analysis is correct and morality is indeed central to the very concept of man and constitutes the way by which man draws close to God, why was this important truth not made explicit in the Torah? Not doing so has resulted in all sorts of distortions and misconceptions! The very least that might have been expected was that moral rules and principles would be listed separately and differentiated from ritual commandments pertaining to cultic worship of God. It is, however, clear from even a casual reading of the main collections of *mitzvot* in the Bible that a deliberate policy of intermixing the various types of commandments has been followed.[19]

Biblical usage and etymology bears out the rabbinic observation that the term *mishpatim*, translated as "judgments," refers to rules confirmed by common sense or as socially useful, while *hukim*, rendered "statutes," denotes cultic or ritual rules. Indeed, moral rules are as a matter of fact generally subsumed under the term *mishpatim*. However, here again the Bible in its general exhortations never emphasizes one over the other, or

---

[16] See Martin Buber, "Imitatio Dei" in *Israel and the World: Essays in Time of Crisis* (Schocken Books: New York, 1948), 66-78.
[17] Gen. 18: 19; Deut. 8:6, 11:22.
[18] Danny Statman and Avi Sagi, "The Relationship between Religion and Morality in the Thought of Buber," *Daat* 17 (1986): 97-118
[19] See Spero, *Morality, Halakha and the Jewish Tradition*, 22-26, especially note 13.

Chapter Thirteen. Toward an Ethical Theory of Judaism

even consistently places one term before the other. What we evidently have here is a deliberate policy to place moral and cultic demands on the same level in terms of their authority and their origin in God.[20] This was necessary due to the contemporary pagan belief that the gods had no real interest in morality. For the pagans, the proper rules by which human society was to be governed were to be found in the realm of wisdom, rather than in prophecy or religion. The radical new concept that the Torah introduced was that the one transcendent Creator, God, was vitally concerned with, and in some sense "affected" by, the way men dealt with each other—not only because God, who is good, seeks the good of others, but because the realization of moral values in the world increases the presence of Divinity and enhances the power and quality of the Holy. Thus, the reason for intermixing the judgments and the statutes, the moral precepts and the ritual commands, in the time of the Torah was to raise the moral precepts in the mind of the reader to the religious level of the ritual, so that they would understand that morality too is religious, that this too brings one into communion with God.

However, at a number of points in the Torah we have evidence that the primacy of the moral over the ritual was recognized:

In his farewell address, Moshe hurls the following challenge at his people: "And what great nation is there that has statutes (*hukim*) and judgments (*mishpatim*) so righteous (*tsadikim*) as all this law (*torah*) which I set before you this day?"[21]

Of course, says Moshe, other peoples, such as the Hittites and the Babylonians, have laws and statutes as well. In this you are not unique. But only you, Israel, have statutes and judgments that are *righteous!* Here the moral principle of *tsedek*, whose meaning is presumably self-evident, is proposed as an objective criterion by which the law codes and religious rituals of different cultures, including the Torah, are to be compared and judged.

That most celebrated document, called the Ten Commandments but referred to in the Bible as the Ten Words of the Covenant,[22] constitutes

---

[20] Lev. 18:4, 5; 25:18; 26:43,46; Deut. 5:1, 28; 6:1, 24; 7:11, 12; 8:12; 11:32; 12:1; 26:16-18.
[21] Deut. 4:8.
[22] "... And he wrote upon the tables the words of the covenant, the ten words" (Exod. 34:28).

the essential terms or conditions of the relationship between God and the People of Israel. Clearly, these words, inscribed on stone tablets, were meant to *represent* in some sense the totality of the demands, all of the 613 precepts that God requires of the people. They might be construed as principles from which the other rules are to be deduced, as chapter headings under which the others are to be subsumed, as a representative sampling, as a model in miniature of the entire Torah. But regardless of how one sees the relationship between the Ten Commandments and the rest of the Torah, the very fact that of the Ten Words of the Covenant (of which only nine have operative clauses), six are clearly moral in nature and appear together as a unit, says something significant about the centrality of the moral component in the Bible.

The Intrinsicality of Moral Value

As society developed in the Kingdoms of Israel and Judea, and economic changes gave rise to inequities and social abuses, the later Prophets, in their exhortations and chastisements, were compelled to address the contemporary reality in which, apparently, fast days, holidays, and the Temple service were generally respected, but basic moral demands of justice and righteousness were ignored. In their attempt to shock the people into a realization of their distorted sense of values, the Prophets cried, in the name of God:

> For I desire mercy and not sacrifice, the knowledge of God rather than burnt offerings. (Hosea, 6:6)

> I hate, I despise your feasts, and I take no delight in your solemn assemblies.... But let justice well up as waters and righteousness as a mighty stream." (Amos 5:21, 24)

> Saith the Lord: I am full of the burnt-offerings of rams and the fat of fed beasts.... Yea when you make many prayers, I will not hear: Your hands are full of blood.... Seek justice, relieve the oppressed. Judge the fatherless, plead for the Widow.... (Isa. 1:11-17)

It is of course clear that the Prophets did not come to declare that the holiday and Temple services ought to be replaced by moral behavior, or that once people were moral, the Temple service was no longer necessary. Instead, they wished to point out that sacrifices and Temple worship could not compensate for unrepentant, immoral behavior, and that worship by an unregenerate sinner is an abomination.

However, whether intended or not, such declarations in effect acknowledge a certain important distinction between moral and ritual commandments, namely that moral commandments have *intrinsic* value, while ritual commandments have only *instrumental* value. In order to see this let us imagine a sort of reversed situation, a society in which morality is being meticulously observed, whereas sacrifices and Temple services are being neglected. Is it conceivable that anyone would arise and preach in the name of the God of the Bible: "1 am full of your mercy and kindness.... I hate and despise your acts of justice and righteousness, for you have neglected my burnt offerings and my solemn assemblies." In Judaism this is inconceivable, yet the reverse was plainly declared by the Prophets!

This is so because acts of kindness, justice, and righteousness, if that is what they indeed are, can never be rejected regardless of motivation and whatever else the individual may or may not have done. Such acts of morality are of *intrinsic value,* good of and by themselves, while cultic acts are valued not because of themselves but only because of what they represent, what they can bring about. Therefore, if these cultic acts are not done properly, with the right intentions, with "clean hands," with a repentant, humble spirit, with a sense of subservience to God, then they cannot have the desired effect and, as such, are worse than worthless.

Morality and the Rabbinic Tradition

Let us now consider whether the Talmudic rabbis related to morality in a manner which preserved the biblical insights. They did of course, affirm the doctrine that biblical legislation in its entirety, ritual and moral, by virtue of its divine origin, is equally and unconditionally authoritative. On the practical level they warned against the consequences of grading the precepts: "Be heedful of a light precept as of a grave one for you know not the reward of the precepts."[23] In applying their special method, *midrash halakhah,* to the legal portions of the Bible, they worked with as much diligence on the moral precepts as on the ritual ones. However, the process of halakhic elaboration often necessitated

---

[23] *Avot* 2:1.

the making of material distinctions among the commandments, making divisions between "Thou shalts" and "Thou shalt nots," classifications of precepts according to the degree of punishment assigned to them by the Torah, and separations between commandments between man and man and those between man and God. Thus, the rabbis were led to articulate the distinction between *hukim* and *mishpatim*, which had only been implicit in the Bible, and to notice and appreciate the different nature of the moral precepts. For example, it has been pointed out that in elaborating the ritual commandments the rabbis used a policy of contraction, restricting the law to the precise conditions mentioned in the text, whereas in regard to precepts between man and man or the moral *mitzvot* they used a policy of expansion, i.e., they widened the scope of the law, since they understood the guiding moral principle behind the precept.[24]

It is well known that the rabbis did not "do" philosophy in the analytic and systematic manner of the ancient Greeks. Instead, in the area of *midrash aggadah,* they formulated their insights in terse and pithy maxims which nevertheless showed their capacity for abstract conceptual thinking. Unfortunately, however, "there is never an attempt to combine isolated conclusions into a coherent framework"[25] or to follow through systematically on the implications of the individual teachings. Unlike the Bible, which contains primarily the content of the religious consciousness itself, the Talmud begins to treat certain biblical ideas and precepts as objects of theoretical reflection; the rabbis begin to consider them philosophically. One of these is the area of the moral precepts. What we have, therefore, in some of the rabbinic teachings is actually the beginning of an ethical theory. Consider the following discussion:

> "Thou shalt love thy neighbor as thyself," this is a great principle of the Torah. Thus said Rabbi Akiva. Ben Azzai said, there is a principle that is even greater: "This is the book of the generations of Adam ... in the likeness of God made He him" (Gen. 5:1).[26]

---

[24] See Yechiel Michel Gutman, *Behinat Ki'um Ha-Mitzvot* (Breslau, 1931), 19-23.
[25] Julius Guttmann, *Philosophies of Judaism* (New York: Holt, Rinehart & Winston, 1964), 39.
[26] *Torat Kohanim,* Lev. 19:18.

Chapter Thirteen. Toward an Ethical Theory of Judaism

Rabbi Akiva seems to be saying several things. First, he is pointing out that this particular precept is a *principle*, i.e., given in general terms (*klal*). This means that although an imperative, the precept of and by itself does not call for any particular action. However, as a general principle it can be used as a criterion to test the morality of any number of particular acts. Thus, anyone wishing to observe this moral principle would feel obligated to visit the sick, invite the hungry, bury the dead, or help the poor as he would certainly wish others to do the same for him. Rabbi Akiva also says it is a "a great principle," or as it seems from Ben Azzai's remark, "*the* great principle." This is not to be taken as a value judgment but as a statement about the extent of its generality. For while a precept such as "Righteousness, righteousness shalt thou pursue ..." is also a general principle (*klal*) in that it is relevant to any number of different situations and mandates any number of different actions, it is restricted to a particular content, i.e., the moral principle called "righteousness." The precept of "Love thy neighbor" is a completely formal principle urging a single moral standard for the self and the other.[27]

Rabbi Akiva has, in effect, discovered a most important characteristic of moral experience, namely that it presents itself to consciousness as a general principle and must be capable of universalization. Because moral experience is primarily intuited as general principles, morality can be taught and learned, particular moral judgments can be justified by appeal to principle, moral rules can be related to moral principles as particulars to universals, making possible moral reasoning and giving to morality the possibility of logical structure. A "great principle" indeed! The fact that Rabbi Akiva calls this "the Great Principle *of the Torah*" even though we are only talking about the moral precepts, again reflects the primacy of morality in Judaism.

Ben Azzai disagrees with Rabbi Akiva and claims that there is in the Torah a general principle that is "even greater than" (more general than) "Thou shalt love thy neighbor." The verse cited by Ben Azzai is not even a precept in the imperative voice, and merely refers to the fact that man was created in the "likeness of God"! However, the key to understanding Ben Azzai lies in the fact that he reaches out to Chapter 5 in Genesis for his source that man was created in the image of God. If that alone was what he wished to teach, he could have found it in Genesis 1:26 and 1:27.

---

[27] See the discussion in Spero, *Morality, Halakha and the Jewish Tradition*, chapter 7.

But it is only in Genesis 5:1 that Ben Azzai finds the introductory phrase: "This is the *book of the generations of man*." This tells us that to have been created "in the likeness of God" is not simply an abstract metaphysical concept with only honorific implications. What makes human history significant and important to God, so that the Bible itself really is "the book of the generations of man," is the fact that man is a moral agent, that the struggle between good and evil takes place within every man, that there is hope that the great drama which is human history will work its intended good because man can become "like unto God."

If Ben Azzai challenges Rabbi Akiva, who is clearly focused on the subject of morality, then it follows that Ben Azzai believes that the concept of "man created in the image of God" has significant implication for morality which, writ large, is the problem of history.

If this interpretation is correct, then the views of Rabbi Akiva and Ben Azzai need not be mutually exclusive. Rabbi Akiva is speaking about the most general principle *within* the system of Torah, whereas Ben Azzai is addressing the question of the *ground* of morality in general, or the conditions which make morality possible altogether. Once this distinction is acknowledged, it is possible to argue that each of those principles is supreme in its own sphere.

In a number of teachings some leading rabbis in the Talmud made it clear that the moral precepts were central to the entire Torah. This could be seen in the celebrated reply of Hillel to the impudent request of a pagan that, preparatory to conversion, he be taught the entire Torah while he stood on one foot: "What is hateful to yourself do not do to your fellow man. This is the entire Torah, the rest is commentary."[28] There is the teaching of Rabbi Phineas ben Yair, who outlined a series of stages in the religious development of the individual wherein the highest stage is described in terms of moral virtue such as "kindliness" or "humility."[29] But all this is already foreshadowed in the early teaching of Simon the Just: "Upon three things does the world stand: on *Torah*, on *Avodah* (service), and on *Gemilut Chasadim* (acts of loving-kindness)."[30] Regardless of the precise meaning of the first two general terms, the fact that a concrete particular such as moral deeds is considered the "third (indispensable)

---

[28] *Shabbat* 31a.
[29] *Avodah Zarah* 20b.
[30] *Avot* 1:2.

pillar" of Judaism, and indeed of the cosmos itself, points to its being seen as much more than simply a certain class of the divine precepts.

All that we have pointed out regarding the biblical and rabbinic understanding of morality serves only to sharpen the question we posed at the outset: why didn't classical Jewish thinkers pick up on the clues and implications, the hints and sometimes overt disclosures, in our primary sources regarding the special significance of morality and develop therefrom a comprehensive ethical theory?

The Major Attribute of God: Knowledge or Morality?

In describing different types of religions, Guttmann points out that much depends upon what we consider to be the major attribute of God: "If it is held that morality is the major attribute of the Deity, then morality will be the way to achieve proximity to God. However, if knowledge is considered the major value then it is by way of the intellect that closeness to God is attained."[31]

The latter type of theology is exemplified in medieval Jewish thought by the writings of Bachya, ibn Daud, and of course Maimonides, whose enormous influence imposed an intellectualist bent on subsequent Jewish thinking. However, what is most curious is that while there were other Jewish thinkers in that general period who did not see "knowledge" as the most important attribute of God nor the intellect as the way to God, nevertheless they did not choose morality as the alternative! For example, in his sharp distinction between religion and philosophy, Judah Halevi sees the pious individual as driven to God not by a desire for knowledge but by his yearning for communion with Him. There is a special religious faculty in every man which is developed into an actual disposition by observance of the ceremonial law which leads to an experience of God felt as love and joyous obedience, a foretaste of the bliss of the world to come.[32] Thus, although knowledge is rejected as a major attribute of God by Halevi, the moral precepts as such are not singled out for special attention. But why not, given what the Bible and the rabbis had to say about morality?

---

[31] Yitzhak Julius Guttmann, *On the Philosophy of Religion* (Jerusalem: Magnes Press, 1976), 189.
[32] Judah Halevi, *Kitab Al Khazari,* Part IV, sections 15, 16.

Chasdai Crescas demolished the Aristotelian metaphysical presuppositions of Maimonides and asserted that the primary content of the God idea is not "thought" but the divine Will and His goodness. This "goodness" is not merely an analogical characterization of the quality of God's personality, but is "the unitary ground which welds the plurality of the attributes into a single whole."[33] God is joyous in that His goodness overflows into creation which is an expression of the divine Will and demonstrates God's love for His creatures. To make possible deeds of loving-kindness is the ultimate purpose of the world, and this cannot be questioned any further since goodness is for its own sake.[34] According to Crescas, man's highest good, which he attains by the observance of the divine precepts, is love of God—which brings him to communion with God and to eternal happiness in the world to come. Yet, even as Crescas rejects the idea of physical perfection and intellectual perfection as possibly constituting man's *ultimate* perfection, so does he reject moral perfection, although he acknowledges its social benefits.[35] What is rather strange here is that Crescas has no problem in making positive statements about the nature of God, namely His absolute goodness, and yet he is unable to see the connection between man's personal moral perfection in the form of a virtuous personality and communion with the good God!

Morality as a Special Kind of *Mitzvah*

I wish to suggest that there are two main factors, operating sometimes separately and sometimes together, which are responsible for the inability on the part of Jewish thinkers during this period to perceive morality as the bridge between man and God. One was the conviction stemming from religious as well as rational considerations that man could not grasp intellectually the nature of God: "For man cannot see

---

[33] Chasdai Crescas, *Or Adonai*, I:3.3. See Julius Guttmann, *Philosophies of Judaism*, 224-241.

[34] The same is true of Saadia Gaon, who acknowledges that we can infer God's goodness from the fact of Creation along with His attributes of existence, power, and knowledge. Saadia also acknowledges the special nature of that class of precepts which have a "reason" in that they bring about beneficial social consequences. However, he makes no connection between morality and coming close to God.

[35] Chasdai Crescas, *Or Adonai*, II:6.1.

Chapter Thirteen. Toward an Ethical Theory of Judaism

Me and live" and "To know Him is to be Him." This agnosticism about the nature of God discouraged any further explication of statements such as "God is merciful, God is compassionate," other than as analogical descriptions of God's actions. The same cloud of obscurity and vacuousness cast by Maimonides over attributes such as "God's knowledge" and "God's existence" was applied to statements about God's moral nature.[36]

The second factor has to do with these thinkers' understandings of morality and the nature of moral value. Aristotle considered morality to be the realm of practical reason. In other words, reason determined the right policy for man, in terms of his nature, which was then up to the individual to carry out. However, from the covenantal perspective of the Bible, as teachings directed in the first instance to the people of Israel, morality is simply that portion of the 613 precepts that deal with man's relationship with his fellow man. Therefore, any question as to the significance of these rules and principles for man has to be found within the context of their being *mitzvot*. The rabbis had indeed noted that these particular precepts had beneficial social consequences, which demonstrated God's benevolence. Yet in terms of their purely religious significance, that is, in terms of relating the individual to God, there appeared to be nothing special. True, the individual in carrying out these precepts is expressing his loyalty and obedience to God, but no more so than when he is fulfilling any of the other precepts.

Indeed, the fact that some of the commandments are "rational" actually constitutes a problem for a certain type of religious consciousness, and their inclusion within a religious system sets up a certain tension with the other elements. There are those who claim that the most distinctive and important element in the subjective religious experience is a sense of the *mysterium tremendum*: a sense of the Holy, a sense of radical dependence.[37] This feeling, which a person can experience in the intense concentration of prayer or in the collective enthusiasm reached at the climax of a religious ritual or dramatic ceremonial, seems to fit our concept of a deity who is "wholly other," mysterious and fundamentally

---

[36] See Chapter 9 in this volume.
[37] See Rudolph Otto, *The Idea of the Holy* (New York: Oxford University Press, 1958), and William Barrett, *Irrational Man* (New York: Doubleday & Co., 1958), both of whom relate these elements of existential philosophy to the Bible and Hebraic tradition and, of course, the writing of Rabbi Joseph B. Soloveitchik.

unknowable, who inspires dread before He inspires gratitude and fear and awe, before it turns to love. All of this flourishes best in the absence of the rational. The individual who straps on his *tefillin* in the morning may feel that there is no significance to what he is doing other than as an act of divine worship. Yet, in terms of the purity of his intentions and the general content of his consciousness, he is free to receive whatever religious emotion awaits him. However, in the performance of moral precepts where there exists a natural human sympathy and an awareness that murder and theft and adultery can destroy the social fabric, can one, in performing these precepts, truly experience the Presence of God? Can it be that the very understandable features of the moral precepts, which enhance our appreciation of their value and urge upon us their fulfillment, may leave little room for the *religious* impulse? While for the Jew it is clear that it is God who has commanded us to be moral, the living experience of God during the performance of the moral rules may be harder to generate and to identify.

The impasse reached by medieval Jewish philosophy in regard to the significance of morality is clearly presented by Joseph Albo (d. 1444), a student of Crescas whose work, in a sense, sums up the Jewish philosophic legacy of the Middle Ages:

> Now it is clear that perfection may be acquired through the theoretical part of the Torah (*helek ha-mada'i*), its negative as well as its positive side. Similarly, perfection may be acquired through the part containing the statutes (*helek ha-chuki*), i.e., the rules concerning those things that are pleasing to God and those which are displeasing to Him. The thing that requires explanation, however, is how can perfection of the soul be acquired through the third part, which embraces judgments (*helek ha-makif ba-mishpatim*)? It is hard to conceive how any of its parts, whether the positive or the negative commandments, can give perfection to the soul. Those positive commandments which deal with injuries caused by an ox or an open pit or a fire, and negative commandments like, "You shall not steal," "Thou shalt not oppress thy neighbor nor rob him" and so on, are no doubt correct rules for the preservation of social life but by what merit does the soul of a moral man acquire perfection by means of them?[38]

---

[38] Joseph Albo, *Sefer Ha-Ikarim*, III:28 (Philadelphia, Jewish Publication Society of America, 1930), 261-262.

Chapter Thirteen. Toward an Ethical Theory of Judaism

In posing the question in this manner, Albo is evidently focusing on the substance of the different commandments. Precepts that deal with "beliefs" are clearly related to the soul, in that they are "spiritual." Precepts that deal with natural or cultic items which have no rational justification other than that they are "pleasing to God" also relate to the spiritual perfection in that they are performed as an expression of humble submission and obedience to God. However, regarding the rather mundane specificity of the precepts called *mishpatim*, which include so much of civil law and are performed in order to achieve their beneficial social consequences, how are they related to spiritual perfection?

At this point, Albo makes a statement which demonstrates that he had advanced in his understanding to a stage beyond that of Crescas:

> And if their virtue [the virtue of the *mishpatim*] consists in the fact that they are a guide to correct morals, which alone enable one to acquire human perfection, then it would follow that the intensive occupations within the Talmud on the part of the Jewish Sages with their study of talmudic questions is of no benefit in acquiring perfection, and their labor is in vain!

But, continues Albo, perhaps we should consider the value of the deeds called *mishpatim* not in their social benefit but rather in the effects those acts have on the doer, i.e., in developing within him a moral personality which may be considered, by itself, ultimate human perfection. This Albo rejects, arguing that were we to see the entire purpose of the *mishpatim* to lie in their effect on the doer and on that alone, then we have no justification for the time and effort spent by the sages in explicating the fine points of their application. "Besides it is not likely that so large a part of the Torah bestows perfection only because it leads to right morals and for no other reason."

What is important here is that Albo recognizes that while the *mishpatim* as laws confer social benefits, they are at the same time moral actions embodying moral principles, such as justice and righteousness and concern for the other. When performed consciously on principle, these deeds can develop a virtuous personality and as such decisively affect the soul of the doer. Albo's objection, however, is not in the unsuitability of moral virtue as a candidate for ultimate human perfection, but in that this theory would leave unaccounted for the intense preoccupation of the rabbis with the minutiae of the Halakhah. Albo's own solution to the problem is to state that the proper fulfillment of a commandment lies in the combination of the action with the proper intention or frame of mind. Thus, in carrying out the *mishpatim* one must have in mind not only the improvement of social life but that the source of the commandment is God, and that one is performing the commandment out of love of God. So performed, these precepts achieve for the doer perfection of soul.

Although Albo does not go into this, it would appear from his analysis that the religious significance of the *mishpatim* performed with the proper intention should be greater than that of the *hukim* performed with the proper intention. For, while both types of precepts confer perfection of the soul by their being motivated by the love of God, the *mishpatim* have the additional virtue that they are benefiting society and are contributing to the doer's moral perfection.

Maharal and the Reinstatement of Morality

Writing in Prague about 100 years after Albo, Rabbi Judah Loeb (d. 1609) is able to ignore the intellectualistic bias of Greek philosophy and sets things straight, as they always should have been, to "we disciples of Moshe our Rabbi."[39] The ultimate goal of man is to achieve communion with God. This possibility was already provided by man being "created in the image of God." Toward this end man was given the system of commandments, which by observance of the negative commandments lifts man above nature, and by performance of the positive ones implants in man proper character traits.

> The commandments of the Torah purify the soul and bring man closer to God until he cleaves unto Him. And by doing all these good things like charity, righteousness and justice (it is unnecessary to explain), man achieves ultimate salvation because those things relate him to God and make him like unto Him since these are the attributes of God who is kindness and justice and

---

[39] Judah Loeb ben Bezalel, *Tifferet Yisroel*, Chapter 9. Known as the Maharal of Prague, the author was probably aware of the empirical spirit of the early science which was developing in that city.

righteousness. And it is precisely by being in such a relationship that one might be said to cleave unto Him...[40]

And likewise theft, robbery, adultery, and murder without doubt bring about eternal punishment, for these are abominable and detestable in the eyes of God for He is the essence of fairness ... incest and sexual immorality and materialism place one outside the fence of Holiness and are far from God who is utter holiness.[41]

The importance of the Maharal's teaching lies not only in his explicit rejection of the idea of the intellect being the supreme attribute of God but in his uninhibited receptivity to the plain meaning of biblical and rabbinic sources. By linking the following pivotal biblical teachings, Maharal arrives at his clear and incisive grasp of the role of morality in Judaism:

1) As a consequence of having been formed in the "image of God," man is a moral agent.

2) God is not only moral in His actions, but morality is the only known quality of His personality.

3) The command to "cleave unto God," which is man's ultimate perfection, links (1) and (2). "You shall diligently keep all the commandments which I command you to do, to love the Lord your God, to walk in all of His ways and to cleave unto Him."[42] The "way of the Lord" (derekh Hashem) has already been defined in Genesis 18:19 as "to do righteousness and justice."

Man's uniqueness lies in his ability to discern, appreciate, and act upon the moral principles of justice, righteousness, and kindness. His task in life is to actualize these values and sense therein the Presence of God. The only positive attribute of God that is explicitly stressed is His morality, His moral character, and His "love" for justice and righteousness and for people who practice justice and righteousness. What, therefore, is more self-evident than that the command to "cleave unto God" and to commune with Him is by means of moral perfection? In striving for moral perfection man "imitates God" not only by realizing (making "real") moral values in the living tissues of human relationships, but also by exercising his freedom and creativity in shaping for himself a unitary

---

[40] Maharal cites proof-texts from the Bible and the rabbis for these assertions.
[41] Judah Loeb ben Bezalel, *Tifferet Yisroel*, Chapter 9.
[42] Deut. 11:22.

moral personality. As He is free so shall you be free, as He is creative so shall you be creative, as He is One so shall you be one and united within yourself.

What remains to be explained is what possible meaning other than as attributes of His action concepts such as "justice" and "righteousness" could have in reference to God Himself? Here we must return to a point stressed both by Saadia Gaon and Crescas: the entire philosophical quest for God must start with the reality of the world of which man is a part, and from there by a process of inference work our way to a Creator with the necessary attributes of life, power, and wisdom who acts by the exercise of His free will. We today find these conclusions in a way confirmed by our personal religious encounter, by our ontological experience as creature and as beneficiary which simultaneously confers a sense of utter dependence-of-being on God, and yet we feel confirmed in our personal identity by God's care. One feels oneself to be completely at the mercy of God, and yet feels that He is *my* God. Together they give man a sense of *relationship* with the Divine.[43]

Most important in the philosophy of Saadia and Crescas is the realization that the entire process of Creation is to be seen as a moral act which implies the Creator's "goodness." In other words, God creates, goes "beyond" Himself, out of His splendid isolation in order to create others whom He can benefit and to whom He can do good. God is to be seen not only as the ground of all being, which means that the real is also rational, but also as having impregnated Creation with value, and being the source of all value. Creation is also a moral act in the teleological sense, for the goals for which God has brought the world into existence are value-laden and serve to increase the good and benefit others. Thus, in spite of the difficulty of speaking of the "wholly other" God in terms of "intending," "willing," "planning," "caring," "loving," "being good," and "moral," the biblical testimony and the living religious experience of the individual require that we speak of Him in this manner.[44]

---

[43] The Aristotelians argued that it was incorrect to speak of having a "relationship" with God. On this, see Eliezer Berkowitz, *God, Man and History* (New York: Jonathan David, 1959), 61.

[44] This is also the view of Rabbi Joseph B. Soloveitchik. See Shubert Spero, *Aspects of Joseph Dov Soloveitchik's Philosophy of Judaism: An Analytic Approach* (Jersey City, NJ: Ktav, 2009).

"Justice" and "righteousness" seem to have significance only in a social context, in regulating relations between human beings.[45] However, God as Creator is in relationship with His creatures, whom He has formed out of His benevolence. Were God to deal with His creatures unjustly or unfairly, it would violate God's "goodness." Thus, the same essential quality of benevolence which is God's "goodness," which we experience in the fruits of Creation, is the basis for the assertion that God is "just and righteous" in history.[46] We are suggesting that according to the ethical theory of Judaism the primary term in morality is "goodness," to which all of the other terms can be reduced.

The Bible frequently asserts that God is "good."[47] As used throughout the Bible, this term in all of its different forms connotes something *positive* and *approving*. Sometimes it is used to refer to moral good.[48] When used as an attribute of God, the word good (*tov*) would seem to fit best our word "value," a term which encompasses all of the basic items and experiences in life which men cherish, desire, and approve of, such as the cognitively true, the morally good, and the aesthetically beautiful. Frequently, the word "value" is used in contrast to the word "fact." The latter is used to refer to the public reality which is "out there," doing its thing independent of our perceptions, and whose existence can in principle be verified. "Values," although in a sense even more important than "facts," do not seem to "exist" in the same sense as the "facts." They seem to be impervious to "facts" and in some sense to float above them, endowing them with meaning.

I wish to suggest that Judaism is compatible with the view that values such as the *true*, the *moral good* and the *beautiful* are not the subjective inventions of man but are integral aspects of reality.[49] However, they

---

[45] It is hard to believe that the following was written by Maimonides: "For all moral principles concern the relation of man to his neighbor; the perfection of man's moral principles is, as it were, given to man for the benefit of mankind. Imagine a person living alone and having no connection whatever with any other person, all his good moral principles are at rest, they are not required and give man no perfection whatever" (Moses Maimonides, *Guide for the Perplexed*, trans. M. Friedlander [New York: E. P. Dutton & Co., 1942], III:54).
[46] Deut. 32:4.
[47] Psalms 100:5, 136:1; Jer. 33:11.
[48] Gen. 3:5; Amos 5:4,15; Psalms 25:8; 34:15.
[49] See Chapters 10 and 15 in this volume

are intuited or known or apprehended by man differently than are facts. They are experienced *immediately* as value, i.e., they are immediately appreciated as something positive and desirable, are accompanied by an emotion such as joy, love, and hope, and are perceived as an attribute of the object.

Thus, when the Torah asserts that "God is good": "Praise God, for God is good (Jer. 33:11), it is stating that goodness is an essential quality of God Himself. But to be good means also to act benevolently to others. Hence, "God is good to all and merciful to all His creations" (Psalms 145:9). However, since at first there were no "others," God in His goodness and out of love creates a world which He impregnates with value: "And behold God saw everything that He had done [was] very good (Gen. 2:31), so that the cosmos itself exhibits a certain beauty and seems to follow certain underlying uniformities called "laws." But, above all, God creates man "in His image" so that now man himself can perceive and appreciate the value that is all about him: "...taste and see for God is good" (Psalms 34:9), and man himself can go on to create things that are true, good, and beautiful:

> And God blessed them and said to them, "Be fruitful and multiply, fill the land and conquer it..." (Gen. 1:28).
>
> And his brother's name was Yuval; he was the father of all sucha s handle the harp and the pipe... (Gen. 4:21).
>
> And do what is right and good... (Deut. 6:18).

Conclusions

The following set of propositions culled from the above are presented as part of an outline of an ethical theory of Judaism. I have argued that all of them are consistent with primary biblical and rabbinic texts; some of them can be directly deduced therefrom; and together they serve to justify Jewish normative practice.

1) The Bible and the rabbis implicitly recognized among the many divine precepts a particular set of normative principles, rules, and virtues as appropriate to the human being *qua* human being. This concept corresponds to what we today call "morality."

2) Moral value, particularly in its instantiation as the quality of *Goodness* and *Benevolence,* is not only an attribute of God's actions but

is of the very nature of God Himself. Hence, God cannot do otherwise but act morally.

3) Man's nature as a being "created in the image of God" confers upon him the status of a *moral agent*, which includes the obligation and the capacity to be good, just, and righteous.

4) The *summum bonum* for man as one created in the image of God lies in self-fulfillment, which is to create for himself a resident moral personality out of love for the supreme Good which is God and ultimately to attain communion with Him.

5) Man acquires the ability to distinguish between the moral good and the moral evil by exercising his intuitive moral sense, which is part of his *tzelem elohim*. The Sinaitic revelation, whose main purpose was to establish the covenantal relationship between God and Israel, does not proclaim a "new" morality but comes to clarify the range and depth of the natural morality, to urge its application in all spheres of life, and to reveal the relationship between morality and God.

6) There is only one meaning to "moral good" and "moral evil" in any particular situation, and it binds both man and God. In judging the morality of God's actions man may err for lack of sufficient information.

7) Of the things demanded of man by God, morality alone (which includes love of God) is to be seen as an intrinsic value: "to love and do good because it is good."

8) One's relationship to God and one's relationship to the question of whether there is a God is in part a matter of morality. Therefore, he who is moral in his relations to man but does not relate to God is not morally perfect. He who worships God but is not moral in his relationship to man or beast is neither pious nor moral.

Chapter Fourteen

What is Self-theory, and Does Judaism Need One?

The study of "self" is located at the intersection of psychology, philosophy, and theology. The particular direction taken in this inquiry is dictated by the context, which is the theoretical aspect of Judaism. However, we shall, of necessity, dip into all three disciplines.

By the term "self-theory" we refer to a set of sentences that explicate what is meant by the "self" of the individual person, that which gives him his sense of personal identity. A theory of this kind is expected to distinguish among the various states of human consciousness, between those that appear to be happening *to* the self and those in which we experience the self as agent. An adequate theory should also deal with a number of questions. Are there parts to the self, or is it unitary? Does the self have any original determinate nature, or is it pure potentiality that is only transformed into something definitive by experience? A preliminary, minimal definition of the "self" might be that it is the referent of the first person pronoun "I," is the possessor of a mind and body, and can initiate changes in both.

The short answer to the second question in the title of this chapter is, in our judgment, an emphatic yes! Judaism needs a self-theory for two different, albeit related, reasons, both of them fundamental. The first stems from the moral outlook of Judaism. If a person is to be able to rule himself and be held accountable for his actions, an ability which is certainly assumed by Judaism, he must understand the forces at work within himself, the constituent elements of his personality, their nature and dynamic. These can only be elucidated in terms of a theory, frequently checked by reference to one's own inner experience. The second reason a self-theory is necessary in Judaism is philosophical. Certain religious beliefs in Judaism, such as freedom of the will, immortality of the soul, and prophecy, presuppose that the human self is one sort of thing rather than another. A self-theory should provide adequate grounding for these beliefs—that is, conditions that make these beliefs possible. In what follows we will elaborate on both these reasons and attempt to sketch the elements of a self-theory for Judaism.[1]

I

The first to think of a theory of self were probably individuals called upon to impart to others what were considered basic rules of behavior. We can imagine their perplexity and frustration when, for the first time, they met up with resistance or contrary responses to what is clearly the right, the proper, and the accepted way to act: "What is wrong with this person?" "What got into him?" "How do we explain what is happening?," they might wonder.

Such a situation would surely generate a strong desire to know the self much better than we thought we did. In attempting to enforce proper behavior, individuals strove to penetrate deeper into their minds, to understand the dynamics of personality and the wellsprings of motivation. In short, these individuals pondered what it is that goes on within the self and what elements are involved.

It has been suggested that it was probably incidents of mental conflict observed in others or experienced by himself that led Plato to his very early self-theory.[2] In an example offered by Plato, someone is very thirsty but does not drink the water available to him because he knows it to be poisoned. The mental conflict this man experiences can be explained by saying that something in the man called Appetite pushes him to drink, while something else called Reason holds him back. In another situation, a person is about to strike someone in anger, but refrains when he realizes that the other person is much bigger. Here, Reason is in conflict with an emotion associated with something in man called

---

[1] In Aaron Rabinowitz's "The Concepts of Self, Mind and Consciousness as Perceived by Judaism," BDD 6 (Winter 1998), which is essentially historical and comparative, Rabinowitz deals with the concepts of self, mind and consciousness as they are understood in psychology and philosophy today in relation to terms such as *ruah, nefesh,* and *neshamah* as they appear in classical Jewish literature. My approach in this essay is to trace the implications of the moral and theological teachings of Judaism for self-theory.

[2] See Leslie Stevenson, *Seven Theories of Human Nature* (Oxford: Clarendon Press, 1974), 26.

Spirit.[3] Given these rudiments of a self-theory, it was a simple matter for Plato, the teacher, to explain that the key to proper behavior is for each individual to organize himself in such a way as to have Reason control both the Spirit and the Appetites. This theory also provides a ready diagnosis should someone behave in ways which appear self-destructive: clearly, Reason has lost control of the other aspects of self.[4]

More than 2000 years after Plato, Sigmund Freud developed another self-thoery. In Freud's case, empirical observations grew out of his interest in cases of hysteria. Freud retained the notion of a tripartite self, although his identification of the parts was much more sophisticated. Instead of "parts," his expositors speak of "three major structural systems" which are: (1) *Id*, which is all the instinctual drives which seek immediate satisfaction; (2) *Ego*, which deals with the real world outside the person; and (3) *Super-ego*, which contains the conscience and social norms acquired during childhood. (Of course, the "mind" is now seen as much more complex, with the addition of the "subconscious.")

While there are obvious differences between these two theories, there is a remarkable similarity between them, not only in terms of the number of discernible elements in the self but also in terms of their essential nature.[5] Both recognize the existence of powerful drives (Appetites, Id) that are the source of much of the energy and motive power of the self. Both theories acknowledge a second element, the *ought-component*, that supplies the goals of one's actions and reminds the self of some of the "don'ts" (Reason, Superego). In both theories, the third element represents the system in charge, the chief executive officer, the part of self that arbitrates between the other two and makes the final decision (Reason, Ego).

---

[3] "Spirit" to Plato was more than emotion. It included all sorts of acts of self-assertion and usually was on the side of Reason.

[4] At this point, we leave open the question as to whether Reason is to be viewed as just another faculty at the disposal of the ego-self or whether it is in any sense to be more closely identified with the self *per se*. Saadia Gaon, one of the earliest Jewish philosophers, concluded that "this soul of man must perform the act of cognition by means of its essence." Saadia Gaon, *The Book of Beliefs and Opinions* (New Haven: Yale University Press, 1948).

[5] Each of these theories is, of course, generated and shaped by a complete world-outlook about the nature of man and the universe. Our purpose in comparing Plato and Freud is solely to facilitate our understanding as to how self-theory is constructed.

Chapter Fourteen. What is Self-theory, and Does Judaism Need One?

The overall picture we get is that of the essential "I" (pure Ego) being exposed on the one hand to powerful instinctual drives and on the other to elements making for constraint and moderation. According to both theories, the appetites are natural, universal, and powerful. The forces for constraint, however, while natural for Plato (Reason), are according to Freud societal in origin (Superego). However, according to both theories it may be assumed that these elements do not occur in all individuals with the same strength or intensity, thus accounting for the phenomenon of individual differences.

The existence of some such tripartite self is supported by the most elementary introspection, which reveals "three departments of the mind," those responsible for : (1) Conceiving; (2) Feeling; and (3) Willing.[6] The first kind of inner experience, conceiving, can be taken as evidence of the intellect or Reason at work. The second, feeling, reflects the activity of the Appetites and the emotions. The third, willing, is the expression of the "I," the real self, maker of decisions and indicator of direction.[7]

The different parts or activities of the self described by these conceptualizations can readily be matched up with experiences that are accessible and familiar to almost everyone. However, none of them enable us to clearly identify and separate out the pure-self (sometimes called *primordial ego*) from its activities, such as "willing" and "imaging," and from various feeling-states that temporarily pass over the self. The self has thus far only been described by what it does or how it feels. Another question remains as well: is Reason to be regarded as a useful faculty only, to be employed by the individual as needed, or is it in some sense a component of his essential self? We will deal with these questions later.

The same need that prompted Plato and Freud to theorize regarding the nature of self has been operative in Judaism from the very beginning. Central to the Torah is the notion of obedience. Man is expected to obey God. When he doesn't, explanations are in order. In the first recorded preventive therapy, God explains the nature of emotions to Cain, the first human born of woman. Cain is taught that while powerful

---

[6] See William James, *Will to Believe* (New York: Dover Publications, 1956).

[7] It is interesting to note that Saadia Gaon (883 CE—941 CE) already perceived the soul of man as expressing itself in the body through three faculties: the power of reasoning (*neshamah*), the power of appetite, i.e. desire or willing (*nefesh*), and the power of anger, i.e. emotions, feeling (*ruah*). All three powers belong to one soul. Saadia Gaon, *The Book of Beliefs and Opinions* , 243-244.

feelings (envy, hate) are somehow within him, he himself is not his emotions! "You," that is to say, your true self, "can rule over it" (Gen. 4:7). Here we have an early picture of a human self that is conflicted. Something called "sin, whose desire is unto you, crouches at the door" (Gen. 4:7).[8] However, there are times when man hears the commanding voice of God, either directly or through the tradition, which counsels obedience and righteousness. And the true self somewhere in the midst of it all, and torn between the opposing forces, must decide.

Somewhat later, the description of God's disappointment with man is accompanied by a more detailed diagnosis: "… Every imagination of the thoughts of his [man's] heart [*yezer mahshevot libo*] is continually evil" (Gen. 6:5). But it is not man, nor his soul, which is called "evil," but rather "the imagery of man's heart." Man's heart thinks images of possible evil, which could be made into the real. "Imagery is play with possibility, play as self-temptation from which ever and again violence springs…. This imagery of the possible is called evil."[9] This seems to place the source of evil somewhere within man himself, but only as a possibility.

Nevertheless, this does not preclude the possibility of moral improvement and change, for ten generations later we learn from the life of Avraham that it is possible for a man to overcome evil and to educate his household "to walk in the way of God to do justice and righteousness" (Gen. 18:19). Yet, Moshe, at the end of his career, grounds his dire warnings about Israel's future loyalty in a knowledge of his people's nature. "For I know your rebellion and your stiff-neck" (Deut. 21:29, 31:7). Surely these statements presuppose some sort of implicit self-theory.

In discussing the implications of the biblical material, the rabbis personalized the internal forces to which the self is subjected and posited that each person possesses a *yezer ha-ra* (evil impulse) from birth and a *yezer tov* (good impulse) which comes with adulthood.[10] It would appear that the *yezer ha-ra* is to be identified with what have been called the "appetites," not only the sexual drive but the acquisitive and aggressive drives as well. Although termed "evil," these drives are not intrinsically so. As natural forces, they are amoral, neither good nor evil. They were

---

[8] For a fuller discussion of this text, see Shubert Spero, *Morality, Halakha and the Jewish Tradition* (New York: Ktav and Yeshiva University Press, 1983), 237-239.
[9] Martin Buber, *Good and Evil* (New York: Charles Scribner's Sons, 1953), 91.
[10] *Berakhot* 61a and b; *Sanhedrin* 91b; *Avot d'Rabbi Nathan* 16.

placed in the soul by God of necessity. Without the sexual drive, "man would woo no woman, beget no children, build no home, and engage in no economic activity."[11] Man's task, therefore, is not to root out the *yetzer ha-ra* but to unite it with the *yetzer tov*. Man is bid to "love the Lord with all your heart (pl.)," which is understood to mean, "with your two united and integrated impulses."[12] The *yetzer ha-ra* provides the energy and passion, while the *yetzer tov* furnishes the direction, which is the love and service of God.

Included in the concept of *yetzer ha-ra* are not only the natural drives that everyone experiences in varying degrees but also those particular dispositions and emotions which may have become part of the individual's temperament. Thus, if one finds oneself at adulthood with a quick temper, an arrogant spirit, or a tendency to violence, for whatever genetic or cultural reasons, that becomes one's personal *yetzer ha-ra*, which one must learn to control.[13] All this implies that not only is knowledge of the human self in general vital for each person, but an insight into one's own peculiar temperament and mix of character traits is also crucial.

The origin and nature of the *yetzer tov*, however, was never clearly defined by the rabbis. One suggestion is that once two alternatives and their consequences are clearly laid out and calmly contemplated, common sense will generally opt for the one that can be described as "good." So construed, "reason" can perhaps be seen as the *yetzer tov*.[14] It has re-

---

[11] Ibid. See Moshe Halevi Spero, *Judaism and Psychology* (New York: Ktav and Yeshiva University Press, 1980), 64-82.

[12] Deut. 6:5. See Rashi on that verse.

[13] "Who is strong (*gibbor*)? He who conquers his impulse [*yitzro*]" (*Avot* 4:1). Judaism has long recognized that all people are not created equal. For example, one's particular genomes may predispose one person to aggressive behavior more than others.

[14] The rabbis recommended making a reckoning of the possible material losses entailed in performing a *mitzvah* against its spiritual rewards, and evaluating the possible short-term gains of transgression against the punishment (*Bava Batra* 18b). This suggests a sort of profit-and-loss accounting similar to Pascal's Wager. In this context, we can see the relevance of Plato, who held that knowledge is virtue and that if a person *knows* what he ought to do he will do it, and that evil is chosen only out of ignorance. Others, however, such as Hume, argued that moral judgments are derived from feelings and not reason.

Already in the Book of Proverbs we are told that the vital task of developing a moral personality and behavior is not simply a matter of will power, of always

Part IV. The Analytic in Action

cently been suggested that universal human nature comes stocked with an emotional repertoire of sympathy, trust, guilt, anger, and self-esteem,

---

choosing the good over the evil, but also involves some sort of knowledge or wisdom.

To know wisdom (*hokhma*) and instruction (*mussar*) ...
To receive the discipline (*mussar*) of wisdom (*haskail*)
Justice, righteousness and equity.... (Prov. 1:2, 3)

Reading on, however, one finds that the "wisdom" and "knowledge" being referred to consist primarily of the knowledge one acquires from life-experiences, either one's own or that of others, as distilled by the wise. It is essentially knowledge about the ways of people in the world and how to recognize the distinctive character-traits of the virtuous, as well as those in the "rogues' gallery" (*kesil, letz, peti, rasha, avil*) and the social consequences of various types of behavior. It is a knowledge that is readily accessible:

Wisdom cries aloud in the street
She sounds her voice in the public square. (Prov. 11:20)

Similarly, the Talmudic sages were quick to point out that it is not enough to have a list of good deeds and to be highly motivated to perform them. One must also have some insight into popular human psychology to know what, when, and how to say and do things to people lest one achieve the very opposite of what was intended (*Avot* 4:23). They also remind us that holding certain philosophic views on the origin and destiny of man and on human freedom and accountability may influence the kind of moral choices one is inclined to make (*Avot* 3:1).

Of course, the "knowledge" most essential to making moral choices is the fundamental one of being able to distinguish right from wrong and good from evil, not only in terms of actions but in terms of character-traits. Disregarding the precise meaning of the account in Genesis 3 as to how man acquired the knowledge of good and evil, it is clear that the Bible assumes man to have it. Maimonides, however, introduces an interesting complication. Following Plato, Maimonides teaches that, "Reason is the power in man by which he distinguishes between base and noble actions" (Moses Maimonides, *Eight Chapters*, chapter 1), so that once he knows what is good, man will always choose the good. However, Maimonides, always the physician, posits the possibility of one developing what he calls "a sick soul," in which case one would imagine "bad things to be good and good things to be bad" (*Eight Chapters*, chapters 3 and 4). Unless the soul is somehow "cured" (restored to health), i.e., unless the individual somehow becomes aware of his self-deception and seeks out the advice and treatment of the wise, he will perish. It follows from this that a most vital bit of information that everyone should have is that it is wise to be suspicious of one's own judgment regarding what is truly right and wrong, and to be alert for the possibility of self-deception. This point is valid regardless of whether you believe, like Maimonides, that a man distinguishes between good and evil by means of his reason or whether you feel the distinction comes from some moral sense or intuition.

"that makes for the good."[15] Vagueness as to the identity of the *yetzer tov* might reflect the assumption that the word of God itself, embodied in scripture and the tradition, constitutes a positive force making for the good. Or perhaps the element of divinity implanted in man ("created in the image of God") expresses itself as some sort of moral sense or moral intuition that guides man toward the right.[16]

The Talmudic rabbis did not posit any theoretical entities beyond the *yetzer tov* and the *yetzer ha-ra*. Their many remarkable observations about the wiles and stratagems of the *yetzer ha-ra*, which show keen psychological insight, were presented as practical advice on how this evil inclination might be overcome.[17] The only rabbinic figure of the medieval period who felt the need to support the moral teachings of the Torah with an overarching theory was Maimonides (1135–1204), who adopted the Aristotelian theory of the soul and the concept of the Middle Way to explain the Torah's concept of moral character.[18] However, as a physician of body and soul, Maimonides' attempt was not a theory of

---

[15] Steven Pinker, *The Blank State* (New York: Viking, 2002), 168.

[16] Pinker (ibid., 271, 435), states that recent research indicates that among a number of Human Universals are to be found "moral sentiments," and that the moral sense can be shown to be made up of four families of emotions which are part of universal human nature: (1) contempt, anger, and disgust, which lead us to condemn others and punish cheaters; (2) gratitude, elevation, and moral awe, which prompt us to reward altruists; (3) sympathy, compassion, and empathy, which lead us to help a needy person; and (4) guilt, shame, and embarrassment, which enable us to avoid cheating and repair its effects.

[17] See *Sukkah* 52a, 52b; *Shabbat* 105b; *Berakhot* 5a.

[18] Maimonides taught that the soul of man (what we have called *neshamah*) is a single unitary soul and is the source of the five life-supporting activities of the human organism, including both the body and the mind. These actions or powers are the nutritive, sentient, imaginative, appetitive, and rational. The first two are essentially physical activities associated with the body. The last three are activities which take place within consciousness and of which the self is aware. The appetitive includes man's desires and fears, loves and hates, and his anger—in short, his emotions. The imaginative is the power that preserves the memory of past experiences and is able to fantasize and compose elements of reality in artificial combinations. For Maimonides the rational part is the source of wisdom and enterprise, which in its theoretical aspect can develop the sciences and in its practical aspect can master crafts and technology. Interestingly, Maimonides states that it is man's reason that "distinguishes between base and noble actions" (*Eight Chapters*, Chapter 1).

self as such, but rather an approach to diagnosis; he perceives human character traits in terms of "health" and "sickness," and recommends a method of therapy.

Even the more recent (nineteenth-century) Musar movement initiated by R. Israel Salanter worked within the traditional framework of the *yetzer tov* and *yetzer ha-ra*. The innovation of Musar was in the particular methodology to be used in order to develop a moral personality. Although the leitmotif of the movement was "Know Thyself," Musar did not attempt to stimulate discoveries of new structures in the human self but was meant primarily as a way for each individual to objectively analyze the weaknesses and foibles of his own particular character. Musar is not interested in the philosophic question of "What am I?" but in the moral question of "What sort of person am I and how can I become better?"[19]

Judaism's insistence upon obedience, with its stress upon individual responsibility, does much to accentuate an awareness of self. It is "I" who is to be held accountable for my deeds. Do I really know myself? Furthermore, the distinction in the Torah between intentional and unintentional transgressions and the rabbis' emphasis upon *l'shma*, doing good "for its own sake," encourages the individual to look inward, to analyze his motives, and to ask himself: what do I really want, and why? Which of my desires speaks for my true self? The belief that punishment and reward might come long after the deed, indeed even after death, creates an acute awareness of the persistence and continuity of the self over time. I know intuitively that, essentially, I am at the core the same "I" that I was 40 years ago, in spite of many obvious changes![20]

Thus, in terms of good and evil, the self seems to have been positioned in a manner which enables it to make free moral choices. The knowledge of good and evil, and the principles through which we determine what is right and wrong in most situations, have been made accessible to man. Except for special circumstances, man will be held accountable for his deeds and for his character because, although the *yetzer ha-ra* is much stronger than the *yetzer tov*, the individual is free to invoke the aid of God and His Torah, which are stronger than both.[21]

---

[19] See M.G. Glenn, *Israel Salanter* (New York: Bloch Publishing Co., 1953); Andrew R. Heinze, "The Americanization of Mussar," *Judaism* 48, no. 4 (Fall 1999).
[20] *Exodus* 21:12-14; *Sukkah* 49b; *Taanit* 7a; *Nedarim* 62a.
[21] *Kiddushin* 30b.

Chapter Fourteen. What is Self-theory, and Does Judaism Need One?

What else can Judaism tell us about the self?

Judaism teaches that permeating a human's entire being is a divine element, a breath of God called *neshamah*. In the words of the morning prayer, "My God, the *neshamah* you gave me is pure. You created it. You formed it and you breathed it into me...."

What is the relation of the *neshamah* to the conscious self? The two do not appear to be identical. The *neshamah* would seem to be the life-force which animates the person as a whole and enables him to function at all levels of being: physical, mental, and spiritual.[22] At the same time, the *neshamah* is that which possesses the potentiality for personality. That is to say, it serves as both "platform" and "raw material" for the building of the individual personality.

We know that the elusive element called "character" is something which develops over time.[23] While various feelings and emotions come and go, repetition of some of them under certain conditions creates resident attitudes and dispositions that may be described as a readiness or inclination to act in a certain way. But in what do these attitudes and dispositions inhere? What unifies these disparate traits and gives them continuity over time? Perhaps it is the *neshamah*, this "breath-of-God," which lends itself to be formed and molded by the experience of the individual; the *neshamah* is able to take on various character traits and become a distinct and unique "self."[24] It is this developing "spiritual" entity which is the referent of the singular first person pronoun "I" and is experienced as pure subjectivity.

---

[22] "Saadia rejects the Platonic dualism of soul and body with their mutual hostility and accepts Aristotle's idea of soul-body that included personality as an active unit. According to Saadia, the soul is immanent, does not enter from the outside, yet is not organically connected with the body but is created and joined to it for a limited time. All the three powers, reason, appetition, and spirit, manifest themselves only through the soul's union with the body through the use of the body as an instrument. But the soul is essentially one and when it leaves the body there is no division." Israel Efros, "The Philosophy of Saadia Gaon," in his *Studies in Medieval Jewish Philosophy* (New York: Columbia University Press, 1974).

[23] See James Davison Hunter, *The Death of Character: Moral Education in an Age Without Good or Evil* (New York: Basic Books, 2000).

[24] This might be called the process by which one's *tselem Elokim*, which is pure potentiality, is developed into an existing moral self that is "like" God and hence achieves the level of *demut Hashem*.Compare Gen. 1:26 to Gen. 1:27 and Gen. 5:1 to Gen. 5:3.

The question of whether introspective analysis yields any evidence for the existence of such a "self" has constituted one of the staples of critical philosophy. Generally, an awareness of self is considered intertwined with consciousness. Although a necessary condition for consciousness, the I-awareness as such tends to merge into the general background and is not seen as an independent force, such as a *neshamah*. The rabbis had, of course, foreseen this, and taught that the soul of man was similar to God in that both "see, but are themselves unseen:"[25] "Just as God dwells in an innermost place, so does the soul dwell in an innermost place." As the substratum in which consciousness appears, the self would have to be something metaphysical, some sort of un-extended, non-spatial reality.

Indeed, Hume had convincingly shown that the most penetrating introspection yields experiences of various sorts, but no self. It would seem that if I *am* self, I should be able to somehow be aware of it. "The subject can never be the direct object of its own experience."[26] "It is like a man who goes outside his house and looks through the window to see if he is at home."[27] Yet, every person feels that there is within his personality "a core or apex which controls his thinking and directs the searchlight of his attention."[28]

All this may explain why one cannot make oneself the object of one's perception. However, does this imply that knowledge of self is only an abstraction? Perhaps one is making an inference of the type, "If there is activity, there must be an agent," or "There must be something that unifies our various experiences." It is at this point that Jewish teaching can help.

Earlier we referred to the divine element in man as the *neshamah*—the breath of life. Elsewhere, however, the divine element is called *tzelem*,[29] which suggests something more distinctive. Indeed, the first word by which God introduces Himself to Israel as a nation is *anokhi*, "I am [the Lord your God]...," and this is repeated scores of times throughout the

---

[25] See Midrash on Psalms 103.
[26] H. D. Lewis, *The Self and Immortality* (New York: The Seabury Press, 1973), 40.
[27] William Barrett, *Death of the Soul* (New York: Anchor Press/Doubleday, 1987), 46.
[28] Arthur Koestler, *The Ghost in the Machine* (New York: Macmillan Co., 1967), 212.
[29] Gen. 1:27.

Torah in the form of *hashem*, "I [am the Lord]." In order to understand the significance of these two words, we should perhaps invert their order to, "*hashem ani*," to be interpreted as "The Lord, am I," that is to say, "divinity lies in my very subjectivity, in my being an "I." The most unique and significant attribute of God is not His omnipotence or omnipresence but the fact that He is *person*, pure subjectivity: "*anokhi, anokhi hashem*"—"I even I am the Lord" (Isa. 43:11).

Perhaps this is the meaning of God's reply "I am what I am" when asked His name (Exod. 3:14). Selfhood cannot be further defined, but must be experienced. "I am": my existence (am*)* is precisely pure subjectivity (I). There is nothing more that I can say about it. And it is this kind of "I" subjectivity, this ego-experience, that God has made available to each human being by endowing him with His *tzelem*. And in all of this unimaginably vast cosmos expanding in all directions into endless space, God has endowed only one creature, man, with self-consciousness, the ability to be aware of himself as an "I" and as an "I" to reach out to the eternal Thou. Consciousness of the self as the abiding entity, which is the "I" that uniquely constitutes my personal identity, is perhaps the primary consequence of being in the "image of God."

The deeper one probes the nature of self consciousness, the more it becomes clear that one never experiences *a* self, only *my* self. That is to say, "the self is known solely in the way each one knows himself to be the unique being he is." Thus, awareness of self turns out to be related to the question of self-identity,[30] for such awareness takes place only when "a being recognizes itself in its difference beyond its immediate identity."[31]

I experience my subjectivity and recognize myself as the same person I was five years ago and not any other. But if selfhood entails uniqueness and recognition of differences, precisely where does my uniqueness lie? Who am I? Is it exclusively a matter of memory, of remembered experiences which I recognize as belonging to myself? In short, what are the main elements in establishing one's self-identity?

Some interesting suggestions are made by Charles Taylor in his penetrating and comprehensive study of the historical sources of the modern

---

[30] H.D. Lewis, "The Elusive Self and the I-Thou Relation" in *Talk of God* (New York: Macmillan-St. Martin's Press, 1969), 168.

[31] Emmanuel Levinas, *Basic Philosophical Writings* (Bloomington, IN: Indiana University Press, 1996), 89.

concept of self-identity, which have striking resonance in terms of Judaism.³² Working back from the condition known as "identity crisis," Taylor concludes that "our identities define the space of qualitative distinctions within which we live and choose."³³ Thus, the process involves a strong element of valuation. "What I am as a self, my identity, is essentially defined by the way things have significance for me."³⁴ When this is broadened, we find that the full definition of identity involves "not only his stand on moral and spiritual matters, but also some reference to a defining community."³⁵ Indeed, when Jonah is suddenly awakened from his sleep in the hold of the storm-tossed boat by the terrified sailors and asked to identify himself ("What is your occupation? Where do you come from? What is your country and of what people are you?"), he simply answers, "I am a Hebrew and I fear the Lord God of heaven" (Jonah 1:8, 9). For, as Taylor points out, "The question of personal identity is the question, 'who am I?'"³⁶ This cannot be answered by giving name and genealogy. What does answer this question is an understanding of what is crucial to us. This most certainly starts with one's concept of the moral good.

But this brings us right back to the teachings of Judaism, for in the view of the Torah, moral experience is not only the crucial element in personal identity, it is the active ingredient in developing and strengthening awareness of the self. It has been said, "Freedom is not the power to act according to moral advice but the inward power to struggle for it … the I lives and becomes stronger in battle. Only in ethics does the 'I' itself appear, struggle, and assume responsibility."³⁷

Only in moral struggle do I begin to know *who* I am. Only then do I realize *that* I am. In the depths of moral crisis, I become aware of a self that deliberates, weighs alternatives, agonizes over outcomes, is awed by the weight of responsibility, and then decides. At that moment I am truly aware of a recognizable entity that is something distinct, abiding, and

---

[32] Charles Taylor, *Sources of the Self* (Cambridge, MA: Harvard University Press 1989).
[33] Ibid., 30.
[34] Ibid., 34.
[35] Ibid., 36.
[36] Ibid., 27.
[37] Israel I. Efros, *Ancient Jewish Philosophy* (Detroit: Wayne State University Press, 1964), 119, 130.

Chapter Fourteen. What is Self-theory, and Does Judaism Need One?

freely choosing. From that moment on, the unique entity that is *my* self has become more distinct and recognizable and has taken on *character*. I am I that has resisted temptation and made the proper moral choice.

There is a well-known saying of Rabbi Akiva whose import, I believe, has not been properly recognized:

> Rabbi Akiva would say, Beloved is man for he was created in the image of God. But it is by a special love that it was made known to him that he was created in the image of God, as it is said: "For in the image of God made He man...." (*Avot* 3:18)

Rabbi Akiva is here coining a new idea in Jewish theology. First, he restates a basic principle of the Jewish concept of man that is plainly stated in the Torah, namely that every man and woman is created in the image of God. He goes on to say that the fact that there is this divine element in man has been *made known to him*. That is to say, this information that man has been formed in His image, which is an expression of God's special love, is available to every person.

Let us ponder the significance of this teaching. The question of "who or what is man?" remains the "mystery of mysteries," with the entire issue of life's meaning and the nature of morality hinging on the answer. But if Rabbi Akiva is correct and somehow we can *know* that we bear the "likeness of God," why are so many still walking in darkness?

What proof-text is given for this revelatory teaching of Rabbi Akiva? Man can know his special nature because it is taught in the Torah that man was created in the image of God (Gen. 9:6)! But the Torah is the special revelation of God to Israel. The publication of certain vital information in the Book of Genesis can hardly be considered a responsible way of communicating with mankind as a whole! What of that large portion of humanity that for most of human history never heard of the Hebrew prophets, and of that other portion that, having heard, gives no credence to *Torat Moshe*?

However, once we read the full text we can understand why Rabbi Akiva had to go to Chapter 9 in Genesis to find his proof, rather than to cite Gen.1:27, the more obvious choice.

> Who so sheds man's blood, by man shall his blood be shed ... for in the image of God made He man. (Gen. 9:6)

Rabbi Akiva's textual evidence lies in the association of "image of God" with the universal moral concept of justice, an association which is found in this verse only. The justification of the death penalty for murder lies in the preciousness of the human being and the fact that man is a responsible moral agent. The fact that man is able to recognize, appreciate, and accept the moral principle of justice informs him that he bears within himself the seal of the moral God.

According to Judaism, therefore, this accretive, life-long process of transforming one's *neshamah* into an ethical self is simultaneously a process of self-creation and a process of growing self-awareness. It is performed by the protean self and results in the appearance of a more recognizable self. The power and freedom to do this is part of what it is to be *tzelem elokim*, as is the sense of responsibility that accompanies it. Once one has realized the potential of the *tzelem* and made moral values a resident part of one's personality, one attains the level of *demut*, to be "like God," *domeh lo*.[38] In the words of Rabbi Joseph B. Soloveitchik, "… that man must create himself is the most fundamental principle of all, the peak of ethical religious perfection." In transforming myself into an ethical personality, I attain true selfhood, "individuality, autonomy, uniqueness, and freedom. For self-creation means that man breaks through the limitations of universality, causality and species-dependence."[39]

In his analysis of the elements that go into the making of the modern concept of self-identity, Taylor draws our attention to the ways we talk about judging the significance of individual lives. We ask whether a life has been "rich and full" or "trivial and empty." We want to know whether an individual's life has been fragmented or has shown "unity and purpose." Most telling of all is the phrase "the *story* of one's life."

Taylor points out that behind all attempts to describe human lives, my own or others', stand certain "inescapable frameworks" that provide

---

[38] This explains why, in announcing the plan, God says: "Let us make man in our image after our likeness" (Gen. 1:26), yet in the implementation we are told, "And God created man in His own image" (Gen. 1:27). "Likeness" (*demut*) is not mentioned because this quality is something acquired by the individual over the course of his life.

[39] Joseph B. Soloveitchik, *Halakhic Man* (Philadelphia: The Jewish Publication Society, 1983), 101-104, 135.

criteria of good and evil, sets of values, and a sense of direction. Since a human life takes place in a temporal context, to judge it requires a narrative understanding, "a sense of what I have become and how I got there, which can only be given in a story."[40]

Thus, as we have seen, when Jonah responds to the questions of personal identity that are suddenly hurled at him, he properly answers by saying, "I am a Hebrew and the Lord God of Heaven do I fear." I identify with the Hebrews and their God. Learn their story and the values of the God of Israel and you will know who I am.

In a similar manner, the entire structure of the Passover *seder* takes on a fresh significance once we realize that behind the many different "questions" that are asked, the underlying quest is for self-identity.[41] Surrounded by a plethora of rituals, the Jews of the next generation want to know where they fit in. And the reaction is always to tell them the story, the *entire* story from the very beginning, so that perhaps they will get the picture and may even find themselves in that framework!

II

From our discussion in the first part of this paper, it should be clear that the self, to the extent that it "exists" and performs the functions we have attributed to it, would have to be something metaphysical, that is, some sort of non-material reality not subject to empirical verification.

This concept of a self or soul has been severely criticized from the beginning of modern philosophy as being purely speculative, with no basis in reality. Indeed, the traditional concept of the soul has variously been called "a grammatical fiction" and the "ghost in the machine," and the illusion of self has been seen as a "mere bundle of perceptions" or "the reification of a set of relations among my thoughts."[42]

We suggested earlier that awareness of self, with its accompanying sense of self-identity, may be viewed as an immediate intuition of a

---

[40] Charles Taylor, *Sources of the Self*, 47, 48.
[41] See Shubert Spero, *God in All Seasons* (New York: Sheingold Publishers, 1967), 111-115.
[42] Alburey Castell, *The Self in Philosophy* (New York: Macmillan Co., 1965), 49.

very unique nature. We should not expect to "know" it as we do other realities. To do so, it has been suggested, is to confuse the existential with the epistemological. "We are aware of ourselves in the radical sense which is involved in our *being* ourselves."[43] In short, it is a mistake to seek the self among the *contents* of our consciousness when it is in reality the very *ground* of our consciousness.

Nevertheless, there are some common experiences which can be seen as testifying to the reality of the self.

1) We are able to distinguish between different experiences, recognizing which ones are the activities of the self. Thus, I often experience sensations or emotions which are occurring *to* me and of which I am conscious, but toward which I am passive. For example, I feel myself getting thirstier and thirstier, or angrier and angrier. These are psychological processes, but are not activities performed *by* the self. A decision not to drink from a possibly-contaminated water source in spite of my growing thirst, on the other hand, is directly experienced as an activity of the self.[44]

2) Consider the difference between subject and object. I direct my attention to the pain in my finger. True, it is *my* finger and I feel the pain. However, I am able to distance myself from the experience, at least to a certain extent. I am able to view my finger as an object. I am in pain, but I am not my pain. I am angry, but I am not my anger. However, I can never distance myself from my self because I *am* my self, a subject.[45]

3) While it is true that we can never catch the self, as such, without some particular perception or sensation, there is somehow the feeling that there must be more to consciousness than the passing scene or memories of past perceptions. There must be "something or someone at the center of such experience that unifies it all, that holds the terms and relations of it together in our consciousness, a sort of organizing center of experience."[46]

---

[43] Stephen Strasser, *The Soul in Metaphysical and Empirical Psychology* (Pittsburgh: Duquesne University Press, 1957), 106.
[44] Alburey Castell, *The Self in Philosophy*, 57.
[45] Stephen Strasser, *The Soul in Metaphysical and Empirical Psychology*, 64.
[46] H.D. Lewis, *The Self and Immortality*, 34.

4) Also revealing is a phenomenological analysis of our use of the terms "being" and "having."

    a. Anything I may be said to *have* exists, at least to a certain extent, independently of me.

    b. With respect to myself, anything I *have* exhibits a certain "exteriority" and "foreignness."

    c. Anything I *have* has the character of an object.

    d. I can, within certain limits, dispose of anything I *have* or cede it to another.

It is evident that none of the above applies to what we call the self.[47] This means that the problem of the self cannot be solved in the realm of "having" but only in terms of "being." Thus it is misleading to say "I *have* a soul," rather than, "I *am* my soul."

There is also the experience we call "exertion of will," which is different from the simple act of choosing. We need not think of the "will" as a separate faculty of the self, but rather as an activity of the total person. Typically we become aware of this in situations in which our desire tends to lead us toward one object while our sense of duty points in another. We become conscious of exerting effort because we are going against certain resistance. In such situations we find the self to be the source of the effort and know we can withhold the exertion or make it in varying degrees.[48]

The above considerations, in addition to the subjective awareness of self-hood, warrant an assertion of the reality of the self. However, in describing its nature we would call it a *spiritual substance*. By saying it is *spirit* we imply that the self did not come into existence as the result of natural processes only. Although "real" and remaining the same over time, it is not composed of matter. The word "substance" (literally, "stand under") is used here as a spatial metaphor: the self "stands under," undergirds, all of the qualities, relations, and changes that it experiences, but is not, in itself, any or the sum total of these qualities, relations, and changes. As "spiritual substance," the self is capable of change and of

---

[47] Attributed to Gabriel Marcel. See Stephen Strasser, *The Soul in Metaphysical and Empirical Psychology*, 71-72.

[48] See John Howie, "Is Effort of Will a Basis for Moral Freedom?," *Religious Studies* 8, no. 4 (December, 1972).

growth in some significant sense. At the same time, however, it is not subject to the same laws of growth and decay, life and death, as the body is. This leaves room for the possibility of the survival of aspects of the self after the destruction of the body.

Even before we get to the more theological issues, such as the survival of the soul or the nature of prophecy, we find ourselves compelled to view the self as something spiritual. This flows from our need to embrace the concept of human free will. The concept that man is a free agent, particularly in his moral decisions, is an absolutely indispensable condition for moral accountability.[49] This is true not only from the point of view of Judaism, but in terms of any rational analysis of the philosophic foundations of the juridical and penal systems of the West.

On the common-sense level, when someone does something subject to moral judgment we say: "He is wrong. He ought to have done otherwise," or "He should have refrained from doing it." However, "ought implies can," meaning that our moral judgment assumes that, all things being equal, he could have *acted* differently and could have *chosen* to act differently. Only due to this can he be called a responsible agent who could be assigned praise or blame.

However, such a requirement for moral agency taken to its logical conclusion would entail what is called "contra-causal freedom," which is incompatible with what is called psychological determinism. This issue must be met head-on.[50] The philosophy of "determinism" has been growing ever more popular with the successful development of the natural sciences. Wherever science has examined the world, it has found that the present is always determined by antecedent conditions. These orderly patterns can be formulated as causal regularities so that, given knowledge of the antecedent conditions, accurate predictions can be made. If the principles of causation and predictability are assumed to prevail in the psychological area as well, you end up with a theory of universal determinism. That is to say, you may think you are a free agent and can *do* as you please, but can you really *please* as you please?

---

[49] Maimonides, *Mishneh Torah, Hilkhot Teshuvah* 5:1-4.
[50] See the full discussion in Shubert Spero, *Morality, Halakha and the Jewish Tradition*, 255-274.

Chapter Fourteen. What is Self-theory, and Does Judaism Need One?

Before we proceed any further, we must recognize the kernel of truth in psychological determinism. One of the necessary conditions of moral responsibility is that the agent retains the self-same identity throughout. The self must be seen as an abiding continuant that generally behaves according to the values and character traits it has developed in its life so far. In fact, much of daily life assumes the predictability of behavior in moral agents and the constancy of character. The Talmud itself is replete with principles of psychological regularity which enable us to anticipate human behavior. Thus, all free will is freedom within the limits of a person's inborn capabilities and the world in which he lives.[51] The one area that must be reserved for the possibility of the exercise of contra-causal freedom is the moral realm, or situations in which the agent believes that his essential character or integrity as a self hangs on his decision.

Taken together, the moral and philosophical requirements of Judaism seem to include contradictory conditions:

1) That I remain throughout the self-same person.

2) That I could have acted "out of character" and chosen otherwise.

Thus, while affirming contra-causal freedom, we are saying that there is some meaningful way to attribute an act to a self even though in an important sense it is not an expression of the self's character as so far formed. This is, indeed, the crux of the matter. Judaism would maintain that this freedom to choose is a capacity inherent in every human being as a consequence of having been created "in the image of God." On such occasions, man can make a choice which no one, even with encyclopedic knowledge, could have predicted, because it may go against the entire lineup of causal conditions. But what causes the person to make that particular choice at that particular time? The answer is: nothing! At least nothing in the conventional sense. For this is precisely the nature of freedom of the self as spiritual substance.

---

[51] Thus, the free act of a moral agent would be "an act which is not the expression of the self's character as so far formed and yet is the self's own act." See C.A. Campbell, "Is Free Will a Pseudo-Problem?," in *A Modern Introduction to Philosophy*, ed. Paul Edwards and Arthur Pap (Glencoe, IL: The Free Press, 1957), 379.

> Certain substances, however, can initiate changes in an absolute Sense, that is, they are capable of originating a change that does not itself issue from some other change.... This ability is alternativelydescribed as "the power of absolute self origination, as a creative power, as the power of agency and perhaps best as "the ability to act as a prime mover."[52]

Here we can perhaps see most clearly how man resembles God. Even as God is the unmoved mover, the uncaused cause in creation, so is man in the realm of moral choice. Even as God created "out of nothing," so can man, on occasion, freely initiate new structures to his character and unpredictable processes in the world. While the conscious portion of the self faces outward and connects into the empirical web of causality, the primordial ego, which is the ground of the self, whose depths man can never glimpse, backs up into the mysterious realm of the spirit. And it is from there that the self can creatively introduce new energy and crucially modify the balance of power in his own personality.

Note the similarity between the self-originating choice of a moral agent as described here and an event usually attributed to God, called a *miracle*.

> A miracle is emphatically not an event without cause or without results. Its cause is the activity of God, its results in the forward direction are interlocked with all nature just like any other event. Its peculiarity is that it is not interlocked backwards. That is to say, in terms of its origin, it is not so interlocked with the previous history of nature.[53]

We can speak similarly about man's moral choices. After the free choice has been made, the event interlocks with the rest of nature, including the decision-maker's own character. We would argue that, in principle, before the choice, what he actually will do is unpredictable.[54]

---

[52] P.D. Gosselin, "C.A. Campbell's 'Effort of Will' Argument," *Religious Studies* 13, no. 4 (1977).

[53] C. S. Lewis, *Miracles* (New York: The Macmillan Co., 1947), 61.

[54] In this sense, the *Sefat Emet* (on *Pareshat Va-yerah*) sees a connection between the words *nes* (miracle) and *nisayon* (trial or test). Every moral test to which a person is put is in reality a challenge for him to overcome his "nature" and by

Chapter Fourteen. What is Self-theory, and Does Judaism Need One?

On the basis of our phenomenological analysis as well as the implications of the concept of contra-causal freedom, we have concluded that the human self can best be described as *spiritual substance*. As such, there is nothing that precludes the possibility of the self's survival after the death of the body. The question remains, however, as to whether the sketch we have drawn of the human self is adequate and compatible with all aspects of the Jewish doctrine of the immortality of the soul. While the eschatological views of Judaism are rather complex, the specific belief that concerns the ultimate fate of the individual is referred to as a belief in *Olam ha-Ba*, the "world to come."[55] According to the most reasonable view, this is an all-spiritual realm in which the souls of the righteous continue to "exist" after the destruction of the body. The rabbis of the Talmud were emphatic that we can have no conception of conditions in the afterworld other than that "there is neither eating nor drinking, nor hatred, nor envy, nor strife, but that the righteous sit with their crowns on their heads and enjoy the splendor of the Divine Presence."[56]

There are two questionable assumptions implicit in the discussion of the medieval philosophers on this subject which created considerable confusion. One assumption, part of the legacy of Aristotle, was that the most distinctive part of the human soul is the rational faculty that exclusively connects the individual to God, and that it is that aspect of the self which survives death and therefore must be most assiduously cultivated by man during his lifetime. The second approach was to view all eschatology in terms of reward and punishment. That is to say, there is a theological need for "heaven and hell," *Gan Eden* and *Gehinnom*. Exile and Redemption were seen as growing primarily out of the moral nature of God, which required each person to receive his just desserts.

Let us first consider the role of reason in the makeup of the human being. It cannot, of course, be denied that the level of intelligence

---

exercising his "free will" to choose the right. Each time this is done we have in essence a psychological "miracle."

[55] Belief in the "world to come" (*Olam ha-Ba*) as the ultimate reward for the individual is included in the eleventh of Maimonides' Thirteen Principles of Faith. For a full discussion, see Joseph Albo, *Sefer Ha-Ikarim* (Philadelphia: Jewish Publication Society, 1930), III:30, 289-306.

[56] *Berakhot* 17a, 34b.

possessed by an individual, his power of reasoning, is one of his most important characteristics and is one of the consequences of having been "created in the Image of God." It does not, however, follow that the rational faculty is man's *telos* or ultimate reason for being. Computer technology and the ongoing development of artificial intelligence has emphasized the dependence of the mind upon the physiological activity of the brain, thus discrediting the belief that it is something spiritual. Furthermore, modern philosophy has undermined the belief that reason is a possible means by which man can attain theological truths of a metaphysical nature. It is true that man could not be man, be a moral agent, engage in scientific discovery, build civilizations, or study Torah without mind, intelligence, or reason. It is a most useful and necessary tool for human life on earth. However, we do not think about our brains as part of our essential selves. I do not identify with my IQ! In the view of Judaism, man was not brought into existence primarily to develop his reason or to think "deep thoughts," even if they were Torah thoughts or thoughts about God.

Just as man becomes aware of his self in moments of moral choice, so does the self grow in substance and in significance the more he embraces moral values. Man can sometimes employ his reason to determine the way of justice and righteousness in particular circumstances, but there is no necessary correlation between intelligence (reason) and moral character. Thus, there is no good reason to believe that it is the rational faculty of the human soul that is immortal.

Medieval philosophers, following the Talmudic rabbis, discussed eschatological events such as the days of the Messiah, the resurrection of the dead, and the World to Come in terms of reward and punishment. That is, God, as the just and righteous Ruler of the world, is bound to provide at the end the reward or retribution for each individual according to his behavior during his lifetime. Although this was indeed the basis for the discussions surrounding the doctrine of the resurrection of the dead it is not the dominating consideration regarding the concept of the immortality of the soul.

As is well known, survival of the human being after death in some form long predates the appearance of Israel or the emergence of Judaism. It has been rightly noted that while we find the idea of immortality in the Bible itself, it is not connected to judgment, to reward and punishment.[57] Where is the idea of immortality in the Bible? Indeed, it is only natural that a person, after experiencing all of the ineluctable wonders of self-consciousness and creativity, would almost instinctively believe that the self is somehow indestructible. Self awareness is too vibrant an experience to permit thinking of non-existence as somehow inevitable.

I wish to suggest that immortality of the soul and the "cleaving" of the self to God after death are to be understood as the original purposes and ultimate destiny of the individual human being. Man was created *betzelem elokim* and given the capacity to be a moral agent so that he could, in the course of his lifetime, exercise his free will and create for himself a personality permeated with moral value. Just as personality itself is incremental, coming into existence over time as the result of the formation of resident character traits and dispositions, so, too, the possibility for survival after death and fellowship with God is developmental and incremental.[58] Nothing is set at birth. The *tzelem* provides potentiality—the rest is up to the individual.

Upon the death of the body, the spark of potentiality that has hopefully been developed by moral action and has grown into a full-blown spiritual substance continues to exist. In the event that the individual has not lived a moral life, his potential remains unrealized and, in the absence of any developed spirituality, the individual self perishes. This is the ultimate "punishment."

In the words of the rabbis: "In the World to Come … the righteous," those that have developed moral personalities, "sit with their crowns on their heads," that is, the crowns of the good names that they achieved as a result of their moral dealings with others, "and enjoy the splendor of the Divine Presence."[59] This means that the souls of the righteous are able to commune with and achieve *de'vaikut* with the *shekhina*. For in some mysterious sense, moral values, which in human terms translate as justice, righteousness, love, kindness, and mercy, are aspects of the

---

[57] See Yehezkel Kaufmann, *The Religion of Israel* (Chicago: University of Chicago Press, 1960), 316.

[58] See D. Bookstaber, *The Idea of Development of the Soul in Medieval Jewish Philosophy* (Philadelphia: Maurice Jacobs, Inc., 1950). Also see Yitzhak Julius Guttmann, *On the Philosophy of Religion* (Jerusalem: Magnes Press, 1976), 89-94.

[59] Albo, *Sefer Ha-Ikarim*.

very essence of God.⁶⁰ Thus the creation by the individual of a moral self makes possible fellowship with God, and this is the ultimate reward.

As we have stated, "Regarding *olam ha-ba*, no eye has seen it, O God, beside Thee."⁶¹ Nevertheless, our analysis of the self permits some tentative observations regarding the question of self-identity in the hereafter.

The most intimate relationship with God is described in the Pentateuch as "cleaving" or "clinging" unto Him (*le-davka bo*),⁶² a mystical experience which seems to include elements of fear and love and "walking in His ways." It has been pointed out that Judaism cannot accept an interpretation that calls for a mystical union with the Divine in which man loses his self-identity.⁶³ This is true as far as the *mitzvah* of *le-davka bo* is concerned, as "cleaving" to God is considered a practical commandment to be observed in this world. However, how shall we understand the ultimate condition of the self in the World to Come? Is this some joyful absorption into the splendors of the *shechina* in which the individual finally loses his sense of self-identity, yielding the spiritual fruits of his life to his Maker? Does it even make any sense to continue to talk of "self-identity" in such uncharted circumstances?

All of the mundane elements which accompany a person's sense of self-identity while alive, such as memories of past experiences, particular human relationships, and aspirations for the future, must surely fade into irrelevance. If a sense of self-identity is retained, it is possibly the self-satisfaction of personal fulfillment suffused with the *korot ruah*, spiritual satisfaction, of moral value.⁶⁴

---

[60] Judaism believes that apprehension of value is getting to know something significant about Being and is a sort of cognition. Thus, for example, the experience of loving-kindness in God's creation is no mere subjective feeling state but a discovery of some objective property called moral value which belongs to an absolute value-realm. See W .H. Werkmeister, *Theories of Ethics* (Lincoln, NE: Johnsen Publishing Co, 1961), 329). This is why the prophet explains that "knowledge of God" consists of the moral principles of righteousness and loving-kindness (Jer. 9:23).

[61] Isa. 64:3

[62] Deut. 11:22.

[63] See Rabbi Joseph B. Soloveitchik, "*U-vikkashtem mi-Sham*" ("*And You Shall Seek Him from There*") in *Ish ha-Halakhah: Galuyi ve-Nistar* (Jerusalem, 1979), 190.

[64] Avot 4:22.

Chapter Fourteen. What is Self-theory, and Does Judaism Need One?

The concept of prophecy is fundamental to biblical religion.[65] It is the general name for the process by which God communicates with man.[66] The possibility for such communication is essential, since according to Judaism man on his own is incapable of discovering his true nature and the reason for his existence. As a nation, Israel, in the absence of revelation, would have remained ignorant of its special vocation. Throughout the Torah, the media by which God reaches out to man are described as His *ruakh* (spirit) and as His *davar* (word).[67]

> And as for Me, this is My covenant with them, says the Lord, My spirit [*rukhi*] that is upon you and My words [*devarai*] which I have put in your mouth shall not depart out of your mouth nor out of the mouth of your seed ... says the Lord, from now and forever (Isa. 59:21).

This "spirit of God," or Holy Spirit (*ruakh ha-kodesh*), which comes in varying degrees of intensity, is felt as an outside force which enters and takes hold of the individual, who then proceeds to successfully bring about matters of great significance. However, the most characteristic way in which the biblical God expresses His will is by means of the *davar*, the word whose power is such that it itself may transmute into the reality that is called for: "And the Lord said, 'Let there be light,' and there was light" (Gen. 1:3).[68] But when spoken to man, the word of God can instruct and encourage, promise and console, warn and condemn, exhort and inspire. From the very beginning, we read of how God speaks to Adam and Eve, Noah, and the Patriarchs. However, the message essentially concerns those spoken to. It is first with Moshe that we hear of *apostolic prophecy* and meet the prophet-messenger.[69] Here an individual who has not sought the mission is selected by God and charged to bring a message to others, to world rulers or to an entire people, in order to effectuate

---

[65] See Abraham J. Heschel, *The Prophets* (New York: Harper and Row, 1962), 431-432.
[66] Ibid., 405-407.
[67] See the section by Andre Neher in Dov Raphael, *Ha-Nevuah* (Jerusalem, 1971), 207-224.
[68] See Isa. 55.
[69] Yehezkel Kaufmann, "The Biblical Age" in *Great Ages and Ideas of the Jewish People* (New York: Random House, 1956), 58, 59.

radical changes in human behavior and in the fate of nations. Here we encounter the truly distinctive characteristics of Hebrew prophecy.

While the history of religions is replete with accounts of a variety of Divine-human encounters, we are able to identify from the subjective side what is different in the experience of the Hebrew prophets.

Unlike mystical experiences of ecstasy wherein the person loses his identity, in the prophetic act there is no collapse of consciousness.[70] In ecstasy, the experience is incommunicable, whereas in prophecy there is a message to be imparted to others.[71] Moreover, the prophetic event has a direction. It is a message to someone in particular, about something in particular. Prophecy is an encounter of the concrete person and the living God. It is the experience of a relationship with a Person.[72] "It is characterized by a subject-subject structure, the self-conscious active 'I' of the prophet encounters the active living 'Inspirer.'"[73]

Most important of all, however, is the *certainty* felt by the prophet of having experienced the impingement of a personal Being, of another "I." Could this not be some illusion, some wishful thinking on the part of an overheated imagination? However, when we consider that often the prophet had to battle contemporaries whom he himself labeled "false prophets" and that his message was often unpopular and greeted with hostility, we can assume that the prophet must have had certain reliable criteria for distinguishing between veridical experience and illusion, and for deciding that the source of his experience was the living God.[74]

From the Biblical evidence it is clear that prophecy was experienced in different forms and in varying degrees.[75] Already in the Torah we hear of "dreams" and "visions," of "oracles" and riddles," of God speaking to man by means of angels, but also of God addressing man directly.[76] Most crucial for Judaism, however, was the need to explicate the unique na-

---

[70] Abraham J. Heschel, *The Prophets*, 357.
[71] Ibid., 360.
[72] Ibid., 437.
[73] Ibid., 366.
[74] Ibid., 418-428.
[75] See Maimonides, *Guide for the Perplexed*, translated by M. Friedlander (London: George Routledge & Sons, 1942), II:40-47.
[76] "And He said: 'Hear now My words: If there be a prophet among you, I the Lord do make Myself known to him in a vision, I do speak to him in a dream. My servant Moshe is not so. He is trusted in all My house. With him do I speak

ture of Moshe's prophecy, upon which rests the entire authority of the Torah.[77] Our interest in this paper, however, is to determine whether the theory of the self we have propounded is consistent with the theoretical requirements of a phenomenon such as prophecy. At the close of the Middle Ages, the general consensus was that the word of God impacts the prophet in the following manner:

> Prophecy is an inspiration coming from God to the rational power in man either through the medium of the imagination or without it, by virtue of which information comes to him ... concerning matters that a man cannot know naturally by himself.[78]

The idea of God speaking to man has always been met by a certain initial incredulity, for how could the spiritual connect with the material, the infinite with the finite, the absolute with the relative? However, if we understand the self in the terms we have presented, then it is clear that within every person, even in his natural state, there is an ongoing interaction between the material and the spiritual, between the person as a physical organism and the self, which is a spiritual substance. The free will of the individual, which is the immediate expression of the self, can set into motion all sorts of bodily activities. Thus, there would appear to be no special difficulty with more powerful spiritual forces such as *ruakh Hashem* or *devar Hashem* connecting with the person's consciousness. Since some prophetic experiences involve dreams and visions, the philosophers spoke of the imaginative faculty being engaged, whereas the "word of God" would be received by the rational faculty.

Heschel has convincingly shown, based on the biblical evidence, that the most outstanding aspect of the prophetic consciousness is its emotional quality. That is to say, the overwhelming realization of the prophet is of the Divine pathos, that God cares for man and needs man to make abstract moral values real by concrete fulfillment in human affairs, that God is disappointed by man's failure and outraged by his treatment of his fellow man. And the prophet responds with an emotion best described as "sympathy," "an overflow of emotion which comes in

---

mouth to mouth manifestly and not in dark speeches [riddles and oracles] and the similitude of the Lord does he behold..." (Num. 12:6-8).

[77] See Maimonides, *Mishneh Torah*, *Hilkhot Yesodei ha-Torah*, 7:6.

[78] Albo, *Sefer Ha-Ikarim*, III:74.

response to what the prophet senses in divinity."[79] Thus, to be a prophet means to "identify his concern with the concern of God." We may therefore say that prophecy consists of the inspired communication of Divine attitudes to the prophetic consciousness.[80] Indeed, this is the way the prophet describes himself:

> But as for me, I am filled with power
> with the *ruah* of the Lord.
> And with justice and might
> To declare to Jacob his transgressions
> And to Israel his sins. (Michah 3:8)

Another aspect of our theory that coincides with the prophetic consciousness is the nature of the prophetic preparation. In the Jewish view, the experience of prophecy is not something that can be obtained naturally or induced by the individual upon reaching some specific level of intellectual or moral achievement. In every case, the prophetic experience depends ultimately on the will of God. However, there are necessary conditions. One rabbi declared that the Divine Presence rests upon a person only when that person is experiencing the joy of performing the commandments.[81] Another rabbi advocated a step–by–step process of personal religious and moral development in which "holiness leads to humility which leads to fear of sin which leads to loving-kindness (*hassidut*), which leads to the Holy Spirit (*ruah ha-kodesh*)."[82]

It would appear that the element most effective in bringing the self into tune with *ruakh ha-kodesh*, divine inspiration, and ready to receive *devar Hashem* is moral development. The human personality that has become good and compassionate, caring and generous, and sensitive to injustice and the suffering of others can best respond to the Presence of a God that is Himself good and is the source of all justice. God reaches out to man because He is concerned about the world and wishes to be intimately involved in the history of man. "This," says Heschel, "is the essence of God's moral nature."[83]

---

[79] Abraham J. Heschel, *The Prophets*, 309.
[80] Ibid., 223.
[81] *Shabbat* 30b.
[82] *Sotah* 9.
[83] Heschel, *The Prophets*, 225.

Chapter Fourteen. What is Self-theory, and Does Judaism Need One?

The ability of the human being, the prophet, to respond to the invasion by the *ruakh* or *devar* of God on all levels of his being, emotionally, intellectually, and imaginatively, is living testimony to man's having been formed in the "image of God." The prophet does not merely constitute a conduit for the divine force but joins it at all levels. Should he receive a *vision*, the prophet seeks out his richest vocabulary with which to describe it; becoming aware of the Divine *pathos*, the emotions of the prophet to their very depths begin to vibrate in passionate sympathy. Should the *word* of God enter his consciousness, the prophet seeks to understand it, to draw its full meaning as he seeks to transmit it to others.

The special nature of Moshe's prophecy has been emphasized by the Torah itself and elaborated upon by rabbis and philosophers. The importance attributed to *Torat Moshe* as containing the legislative core of God's revelation reflects the belief that we have here verbal inspiration (*devar Hashem*), that is, that the words of the text are the very words selected by God. The role of Moshe was to understand them and record them for transmission down the generations. By contrast, the literary prophets experienced the *ruakh Hashem* as divine pathos and were sent primarily to exhort and chastise, to comfort and console. They express their prophetic experience in words drawn from their own vocabulary.

The only type of prophecy in which it could be said that the *ruakh Elokim* was in exclusive control was in that singular prophetic act known as the *writing* of the Torah.[84] This was the final step in the creation of the Torah, in which the Divine takes over the consciousness of Moshe and dictates word for word what he is to write. What emerges is a melding of records of earlier primary revelations, memories of events in the life of Moshe, and material from existing historical archives and folk traditions in the fires of prophecy to produce *Torat Hashem*.[85] Here we may use the words of Maimonides to describe what took place:

> In receiving the Torah, Moshe was like a scribe writing from dictation the whole of it, its chronicles, its narratives and its prescriptions.[86]

---
[84] Exod. 24:4; Deut. 31:24.
[85] See Chapter 8 in this volume. .
[86] Commentary on the *Mishnah Sanhedrin, Perek Helek*.

We have acknowledged from the outset that "the self which has ultimate responsibility for man's actions, can never be caught in the focal beam of his own awareness,"[87] and doubts have therefore continually arisen among philosophers to its "reality." Nevertheless, we have argued that Judaism as a worldview is compelled to articulate a theory of the self as *spiritual substance* which is able to (1) account for its moral outlook, and (2) support its belief in such concepts as freedom of the will, immortality of the soul, and prophecy. We submit that the dynamics experienced within consciousness, such as moral deliberation and self-identity, are adequately accounted for by the theory we have outlined, which is completely compatible with Judaism's traditional beliefs. While there is no way in which to empirically verify the existence of *spiritual substance*, there is much to commend the observation that, as Shakespeare might put it, "there may be more things in heaven and earth than we have dreamed of in our philosophy."

---

[87] Arthur Koestler, *The Ghost in the Machine*, 217.

Chapter Fifteen

Judaism and the Aesthetic

The difficulties encountered in the past by those addressing broad questions of the type "What is the relationship between Judaism and science/ Judaism and morality/ Judaism and the arts?" have not all come from the side of Judaism. These very familiar but terribly elusive concepts such as "science" and "morality" to which Judaism was juxtaposed have, sometimes, for reasons pertaining primarily to lags in their own philosophic development, not properly been understood. If this observation can be shown to be true in relation to "science" and "morality," how much more so can it be in regard to the "arts." For the very idea of the arts considered as a unitary group, or of aesthetics deemed a separate discipline, is philosophically of relatively recent vintage. Little agreement can therefore be found, even on basic questions.

I wish to suggest, nevertheless, that a number of seminal approaches can be found in the philosophy of art which warrant a fresh look at the relationship between Judaism[1] and the arts. Early thinkers did not conceive of the different art forms as united by any common quality. Music had its educational uses, poetics had its unities, and the relation of the arts to the emotions caused Plato to view them with suspicion. For a long time the artist was considered simply a special kind of fabricator, no different in principle from a carpenter or a builder.

Any possible interest in the arts on the part of Judaism was virtually precluded by two restricting characteristics of the traditional approach to the arts. The first of these characteristics was the almost exclusive focus on the artist and his work of art. The second was a preoccupation with the graphic and representational art forms, such as painting and sculpture. These two factors, taken together, created the impression that the world of art consisted exclusively of a certain mysterious

---

[1] By "Judaism" I refer to the religious beliefs and practices of the Jewish people based on the biblical-rabbinic traditions as reflected in the codes and treaties of the High Middle Ages, prior to the liberating tendencies of the Enlightenment and Emancipation, here perceived as a coherent theological world view.

kind of *making*, unrelated to function. This, combined with Judaism's stricture against the making of "graven images," created in the mind of the religious Jew an enduring impression of the arts as an activity which was at best frivolous and at worst blasphemous.[2]

However, as the term "aesthetic" began to be introduced into discussions of the arts, approaches developed which broaden considerably our understanding of the subject matter of the philosophy of art. It can no longer be limited to an investigation of "beautiful" as a concept, nor can it be linked solely with the "fine arts," nor even confined to objects that are man-made. The new term "aesthetic" encouraged an examination of the connection between the production of art on the one hand and the appreciation of art on the other. Both artist and audience may be said to participate in an aesthetic experience, with each party performing both roles in somewhat different forms and sequences. The very use of the term "experience" in this context hints at the widened view of what the arts are thought to be about. No longer confined to a certain kind of "making," we are talking about experience in its broadest sense, and the materials involved are all natural.

Put this way, even to a religious Jew the subject matter of aesthetics hardly seems threatening. However, this does not mean it can be ignored. Once we clearly perceive the extensive nature of the aesthetic experience, that its field is "spread over all heaven and earth and their total content,"[3] we realize that this view of the arts now constitutes a real challenge for a religious Jew, For it has been rightfully said: "If you are not sensitive to the aesthetic dimension you are losing full satisfaction in the world as it is actually and really present.[4] But it is precisely the religious Jew who has been told, by thinkers from Maimonides to Soloveitchik, that only by contemplating the universe can one arrive at a love of God, and that "the white light of divinity is always refracted through reality's 'dome of many colored glass,'" so that "the cognition of this world is of the innermost essence of the religious experience."[5]

---

[2] Exod. 20:4. See Shubert Spero, "Towards a Torah Esthetic," *Tradition* 6, no. 2 (Spring- Summer 1964); S.S. Schwarzschild, "The Legal Foundation of Jewish Aesthetics," *Journal of Aesthetic Education* 1 (Jan. 1975). Harold Rosenberg, "Is There a Jewish Art?" *Commentary* 42, no. 1 (July 1966).

[3] D. W. Prall, *Aesthetic Analysis* (New York: T. Y. Crowell. 1967), 5.

[4] D. W. Prall, *Aesthetic Judgment* (New York, T. Y. Crowell, 1967), 37.

[5] J. B. Soloveitchik, *The Halakhic Mind* (New York: Macmillan, 1986), 46.

Chapter Fifteen. Judaism and the Aesthetic

In my approach to aesthetic theory I shall mainly follow the works of John Dewey and D. W. Prall, whose theories rest on an empirical analysis of sense perception and a broad knowledge of the various art media, thus entailing a minimum of metaphysical suppositions. In my judgment, these theories give an adequate account of the world of art in all its forms, from the points of view of the artist and the art object, as well as that of the observer.

I

Aesthetic experience results from the discriminating perception of an object as it appears directly to the senses, with no ulterior interest whatsoever.[6] One's interest is concentrated on appearance only, on the surface qualities: how the object looks, how it sounds, how it feels. One's interest is not focused inward, to understand the underlying structure of forces which give rise to the appearance. One's interest is not forward-looking, to wonder to what purpose this object can be put or what future event can be predicted from its appearance. Nor is one's interest outward, to wonder what the relations are between an object and its surrounding environment. Only if a person frees himself from these familiar and often necessary ways of looking at things, and is able to concentrate solely on an object's *appearance to the senses,* can an aesthetic experience take place. Says Prall: "Aesthetics is not physics nor psychology nor yet physiology. Its direct object is presented conscious content; objectively discriminable sensuous presentations."[7]

However, because of our basic dependence upon the practical and the useful, and because of the tremendous prestige of science, with its unchallenged claim to have achieved the only cognition of the world available, we have tended to ignore the qualitative universe. The scientist can deal only with those aspects of reality which can be quantified and which fit his instruments. The impression was thus created that for really "serious" people, the qualitative world, i.e., the world of appearance, is not that important and may safely be left to the frivolities of the "aesthete," which name itself became a term of derogation. However, this very bifurcation is foreign to the stance of the religious individual, "who moves

---

[6] Prall, *Judgment,* 57.
[7] Prall, *Analysis,* II.

in a concrete world full of colors and sound and lives in his immediate, qualitative environment, not in a scientifically constructed cosmos. The world he knows is identical with the world he experiences."[8] This is a precise description of the aesthetic field, whose properties are open before us to experience. "All that is directly presented to our senses is qualitative presentation; qualities not only distinguished by our senses but felt emotionally in their full present character."[9]

It is a simple matter of fact that in our world the surface of things, the color of the sky, the fragrance of fresh-cut grass, the chirping of birds, a clap of thunder, is always an immediate sense perception, to some degree pleasant or unpleasant.[10] That is to say, the sense perception is always accompanied by some quality of feeling which is apprehended by the subject, and then attributed to the object. In the words of Santayana: "Beauty is a pleasure regarded as the quality of a thing."[11] The aesthetic experience is thus a transaction between the surface of our world and the senses of the individual.

All the possibilities of aesthetic creation and enjoyment depend upon these facts, and upon the ability of the human being to discriminate between the sensuous elements offered to us in nature. What the artist does is to compose various unified structures by utilizing the sensuous materials he finds in nature, employing certain skills and techniques in accordance with human imagination. However, the existence of sensuously qualitative materials, while sufficient to account for aesthetic experience, is not enough to have made possible the impressive artistic creations we find in the fine arts. To make his point, Prall asks why it is that art never developed in the areas of taste and smell, despite the fact that these are qualities which are as subtle, specific, and characteristic as those of colors, shapes, and sounds.[12] His answer is that, unlike colors and sounds, the sensuous qualities of taste and smell do not fall into any known or felt natural order or arrangement, nor can their variations be defined in such intrinsic natural structures as colors and sounds. While tastes and fragrances may be blended, they do not constitute an art

---

[8] Soloveitchik, *The Halakhic Mind*, 40.
[9] Prall, *Analysis*, 6.
[10] Prall, *Judgment*, 19.
[11] George Santayana, *The Sense of Beauty* (New York: Dover Publications, 1955).
[12] Prall, *Judgment*, 62-63.

Chapter Fifteen. Judaism and the Aesthetic

form, for there are no structural or critical principles: the very elements with which they work have no intelligible structure or order in variation. Says Prall, "In order to create objects of more than elementary aesthetic value, artists must work with materials that have relations, degrees of qualitative differences, established orders of variation and structural principles of combination."[13] One of the fortunate facts about the world we live in is that colors, sounds, and shapes do have these characteristics.

Sound is one of the primal marks of life and vitality: "the babbling brook, the roaring surf, the whispering breeze, the calls, cries and songs of beasts and birds, the speech of man."[14] The basic aesthetic materials of sound that are employed by the artist of music are tones and the principle of discrimination is the continuous range of pitch.[15] A tone lies between other tones in an order of pitch which is a one-dimensional series running from high to low. This gives to music the possibility of melody. There is another ordering principle made possible by the natural constitution of physical instruments of sound production. Due to the mechanics of vibration, "when we hear a sound of a given pitch produced by any sort of vibrating body we are also hearing at least one other pitch which seems to us simply the fullness or richness or characteristic quality of the sound of the former."[16] We name the second note the octave of the first. In addition, there are two other kinds of variation in sound, that of timbre and that of intensity (loudness and softness).[17]

We see that not only are the surface qualities of sound elements expressive of significant feelings but they are also intrinsically ordered by their own nature so as to be capable of infinite variety, both in specific details and in composed structures, all for the ear alone. All are elements of one sensory domain.[18]

---

[13] Ibid., 76-77.
[14] Ibid., 82. Prall points out that sound enjoys a certain primacy as having been the very first creation, or at least the vehicle of creation ("And the Lord Said"): "It was the sounding word that made intelligible the creation of an ordered world out of the chaos of sheer nothingness" (p. 80). See also *Avot* 5:1.
[15] Prall, *Judgment*, 89.
[16] Ibid., 87. The Bible indicates its awareness of the importance of musical instruments by recording that a particular individual was "the father of all such as handle the harp and pipe" (Gen. 4:21).
[17] Ibid., 91.
[18] Ibid., 80.

The corresponding element in the medium of color to that of pitch in the medium of sound, is hue. Color variations can also be shown to be serially ordered along a scale, although not as precisely the way sound is.[19] First, there are hues from yellow through orange and red, and through purple and violet to blue and blue-green, and through green and green-yellow back to yellow. Secondly, there are the lighter tints for each hue, running up into white in all of them, and the darker shades running into black. Thirdly, there are the variations in intensity, encompassing all the degrees of lightness and darkness, from maximum saturation to the natural grays. Every color variation is to be found somewhere along these different scales. We see, therefore, that every variation of color lies at a measurable distance from others along any single dimension chosen.[20]

It is interesting to note that colors as they actually appear have nothing qualitative in common, but are simply a set of intrinsically ordered differences. Thus, "it is a brute natural physical fact (including the physical and nervous condition of the eyes) that presents us with the differences and these differences, these specific, irrational, inexplicable, ultimate, qualitative natures, are the materials of visual beauty of which the complex beautiful structures of the visual arts are composed."[21]

Prall goes on to demonstrate that there are intrinsic ordering principles specific to shape and space-relations by which we intuit genuinely composed structures rather than a blurred jumble of lines and shapes.[22] Spatial features are elements of structured compositions. Lines, areas, and volumes—each has its own peculiar character depending upon its dimensional complexity, making possible certain types of relations only: one-dimensional lines give direction only; two-dimensional areas give expanse, flat or curved surfaces; three-dimensional volume gives depth, fullness, solidity. Also, because of the specific character of space, notions of balance, symmetry, and proportion are perceived.[23]

Another factor which is fundamentally significant in the aesthetic experience of music, poetry, and dance, and must be seen as a unique

---

[19] Prall, *Analysis*, 49.
[20] Ibid., 51.
[21] Prall, *Judgment*, 105-106.
[22] Ibid., 123.
[23] Ibid., 130.

Chapter Fifteen. Judaism and the Aesthetic

part of the intuited character of the aesthetic surface of our world, is the element of rhythm. "Rhythm is always perceived through feeling, distinguished by feeling and introduced by the body to the mind."[24] What is experienced is the rhythmic character of the sensuous content, which can be evoked by any sensory elements that occur in time. Rhythm is temporal, durational order, involving recurrence or regularity. Its variations can also be ordered by rate (slow or fast), and by division into all sorts of combinations by intervals.[25]

It follows from this analysis that the entire enterprise we call art, in all its forms, from the vantage point of both the producer and the consumer, this activity which has interested and enchanted man from the cave drawings of prehistory through the masterpieces of the Renaissance to the complex institutionalized world of contemporary art, is essentially man's appreciation and creative response to certain fortunate characteristics of our world. First, the surface qualities, when contemplated in an impartial manner and appreciated for their own sake, are a source of pleasure and delight. Secondly, sound, color, space, and shape relations occur in nature with their own intrinsic scales of order and structural principles of variation; these make it possible for sounds, colors, and shapes to serve as compositional elements for artists. Only because of these "accidental" features of sound, color, and shape can unitary works of art possessing an articulated manifold be composed by artists.

The implications of such an analysis of aesthetic experience are extremely important for the religious Jew, for whom the physical universe, after the Torah, is the sole avenue through which one can learn about God, the Creator, and in which one can apprehend a sense of the Presence of the Transcendent. Prophet and Psalmist alike urge the individual to "cast thine eyes heavenward"[26] and see therein "the glory of God."[27] Those who do so are inspired to cry out, "How great are Thy works O Lord, Thy thoughts are very deep,"[28] and, "How manifold are Thy works O Lord, in wisdom hast Thou made them all."[29]

---

[24] Ibid., 143.
[25] Ibid., 145.
[26] Isa. 40:26.
[27] Psalms 19:2.
[28] Psalms 92:6.
[29] Psalms 104:24.

But precisely what is a contemplation of nature supposed to teach about God? Maimonides is quite clear on the point:

> And what is the way that will lead to the love of Him and the fear of Him? When a person contemplates His great and wondrous works and creatures and from them perceives this wisdom which is incomparable and infinite, he will straightaway love Him, praise Him, glorify Him and long with an exceeding longing to know His great Name.... And when he ponders these same matters he will recoil, frightened and realize that he is a small creature....[30]

The contemplation of nature advocated by Maimonides seems to be a sort of scientific study of the world which, through a revelation of the underlying forces and micro-structures by which all things exist and function, can indeed make manifest the incomparable wisdom of the Creator. However, can displays of God's wisdom necessarily lead man to love Him? To fear or revere Him, perhaps, when an awareness of God's wisdom is combined with a realization of His awesome power; love, however, would seem to be more appropriately connected to evidence of God's goodness. A scientific study of nature, on the other hand, would simply provide additional instances of God's engineering skills in fashioning a remarkably efficient universe in line with His purposes. But, of course, for Maimonides, "love of God" is identical with the philosophical and intellectual "knowledge of God." Thus, to know the world, cognitively, is to know something of God's wisdom and hence of God Himself.[31] But this could hardly have been what the Prophet or Psalmist had in mind!

I wish to suggest that a primary element in Judaism's celebration of nature is precisely the aesthetic aspect in the sense that we've been using the term. For it alone, by opening our senses and selves to the surface qualities of this world and to the intrinsic beauties and delights of color, sound, shape, taste, and fragrance, enables us to truly apprehend God's goodness and gain an intimation of His love for man. For, conceivably, God could have brought into existence a more "no nonsense," "business-like" universe, retaining all of the existing micro- and macro-engineering marvels—from the laws of gravity and molecular motion

---

[30] Maimonides, *Mishneh Torah, Hilchot Yesodei HaTorah* 2:1, 2.
[31] See Chapter 10 of the present volume.

Chapter Fifteen. Judaism and the Aesthetic

to the intricacies of the double-helix—without providing nature with those sensuous qualities which make it possible for man to experience the aesthetic. But even if God had only given us the beauties of color and sound without their intrinsic ordering principles, as He has given us the delights of taste and smell, we should have said *"dayainu"*! What shall we say then to the *hiba yetaira,* the "special love" that is manifest in the intrinsic scales of order and structural principles of variation to be found in color, sound, and shape, which make it possible for man to create aesthetic objects! Perhaps the primary thrust of the exhortations in Judaism to contemplate nature is not to help us develop love for God, but rather to help us become aware of God's love for us, a love which we are daily assured is not merely everlasting love, *ahavat olam,* but abundant love, *ahava rabbah.*[32] Surely if God loves man "abundantly," it can be expected that the world will reflect that love, that God will endow human existence with "plus" factors which are not strictly necessary for His purposes but which impart to the world qualities and values which man can apprehend, from which he can derive pleasure, and which he can use as raw material for creating objects of beauty.

Realization of the centrality of the aesthetic gives us a new perspective on the biblical account of the creation. On the words, "there is no rock *(tzur)* like our God,"[33] the rabbis comment: "There is no sculptor *(tzayor)* like our God," and proceed to show that God's forming of primal man was, in several respects, superior to the work of a human sculptor.[34] In so commenting, the rabbis are asking us to view God as an artist and man as an aesthetic object. As Rashi comments, while everything else was created by the "word," man was created by the "hands" of God.[35] This implies that man and woman were endowed with the surface qualities which give rise to aesthetic pleasure. Their appearance, their shape and form, can provide visual pleasure, their movements can be graceful, the sounds they utter can develop into song. In commenting on the comeliness of Rav Kahana, the Talmud traces it to Jacob, and thence to primal man, and concludes "… and the beauty of Adam was of the beauty

---

[32] Opening phrases of the second of the blessings that precede the *Shema* prayer in the morning and evening services.
[33] I Sam. 2:2.
[34] *Megillah* 14a.
[35] Rashi on Gen. 1:27.

of the Divine Presence itself."³⁶ This is consistent with the fact that the human form and its physiognomy has been a constant subject for artistic rendering throughout the ages. Michelangelo is reported to have said that the human figure is the most beautiful object in the world. Cynics may see this as a classic case of megalomania. We may see it, however, as a tribute to Divine artistry and a glimmer of the Divine spirit which shines through the physical. Indeed, in enumerating the different contributions made by the "three partners" in the formation of the human being, God is said to have contributed the soul and "the splendor of his face."³⁷ Even as the Psalmist proclaims, "... with glory and beauty hast Thou crowned him [man]."³⁸

Our broadened understanding of the aesthetic experience and its centrality in Judaism can warrant the judgment that not only man, but the entire cosmos and particularly our planet, may be viewed as an aesthetic object, and perhaps was so intended by its Artist-Creator.³⁹ Indications of this can be found in a number of texts which, for all their familiarity, have always been thought somewhat curious. Beginning with the creation of light, the same formula is followed in the Torah with each phase of the creation: "And God said: 'Let there be light.' And there was light. And God saw the light that it was good *(tov)*."⁴⁰ The seventh such pronouncement, at the end of the sixth day, varies somewhat: "And God saw everything that He had made and behold it was very good.⁴¹ Now, what does the word "good" mean in this context? What does this judgment by God about each phase of His creation and about His creation as a whole tell us? After God said "Let there be light," we are told that it did in fact come to pass: "and there was light." Similarly, after each such utterance we are explicitly told that what was ordered came into being, presumably as specified: "... and it was so and the earth brought forth grass, herb-yielding seed after its kind and tree bearing fruit wherein is the seed thereof, after its kind." What is being

---

[36] *Bava Batra* 58a.
[37] *Nidah* 31a.
[38] Psalms 8:6.
[39] The astronauts, on returning from the moon, are reported to have marveled that, from space, the only colorful and hospitable-looking body visible was the planet Earth.
[40] Gen. 1:3, 4.
[41] Gen. 1:31.

Chapter Fifteen. Judaism and the Aesthetic

added when, in the following verse, we are told: "And God *saw* that it was *good*" (emphasis mine)? Surely there is every reason to believe that the earth heeded the command exactly as ordered by God. What is God checking on? Furthermore, since everything happens *in* God, He knows all because He knows Himself, so He doesn't have to look *out* to *see* what has happened!

I wish to suggest that the word "good" *(tov)* in this particular context must be interpreted as referring to "aesthetic value."[42] That is to say, despite knowing that this phenomenon called "light" had indeed come into existence as specified, the Torah wishes to make us aware of another of light's dimensions, that it is *good*. God intended that light not only be useful, but also have the sensuous surface qualities from which man could derive visual pleasure. And so God, as it were, is described as "viewing" His creation from a human sense perspective ("... and God saw"), so as to inform the reader that the world has aesthetic value.[43] It is precisely in aesthetic terms that we can best explain God's final judgment after seeing *all* that He had made, and *"behold* it was *very* good" (emphasis mine). How do six "goods" add up to a seventh *"very* good"? One of the basic characteristics of a work of art is its unity. In the most elemental sense, this means that what is being presented for our attention is a simple whole distinguished from all else around it. Since art is a composition of various elements, the condition of unity requires that all be perceived as a coherent organic unity: there should be no gaps, nothing should seem to be missing, no part should seem to be superfluous; the parts should seem to be interdependent upon each other so that the whole appears to be greater than the sum of its parts. It is in all of these senses that God's final judgment on His universe must be understood. God makes the pleasant "discovery" ("behold") that the cosmos, aesthetically, exhibits an organic unity ("all") in which all of its parts, individually pronounced "good," taken together cohere into a perception that is "very good." If this interpretation is correct, then the Torah would appear to be stressing the importance of the world's aesthetic features, for it is, primarily, sensitivity to the aesthetic aspects of life and to man's capacity for aesthetic experience that can increase our awareness of God's love for man.

---

[42] See Gen. 2:9, where *tov* is used in a clearly aesthetic context.
[43] See John Dewey, *Art as Experience* (New York: Capricorn Books, 1934), 49.

It is instructive in this regard to examine the original environment into which primal man was introduced by God, the so-called "paradise": "And the Lord God planted a garden east of Eden and there He put the man whom He had formed. And out of the ground, the Lord God made to grow every tree that is pleasant to sight and good for eating...."[44] God does not simply find a naturally pleasant spot near a quiet pond but, like a true artist, uses the already existing natural elements which themselves have aesthetic quality to compose a new manifold, a newly-structured unity: "He plants a garden," which in itself can be viewed as an aesthetic object, for "garden" implies that the trees, shrubs, plants, grass, and paths were set out in accordance with formal aesthetic principles. Not only were man's nutritional needs provided for, but planted in the garden was "every tree that was pleasant to the sight," an explicit reference to the purely aesthetic value of the garden! Even the phrase "good for eating" refers to the fruit tasting good to the palate rather than to its health-enhancing properties.[45] In thus describing the original environment designed by God for man, the Torah seems to stress the importance of a setting in which man is afforded the possibility of aesthetic experience.

There is another curious occurrence of the word *tov* in this portion of Genesis. In describing the four rivers which flow from Eden, the names of the rivers are accompanied by a brief indication of their general geographic location. However, in connection with the river Pishon we are told, "it is that which encompasses the whole land of Havilah where there is gold; and the gold of that land is good *(tov)*; there is bdellium and the onyx stone."[46] Here again the Torah seems concerned to point out God's conscious intent to stock the world not only with basic necessities but also with precious metals and stones,which are visually attractive, provide aesthetic pleasure, and are workable by man for the creation of objects of art.

Biblical commentators have experienced difficulty in explaining why God should have chosen the rainbow as a sign of the covenant He made with Noah and all mankind never again to bring a flood upon the earth. The text lovingly mentions "bow in the cloud" three times, and the fact

---

[44] Gen. 2:8, 9.
[45] This is evident from Gen. 3:6.
[46] Gen. 2:11.

Chapter Fifteen. Judaism and the Aesthetic

that it is a "sign of the covenant" five times![47] After all, the rainbow is a natural phenomenon which may occur after any rain, and presumably rainbows had been seen even before the flood. However, in view of the aesthetic importance of colors and the marvelous nature of its intrinsic order, God finds in the rainbow an appropriate "sign" of His essential love for man. The droplets of rain act as a prism, breaking up light into its various component colors. What better token of God's commitment to undertake the slow education of, rather than to severely punish, man than the beautifully colored rainbow arching across the heavens?

In order to better understand the relationship between the aesthetic contemplation of nature and God's love, we must analyze the relationship between aesthetic experience and emotion in general. From the very beginning, philosophical analysis of the arts has revealed basic connections with the emotions. Early on Aristotle had developed his influential theory of drama as effectuating a catharsis of emotions. Wordsworth is remembered for saying, "Poetry takes its origin from emotion recollected in tranquility." The effect of music on man's emotions was, of course, quite obvious to the writers of the Torah.[48] Tolstoy concluded that art is a means of communication, a language for the communication of feeling.

So what, precisely, is the connection between art and emotion? On the most basic level, it should be remembered that all aesthetic experience begins with a sensory awareness in which the act of feeling and the content felt are not distinguished, such that we feel things like the "gaiety of yellow" and the "dark sorrow of violet."[49] Emotion is also involved on the level of representation. Most often, what is represented in painting and in sculpture, the subject matter of poetry and drama, and the movement of the dance are items which have deep emotional resonance—they are of universal, national, or religious significance.

But by far the most widespread theory, which places emotion at the center of the aesthetic experience for both the artist and the contemplator, is some variation of what is known as "art as expression of emotion." This theory stipulates that the art object does not refer to or represent

---

[47] See Nachmanides on Gen. 9:12-17.
[48] See I Sam. 16:23.
[49] See Arthur Berndston, *Art, Expression and Beauty* (New York: Holt, Rinehart & Winston, 1969), 17.

emotion, nor does it necessarily arouse emotion, but rather, that both the artist in creation and the spectator in contemplation experience an actual emotion that has been modified by having been fused with form.[50]

We will leave it to the philosophers to debate the question of how, precisely, such a "fusing" takes place. For our purposes it shall suffice to adopt this minimal phenomenological description: "Expression is a relation of form and emotion by virtue of which emotion is clarified and made free and beauty is brought into being."[51] From the perspective of the contemplator we can use the term, "embodiment": "The spectator perceives the developed emotion as incorporated in form." Clearly, a theory such as this can work for those art forms created by the human imagination using special techniques. However, can our appreciation of the aesthetic surface inherent in the natural world, where things appear beautiful "accidentally," be explained by this theory?

Prall reminds us:

> ... if the beauty of art is sensuous at all, it is nature that furnishes both its materials and its structural principles. The beauties of nature offer all the possibilities that there are of beautiful sensuous elements, all the possible kinds of structure native to these elements as well as all the spatial and temporal possibilities for variety and for combination that could be imposed upon them by men as artists ... and they may occur on a scale quite beyond men's powers. As nature offers us color and light and shape and perspectives, color harmonies and even musical sounds, so she offers us such refined and sophisticated forms as animal and human bodies among which sculpture finds its models and patterns.[52]

But in what sense may nature be said to be expressive of emotion? A violent mountain storm will certainly arouse all sorts of emotions in people. Even if the spectator is not personally threatened, by association the violence and destruction bring to mind the emotions of anger, wrath, and fearfulness. Be the language figurative, symbolic, or analogical, man constantly turns to nature to find expression for his emotions, and to describe the features of various qualities, ascribing to them admired human and even moral traits: the purity of a white lily, the fragility of

---

[50] Ibid., 64.
[51] Ibid., 147.
[52] Prall, *Judgment*, 302-303.

flowers, the strength of an oak, the reliability of the Rock of Gibraltar, the power and swiftness of lightning. "Nature's actual surface in its aesthetic particulars thus gives us the ultimate terms in our definitions of even the most humanly or the most divinely significant meanings."[53] This is graphically seen in the biblical "Song of Songs," where the lover describes the qualities of his beloved in terms of the surface qualities found in nature. The text abounds in a variety of references to the sights, sounds, and colors of the countryside. The rabbis insist that the love so aesthetically described is in reality the love between God and the people of Israel.

Judaism is not, of course, committed to the doctrine that every threatening situation in nature is a sign of God's wrath. However, the fact is that the Torah does describe a violent destructive deluge early in man's history as being brought about by God in response to man's corruption. Furthermore, natural disasters are included in the list of punitive consequences that should be anticipated in the event of Israel's disobedience. It is, therefore, fair to say that unusual displays of nature's violent and destructive power in storms, earthquakes, floods, and volcanoes are, for a religious Jew, expressive of a great range of emotions. At the very least, in the words of the blessing over thunder, they remind us "that His power and might fill the universe."

But what is our reaction as we contemplate the many instances of natural beauty? What emotion is expressed by a multi-colored sunset, or a sun-splashed meadow full of yellow flowers? The essence of beauty is an emotion of joy which makes of beauty an axiological entity. That is to say, the spectator experiences the beauty and his emotion as intrinsic values. When I am intuiting beauty, the pleasure I am experiencing is obviously *my* pleasure; but it is experienced in an impartial and distanced fashion. Neither the object nor the emotion are considered in relation to the self but objectively, as an intrinsic worth which I may associate with God. This apprehension of value feeling which is experienced as preferring, as desired and desirable, is already a form of loving. Our wish is to get closer to the object of value, to remain in its presence, to unite with the source of value. And although beauty (like color) is existent only for and in the mind, its ontological status is not affected. Beauty is real and a part of nature. For the religious consciousness, the recognition of

---

[53] Ibid., 304.

intrinsic value in the universe, be it in the moral teachings of the Torah or in the aesthetic experiences of natural beauty, testifies to the love and benevolence which God has for His creatures. We see this in the fact that God endows human existence with positive pleasure-giving factors which are not strictly necessary for His essential purposes. This leads man to a love of God which can be called "love of admiration," i.e., pleasure in the valued qualities of another.[54] It has been noted that "when a person notices a beautiful object and approves of it, he will love and desire it and when he attains it he will experience joy: as when a person sees a precious stone or a beautiful and stately house, immediately his soul will desire to reach it and cleave to it."[55]

We are suggesting that it is precisely this sensitivity to and appreciation for the aesthetic aspects of the universe that can lead us to experience the love that is being expressed therein by the Divine artist. In some special sense. the experience of holiness or the sacred which is associated with God is intuited as value. "God is good"[56] and God is "clothed with splendor and beauty."[57] He is also the source of these qualities as they manifest themselves in the natural life of man. "The voice of God is in power, the voice of God is in beauty."[58]

As Maritain wrote, "God's love causes the beauty of what He loves whereas our love is caused by the beauty of what we love."[59]

II

In the first part of this chapter we attempted to demonstrate the importance to Judaism of the aesthetic perspective as the path which leads to love of God. However, the aesthetic may also play a key role in the dynamics of certain particular observances within Judaism. We will now seek to demonstrate how our appreciation of a vital institution such as the Sabbath can be deepened by an understanding of the relationship between aesthetic and ordinary experience.

---

[54] Berndston, *Art, Expression and Beauty*, 264-265.
[55] See *Peirush* (commentary) on Maimonides, *Mishneh Torah, Hilchot Yesodei HaTorah*, 2:2.
[56] Psalms 136:1.
[57] Psalms 104:1.
[58] Psalms 29:4.
[59] Jacques Maritain, *Art and Scholasticism* (London: Sheed and Ward, 1947).

Chapter Fifteen. Judaism and the Aesthetic

John Dewey has maintained that the aesthetic is no intruder in experience from without, but is simply the clarified and intensified development of traits that belong to every normally complete experience.[60] Experience usually occurs continuously without beginning or end; it is seamless. We interact constantly with our environment in all sorts of ways, big and small, trivial and significant. Even when the stream of experience is broken up into segments, for various purposes, the parts are usually jagged and fragmentary. Sometimes, however, we encounter what we characterize as "an experience" which stands out from the rest of the vast flux which rushes by: a special meal with friends in a quiet restaurant, a game of chess that is played through, a meticulously planned trip abroad that takes place without a hitch. We might be heard to exclaim: "That was an experience!"[61] According to Dewey, such an experience has a unity which is characterized by a simple quality that pervades the entire experience. Upon later analysis we may distinguish emotional, intellectual, and practical elements within it, but the experience is not the sum total of these different components: "The experience itself has a satisfying, emotional quality because it possesses internal integration and fulfillment reached through ordered and organized movement ... that which rounds out an experience into completeness and unity and which is immediately felt emotionally is the aesthetic quality."[62]

According to Dewey, an experience will have aesthetic character when:

1) every successive part flows freely into what ensues without the parts losing their self-identity;

2) there is dynamic organization, growth over time. There is inception, development, and fulfillment, which give the experience form and structure;

3) there is a rhythm of intakings and outgivings divided by regular intervals;[63]

4) the conclusion is not experienced as a separate and independent thing. It is a movement of anticipation and cumulation. It is the consummation of a movement.[64]

---

[60] John Dewey, *Art as Experience*, 46.
[61] Ibid., 37.
[62] Ibid., 41.
[63] Ibid., 55.
[64] Ibid., 38.

I wish to suggest that the institution of the Jewish Sabbath, as it is understood and practiced today against the background of its biblical and rabbinic development, is fully comprehended only when its aesthetic character (along the lines discussed by Dewey) is taken into consideration.

Clearly, the Sabbath should be regarded as a predominantly religious observance, and the ultimate quality to be experienced is that of *kedusha*—Holiness. Nevertheless, if we wish to understand how the Sabbath works and what contributes to its effectiveness, we would do well to recognize its aesthetic dimension. The biblical material taken alone easily lends itself to a perception of the Sabbath as a cold, cheerless day during which one remains confined to one's quarters and contemplates the power of the Creator. More so, perhaps, than other *mitzvot*, the Sabbath has undergone extensive clarification by the rabbis regarding its Halakhic aspects, and interpretive embellishment and deepening in its philosophic and Aggadic aspects. But beyond the Talmudic-rabbinic contribution to the Sabbath, every individual seems called upon not only to "observe" and "remember" the Sabbath but in some important sense "to make the Shabbat throughout their generations."[65] The Sabbath, for all its detailed *halakhot*, its prescribed "dos" and "don'ts," must be perceived as a total experience to be made anew each week. Each individual Sabbath is to be meticulously carved out of time with an "inception, development and consummation" which has to be "made" or recreated anew each seventh day. In regard to the aesthetic aspect of the Sabbath, the individual is both artist and spectator, producer and consumer. The Sabbath in its main outline is given to Israel to be "observed" and "remembered."[66] Whether the individual makes something further out of the Sabbath materials so that he can call the experience a "delight," may depend on whether he sees himself as an artist determined not only to carry out the minimal requirements but also to fashion an aesthetic experience through which God will be served.[67]

If we compare the structure of the Sabbath to the properties required by Dewey to qualify for an aesthetic experience, we find an impressive correspondence:

---

[65] Exod. 31:16-17.
[66] Exod. 20:8; Deut. 5:12.
[67] Isa. 48:13.

Chapter Fifteen. Judaism and the Aesthetic

1) The Sabbath experience is inaugurated with the kindling of Sabbath candles and the Kiddush ceremony, and concludes with the *havdalah*, which dramatically sets the Sabbath apart from the rest of the week.

2) The structure of the Sabbath is built around the three festive family-centered meals, each of which has a distinct character and significance:
   a. Each *seuda* (meal) is held at a characteristically different time of day in the following sequence: evening, midday, late afternoon.
   b. Each *seuda* presides over a different part of the Sabbath—arrival, set-presence, departure—with each generating a mood of its own. But even as darkness gives rise to dawn and noon to dusk, and even as in Jewish theology Creation leads to Exodus and thence to Messianic redemption, so each part of the Sabbath leads to the next without any part losing its self-identity.
   c. Each *seuda* celebrates a different conceptual aspect of the Sabbath: Creation, Exodus, Messianic redemption.[68]

3) In actual practice, the three *seudot* create a special rhythm within the Sabbath day as each is preceded by a different synagogue prayer service. Thus, the natural rhythm of the three meals during a 24-hour period is punctuated by intervals of public prayer. However, both the physical experience of eating and drinking and the spiritual experience of prayer are given a strong social dimension by the first taking place within the family and the second taking place within the circle of the community.

One of Dewey's important insights is the observation that "conscious experience is a perceived relation between doing and undergoing." However, what makes a particular doing artistic is when "the perceived result is of such a nature that its qualities as perceived have controlled the question of production."[69]

---

[68] Compare the main text in the Amidah prayer of the *Kabbalat Shabbat, Shachrit,* and *Mincha* services.
[69] Dewey, *Art as Experience*, 46.

One of the most unusual features of the techniques used by the "artist" who is "making" his Sabbath is that all of his preparations, his "doing," must be done before the onset of the Sabbath. Once the Sabbath begins, the individual must cease his preparatory "doing" and begin "undergoing." His role now becomes that of one who perceives, appreciates, and enjoys. But, as Dewey points out, this is not a purely passive role because to truly surrender oneself to the aesthetic experience, to be truly receptive, involves "an act of the going out of energy; to steep ourselves in a subject matter we have first to plunge into it."[70] In describing the attitude necessary for Sabbath preparation, the rabbis pointed to the verse: "Six days you shall labor and do *all* your work."[71] Unlike the Creator, the Jew who staggers through the work-week and reaches the Sabbath knows that his work is not completed. He has not done *all* of his work! "Yet," say the rabbis, "let it appear in your eyes *as if* all your work was done."[72] The individual must indeed surrender totally to the Sabbath, in thought as well as in deed. He must focus completely on the joys of existence, on the goodness of being. This special relationship between "doing" on *erev Shabbat* and "undergoing," on Sabbath itself is what helps mark the Sabbath as "an experience," and gives it its aesthetic quality of unity. This experience heightens the conceptual understanding that man's cessation of creative "doing'" on the Sabbath is a demonstration and testimonial to, the belief that it is God who created all and gave man a *completed* universe capable of satisfying his deepest needs and of giving expression to his uniquely human capacities.

This leads us to a basic concept of the Sabbath, which throws new light on the role of the aesthetic in Sabbath observance. From a plain reading of the biblical text one arrives at the following rationale for the command "not to do any manner of work on the Shabbat": (1) the Lord rested on the seventh day from His work of creation; (2) the Lord blessed the seventh day and hallowed it; (3) therefore, the Israelite is commanded not to do any manner of work on the seventh day. By consciously abstaining from work ("remember'" and "keep"), one hallows or sanctifies the Sabbath. From whence, however, and for what purpose is

---

[70] Ibid., 53.
[71] Exod. 20:9.
[72] See Rashi on Exod. 20:9.

Chapter Fifteen. Judaism and the Aesthetic

all of the rich sensuous content that fills the Sabbath today? How do the *oneg* and the three *Seudot* fit into the scheme of the creation?

The answer to this is subtly implied in the biblical account, but is generally overlooked. God rested on the seventh day *not* because He was tired, but because "the heaven and the earth and all their host were completed."[73] What we are doing, therefore, each seventh day is not merely commemorating the fact that God rested, but primarily celebrating the fact that God has placed us in a universe that He in His wisdom and goodness considers complete, finished—perfect in terms of His purpose for man. Indeed, God is so confident that His world contains all of the elements necessary for man's happiness that He presents Israel with this "gift" of the Sabbath, with the promise that every seventh day of their lives they can create for themselves as psycho-physical-spiritual beings an experience of "*oneg,*" and be socially, intellectually, and religiously united by its aesthetic quality. As the grateful Jew acknowledges in his Sabbath prayer: "The people that sanctify the seventh day, even all of them, shall be *satiated* and *delighted* with Thy goodness." The word "satiated'" implies that the Sabbath experience is not just another "good time" but is a demonstration that the individual can, with all of his senses open and engaged, experience fulfillment in its profoundest sense—which testifies to the sublime goodness of God. "Taste and see the Lord is Good"[74] is a challenge taken up by religious Jews every seventh day.

However, not only is the Sabbath as a whole to be seen as something artistically "made" each week by the individual, who then appreciates it aesthetically in Dewey's sense of "an experience," but it is filled with many observances which, in addition to their conceptual rationale, exhibit a clear sensuous quality. A brief survey reveals the following: appealing to our sense of taste are all of the special Sabbath delicacies, food and drink honed to gourmet perfection by centuries of tradition, with the halakhah prescribing meat, fish, whole loaves of bread, and of course wine, all to be served in quantities that do honor to the Sabbath. The consumption of fruit and confections between the *Seudot* is encouraged by the tradition that would have each individual recite a

---

[73] Gen. 2:1.
[74] Psalms 34.9. The rabbis assert that the experience of the Shabbat rest is a sixtieth of the spiritual bliss of the World to Come (*Berakhot* 57b).

hundred blessings over the course of the Sabbath. Sound is celebrated by the singing of *zemirot*, traditional tunes, during the three *seudot*, during the services in the synagogue, and in the poetry of the liturgy, during the recitation of which dancing may also take place. The visual sense is engaged by the light of the *nerot Shabbat* (Sabbath candles), the special Sabbath clothing, and the artistically designed vessels for Sabbath use, such as goblets, candlesticks, silverware, *challah* covers, and spice boxes. The sense of smell is stimulated by flowers brought into the home for Sabbath, the Havdalah spices, and in some traditions by perfumed snuff passed around in the synagogue. And, of course, husband and wife are encouraged to engage in marital relations on Sabbath eve.

It would seem that the rabbis were well aware of the special pleasures experienced on the Sabbath, but had difficulty relating them to the day's religious theme. One finds oneself thoroughly relaxed: the tensions of the workaday world have been put aside, and pleasures suffused with the warmth of fellowship flood in through all of one's senses. True, there is an intellectual awareness that by observing the Sabbath one is serving God, but the immediately-perceived quality of each individual experience is simply sensuous pleasure. Was there not a danger that somehow, all of this might become disconnected from the spiritual? It is recorded that a Roman emperor once asked one of the rabbis to explain why the Sabbath foods tasted so good. He replied: "We possess a spice named 'Shabbat' which we include, which gives it its taste." And when the emperor asked to be given some of the special spice, he was told: "It only avails him who observes the Shabbat."[75]

Perhaps what the rabbi was trying to say was that the individual sensuous pleasures of the Sabbath in themselves are not what constitutes the *oneg* of "making" Sabbath. Each activity becomes enhanced when it is performed as part of the total Sabbath experience, which itself becomes "an experience." There is another rabbinic teaching to the effect that "an additional soul is given to man on the eve of the Shabbat and is taken from him at the termination of the Shabbat."[76] One might think that this "additional soul" is given to man in order to heighten his spiritual capacities, but Rashi comments, "It is to deepen his sensitivity

---

[75] *Shabbat* 119a: *Bereishit Rabbah* 11:4.
[76] *Ta'anit* 27b.

Chapter Fifteen. Judaism and the Aesthetic

for eating and drinking."⁷⁷ Perhaps this, too, has to be understood in terms of the unique significance of sensory pleasures on the Sabbath. Ordinary eating and drinking on this day affords a special enjoyment, since it is part of the overall Sabbath experience, which itself is artistic in its making and aesthetic in its enjoyment. To be able to integrate all of the separate pleasures of the day into a unitary experience of joy in existence itself and love for God may indeed require an "additional soul." What emerges from our discussion is that those surface qualities of our universe which make possible artistic creativity and aesthetic experience were recognized early on by Judaism, and were considered to be highly significant manifestations of God's goodness and love for man. Contemplation, appreciation, and enjoyment of the aesthetic aspects of our world should lead a person to adore its creator: "Blessed art Thou, O Lord our God, King of the Universe, who hast made thy world lacking in naught but hast produced therein goodly creatures and goodly trees wherewith to give delight to the children of men."⁷⁸ It is in this mutual turning to each other in love—"I am for my beloved and my beloved is for me," that the God-man relationship reaches its apex.⁷⁹

The seven-day week is a creation of Judaism, and mankind has sufficient reason to see it as a great blessing. While the cosmic and theological origins of the Sabbath are given in Genesis, it first enters the institutional life of man as a command to the People of Israel after the Exodus from Egypt—it is the only ritual command included in the "words of the Covenant" known as the Ten Commandments. The rabbis saw the giving of the Sabbath to Israel as a "gift," as a gratuitous gesture.⁸⁰ Unlike the

---

77 Rashi explains "Harkhevet ha-da'at," widening the understanding, as referring to eating and drinking. Jastrow renders it as referring to contentment. The implication seems to be that the additional soul enables the individual to experience greater "contentment" or "satisfaction" from his eating and drinking.
78 Shulkhan Arukh, *Orach Chaim, Hilkhot B'rakhot*, 226.
79 Song of Sol. 2:16, 6:3.
80 "The Holy One blessed be He said to Moses, I have a precious gift in my treasury named Shabbat and I wish to present it to Israel; go and inform them" (Shabbat 10b). Cf. Prayer for the Shabbat eve composed by the rabbis: "From Your love, O Lord our God, wherewith you did love your people Israel, and from your compassion, O our King, which You did feel for the children of Your covenant, You did give us O Lord our God this great and holy seventh day in love" (*Tosefta Berachot* 3:11).

Festivals, which "pertain" to Israel by virtue of their celebrating events in the history of the nation or in the religious life of the individual, the theological significance of the Sabbath is cosmic and universal with no particular connection to Israel. Thus, God in love presents the Sabbath to Israel, "for their generations," so that they may *make* of it a multi-dimensional aesthetic experience. As they relive weekly the "goodness" of God and intensify their love for Him, they constantly demonstrate the mutuality of the God-man relationship. "It (the Sabbath) is a sign between me and you throughout your generations, that you may know that I am the Lord who sanctify you."[81]

God, in His love for Israel, has given them the Sabbath. They, in experiencing the beauty and joy of existence by means of the Sabbath, turn to Him in love. "It is a *sign between you and Me* ... that you may know that I am the Lord who sanctifies you."[82]

---

[81] Exod. 31:12.

[82] The Shabbat has both an outer-directed as well as an inner-directed aspect. As regards the outside world, the Jewish Sabbath presents the impressive picture of an entire community "closing down" each seventh day, turning from the mundane world, often at great cost and self-sacrifice, in order to testify to the fact that our universe is the handiwork of the One God: "It is a sign between Me and the children of Israel forever, that in six days the Lord made heaven and earth and on the seventh day ceased from work and rested" (Exod. 31:17). Willful violation of the Sabbath by a Jew is considered a betrayal of the covenant and is severely punished.

Chapter Sixteen
Providential History and the Anthropic Principle

This chapter argues that the Anthropic Principle, which is believed to have heuristic and predictive value in science, can be fruitfully employed in explicating a central problem in Jewish historiography: the complete lack of any guiding principle by which to judge the significance of the events of Jewish history since the destruction of the Second Temple. We suggest that the establishment of the State of Israel in 1948 be regarded to have been the goal of Providence since 70 CE. By so doing, we can then identify and trace four lines of development in Jewish history and four lines in world history, which together constitute the necessary and sufficient conditions for the Jewish return to Zion in our day. This gives us, in effect, a theory of progress for Jewish history.

Nathan Aviezer gives us an explanation of the meaning of the Anthropic Principle in science and its importance for the believing Jew[1]. In terms of the latter, he quite correctly points out that recent discoveries in cosmology may be taken as further evidence of the universe being the result of purposeful design:

1) The earth just happens to be sufficiently distant from the sun so that surface water does not evaporate or decompose (as on Venus), yet is sufficiently near the sun so that oceans do not freeze permanently (as they may have on Mars).

2) The nuclear force just happens to be in the narrow range in which the protons (in the hydrogen) of the sun can combine with a neutron to form a deuteron, which "burns" gradually to give us the intense "heat" and brilliant "light" which makes life possible. Were protons able to combine with protons, the sun would instantly explode!

---
[1] Nathan Aviezer, "The Anthropic Principle," *The Journal of Torah and Scholarship (B.D.D.)* 5 (Summer 1997): 41-54.

However, it could be argued, after all is said and done, that the cause of the believing Jew has not been advanced all that much, for this new evidence, while fascinating in itself, merely constitutes additional examples of design which, ultimately, are only as effective as is the logical validity of the traditional Teleological Argument for the existence of God as a whole.[2] And this, it is generally agreed today, does not constitute a "proof"-yielding certainty but only a certain degree of probability, and that only after making a certain assumption: "If you believe that human beings are the most important creatures in the world."[3]

Nevertheless, it should be pointed out that this new evidence from cosmology is, in a sense, more significant than much of the earlier evidence given in support of the Teleological Argument, from the days of Aristotle to the classic formulation of William Paley (1743-1805). These early thinkers were impressed by the harmonious relationship between living creatures and their environments, which suggested that "the world in all its richness and subtlety was contrived for their benefit alone."[4] In searching for supporting evidence, they "focused primarily upon the biological realm." Thus, for example, the human eye was a favorite example of what Hume was later to call "the curious adaptation of means to ends."[5] Who could deny the common-sense conclusion that the human eye was exquisitely and ingeniously designed as a self-cleaning organ to provide steady, wide-angle vision in living color?

However, what dealt a massive and almost fatal blow to this Teleological Argument was not so much the logical refutation of Hume but the publication of Darwin's *Origin of Species* (1859). Darwin's hypothesis of "natural selection" seemed to provide a "plausible alternative explanation for the very facts upon which the anthropocentric design argument was based."[6] Thus, the eye and many other "happy" adaptations of the human being to its habitat came about not because

---

[2] See John Hick, *Arguments for the Existence of God* (New York: Seabury Press, 1971), 1-33.
[3] See Nathan Aviezer, "The Anthropic Principle," 53.
[4] See John D. Barrow and Frank J. Tipler, *The Anthropic Principle* (New York: Oxford University Press, 1986), 27.
[5] David Hume, *Dialogues Concerning Natural Religion*, ed. N. Kemp Smith (Indiana: Bobbs Merrill, 1997), Part II.
[6] John D. Barrow and Frank J. Tipler, *The Anthropic Principle*, 81.

it was originally so purposed, but because of the operation of certain impersonal phenomena in nature, such as random mutation and survival of the fittest. This certainly weakened the Design Argument, which was based heavily on examples from the realm of biology.[7]

However, for the new evidence from cosmology, such as the examples cited above, which deal with the cosmic constants of nature, there are no alternative explanations, and the scientist qua scientist must resort to expressions such as "happy coincidence" and "fortunate accident." And ironically, today, even in the biological realm, it no longer appears that the principle of natural selection can explain the appearance of new species—and certainly not *Homo sapiens*. As Aviezer points out, the fossil record has not lived up to Darwin's expectations, so that even in the area of biology the so-called "evolutionary process" is largely determined by such unusual events as drastic climatic changes and the impact of meteors.[8] Indeed, with respect to the explanatory power of evolution in regard to the origin of intelligent life, we are told, "There has developed a general consensus among evolutionists that the evolution of intelligent life, comparable in information-processing ability to that of *Homo sapiens*, is so improbable that it is unlikely to have occurred on any other planet in the entire visible universe."[9]

The "Weak" Version

So much for the religious uses of the Anthropic Principle in its "strong" version, in which it is similar to the Teleological Argument. I should like to suggest another use for this principle by believing Jews in the realm of history, a use which brings it closer to the way it is actually employed in science. In their massive work on this subject, Barrow and Tipler point out that in one of its formulations (called the Weak

---

[7] It is pointed out that Paley, in his classic presentation of the Design Argument, in seeking out examples of design, does devote considerable attention to the laws of motion and gravitation and their role in astronomy, which obviously are outside the jurisdiction of Darwinian natural selection. However, according to Barrow and Tipler, "they were ignored in subsequent evaluations of his work" (p. 82).

[8] Nathan Aviezer, "The Anthropic Principle," 46-48.

[9] John D. Barrow and Frank J. Tipler, *The Anthropic Principle*, 133.

Anthropic Principle, or W.A.P.) this principle has heuristic value and may even have predictive force:

> The observed values of all physical and cosmological quantities are not equally probable but they take on values restricted by the requirement that there exist sites where carbon-based life can evolve and by the requirement that the universe be old enough for it to have already done so.[10]

In other words, the fact that carbon-based life did eventually evolve on earth imposes certain constraints on what the fundamental constants of nature may ultimately turn out to be; that is, the relative strengths of the nuclear and electromagnetic forces have to be such as to make it possible for carbon atoms to exist. Also, after learning the composition of those complex elements which are the building-blocks of life, such as carbon, nitrogen, oxygen, and phosphorous, and how they are formed, we are able to predict something about the size and the age of the universe: there has to have been enough time for these complex elements to have been synthesized out of the simpler elements of hydrogen and helium. And this had to be done at a more moderate temperature and for a much longer time than was available in the early universe. These conditions were present in the interiors of stars. Hence, the universe would have to be at least ten billion years old!

It should be noted that in so employing the W.A.P. it is not necessary to conclude that the appearance of carbon-based life somewhere in the universe was in fact the goal from the very beginning. From the point of view of science, all that can be concluded is the following:

> We have found nature to be constructed upon certain immutable foundations which we call fundamental constants of nature. As yet we have no explanation for the precise numerical values taken by these unchanging dimensionless numbers. They are not subject to evolution or selection by any known natural or unnatural mechanism.[11]

Yet it is this precise combination of initial conditions and cosmological coincidences that make the existence of intelligent life possible.

---

[10] Ibid., 16.
[11] Ibid., 31.

Chapter Sixteen. Providential History and the Anthropic Principle

Loss of the "Story Line"

I wish to apply something like the W.A.P., or at least a similar form of reasoning, in order to help resolve a most vexing problem confronting those believing Jews who seek a coherent philosophy of history.[12] The problem, in brief, is as follows: For all of their emphasis on historiography, our biblical and rabbinic sources are far too sketchy to provide us with a complete outlook on history. The Pentateuch had much to tell us about the meaning of the beginnings of Jewish history, while the Prophets disclose a great deal about its ultimate eschatological goals. However, there is a lacuna in regard to the in-between; that intermediate period between the end of the beginning and the beginning of the end, between the destruction of the Second Temple and the Messianic redemption, a period that has turned out to be very long. There was little in the Pentateuch to guide Israel as to how long the Exile would last. As to the Exile itself, only the bleakest conditions are indicated. However, the Pentateuch predicts an ultimate spiritual regeneration on the part of Israel, followed by a response from the God who "remembers" and an ultimate return.[13] However, toward the end of the First Temple period, Israel has the benefit of the word of Jeremiah, who prophesies a short and tolerable exile.[14]

During the entire Second Temple period it was reasonable to believe that, although the period of independence under the Hasmoneans had ended and Israel was now under Roman rule, so long as the people were in their land Israel was being given another chance to fulfill its original goal of building a just and holy society that would make its impression on mankind. It was still possible to dream the old dream and to function on the basis of the original plan. Operating on this premise, Bar Kochba, even after the Temple was destroyed, made a desperate effort to throw off the yoke of Rome, but failed. After that, Judaism's historiographic crises began in earnest and continued to intensify as time wore on.

As the Jews were removed from the soil and soon were no longer a majority in their own land, and as the exiles were driven further and

---

[12] The thesis advanced here is developed in my work *Holocaust and Return to Zion: A Study in Jewish Philosophy of History* (Jersey City, NJ: KTAV, 2000).
[13] Lev. 26:36-38; Deut. 28:65-69, 30:1-6.
[14] Jer. 29:10-11; 37:7-8.

further away, the very notion of an "ingathering of the exiles," which would seem to have to precede all of the other restorative and utopian elements of the Redemption, became so unrealistic as to be relegated to the sphere of the supernatural and the realm of special Providence. Hence, for people in the present, locked into a situation with no apparent possibility for human initiative except prayer and good works, the practical relevance of the entire forward-looking aspect of Judaism's historiography began to evaporate. "Waiting for the Messiah" became a pious ideal that was literally "out of this world"!

To better appreciate the nature of the problem, let us compare the post-exilic period with the earlier biblical period, which we may term the *ascendancy*, i.e. the progressive development of Israel from patriarchal prehistory to becoming a people in their own land. Here, at every intermediate stage, we are able to discern a "pointing" in a certain direction. All of these, taken together, show an overall pattern. Toward the end of the Patriarchal period, the direction is clearly towards Egypt, there to become a people. Then they were to survive the servitude, then to be liberated, then to experience the Covenant at Mt. Sinai, then to overcome the Wilderness, then to conquer and settle of the land, then to unite the people around a central religious sanctuary. Thus, aside from the *overall* goal of fulfilling the vision given to Abraham of becoming a "blessing to all the families of the earth," which still remained in the distant future, there was at every point a *concrete intermediate goal* understood as a station along the way. Jewish history could then be understood and events evaluated in terms of "progress" made in the short term, in achieving interim stages which were necessary steps in arriving at the ultimate goal. We see this at certain pivotal junctures where the Bible links present events to the past as well as to the future, thus indicating that all are part of an overall pattern. For example, Joseph in Egypt, before his death and while conditions are still quite favorable for his people, reminds them that their history extends beyond Egypt.[15] Moses is told that after the Exodus he is to bring the people "to serve God" at Mt. Sinai, and that afterward the Lord will bring them to the Promised Land.[16] In his Song of the Sea, Moses, while still in the Wilderness, points to a future arrival at the "mountains of the Lord's inheritance

---

[15] Gen. 50:25.
[16] Exod. 3:12; 6:8.

Chapter Sixteen. Providential History and the Anthropic Principle

where He dwells in His sanctuary."[17] Joshua, having conquered and settled the land, traces the Jews' entire history from Abraham on through Egypt and the Exodus, the splitting of the sea, the vicissitudes in the Wilderness, the conquests on the eastern side of the Jordan, and on to the present.[18] Finally, Solomon perceives his united kingdom and the visible Presence of God in the newly dedicated Temple in Jerusalem as signifying the fulfillment of all the promises made to Moses.[19] With this we reach the highest point in this initial period of ascendancy, insofar as it relates to the national and political framework.

Can Jewish History Support a Theory of Progress?

Another way of presenting our problem is to ask whether Jewish historiography contains a theory of progress. Historians trace the origins of the theory of progress to Christianity, which received from the Jews the basic ideas of history as having a transcendent purpose, of there existing a future Golden Age on earth and of there being a unity of mankind, whereas other vital ideas came from the ancient Greeks and Romans.[20] The ideas received from the Jews are necessary but do not by themselves constitute a theory of progress. For while the concept of progress relates the past to the future, it does so in a manner which is far more complex than merely positing a promise made in the past which somehow is to be fulfilled in the future.[21] Any credible theory of progress would have to be based on a special type of historical explanation which points to a series of successive temporal events that: (1) seem to possess continuity by exhibiting a) a certain direction of development and b) a persistence of certain similar elements; and (2) by showing how what comes later *depends* upon what came earlier in the sense that, but for the latter, the former could hardly have occurred in the way it did.

Thus, to claim for Judaism a theory of progress we must be able to point to a converging series of temporal events occurring over the entire

---

[17] Exod. 15:17.
[18] Josh. 24:1-15.
[19] I Kings 8:16, 8:56.
[20] See Robert Nisbet, *History of the Idea of Progress* (New York: Basic Books, Inc., 1980), 3-47.
[21] See W.B. Gallie, "Explanations in History and the Genetic Sciences," in *Theories of History*, ed. Patrick Gardiner (Glencoe, IL: Free Press of Glencoe, 1959), 395.

course of the last 2,000 years which exhibit *continuity* and *dependency* in the sense described above, and which seem to be leading in the direction of the eschatological goals. It has been suggested that "explained history" is actually "reasoned narrative." One of the reasons the Bible reads so well is because the history it presents is adequately "explained" by constantly bringing out the continuity between the successive phases, the dependence of the later phases upon the earlier, and the fact that all are leading to the promised goal. This "thickens up" the narrative.

It is quite clear, therefore, that for the period of the ascendancy covered in the Bible we do have a recognizable progressive development, i.e. a selective presentation of the main historical events showing Israel's development from earlier stages to more advanced stages, from promise to fulfillment. However, it is the post-Exilic period, a vast time-sequence of some 2,000 years for which we do not have the benefit of a prophetically-written history, that poses the real challenge to Jewish historiography. Does the material here lend itself to a theory of progress? Aside from the "constants" of suffering and literary creativity, do we find here any patterns or lines of development which can in some sense be termed "progress" towards the historic goal of Redemption?

It would seem that the real difficulty relates to the very amorphous character of the concept of Redemption, the presumed goal of history. In terms of its ultimate utopian expression in the form of a morally-reformed and spiritually-regenerated mankind, there are certainly no obvious lines of progress that may be said to be leading to that particular goal. Indeed, it is not at all clear that a condition such as "spiritual-regeneration" comes as a result of gradual evolutionary development. Whereas, if one focuses upon some of the more concrete restorative elements of the Redemption, such as the reconstitution of the Sanhedrin, the rebuilding of the Temple, or the appearance of a Messianic figure, the problem is twofold: first, we saw nothing which would indicate progress toward any of these events. Secondly, we do not know if any of these events precede or follow the Redemption and in what sequence they would appear.

Messiah in Zion or Universal Redemption?

Toward the end of the eighteenth century, the heavy fog that had enveloped the course of Jewish history seemed to lift ever so slightly. The first glimmers of the modern age with its promise of civil rights for all,

Chapter Sixteen. Providential History and the Anthropic Principle

freedom of movement, and the stirrings of national unification began to be perceived. And, for the first time, two possible directions opened for the Jewish people which could be taken as authentic goals indicated by Jewish historiography:

1) To retrench in the Diaspora, continue to fight for full civil rights, become everywhere respected citizens and thus spread the values and ideals of Judaism, i.e. the "universal mission"; or

2) to ride the waves of rising nationalism and support Jewish colonization in the Holy Land, i.e. the "ingathering of the exiles."

What happened, of course, was that events themselves decided the issue, and today almost six million Jews are living in a 65-year-old sovereign Jewish state, economically vibrant and militarily strong within the borders of historic *Eretz Yisrael*.

I wish to suggest, on the basis of the reality of the present and on the basis of what Jewish historiography has led us to expect, that we may assume the 1948 re-establishment of the Jewish State to have been the concrete intermediate goal of Providential history during the entire preceding nineteen centuries of world history.[22] We can then go on to identify those necessary and sufficient conditions whose confluence at precisely that time made the realization of the goal possible. Then, looking back, we may review the entire sweep of world history to trace the emergence and development of those factors which led to the coincidence of these conditions in 1948.

This type of reasoning seems analogous to the way the W.A.P. is used in science. The latter takes the fact of intelligent life on earth as its starting point. Science then ascertains the physical conditions necessary for the appearance and continuance of human life on earth, and seeks to trace the origin of the necessary chemical elements to processes that started in the early universe. Similarly, by assuming the re-establishment of Israel in 1948 to have been the goal of Providential post-Exilic

---

[22] Regarding the debate as to how the Jewish State of '48 should be identified according to Jewish tradition, see Menachem Kasher, *Hatekufa Ha-Gedola (The Great Era)* (Jerusalem: Torah Shelema Institute, 1968); Issachar Shlomo Teichtel, *Eim Ha-Banim Smecha (The Mother of the Sons is Happy)* (Jerusalem: Pri Haaretz Institute, 1983); Yehuda Amital, *Hama'alot Mima'amakim* (Jerusalem: Elon Shvut: 1964).

history, we may trace the major necessary conditions that had to come to pass and had to be completed and in place by 1948 in order for the event to occur. This will suggest patterns of development apparent over centuries and may even provide material to "fill out" a progress theory of Jewish history.

World Conditions Necessary for Redemption

However, before we can do this, we must take into consideration the limiting conditions that Providence imposed upon itself. That is to say, according to the tradition what was sought was not an "ingathering of the Exiles" regardless of the means by which it was achieved. The return of the Jewish people to their land, this time, had to be made in such a way as not only to arouse the response "This was the Lord's doing,"[23] but also to reflect the moral values appropriate to an age which was drawing closer to the Redemption. The following conditions, therefore, had to be met:[24]

1) In order for the act to have religious and moral significance, the declaration of Jewish statehood had to be made "voluntarily," i.e., those there at the time had to have had a reasonable alternative, and nevertheless choose the responsibilities of Jewish statehood.

2) Leaving the lands of the Exile and the acquisition of land in *Eretz Yisrael* was to be nonviolent and lawful by generally prevailing moral and legal standards.

3) Conditions had to be such that the right of the Jewish people to this land before and after statehood would be recognized by some form of international community.

Since the "end" so conceived could not be "forced," it had to wait upon the natural development of men and institutions that would make the above possible.[25] It is now clear why the Exile lasted so

---

[23] Psalms 118:23.
[24] *Ketuvot* 111a.
[25] Already in the Pentateuch the principle had been demonstrated that Divine Providence will often prefer to work within the physical and psychological limitations of the situation, even if it means delays and detours. See Gen. 15:16; Exod. 13:17, 18; and Num. 20:14-21.

Chapter Sixteen. Providential History and the Anthropic Principle

long.[26] It was not Israel's sins alone that delayed the Redemption.

---

[26] We should not be surprised by the need for long stretches of time in order for certain basic conditions to come about either in nature or in history. According to the physical laws now known, the gradual development of the universe from the stuff of the Big Bang was necessary to bring about the development of man. The solar system and all it contains are a mix of matter that has come down to us "after uncounted cycles of super compression within the cores of stars."

"The birth of stars and their death were all needed to recook the hydrogen and helium formed in the first few moments following the Big Bang into the heavier elements such as carbon, iron and uranium needed for life as we know it" (G.L. Schroeder, *Genesis and the Big Bang* [New York: Bantam Books, 1990], 49). Thus, most of the 15 billion years of the universe has been taken up with bringing into existence the basic ingredients necessary for life. The appearance of intelligent life on earth is truly a "last minute" development.

The difference between the long stretch of time needed for the development of basic conditions and the accelerated pace of later development, can also be seen in the relationship of history to prehistory even as conceived by the Bible. The first important positive religious development recorded in the Bible takes place in connection with the stories of the Patriarchs (c. 2000-1800 BCE) during the Bronze Age. It might therefore be assumed that the preceding 20 generations, also listed in the Bible, were of no positive significance and were irrelevant to the appearance of the Patriarchs. Indeed, the rabbis called this period one of *tohu vevohu* (see *Avot* 5:23).

However, archeology, supported by hints in the Bible, reveals that it was precisely during the millennia preceding the Bronze Age—the Neolithic and the Chalcolithic periods—that the major advances took place in agriculture, animal domestication, metallurgy, and urbanization. These giant steps in human development did not merely precede Abraham chronologically but were, in some fundamental sense, a prerequisite for his entire religious breakthrough. There is no real alternative to the rabbinic teaching that Abraham, on his own, came to an awareness of a single moral, transcendent Creator-God before he received the divine call,but is it reasonable to believe that anyone could come to such a conception before man *as a species* learned to know himself, had developed his basic capacities, before man had learned to provide for his basic needs and comforts, before man had demonstrated his superiority over the animals, as being more than a two-legged, fire-using cave dweller? In short, could there have been an Abraham before there appeared conditions in which human existence could be seen as something to be thankful for?

Once again. the amount of time needed to prepare the groundwork, form the ingredients, and bring into existence the necessary conditions was far greater than what would be needed for subsequent developments. To prepare world conditions for a return of Israel to its land took some 1,800 years. Once the Zionist Organization was formed, it took but 50 years to achieve a state!

Developments of world-historic scope had to take place, such as the secularization of society and the weakening of the influence of Christianity and Islam on political events, the increase in access to general education, and the development of a new system of international relations so that Jews could enter the modern world. Moreover, ways of overcoming military threats and economic problems which had beset a small state, poor in natural resources and surrounded by hostile neighbors, in the past had to be provided for. Thus, the nascent Jewish state could hardly have survived the onslaught of its Arab neighbors without the qualitative edge made possible by modern technology. Nor could that thin sliver of land have been expected to support a population of over six million without the benefits of recent science and high tech inventions.

Clearly, the conditions we have been describing as necessary for the re-establishment of a Jewish state are all essential elements of modernity, which had been developing in the West, gradually and painfully, over the preceding two centuries.

Accordingly, a prescient believing Jew, contemporary with the Maharal of Prague, if asked for signs of the coming Redemption, might have pointed to Tycho Brahe and Kepler, and explained that they were laying the foundations for a science whose development would be a necessary condition for the Ingathering of the Exiles in the middle of the twentieth century. Similarly, the Declaration of Independence of the American colonies and their adoption of a constitution (1776-89) could be pointed to as significant progress towards the Redemption, in the sense that the development and spread of democracy was another necessary condition for the events of 1948. This is to be understood both in the sense that democracy would be the only viable political form that a pluralistic Jewish state could take, and that the spread of democratic values and human rights would bring Great Britain to relinquish her empire.

Jewish Conditions Necessary for Redemption

Up to this point we have emphasized those factors necessary for the occurrence of an important event in *Jewish* history which could have been created only by forces operating in *world* history. This interaction between these two overlapping arenas has often been overlooked by

Chapter Sixteen. Providential History and the Anthropic Principle

believing Jews committed to a simplistic notion of the dynamics of history and the role of Providence therein. However, the re-establishment of Israel in 1948 most certainly could not have happened in the absence of certain basic facts regarding the Jewish people themselves:

1) Their physical survival in numbers sufficient for the Jews as a whole to be considered a "player" on the international scene. Shortly before the fall of Jerusalem in 70 CE, Jews worldwide numbered about eight million. As the result of wars, persecution, and assimilation, the Jews at the beginning of the seventeenth century numbered less than one million souls! They increased to 2.25 million by the beginning of the nineteenth century, but were said to be 7.5 million by the 1880s![27]

2) Their preservation of a historical consciousness and sense of self-identity as the descendants of the Jews of the Bible and Talmud, whose language they understood, whose religious beliefs they espoused, whose religious practices they observed, and whose vision of the future they shared.

3) Their continued interaction with and elaboration of all aspects of the Torah tradition by means of translation and commentary, their remaining halakhically responsive to changing conditions, philosophically alert to diverse challenges, and spiritually receptive to mystical movements. This made the Torah accessible to all and transformed a piece of writing into a practical, edifying, and comprehensive way of life.

4) Their migrational patterns, seemingly fortuitous, which transformed them from an Oriental people living largely in the East (Babylon, Parthia, North Africa, Asia Minor) to a Western people living largely in Europe (of the 7.5 million Jews worldwide in 1880, 7 million lived in Europe!). This exposed them to the political and economic changes and intellectual currents which were heralding the birth pangs of modernity. Being in Europe placed the Jews in a position to appreciate the promise of the New World and to think in terms of emigration.

---

[27] See *Encyclopedia Judaica*, vol. 13, under "Population," by S.W. Baron, and vol. 5, under "Demography," by Schmelz.

Each of these four lines of development of the Jewish people can be traced in detail from the very beginnings of the post-Exilic period until the present. When this is done, we shall be provided with an account of how, in 1948, 1,878 years after the destruction of the Second Temple in Jerusalem, it just so happened that there had survived a viable number of Jews, positioned in the right place, aware and proud of their identity, yet no strangers to the modern world, who responded to the opportunity to return to their homeland.

Perhaps when these facts are laid out the material will provide us with a progress theory of history. That is to say, we will be able to perceive how these lines of development involving the Jewish people, and internal to their own history, interacted and coalesced with certain conditions created by the following four major lines of development within world history:

1) The secularization of society. This refers to the gradual removal of institutional religion from the economic, political, and ultimately social spheres, making it possible for Jews to enter and participate in general society.

2) The growth and spread of democracy as the only effective and moral form of political rule.

3) The development of a structure of world government based on values of human rights and social justice.

4) The development of science and technology based on the empirical method and the spirit of free inquiry.

Each of these factors had to be developed and nurtured over the course of time, and all of them had to converge at the precise moment when each had reached its peak of appropriateness, both in relation to the others and in relation to the goal. The establishment of the State of Israel could not have happened much earlier than it did, nor could it have been much delayed. For those who could make no sense of the preceding 2,000 years of Jewish history, the establishment of the Jewish state in 1948 made possible a resumption of the story line, the closing of a circle, which shed light on all that went before. Once the end point is discerned, we are able to pick up the thread and trace it all back to see how we got here.

Chapter Sixteen. Providential History and the Anthropic Principle

Punctuated Evolution

However, amidst all of this talk of "development" and "evolution" we must not lose sight of the role of the fortuitous, the singular, the unexpected. Just as in cosmology and biological evolution there is a need to speak of "happy coincidences" and "sudden extinctions," all of which, together with the law-like and the evolutionary, made possible the appearance of intelligent life, so too we must consider such matters in history. The lines of evolutionary development alone do not account for the establishment of the Jewish state. We must be able to perceive as well the integration of some of the side-effects and consequences of the great tragedies and disasters of Jewish history.

The "lines of development" that we speak of consist in the main of the consequences, intended or not, of the actions of human beings as individuals or collectives who, in following their own inclinations and pursuing their own goals, are usually unaware that they are part of any "line of development" and are oblivious to having a role in any Providential scheme. However, such is the manner of general Providence in history: to bring about desired results by sheer coincidence and to bring together the consequences of different human actions in ways that seem perfectly natural and unobtrusive, so that, looking back over long stretches of history from a certain specific perspective, one is able to perceive particular patterns.

The tradition tells us: "The Lord hath made everything for His own purpose, even the wicked for the day of evil" (Prov. 16:4). This can be interpreted to mean that the Lord, in working out His plan in history, makes use of the multifarious events constantly occurring—including even the consequences of the deeds of evil men. This does not mean that God causes or mandates these deeds, or that all suffering is necessarily to be construed as divine punishment, for man has been given the freedom to will evil and to act in the natural world, and God does not systematically intervene to save the innocent.[28]

---

[28] I have elsewhere (*Morality, Halakha and the Jewish Tradition* [New York: Ktav and Yeshiva University Press, 1983]) treated at length the general problem of theodicy: the fate of the individual and the nation in light of the moral nature of God, that is to say, the relationship between Divine Providence, human freedom, and the moral principle of desert. I deal with the question of the historical

Thus, Israel's suffering in ancient Egypt was caused by the cruelty of Pharaoh and the indifference of Egyptian society. The destruction of the Second Temple was brought about by the decision of Titus. The expulsion of the Jews from Spain was caused by King Ferdinand and Queen Isabella. The Holocaust was brought about by Hitler and the conditions of World War II. However, once these events occurred when they occurred, they had all sorts of ramifications, some of which the Lord of history wove into the "lines of development" which had been leading toward the fulfillment of His long-term goals.

Thus, for example, at the birth of the Israelite nation, the "iron crucible" of Egyptian servitude provided an insulated cocoon for the people's physical growth and slowed assimilation and loss of identity. The failure of dynastic monarchy and Temple priesthood as institutions of leadership democratized Judaism and pressed the people toward direct involvement with the living text of their tradition. The expulsion from Spain shattered confidence in the "protection" afforded by Jews in high places and scattered the most sophisticated branch of our people to northern Europe and the Ottoman Empire, which became staging areas for migration to the New World and to the Holy Land. World War I expelled the Turks from Palestine, placed the area under a British Mandate, and popularized movements of national liberation. World War II, and the unmitigated horror called the Holocaust, sent thousands of Jewish refugees streaming towards *Eretz Yisrael*, driving the Palestine Question to a rapid and historic resolution.[29]

We have suggested that the re-establishment of the Jewish state may be taken as the conscious goal of Divine Providence during the previous 2,000 years of history. This enables us to identify four lines of development in Jewish history and four in world history which, in

---

significance of the Holocaust in my *Holocaust and Return to Zion: A Study in the Jewish Philosophy of History* (Jersey City, NJ: KTAV, 2000). These questions are not within the scope of this paper.

[29] This approach may give us a criterion by which to distinguish between the many different disasters which beset the Jewish people in the course of their history. Thus, the aftermaths of the Bar Kochba Rebellion, the Spanish Expulsion, and the Holocaust were different by virtue of their effects in bringing about major geopolitical dislocations, demographic changes, and patterns of immigration, all of which coalesced in various ways with the Providential "lines of development."

combination with the consequences of various upheavals, were necessary and sufficient to bring about the sought-after goal. Tracing these lines of development over the centuries enables us to view history as progressing toward this intermediate stage in the Redemption process. The absence of any one of these conditions, or the failure of any one of them to reach the necessary stage of development at the given time, would have rendered the events of 1948, in the form in which they occurred, impossible. The Jewish believer chooses to see in this astonishing instance of "curious adaptation of means to ends" the guiding hand of the Lord of history.

Chapter Seventeen

The Role of Reason
in Jewish Religious Belief *

I

It is generally thought that the Hebrew Bible takes for granted the issue of religious belief. That is to say, it considers the reality of God self-evident, and does not deal with the questions so important to the Jew of today, such as "How may one who is committed to the God of Israel rationally justify his belief that there is a God?" and "How may one who does not believe come to believe in the God of Israel?" However, a more focused examination of the Bible indicates that this may not be the case. Moses, at the beginning of his commission, protests: "But behold they will not believe me!" (Exod. 4:1).[1] In response to this statement, God gives him the power to perform signs designed to convince them (Exod. 4:2-10). After the people experience a miraculous salvation, we are told, "And they believed in the Lord and in His servant Moses" (Exod. 14:31), implying that they went from a state of unbelief to one of belief. One of the reasons given for the theophany at Sinai was "that the people may believe you [Moses] for ever" (Exod. 19:9). In his farewell address, Moses presents reasoned arguments that their unique historical experiences are reliable signs of the agency of God (Deut. 4:32-35).[2] Some of the later Prophets, as well, appeal to rational arguments from

---

* This chapter draws upon two earlier more tentative treatments by the author of the meaning of *emunah*. The first was delivered as a lecture entitled "Emunah: Knowledge, Grace or Leap?" at the Third National Convention of Yavneh (National Religious Jewish Student Association) in September 1962, and reprinted in *Yavneh Studies* 1, no. 1 (Fall 1963). The second appeared as Shubert Spero, "Faith and Its Justification," *Tradition* 13, no. 1 (Fall 1971).

[1] In this context, to "believe Moses" is to believe that there is a God, and that He spoke to Moses and sent him on his mission as he (Moses) reports.

[2] By the word "reason" used as a noun I denote the intellectual faculty by which we have conceptions, judge arguments, draw conclusions from premises, and recognize means-ends relationships. It is reason that has developed the formal science of logic, which is the most general of all the sciences, whose rules are

Chapter Seventeen. The Role of Reason in Jewish Religious Belief

natural phenomena to demonstrate the reality of a moral God and His Presence in history (Jer. 33:20-26; Isa. 40:26). As David Neumark has suggested, "That the existence of God in Judaism is a matter of course is true only in the sense that those who spoke in His name are not in doubt of His existence..."[3] However, these very spokesmen themselves were perfectly aware of the possibility of encountering skepticism and disbelief on the part of others. Indeed, the rabbis understood that Abraham came to his belief in God at a particular age, after a process of searching and reasoning.[4]

It would thus appear that from the very beginning there was an awareness that there would be many who would not share the prophets' beliefs about God and a concern as to how skeptics might be brought to belief. Clearly, however, the belief in God possessed by those at the founding of the Tradition was based on their immediate personal encounter with the Divine and on their witnessing of various wondrous events. On the whole, there seems to be nothing in biblical theology that would in principle oppose exploring the rational basis for religious belief, certainly not if it comes to the fore, in cases such as convertions or in responses made to hostile critics.[5]

Ever since the encounter between Judaism and Greek culture, there has been intensive, prolonged, and often acrimonious debate regarding the proper relationship between what was termed "reason" and "revelation"—in other words, between philosophy and tradition—and their respective roles in the formation of religious belief.[6] A recent discerning study traces the ascendancy and decline of these two basic approaches

---

    those by which all possible objects can be combined. See Morris Raphael Cohen, *A Preface to Logic* (NY: Meridian Books, 1957).

[3] See David Neumark, *Essays in Jewish Philosophy* (Amsterdam: Philo Press, 1971).

[4] See *Bereishit Rabbah* 39:1.

[5] See *Avot* 2:19: "Know what answer to give to the unbeliever (*apikoret*)." Judah Halevi has been called "the most Jewish" of our medieval Jewish philosophers, and in his philosophic dialogue, *Kuzari*, he sets out to defend rabbinic Judaism against Aristotelian philosophy, Mohammedan theology, and Karaites, armed only with the power of critical reason.

[6] See Julius Guttman, *Philosophies of Judaism* (New York: Holt, Rinehart and Winston, 1964), 21-29, and Isaac Husik, *A History of Medieval Jewish Philosophy* (Philadelphia: Jewish Publication Society, 1941), Introduction.

to religious faith in different communities during different periods of Jewish history.[7] The two contending approaches are termed *emunah temimah*, simple or naive belief, versus *emunat da'at*, reasoned belief. In the first, the individual embraces the Torah way of life on the basis of the tradition of the forefathers and finds no insurmountable difficulty in questions such as the presence of evil or the dating of biblical texts. In the second approach, religious belief is submitted to examination by reason, one's own and conventional wisdom, resulting in attempts to ground religious belief in a broader metaphysical framework which includes God, man, and the cosmos. Alternatively, one may, after some introspection, base one's belief on some immediate personal mystical experience. However, even that could nevertheless be considered a "reasoned faith," for he could tell you "why" he believes the way he does.

It can be said that for nine hundred years after the Talmudic period Jewish thought was dominated by the approach of "reasoned faith" in either its rationalistic or its mystical (Kabbalistic) form. These two world views fought each other for the allegiance of Jewish thinkers, with Kabbala emerging the victor. However, both held *emunah temimah* in high esteem, recognizing it as the starting point for further development. The end of the eighteenth century, and particularly the nineteenth, saw a change in the views of the Jewries of Central and Eastern Europe. Kabbala lost its hegemony, and *emunah temimah* rapidly overcame reasoned faith as the model for the ideal religious faith.

While Kabbala continued to be highly regarded as sacred (*kadosh*), it was neutralized as popular theology by being reserved for the pious elite who alone were "worthy" or "ready" for it. However, "reasoned" belief in its systematic philosophical form was practically delegitimized in spite of its cultivation by some of the most illustrious figures in medieval Jewish philosophy. The argument was that it did not provide a strong enough basis for religious faith, particularly in the face of brutal persecution. This brief history helps explain the entrenched prejudice against "philosophy" which exists today within traditional Judaism.

I wish to suggest that this entire subject is in need of fresh examination, not with the usual historical approach but from the perspective of a practicing Jew today, aware of the world around him. The understanding

---

[7] Binyamin Brown, "The Return of *Emunah Temimah*," in *On Faith*, ed. Moshe Halbertal, David Kurzweil, and Avi Sagi, 403-444 (Jerusalem: Keter, 2005).

Chapter Seventeen. The Role of Reason in Jewish Religious Belief

that past generations had of these basic concepts of reason and philosophy, faith and *emunah*, has been radically superseded by developments which have enhanced our insights. Today we have a much clearer grasp of the power as well as the limitations of human reason.

On the one hand, science and technology have advanced the frontiers of our knowledge of the universe to an unimaginable extent, from providing evidence as to the origins of the cosmos to deciphering the genome code, one of the bases of life itself. So resourceful is human reason that it is capable of inventing artificial intelligence that is able to increase the analytic and imaginative power of the human mind manyfold. On the other hand, the philosophies of radical empiricism and logical positivism have demonstrated the incompetence of deductive reason in the metaphysical realm, and its severe limitations in the creation of formal systems or definitions of concepts such as probability, degree of belief, and weight of evidence.

In light of these developments, we can no longer address the issue of reason versus revelation in terms of medieval Jewish theology. The question must be examined anew, starting from the very beginning, using the only tool at our disposal, our very common God-given reason, the analytic power of the human mind.

Even from the side of tradition and revelation, it is unquestionable that the main arbiters in determining the meaning (*pshat*) of the canonical texts and the validity of received traditions were the common sense, rules of language-usage and simple logic.[8] The literary prophets in their condemnations of idolatry used logical arguments, such as argumentum ad absurdum. In the *Chumash*, the Five Books of Moses, a prime consideration urging obedience to God's commandments was the intuitive moral principle of gratitude.[9] In short, the tradition itself, in interpreting the text and urging its acceptance as the word of God, employed analytic reason. Indeed, the evidence tends to support the proposition that in Judaism, "reason is prior to tradition."[10]

---

[8] While the syntactical and semantic rules of a national language are hardly all logical, the very fact that language enables human beings to communicate effectively indicates that it follows basic rules of consistency and material implication.

[9] See Deut. 32:1-15 and Mechilta on Exod. 20:2.

[10] Israel Efros, *Studies in Medieval Jewish Philosophy* (New York: Columbia University Press, 1974), 33.

Part IV. The Analytic in Action

Let us start with an examination of the terms central to our inquiry. The Hebrew verb "to believe" (*le ha'amin*) and the noun "belief" (*emunah*), whether used in the ordinary or a religious sense, has two main uses, best expressed in the distinction between "belief-in" and "belief-that." The latter refers to a cognitive assertion that something is the case: "I believe *that* it is now raining outside," while the former is an expression of trust: "I believe *in* my invention." The logical relationship between the two is that "belief-that" is logically prior to "belief-in," which in turn implies belief-that, that is, you cannot have belief *in* somebody or something unless you believe *that* he or it exists.

The term *emunah* as found in different grammatical forms throughout biblical-rabbinic literature is used primarily in the sense of "trust" both in the form of "having trust in someone" and in the form of "being trustworthy," i.e. possessing moral character.[11] This supports what was said earlier, that "those who speak in God's name are not in doubt of His existence" and therefore have no need to make assertions of the type "I believe *that* God exists" and deal only with the degree of our trust *in* Him. On the other hand, medieval Jewish philosophers in their own writing use *emunah* even in a religious context to mean "belief-that" something is real or true, i.e., a cognitive judgment. In the words of Maimonides,

> Bear in mind that by "faith" [*emunah*] we do not understand merely that which is uttered with the lips but also that which is apprehended by the soul, the conviction that the object of belief is exactly as apprehended ... that the thing apprehended has its existence beyond the mind [in reality] exactly as it is conceived in the mind. If in addition to this we are convinced that the thing cannot be different in any way from that what we believe it to be and that *no reasonable argument can be found* for the rejection of the belief ... then the belief is true.[12]

Use of the verb *la-da'at* (to know) and its noun *da'at* (knowledge) enables us to distinguish between "belief" and "knowledge." To say, "I *know* that something is the case" is to imply that one's belief is based upon

---

[11] See Yoel ben-Nun, "*Emunah*," in *On Faith*, ed. Moshe Halbertal, David Kurzweil, and Avi Sagi, 403-444 (Jerusalem: Keter, 2005)

[12] Moses Maimonides, *Guide for the Perplexed*, trans. M. Friedlander (New York: E. P. Dutton & Co., 1942), I:50.

Chapter Seventeen. The Role of Reason in Jewish Religious Belief

conclusive, publicly verifiable evidence, whereas to say "I *believe* that something is the case" is primarily to assert something about one's own state of mind without any implication as to what the belief may be based upon and whether the belief is "strong" or "weak."

However, the use of *da'at* in the Prophets in conjunction with God, as in "For the earth shall be full of the knowledge [*da'at*] of the Lord" (Isa. 11:9) and "...that he understands and knows [*yadoah*] Me..." (Jer. 9:23), is best understood as referring to "knowledge" in the sense of "acquaintance" ("connaitre" rather than "savoir"), i.e., empathetic understanding based on direct and immediate personal experience.

In English we have the word "faith," which primarily means "trust" but when used in a religious context takes on an added nuance, lending it a sense of certainty well beyond that which could be justified by available evidence, a sort of privileged "knowledge."[13] However, there is no evidence in our biblical-rabbinic sources or in the writing of medieval Jewish philosophers that they understood *religious* belief to be any different, epistemologically, from mundane belief. Use of a special term such as "faith" to denote a person's relationship to God is important in a religion such as Christianity, which considers it a special state of mind conferred upon a person as a gift from God. However, there is no comparable term in the Jewish tradition.[14]

In attempting to develop an understanding of the necessary and sufficient components of the state of mind which might properly serve as the referent of the term "religious belief" (*emunah*) in Judaism, our diagnostic tools will be the terms "belief-in," "belief-that" and "knowledge," as defined above. Accordingly, any statement such as "I trust *in* God," or "I believe *in* God" or "I am committed *to* God" presupposes that "I believe *that* there is a God," and is a statement that is subject to the same rules of usage as ordinary belief statements, i.e., open to calls for rational justification.

Let us consider today's young practicing Jew, born into and raised by an observant family, with a yeshiva and college education, happily pursuing his social and intellectual interests within the Jewish community, quite comfortable with his religious commitment. Living as he

---

[13] See Martin Buber, *Two Types of Faith* (New York: Macmillan Co., 1951), 7-9.
[14] In Christian theology this is called "grace," that is, the unmerited favor of God as a divine saving influence.

does in an open society with access to modern information media, he is certainly aware that people have different approaches to religious values, even including the possibility of atheism or complete indifference to religion. At some point he may realize that it is only seemingly fortuitous circumstances that account for him living the life he does and having the beliefs he has. He also knows that there are true beliefs and false beliefs, and that the strength with which a particular belief may be held is no indication of its validity.

Some day, as the result of some unexpected event, some unusual encounter, or some particular reading, the implications of these considerations for him personally might impel him to seek reasons for his beliefs and his way of life: "Why *do* I think that my religious beliefs are true?" What emerges may appear to be simply an ad hoc response to an outside challenge, but should this lead the individual to develop a rational justification for his belief, he will begin to experience a heightened sense of self-respect. Faith is no longer a mere "given" but an achievement brought about by exercising that faculty which is God's gift to man. Particularly regarding questions of such singular significance as, "Is this a purposive universe?," or, "Is my being here an accident?," each individual has the obligation to seek answers and freely choose his response. In practice this means that I give the matter serious thought, examine the alternatives, weigh the pros and cons, trace out the consequences, and make my decision, for which I assume full responsibility.

But what if one is not merely comfortable with his beliefs but completely consumed by an overwhelming love for God, and constantly senses His abiding Presence? Should we feel obligated to disturb the strong moorings of his traditional beliefs by raising provocative questions so that he may develop a rationally justifiable religious belief? Perhaps not.[15] Yet man's God-given rational nature imposes upon him a general duty to submit all aspects of his life to rational scrutiny. Can this be done while the man at the very same time fully and thankfully

---

[15] However, this does not mean that the criteria for judging a belief reasonable in one domain necessarily hold for other domains. For it may be that the individual finds that his relationship to God is founded on experiences and emotions of such profundity and singularity that reason itself understands that it is confronting something that transcends its usual criteria of reasonableness. That is to say, in such an instance, in the face of a personal experience so compelling, the belief it generates is adequately justified for that individual.

Chapter Seventeen. The Role of Reason in Jewish Religious Belief

recognizes that his own relationship to God (whose reality he has never questioned) rests convincingly upon the immediate experiences of personal encounter?[16] Some have argued that the very raising of the question: "How do you know your beliefs are true?" generates an element of doubt, as it implies the theoretical possibility that those beliefs may be wrong! It should be noted that the word "doubt" may be used to refer to two different states of mind. The first is an actual inclination to disbelieve (like "I doubt it"). The second, which is the one relevant to our discussion, has been called "methodological skepticism"—that is to say, an objective recognition that my personal sense of conviction, while properly decisive for myself, is of little value in the public arena. Thus, in order to participate in open discussion of these matters I must fashion a rational justification of my belief. Indeed, I may even have a religious obligation to work out a reasoned set of arguments for my belief, for this may be a corollary of Judaism's demand that God be worshipped by the total person, by all aspects of his being, including his reason. This is expressed by, "May the soul *in its entirety* [*kol hanishamah*] praise the Lord" (Psalms 150:6), and even more specifically by, "*Know* this day and lay it to your heart that the Lord He is God in heaven above and upon the earth beneath, there is none else" (Deut. 4:39).[17]

Every mature individual is capable of introspectively distinguishing between three levels of experience: feeling, thinking, and doing. Thus, while our hypothetical religious young man may be relating to God with his emotions and serving Him with deeds, he has not yet exercised his reason to explicate his beliefs or their bases. In this context we can understand Moshe's turning to God in Sinai and beseeching Him, "Make

---

[16] A study of hasidic sources on the subject indicates that the nature of a person's religious consciousness in regard to its epistemological base may be a dynamic one. There are of course instances where one's initial state is one of *emunah temima*, but circumstances launch one on a search for rational justification, where one eventually ends up. But surprisingly enough there are cases of religious belief which start out based upon rational underpinnings, which after a while are seen as inadequate, and the individual graduates into *emunah temima*. Which type of *emunah* is "high" or "preferable" has long been debated inconclusively. (See Yoel Ben Nun, "*Emunah*," 208-210.

[17] Bachya ibn Pakuda sees this as the source of our obligation to engage in philosophical reasoning in order to demonstrate rationally the singularity of God (*Duties of the Heart*, Gate I, chapter 3).

known to me, I beseech You, Your ways." His overwhelmingly rich direct experiences of God notwithstanding, Moshe wishes to deepen his intellectual understanding and thus his relationship. Similarly, I have shown elsewhere, while Rabbi Joseph B. Soloveitchik bases the Jewish relationship to God on immediate personal experience, he nevertheless offers various philosophical arguments to demonstrate the reasonableness of belief and the reality of the transcendent. Thus, one may at least embark upon a process of rational justification without diminution of one's religious convictions.[18]

Therefore, if we wish to usefully differentiate between belief systems which undergird the different Jewish life styles and degrees of observance, we might speak of the following categories of people:

1) Those whose level of observance, intensity of belief, and sense of Jewish identity are so seamless that their precise beliefs concerning God, Revelation, and reasons for the commandments have never been articulated, much less examined philosophically.

2) Those whose conscious beliefs concerning the above are straightforward and traditional and considered to be self-evidently true. They have never had the occasion to question them. These beliefs are confirmed for them daily by their personal experience of the Presence of God in the Torah way of life.

3) Those who have examined the basis for their belief in God and the source of the authority of the Torah and its commandments and have found that it rests upon a number of cognitive truth-claims, including that there exists a moral Creator God whose Will is reflected in the Written and Oral Torah and who is active in human history.

It is members of this latter group who one day may feel challenged by their own senses of intellectual integrity or by their desires to discuss

---

[18] See Shubert Spero, *Aspects of Joseph Dov Soloveitchik's Philosophy of Judaism: An Analytic Approach* (Jersey City, NJ: KTAV, 2009); also, "Feeling is always seen as a conative experience and this aspect is analyzed in light of rational criteria. The meaning is analyzed, the worth of the striving is examined [evaluated] and the possibilities of attainment scrutinized" (Joseph B. Soloveitchik: *Worship of the Heart*, [Jersey City, NJ: KTAV, 2003], p. 8.)

Chapter Seventeen. The Role of Reason in Jewish Religious Belief

these matters with others to seek a rational justification for their beliefs. It is primarily to this group that the second part of this chapter is directed.

II

How would a traditional Jew from Group 3 go about justifying his religious beliefs? Are there generally agreed-upon criteria as to what constitutes rational justification? Does one have to first commit oneself to some existing philosophical school with a developed epistemological theory in order to establish accepted conditions of adequacy?

I wish to suggest an approach which combines the sparse, commonsense epistemology of Saadia Gaon with some insights from philosophy of science. Of all the medieval Jewish thinkers who dealt with this question, the one who in my judgment came closest to the requirements of the Torah was Saadia Gaon (882-942).[19] This is to be seen in his realization that a philosophy of Judaism can be properly constructed only on the basis of a general theory of epistemology, for our acceptance of Judaism and our belief that it is true are based on the same principles as are our general knowledge. This is expressed in Saadia's opening remarks to his philosophic work, *The Book of Beliefs and Opinions*:

> Blessed be God, the God of Israel, Who is alone deserving of being regarded as the Evident Truth, Who verifies with certainty unto rational beings the existence of their souls, by means of which

---

[19] There are several factors which uniquely positioned Saadia to grasp this vital issue. Called the "father of medieval Jewish philosophy of religion" (JuliusGuttman, *Philosophies of Judaism*, 61), Saadia was the first Jewish thinker to construct a *system* of Jewish philosophy (David Neumark, *Essays in Jewish Philosophy*, 163). That is to say, he endeavored to show the logical relationship between the various basic concepts of Judaism, starting with Creation, God, God's attributes, His relationship to man, and the goals of history. As the head of the famed Yeshiva of Sura in Babylon, and possessing the title of Gaon, Saadia was heir to the full talmudic-rabbinic tradition and, at the same time, was schooled in Islamic theology, whose roots were deep in Greek philosophy, unfettered by the authority of Aristotelianism. His grasp of both was incisive and comprehensive. Also, as one called upon to confront the fully developed Karaite heresy, he fully appreciated the role of critical reason as the only universally recognized tool available in intellectual controversy.

they assess accurately what they perceive with their senses and apprehend correctly the objects of their knowledge."[20]

Whereas others might have started with praise to God for revealing His Holy Torah to Israel, Saadia begins with that which is prior to and the basis of all: God's gift of reason to man, a self-correcting tool which enables him to attain knowledge of himself and the world around him. Indeed, for Saadia, agreement with reason was seen as a necessary precondition for the acceptance of any doctrine claiming the status of revelation.[21]

According to Saadia, there are three sources for knowledge: (1) sense perception; (2) certain self-evident intuitive principles; and (3) conclusions drawn rationally from the data supplied by the first two sources. However, since it is possible to be in error regarding any of these, it is the task of reason in its critical mode to make certain they are accurate. To these sources, Saadia adds a fourth, which is knowledge that is based upon a reliable tradition. There is really nothing included here to which a modern mind might have serious objections, nor are their objectionable omissions.

While Saadia will use this fourth source in order to help explain religious knowledge, it is clear that there are many areas of everyday life in which we rely upon information that we derive from others—subject, of course, to common-sense safeguards against error and deceit. *Religious* tradition need be no different. Thus, when we analyze the rational basis for belief in a religious tradition, according to this theory, we find that it is, at least at the outset, not a new source of knowledge, but is based upon the original "three": sense perception, self-evident intuitive principles, and reasoned conclusions drawn from sense perception and self-evident intuitive principles. For example, reports of miracles must be validated by sense perception, and the moral prescriptions of the Torah must be concurred to by our own moral intuitions. Therefore, to the extent that religious belief attains the level of "knowledge," it turns out to be a specialized form of "historical knowledge."[22] While the *event*

---

[20] Saadia Gaon, *The Book of Beliefs and Opinions* (New Haven: Yale University Press, 1948), 3.
[21] Julius Guttman, *Philosophies of Judaism*, 63. Compare with David Neumark, *Essays in Jewish Philosophy*, 208.
[22] Guttman, *Philosophies of Judaism*, 64-65.

Chapter Seventeen. The Role of Reason in Jewish Religious Belief

of revelation is supernatural and may be seen as a source of special "religious truth," the *belief* that revelation actually took place and that its content was reliably transmitted to us must pass all the general criteria of rational belief pertaining to any historical knowledge.

Given this analysis, then, how would a Jew of Group 3 today go about justifying his religious belief?

Before we can answer this question we must fully understand the nature of the material before us. If we are dealing here simply with the belief that certain events happened in the past, then the primary focus of an inquiry will be on the reliability of the texts before us and of the oral transmission. However, if the main element is a belief in a metaphysical entity called God, then the primary question is not the truth of the belief but rather its meaningfulness. Furthermore, religious belief may include a commitment to behave in a certain way and to accept a moral norm. In that case, what is involved is a value judgment which requires a more complex decision-procedure in order to test its rationality. Until this is clarified, we cannot determine the sort of evidence needed befor the belief to be deemed worthy of acceptance.

As Aristotle stated early on, but many seem to have forgotten:

> The same exactness must not be expected in all departments of philosophy alike. Our treatment of this science will be adequate if it achieves the amount of precision which belongs to its subject matter. It is equally unreasonable to accept merely probable conclusions from a mathematician and to demand strict demonstrations from an orator.... Nor again must we in all matters alike demand an explanation of the reason why things are what they are: in some cases it is enough if the fact that they are so is satisfactorily established.[23]

Indeed, it is clear that even by today's standards of science, if one is seeking knowledge of past events or dealing with questions of the reliability of certain literary documents, our criteria of rational belief cannot be the same as it is in the physical sciences.

The concept of *emunah* in Judaism has long been recognized as being much more complex than simply intellectual assent to particular propositions. This can be seen in the rabbinic phrase, "Acceptance of the Yoke

---

[23] Aristotle, *Nicomachean Ethics*, chapters III and VII.

of the Kingdom of Heaven," which is used to describe the first portion of the *Shema*, which is seen as the primary phase of the individual's entrance to Judaism.²⁴

This concept of "Accepting the Yoke of the Kingdom of Heaven" includes a number of "belief-that" propositions such as: there exists a single all-powerful, omniscient spiritual Creator, God, who is concerned with mankind and has covenanted with Israel and revealed His commandments, which may be found in the Five Books of Moses. To "*accept the yoke*," of the Kingdom of Heaven implies, first, that one assents to the truth of these propositions and, second, that one personally takes upon oneself the "authority" of God (*our* God) and His demands. To be sure, the thoughtful individual must at some point consider each of the cognitive components of the "Kingdom of Heaven" separately, so as to simply "understand" them.²⁵ But he must also judge how they can cohere with the other components to form the world-view which is Judaism. Finally, as we learn from the *halakhah* of conversion, the crucial concluding step involves a decision to embrace the new religion as a *totality*.

There are several factors which make for the consideration of Judaism as a "package." First, there is the notion of "authority." In Judaism, God's revelation is said to have taken the form of a prophetic transmission preserved in the words of a particular document. Thus, various narratives and teachings are accepted as true because they emanate from the same authoritative source, i.e., the Torah. Second, the unitary character of Judaism is reinforced by the fact that scripture takes the

---

[24] In seeking the Torah sources for the *mitzvah* of *emunah* or "faith" (can it be a Divine commandment to have faith?), the discussion between Maimonides and Nachmanides focuses on the introduction to the "Ten Words": "I am the Lord your God..." (Exod. 20:2). The sages, however, had already identified the "Ten Words" with the *Shema*, "Hear O Israel..."(Deut. 6:4), so that this first verse which the sages called "Acceptance of the Yoke of the Kingdom of Heaven" (*Berakhot* 6) is paired with the first of the "Ten Words" (Yerushalmi, *Sukkah* 4:3). When we juxtapose these two verses, there is a suggestion that the "I am the Lord *your* [singular] God ..." represents the self disclosure of God in Revelation, while the "Hear O Israel the Lord is our God ..." represents the human response, "...the Acceptance...."

See Jonathan Steif, *Sefer mitzvot Hashem "Emunah"* (Budget, 1931). See also Elimelech Bar-Shaul, *Mizvah va-lev: "Emunah"*(Tel Aviv, 1956).

[25] See Rashi on Deut. 6:4, who interprets the *Shema* to include an affirmation that ultimately all of mankind will accept the authority of the One God.

Chapter Seventeen. The Role of Reason in Jewish Religious Belief

form of historical narration about a central subject, whose development is given in a connected account. To accept Judaism is, in effect, to accept the veracity of a continuous story from its historic origins to its eschatological future, a dramatic narrative which attempts to explain nature and history. Thus, statements about God and His actions are part of a continuous coherent story. Finally, once Judaism is submitted to philosophical analysis (performed by such thinkers as Saadia Gaon and Maimonides), the logical relations between the various concepts within Judaism are worked out to reveal the coherent conceptual framework which undergirds Judaism and gives it a systematic character.

How then shall we characterize this total package, this conceptual whole which is Judaism? I wish to suggest that it is, first of all, in terms of logic, an *explanatory theory*, an interpretation of experience in its broadest sense, as well as of particular phenomena in nature and in history. Thus, the philosophical theory which is Judaism comes to render intelligible events such as the epiphany at Sinai and the survival of Israel as a people as well as what appear to be instances of design in nature, and the mystery of moral experience. In this respect it may be said to be similar to some of the more general theories of science, whose function lies in their abilities to "explain" various natural laws.[26] Ostensibly, Judaism would appear to be unlike scientific theories in that it performs

---

[26] It will be recalled that scientific discoveries are presented as both "laws" and "theories." "Laws" are sentences which assert invariable relations between particular events, while "theories" are sentences which explain "laws." They do so by showing that these laws can be deduced from ideas that are more familiar and more general. The classical example is the scientific study of gases. Several laws had been discovered concerning the physical properties of all gases. Boyle's Law states that pressure is inversely proportional to volume. Gay-Lussac's Law states that at a constant volume, the pressure increases proportionately to the temperature. These laws were subsequently "explained" by what is known as the Dynamic Theory of Gases. This states that a gas consists of an immense number of very small particles called "molecules" which behave as if they were elastic and spherical, flying about in all directions and colliding with each other and the walls of the container. The known properties of the gas (as described in the laws) could now be presented as due to the motion of the molecules which follow the general laws of moving bodies. Of course, the most important feature of this theory is that it states that there are such things as molecules and that gases are made up of them (Norman Campbell, *What is Science?* [New York: Dover Publications, 1952], 79, 85, 93).

its explanatory function by appealing to theoretical entities, such as "God" and "souls," which cannot be directly observed. Terms referring to such metaphysical entities are said to be without real meaning or significance. Such theories, it has been argued, can hardly be considered "explanations." Yet science itself often employs terms such as "electrons" and "molecules," which are likewise in themselves non-observable.

Recent trends in scientific theory-construction suggest the following pragmatic approach: the significance of a linguistic expression (such as an electron) shall be judged in terms of its function and utility within the system as a whole, even though the particular sentence in which the term itself appears has no direct empirical consequence. This can occur when the inclusion of this sentence in the theory may influence the prediction of observable events. Essential for such a theory are a set of interpretive sentences or correspondence rules which connect certain terms of the theoretical vocabulary with observational terms which describe empirical phenomena.

I believe such a scheme can be constructed for Judaism as seen as an explanatory theory: The Jewish World View (J.W.V.)

Postulates:

P.1 There is exactly one God

P.2 God is a transcendent reality

P.3 God has the attributes of Divine Goodness, Divine Justice, Creativity and Divine Purposiveness, Divine Relatedness (capable of covenanting with particular individuals and groups), Divine Omniscience, Divine Omnipotence.

Rules of Correspondence:

CR 1.1 If God is Divinely Good then He will create a universe in order to benefit His human creatures.

CR 1.2 If God is Divinely Good then He will make Himself accessible to some men under certain conditions through religious experience.

CR 2.1 If God is Creative and Divinely Purposive then the universe will have come into existence at a point in time and will exhibit instances of design.

Chapter Seventeen. The Role of Reason in Jewish Religious Belief

CR 2.2 If God is Creative and Divinely Purposive then persons generally will be capable of moral experience and of assuming moral responsibility.

CR 3.1 If God is Just then the universe will not run down or end in cosmic disaster.

CR 3.2 If God is Just then death is not always the end of human personality.

CR 4.1 If God has covenanted with Israel, then

a) it will have been liberated from Egyptian bondage in the thirteenth century BCE to the accompaniment of unusual events;

b) in the course of their history, it will prove indestructible as a group;

c) it will ultimately be restored to its historic homeland as a sovereign nation and be so recognized by the international community.

This ability to show certain correlations between specific aspects of God and particular empirical phenomena, presented as both explanations and predictions, demonstrates that these terms are not empty of cognitive content. It is enough if some of God's attributes have empirical implications in order to confer significance upon the theory as a whole. Furthermore, these implications make it possible to falsify the theory at least theoretically, which is another sign of its empirical significance. It will be noted that this theory, for obvious theological limitations, does not provide a complete definition of God. However, in this respect, it does not differ from science, in which comprehensive information about theoretical entities is generally not required.

There are, of course, certain basic differences between theory-construction in science and our attempts to present the belief-system of Judaism as an explanatory theory. In science, theories are deliberately fashioned in order to explain particular laws, and each is given its distinctive features with an eye to the phenomena it is designed to explain. However, in Judaism, as a religion and way of life into which we may have been born, we *start* with a belief that God is a reality, possessing a particular character. Tracing the belief's explanatory implications is quite secondary. Nevertheless, as I shall show, it can provide the basis for a rational justification for accepting the theory.

There is another difference which emanates from the contrast in the view of man held by the scientist *qua* scientist and that held by the religionist *qua* religionist. The former is interested in man primarily as a problem-solver and tool-designer, while the latter is most concerned with the question of human destiny and whether this is a purposive universe. Differing interests dictate, early on, the choice of phenomenon to be explained. Thus, while one may argue that Judaism seen as an explanatory theory offers a reasonable account for the existence of a universe which exhibits features of design, others may maintain that the universe, as we find it, needs no "explanation" beyond the discoveries of science. Therefore, prior to judging whether a particular explanatory theory is the best or most acceptable, one must decide whether the phenomenon to be explained is important enough to warrant the effort.

This introduces what has been called a "coefficient of value" into the judgment, to which we shall return later.

However, how are we to judge whether this is an acceptable theory at all? Generally, in regard to this type of argument, the evidence which might be marshaled in its support comes mainly from the phenomena which it seeks to explain, and the weight or the strength of the evidence is a function of the number and variety of the phenomena and how well the theory performs the function of explanation. In this respect, our theory would seem to be well placed inasmuch as the phenomena to be explained come from a variety of different aspects of nature and history. It draws upon the suitability of the planet for the development and maintenance of intelligent life and the complexity of the DNA mechanism, the moral nature of man, the survival of Israel as a people, and the phenomenon of Hebrew prophecy, among other things.[27] As we have noted, its very ability to make predictions confirms its empirical signifi-

---

[27] Each of these areas merits careful study, so that the individual may judge for himself whether they are candidates for our Explanatory Theory (Jewish World View). While the literature is vast, we might recommend the following as starters: John D. Barrow and Frank J. Tipler, *The Anthropic Cosomological Principle* (New York: Oxford University Press, 1986) for nature; Shubert Spero, *Holocaust and Return to Zion* (New York: Ktav, 2000) for history; and Abraham J. Heschel, *The Prophets* (New York: Harper and Row, 1955) for the phenomenon of Hebrew prophecy.

Chapter Seventeen. The Role of Reason in Jewish Religious Belief

cance; the fact that some of them, like the return of Israel to its land as a recognized sovereign nation and the discovery that our universe came into being at a certain time, have already been verified, constitutes credible evidence in favor of our theory.

However, precisely because our theory seeks to explain diverse phenomena before judging its acceptability, we are obliged to examine each one of these areas to ascertain whether there are any other more likely alternative explanations for these specific phenomena. Thus, for example, consider above, CR 2:1: "If God is purposive then the universe will exhibit instances of design." Before we judge this confirmed, we are obliged to consider the current Evolution/Intelligent design (I.D.) controversy and the arguments being offered against I.D., and consider whether indeed the given phenomenon confirms our hypothesis. The same must be done in connection with other areas where alternative explanations have been offered.

We stated earlier that acceptance of a theory as meaningful and worthy of our belief as rational persons depends upon the number and variety of phenomena it can successfully explain and predict. Can this be reduced to a formula? Can we state how *much* of this type of evidence or how *heavy* the weight of the evidence must be in order for the theory to qualify for acceptance? The answer seems to be in the negative.

How large must the number and kinds of positive instances be in order that a theory can be taken as adequately established? No general answer can be given to such a question.[28]

This is because in all matters except for academic logic, arguments can only aim at demonstrating degrees of probability, rather than certainty. Therefore, the beliefs that are based upon such arguments, while rational if the argument has demonstrated an adequate degree of probability, are also not certain. For as already noted by Aristotle, the degree of probability required for a positive conclusion depends upon the subject matter. Sometimes greater probability is simply not possible, and sometimes it is not needed.

What is it about the subject matter of our theory—J.W.V., i.e., the phenomena dealt with in the various Rules of Correspondence, which

---

[28] Ernest Nagel, "Probability and Degree of Confirmation or Weight of Evidence," in *Probability, Confirmation and Simplicity*, edited by Marguerite H. Foster and Michael L. Martin (Odyssey Press, NY, 1966) p. 191.

would render it acceptable as rational even on the basis of a less-than-conclusive degree of probability? As we indicated earlier, in a theory such as ours we are dealing with the crucial questions of human destiny and the nature of our universe, conclusive answers to which will probably forever be beyond the competence of empirical science. Thus, we have before us what has been called a "forced option." That is to say, there is no possibility of remaining neutral on this issue. Acceptance of the theory leads to one way of life, while suspending judgment warrants a way of life identical to that of one following a rejection of the theory as false. Therefore, no matter what one does, we will be living in accordance with principles which have not been conclusively demonstrated.[29]

However, unlike the scientist in his quest for knowledge, we do not have the privilege of suspending judgment. For the scientist *qua* scientist, there is no urgency to reach conclusions. In due time, science will discover the answers and mankind will benefit. But for the individual torn by these existential questions there will be no second chance. Unlike the scientist, his great disvalue would be to lose the truth. He must therefore make his decision on the basis of the best possible evidence. To do this is to act rationally.

However, accepting a theory on the basis of evidence which provides only a *degree* of probability would seem to warrant only a *degree* of belief. Can the Jewish concept of religious faith accommodate itself to the notion of *degrees of belief*? Judaism has traditionally been seen as demanding a "full" or "perfect" faith, as we find in the formulation of the Maimonidean Thirteen Principles as they appear in the *Siddur*: "I believe in *perfect faith* … (emunah sh'leima)." Does not the acknowledgement of a less than total belief imply the presence of some "doubt"?[30] Can one pray wholeheartedly to a God of whose existence one is not completely certain?

Actually, the concept of "*degrees* of belief" itself in philosophical literature has not lent itself to quantitative elucidation. Attempts to explore the matter introspectively in order to identify discernable levels of belief

---

[29] See William James, *The Will to Believe* (New York: Dover Publications, 1956), 2-4.
[30] See Norman Lamm, "Faith and Doubt," *Tradition* 9 (1967): 14-51, who takes a very different approach.

Chapter Seventeen. The Role of Reason in Jewish Religious Belief

have not been successful.[31] The only way to measure degrees of belief would seem to be by the actions one is prepared to take on the assumption that the belief is true. In other words, how much you are prepared to "bet on it"? Thus, a person who is ready to stake his life on a bridge being safe is demonstrating a high degree of belief. However, from that alone we could not infer the actual degree of probability that the bridge is safe. That would depend upon how much importance the individual places upon his getting to the other side. The greater the importance, the greater the risk the individual could reasonably be expected to take. This is another instance of the role of value judgment in determining the rationality of particular policies.

Let us look at religious belief from a psychological perspective. It has been convincingly argued that the decisive faculty in man which represents the distinctive "self" and determines one's actions is the "will" rather than reason.[32] While it may be assumed that the rational individual will consult "reason" before deciding upon action, there is no assurance that he will follow its advice. In seeking the allegiance of the individual to God, Judaism requires first and foremost *action (ma'asim)* in the form of observance of the *mitzvot*, preceded of course by a free and deliberate decision to make this unconditional commitment.[33] Can this be done at the same time that the rational grounds for belief are only probable? The answer is, in my judgment, affirmative.

At this point we must apply our distinction between "belief-in" and "belief-that." That is to say, in regard to our "belief-that," the cognitive propositions that undergird Judaism are true, and the available evidence yields not certainty but a degree of probability. This, as we have seen, is the necessary consequence of the nature of the subject matter. However, this need not affect the intensity or the unconditional nature of our belief-in. One can indeed love God "with all one's heart and with all one's soul and with all one's might," even though a conclusive demonstration of God's "existence" is not possible under the rules that govern

---

[31] See Frank P. Ramsey, "Degrees of Belief," in *Probability, Confirmation and Simplicity*, ed. Marguerite H. Foster and Michael L. Martin, 108-118.

[32] See David Hume, *A Treatise of Human Nature* (Oxford: Clarendon Press, 1964), Book II, Part III, Section 3; see also Book III, Part I, Section 1 (pp. 413, 459).

[33] Were it not so and were the evidence for the postulates of the Jewish World View overwhelmingly conclusive, it turning to God would be rendered coercive, and thus not at all expressive of the deepest reaches of a man's personality.

the attainment of knowledge. This is quite reasonable once one factors in the nature of the issues, the value of the outcomes, and the circumstances involved. Thus, in regard to our relationship to Judaism viewed as an explanatory theory, the evidence gleaned from an examination of the Rules of Correspondence may be said to confer a degree of probability sufficient to justify its acceptance.

In light of the above, our young observant Jew may continue to recite the *ani ma'amin* with the utmost sincerity, understanding what he says as follows:

> *ani ma'amin*—I believe (on rational grounds that provide a sufficient degree of probability) *that* God, the ground of all Being, is alone the Creator and *Guide* of all that is.
>
> *be'emunah shlaima*—in whom I place my total trust and to whom I am unconditionally committed.

In so doing, the Jewish believer may be said to have activated all of his faculties in seeking out his God. First, he identifies with the *values* of Judaism which he does for their intrinsic worth and not as a command. Then, he employs his *intellectual* capacity to analyze the cognitive aspects of Judaism and seek rational justification for their acceptance. Finally, he freely decides, after examining alternatives, to live the *halakhic* life-style.

> *vechol koma*—And having reached full stature as a person formed in the Divine Image,
>
> *lecha tishtacheveh*—he is ready to subject himself to Thee.

PART V

HISTORY COME TO LIFE

Chapter Eighteen

The Religious Meaning of the State of Israel

> In my view, the time of the redemption has come and we today stand at the end of the Galut..... I do not insist that what has been said in this essay is absolute truth. We have not come upon this through prophecy nor have I received it from my teachers as a tradition through Moshe from Sinai. However it appears to me that the matter is so from the words of Daniel and his visions.... But whether it is or it is not, I pray to the God of my salvation that he come and not delay the good things of which he has spoken through his servants, the prophets.
>
> Isaac Abarbanel (d. 1508)

To an individual committed to a traditional Jewish orientation, the question regarding the nature of the significance of the State of Israel remains a disquieting one. Unlike some other kinds of questions, whose resistance to easy elucidation can merely be shrugged off with judgement suspended until some illumination reaches us in the future, the question of the significance of the establishment of the State of Israel seems to be the sort of thing William James once called a. "forced option," a situation in which not taking a position in itself constitutes a position with possibly fateful consequences.

During the past 65 years American Jews have followed the story of Israel's development with great interest. Indeed, many of us followed up our interest with concrete involvement in varying degrees and through different conventional forms: UJA, bonds, tourism, and educational opportunities for our children, among others. However, the expected has not happened. We have not grown used to the idea of "having" a Jewish State. We have not learned to take the State for granted and file it away among our other nice Jewish institutions, and the phrase "living in historic times" has not become a cliche. An unease of spirit has persisted, suggesting that perhaps Jews in the free world have not yet made the appropriate response.

Chapter Eighteen. The Religious Meaning of the State of Israel

No doubt, what has contributed to this feeling has been the very eventful character of these past 65 years. Israel did not become yet another somnambulant state: dramatic internal growth has been accompanied by explosive changes in Israel's relationships with her neighbors and the world.

These events have been of such a complex and sometimes contradictory nature that they have been of little help in suggesting a trend or indicating a direction. On the contrary, recent events have, if anything, called into question some of the most cherished assumptions of Zionist ideology.[1]

But why should we think in terms of responses at all? Perhaps our traditional model of thinking is surfacing here. Essential to our world view is the belief that the God of Israel is the God of History, meaning that manifestations of God are to be sought more in the events and social process of history than in the area of nature. Since Israel is the people of the Covenant, every major event in its history is to be viewed as revelational and ultimately of universal significance. However, if the major occurrences of our national life are signs and manifestations of God, then the question of our people's responses to these signs becomes crucial. For it has been well stated that "the basic doctrine which fills the Hebrew Bible is that our life is a dialogue between the above and the below."[2] Upon the nature of our response rests the question of the quality of our relationship to God.

For the religious Jew, therefore, the question of the significance of the State of Israel is no mere academic exercise. Faced by the most unusual and exciting events to have occurred to our people in close to two millennia, we feel in our bones that these events are revelatory of something, that the God of History is trying to tell us something. But what is it that the Lord is saying to us, or perhaps demanding from us, by means of these momentous occurrences?[3]

---

[1] I make reference here to the general principle of secular Zionist nationalism that once "normalcy is restored to the Jewish people in the form of a national home, problems of anti-Semitism and the meaning of Jewish identity will be solved." This clearly has not happened.

[2] Martin Buber, *At the Turning* (New York: Farrar, Straus and Young, 1952), 47.

[3] A beautiful analysis of Israel's rebirth in terms of call and response was given by Rabbi Joseph B. Soloveitchik in his now-classic address "*Kol Dodi Dofek*" (The Sound of My Beloved Knocking), given in 1956 and published in *Torah*

The bewilderment among religious Jews is quite upsetting. Is our tradition, our leadership, our faith of no help to us at such a moment? A disturbing thought crosses the mind. Is our perplexity purely intellectual? Ever since the days of primal man, the temptation has been to hide from the call of God: to pretend that no voice is heard; that no event calls attention to itself; that no sign beckons. Is this, perhaps, our subconscious motivation? Paralyzed by conflicting theories, its hopes cancelled by its fears, religious Jewry, so forthcoming about God's actions in the past and future, is curiously reticent about His mighty acts in the present. The anxiety of many of us is that our silence may be taken for an answer by a Providence grown tired of waiting.

What are the difficulties that stand in the way of an analysis that could lead us from our religious tradition and its categories to an understanding of the religious meaning of the State of Israel and from there to a formulation of the appropriate response required of us?

Oddly enough, one of the main problems seems to be that we suffer from an overabundance of categories. Rather than lacking the conceptual tools to handle contemporary events, we seem to have too many. Shall we speak in terms of the *mitzvah* of settling in the land or in terms of the religious experience awaiting those who live in the holy land where the *shechina*, the divine presence, may be encountered?

Shall we speak of the redemption, the *geulah*, or the beginning of the redemption, *atchalta di-geulah*, or only of the birth pangs of the messiah? Shall we apply the term *shibud malkhuyot* and speak of the end of the servitude to the kingdoms? One eminent rabbinic personality is reported to have observed that the State marks "the end of the *galut*, exile, not the beginning of the *geulah*."[4] Once one enters the semantic thicket, extrication without bruises would seem well-nigh impossible.

Let us for the moment attempt to avoid these overly rich and emotive terms and examine our situation in language less inviting to passion and ideological bias.

Umelucha (Jerusalem: Mosad Harav Kook, 1961). However, Rabbi Soloveitchik stopped short of calling for all-out *aliyah* by American Jewry as the appropriate response to the providential events of the rebirth of the State of Israel. See my book, *Aspects of Joseph Dov Soloveitchik's Philosophy of Judaism: An Analytic Approach* (Jersey City, NJ: KTAV, 2009), for further discussion.

[4] Attributed to Rabbi Abraham Isaiah Karelits, the famous *Chazon Ish*, by Moshe Schonfeld in *Jewish Observer*, October 1974.

Chapter Eighteen. The Religious Meaning of the State of Israel

1) The establishment of a Jewish State with control over its own immigration and increasing power to defend itself comes at a time when the continued existence of Jews in European and Muslim countries has become extremely problematic. As an immediate solution to the problem of Jewish homelessness, Jewish discrimination, and threats of destruction, the Jewish State was and is of great benefit. Since Jewish survival, as such, is a religious value, the birth of the State and its continued existence is, for that reason alone, already of inestimable religious significance.

2) Judaism addresses itself to the totality of human life. Diaspora Jewish living, no matter how intensive, will always suffer from its being the application of Torah values to certain aspects of the life of the individual only. In the larger areas of national and communal life we have not been in control. A Jewish state affords the Jewish people the opportunity to live a full Jewish life in both the individual and the corporate sense, to apply Torah values to the full range of national existence.

3) The Jewish State and its achievements have been the means of awakening Jewish loyalties among many otherwise alienated segments of our people. The galvanizing effects of the Jewish State on elements of Soviet Jewry and upon portions of the American Jewish community are well known cases in point.

If we accept the claim that the aforementioned statements exhaust our understanding of the religious significance of the State of Israel, there would be no difficulty in arriving at an agreement as to the response called for.[5] No matter what label one chooses to apply to these events, their essential character remains the same. We the Jewish people are the recipients of a glorious Good and Blessing from the hand of God. We have been brought from darkness into light. In the State of Israel we have experienced the saving Presence of God and have been made to feel

---

[5] It should be noted that not all religious Jews would agree to even this minimal statement of Israel's religious significances. Moshe Schonfeld, writing in the *Jewish Observer* (Oct. 1974), draws up a "score sheet" for the Jewish State and finds that there are many debits in religious development in the last decades, while the credits, such as the Torah renaissance, are all *in spite* of the State or were there before the State. His conclusion: "Israel is not a Jewish State and certainly not the yearned for *Atchalta Di-Geulah*" (p. 17).

His love and mercy. The response indicated is clear. Whenever man experiences the goodness of God, he must fall to his knees in thankfulness and gratitude. We must, therefore, worship God with renewed spirit and sing His praises. (Sing *Hallel*, with or without a *Brachah!*) We must all strive to support and preserve this historic and precious gift of a Jewish State. Those of us who might be inclined to participate personally in the religious challenges offered by living there should be encouraged to do so. Such is the type of response adequate and appropriate to manifestations of divine bounty.

However, the nub of our problem is precisely the question of whether the rebirth of Israel may be saying more to us than the above three points. Are there any dimensions to the religious meaning of the Jewish State that we may have overlooked? Indeed, the question can be broadened to ask whether our tradition in general provides any basis for understanding revelatory events as expressing more than simply the principle of God's judgment in history.

It is clear that in the rabbinic view any discussion of God's presence in history and the revelational nature of certain events must exclude the theophany of Sinai which is seen as *sui generis*. At Sinai it was not the event that was revelatory, nor was it only that the "Presence" was experienced as having a certain quality, such as a commanding nature, but rather it was the content expressing the will of God *(mitzvot)* that was revealed. Thus, to speak of revelatory events is to refer to such occurrences as the exodus and the crossing of the sea, the events of Purim and Chanukah, and the destruction of the Temple.[6] The common view limits the revelatory element in these events to the working out of God's judgement: "good" events reveal God's love and kindness; "bad" events reflect His wrath and punishment. But in truth, there is something more. The exodus from Egypt, for example, did not merely reveal the saving presence of God. It was not as if the God of justice and righteousness had decided to liberate all slaves held in bondage. At that time, only Israel was remembered. Why was *Israel* brought forth? Why was *Egypt* smitten?

---

[6] Compare Buber's distinction: "Miracle is revelation through the deed which precedes revelation through the word." *Moses* (Oxford: East-West Library, 1947), 79.

> And you shall say unto Pharaoh, thus sayeth the Lord: Israel is my first-born son. And I say unto you, send forth my son so that he may serve me. And if you shall refuse to send him forth, behold I will smite your first-born son."[7]

An important meaning of the exodus was its revelation of the existence of a special relationship between God and Israel—a covenantal relationship. It may therefore be concluded that some events in Israel's history also reveal a choosing presence, a God who selects one people from among many, one individual from among many, one land from among many, for His purposes and charge.

Scholars have pointed to yet another, almost unique, characteristic of God's relationship to Israel. Starting with the patriarchs and continuing through the wilderness experience and beyond, the biblical God is experienced as a *leading* God.[8]

> The God of Abraham was a guardian deity ... who goes with those He guards.... He is a God who tells a man He is leading him ... but whither is He leading him? Not to the place where man wished to come. The God guides as He himself wills and He leads man whither He wills. He leads man whither He sends him. He brings Abraham safely to Haran. Here the man settles desiring to remain, but the God wills otherwise. He sends the man further, leads him further to the foreign land which He promised him. He makes this man a nomad of faith ... the whole of Abraham's Hegira is a religious act.[9]

When events conspire to bring Jacob and his family to Egypt, God appears to the patriarch and says: "Do not fear to go down to Egypt, for unto a great nation will I make you there. I will go down with you to Egypt, and I will surely bring you up...."[10]

---

[7] Exod. 4:22, 23.

[8] Emil Fackenheim's attempt to describe the structure of the Jewish experience of God in history in terms of the commanding and the saving Presence (*God's Presence in History* [New York: NYU Press, 1970]) seems to me inadequate for the reason that he does not account for the experiences which I have described here as choosing and leading.

[9] Martin Buber, *The Prophetic Faith* (New York: Macmillan Co., 1949), 33, 34.

[10] Gen. 46:3, 4.

Later, after the exodus, God again *leads* the people.

> The historical reality of Israel leaving Egypt cannot be grasped if the conception of the accompanying, preceding, guiding God is left out. This is the "God of the fathers," with whom the tribes have now established contact. He has always been a God who wandered with his own and showed them the way.... He leads them by a way differing from the customary one of the armies and caravans.... And the Lord went before them by day in a pillar of cloud to lead them the way and by night in a pillar of fire.... Moses himself, when he leads, follows a leader ingenuously and undauntedly....[11]

The significance of all this is profoundly bound up with the dynamics of galut and geulah as well as with the tension created by Israel as a people, and Israel as witness to God with a universal task. Destruction and dispersal are not merely divine punishment but a "sowing" of God's people in the "wilderness of the nations," so that a harvest of the spirit can later be gathered. What the destruction of the Second Monarchy "said" to Israel was that the arena of Jewish activity must now shift to the world scene. The Lord is now leading His people out of the shattered national frame on the Mediterranean littoral where the "action" was for over two millennia to follow the path of civilization, culture, science, and technology. Israel, by her migrations, is transformed from an oriental into an occidental people. Out of the Greco-Roman world, through the vicissitudes of medieval Europe, the Industrial Revolution, the agonies of two World Wars, and the post-industrial societies of America and Western Europe, Israel as God's Witness People is exhibited to the world, and at the same time significant segments of her people participate in the explosion of human discovery and invention.

Rhythms and patterns are obliterated with the Holocaust and the rebirth of the State of Israel. The former remains an impenetrable mystery, unspeakable horror, *Hester Panim* (the hiding of the Face). Seen in conjunction with the establishment of the State, however, both events may be seen as revelatory in the sense of the *leading* God. "And the Lord spoke unto us in Horeb, saying, You have dwelt long enough on this mountain. Turn yourself and journey to the hill country.... Behold,

---

[11] Martin Buber, *Moses* (Oxford: East-West Library, 1947), 76.

Chapter Eighteen. The Religious Meaning of the State of Israel

I have set before you the land: go in and possess the land which the Lord swore unto your fathers."[12]

What theologically is seen as being led by God out of our land into a two-thousand year *hegira* was historically our being overrun by a brutal world power who forcibly drove us out. What we must understand theologically as constituting our being led by God back to our land is historically the real possibility of our being able to do so. Today, when as a result of the combination of Jewish devotion and sacrifice and the interplay of power politics the possibility has become a reality; when today, in fact, a Jewish population of close to six million inhabits the land in its biblical boundaries, including Jerusalem, residing in the sovereign State of Israel, then the message of the events comes into even sharper focus. The God of Israel is *leading* His people back to the land. Conditions are now such that the Witness People can achieve its divine task through a national existence.[13] The invitation has turned into a summons.[14]

---

[12] Deut. 1:6.

[13] The Gaon of Vilna in his teaching regarding the redemption is reported to have assigned considerable importance to the rise of science and technology as contributing to the creation of conditions facilitating the return to Zion. (See Hillel Rivlin, *Kol Hator*). In this vein, it might be pointed out that whereas in the past it was doubtful whether the land of Israel, poor in natural resources and water, could possibly support the population necessary for a viable state, today with desalination plants, solar and nuclear energy, chemical farming, and an electronic-based industry, the economic viability of an Israel with a population of many millions is entirely feasible.

From a purely historic viewpoint, Judea fell in the past because it was overwhelmed by vastly superior world powers. Given the hostility of the Muslim world and the indifference of the others, what hope does Israel today have of surviving, short of miracles? With the development of thermonuclear warfare, victory is no longer necessarily on the side of the bigger battalions. Today, a small country with nuclear capability possesses an effective deterrent which can lead to a "balance of terror."

If Israel is to be a Witness-People and a "light to the nations," it must be visible. Perhaps this was one of the reasons for the dispersion. Today, with the development of communications media, anything of significance done in Israel (and almost anywhere else) can instantly be brought into the living rooms of the entire civilized world. The Witness-People no longer needs to make "house calls." We can "work" out of our "home."

[14] One of the few writers to call for *aliyah* as a response to the phenomenon of Israel is Rabbi Nachum Rabinovitch, "The Religious Significance of Israel,"

In this context, the Holocaust can be seen as providing the *push* to Israel's *pull*.[15] In the words of Eliezer Berkovits, "the proper name for the Holocaust is not *Shoa* but *Churban*, annihilation. For the first time in our history, the exile itself was destroyed."[16] It should be noted that I offer this link between the Holocaust and the rise of the State of Israel as neither a causal nor a teleological explanation but as a matrix for developing an appropriate response.[17]

In reality, the establishment of the State of Israel signifies more than a summons by the God of Israel to the Jewish people to return home. After all, the phenomenon of a people coming together after an absence of close to two thousand years in their ancient homeland, speaking their ancient tongue and constituting a sovereign nation must be regarded as a most unusual one. But can religious Jews ignore the fact that this has happened to the only people about whom it was foretold at least some 2,500 years ago?

Already in the Bible, the basic principles of a Jewish theology of history are clearly set forth:

> And it shall come to pass when there has come upon thee all these things ... and thou shalt call them to mind among the nations whither the Lord thy God hath driven thee ... and thou shalt return unto the Lord thy God ... then the Lord thy God will turn thy

---

Tradition 14, no. 4(Fall 1974), "The sad truth is that we are afraid.... We are afraid to open our ears to hear the urgent summons to leave the diaspora and to settle the waste places and fill the land with Jews" (p.26). See also the fine article by Yosef Goldschmidt in *Word & Deed* (Vol. 1, No.2) "If we believe that the signs are true then we are obliged to act in accordance with them, e.g. offering praise to the Lord, going up to Eretz Yisrael, making an effort to bring about progress in the land..." (p. 36).

[15] In every past redemption there was some sort of *push*. Even during the Exodus from Egypt we are told, "... we were *driven* out of Egypt and we could not tarry ..." (Exod. 12:39). Some see this as the meaning of the "strong hand" with which God took us out of Egypt. The "outstretched arm" symbolized the repeated punishments to Pharaoh, but the "strrong hand" refers to the various pressures by which Israel was *pushed* out of Egypt.

[16] Eliezer Berkovits, "Crisis and Faith," *Tradition* 14, no. 4 (Fall 1974): 14.

[17] See Emil Fackenheim, "The Holocaust and the State of Israel," *Encyclopedia Judaica*, Yearbook 1974, 154.

Chapter Eighteen. The Religious Meaning of the State of Israel

captivity and have compassion upon thee and return and gather thee from all the peoples ... and will bring thee unto the Land thy fathers possessed and thou shalt possess it.[18]

We are not dealing with interpretations of apocalyptic imagery or computations of Kabbalistic calculus but rather attempting to understand a historic reality by the light of a proposed principle. The Jewish people were promised a restoration.[19] They were assured again and again by the prophets that while *galut* will result from their disobedience, that condition will not be the end. No matter how far in time or distance they may be scattered, they will be restored to their land, identity intact. The *galut*, understood as involuntary separation from the land of Israel and servitude to a foreign power, will at some point be terminated. Against the most improbable odds, this has now come to pass. Jewish national sovereignty has been restored. No terminological obfuscation can hide this fact. Prophecy has been fulfilled. It is extremely doubtful whether religious Jews can continue to evade the challenge posed by this fact without forfeiting their authenticity and consistency.[20]

The act of recognizing the fulfillment of divine promise would appear to have far-reaching religious implications. Consider the comment of Rashi on the passage, "And I appeared unto Abraham, unto Isaac and unto Jacob as God almighty but by my name YHVH I did not make myself known to them."[21] Says Rashi, "I made promises to the patriarchs as God Almightly (One in whom it is proper to rely) but I was not recognized by them by my attribute of faithfulness (YHVH) for I have promised them but I have not fulfilled."

---

[18] Deut. 30:1-5.
[19] See comment of Nachmanides on Deut. 32:40.
[20] Even in non-Zionist publications there occasionally burst forth expressions of wonder over the way in which current events in Israel seem to be the fulfillment of biblical prophecy. In an unusual article in *Dos Yiddishe Vort* (Kislev-Tevet, 5734), Rabbi Shlomo Rottenberg spoke of the miracles and prophetic fulfillment that are occurring in Israel. In order to avoid having to designate our period as messianic, Rabbi Rottenberg found an interesting passage in Isaiah (42:9) which he interprets to say that before any redemptive events begin to sprout, the Almighty will give us a "foretaste" of what is to come by performing wondrous events similar to the real thing, in Israel.
[21] Exod. 6:3.

To be able to perceive in one's life the fulfillment of God's promises opens up dimensions of religious experience which touch upon the mysteries of the tetragrammaton itself. The individual who continues to live solely in the faith of God's promises has not penetrated to an appreciation of God's attribute of truth. As religious Jews, therefore, our thankfulness to God for the State of Israel must express itself, at least in part, as recognition of the fulfillment of the divine promise, as the realization of prophecy, as the coming to fruition of His word.[22]

To sum up our analysis to this point: in addition to the three dimensions enumerated above, the religious significance of the establishment of the State of Israel resides in: (1) its being the fulfillment of the divine promise; (2) specifically, the divine promise predicting the end of the *galut* and the restoring of a sovereign national existence; (3) these events revealing the leading presence of God, which summons Jews everywhere to leave the Diaspora and go up to the land.

We can no longer avoid the question of the applicability of the traditional categories. Actually the only real controversy has centered around the question of messianic terms, or whether we have in the State of Israel *the geulah* as opposed to *a geulah*. If, however, we have been correct in our analysis up to this point, the material for the answer has already been provided.

However, we must bear in mind that the criterion for the application of messianic terms cannot be a simple correspondence with this or that rabbinic text or passage from the prophets. It must rather emerge out of a comprehensive analysis of the total concept in all of its complex variety as found in biblical and rabbinic literature. Fortunately, this task has already been done with remarkable insight.[23] It has been observed that the messianic idea consists of three basic elements: the restorative, the utopian, and the catastrophic or apocalyptic.

By the "restorative" we mean the belief in the return and recreation of past conditions which are seen as ideal, such as the ingathering of the exiles, the reestablishment of the Jewish state, the Davidic monarchy,

---

[22] Recent analyses of the religious significance of the State of Israel give little attention to this point. For example, consider Walter Wurzburger, "The Jewish View-Messianic Perspectives" in *Encyclopedia Judaica*, Yearbook 1974, 148-151.

[23] See the works of Gershom Scholem, in particular *The Messianic Idea in Judaism* (New York: Schocken, 1971).

Chapter Eighteen. The Religious Meaning of the State of Israel

and the rebuilding of the Temple. By the "utopian" we mean the vision of a future state in which things will come about which have never yet existed, such as the abolition of wars, a sense of universal brotherhood, and the earth being full of the "knowledge of the Lord." By the catastrophic we mean an anticipation of an abrupt and radical break between the established present and the messianic future, in which the evil and corruption of the present will be removed by violent upheavals. Various tensions exist between these elements, which never appear as pure cases and which have received varying emphases in different periods, in different sources, and among different movements. While the restorative and the utopian elements are necessary components of the messianic concept, the catastrophic is treated as ambivalent in Jewish tradition. Thus, while in such a sober work as the Mishnah there is an account of some of the catastrophic "signs" which will usher in the messianic age, the Amidah prayer, which refers to almost all of the components of the messianic age, omits completely any reference to the apocalyptic element. However, we need not go into the reasons for this, at this point.

What seems undeniable, however, is that certain restorative elements which have always been considered necessary components of the messianic concept have in fact come to pass. What is equally certain is that neither other restorative elements nor any of the utopian elements have as yet come to pass, nor has there been any hint of the appearance of an individual claiming to be the Messiah. However, Maimonides has already observed that we have no clear tradition regarding the sequence of messianic events nor exactly how they will come about. Since we are dealing with a temporal process of a certain duration and we have no reason whatsoever to believe that it will come about instantaneously, we have every reason to expect incomplete yet unmistakably messianic occurrences. We have no alternative, therefore, but to observe that there have already occurred today events which by virtue of their prophetic restorative character are messianic. Whether these will be followed by the other necessary components we do not know. To say that what has already happened is messianic does not imply that the rest must follow inevitably, or that Israel must continue to win wars in the Six-Day War manner, or that one is denying the need for a personal Messiah.

The following objection has been raised. If, according to the view just outlined, necessary messianic components are still unfulfilled and it may turn out that they will not occur, what in fact does one achieve or meaningfully imply by calling what has already occurred "messianic"? Why not be satisfied to call the State of Israel "pre-messianic" or "potentially messianic" or "the end of the period that is to introduce the Beginning"?[24]

Our reply to this objection is threefold:

1) By designating the State of Israel *messianic,* we are affirming our recognition and gratitude in categories commensurate with the character and magnitude of the event. The Almighty has fulfilled his promise to us after close to 2,000 years. We wish to say that this is more than simply *a* redemption.[25]

2) By speaking of the State in messianic terms, we are giving expression to the evocative nature of these events in the sense that they demand of all Jews a response in terms of *aliyah*; to follow the *leading* God out of the *galut* to the land.

3) "Pre-messianic" or "potentially messianic" are meaningless expressions in our context, because theoretically the Messiah may come tomorrow or any day. ("I wait for him everyday that he shall come.") Therefore every period and every event is "pre-messianic" or "potentially messianic." Neither of these terms does justice to the present; to the wondrous fulfillment embodied in the State of Israel.

It has been argued in regard to our second point that *aliyah* is a *mitzvah* in any case, so that the employment of messianic categories to

---

[24] Some of these alternatives are suggested in Wurzburger, "The Jewish View-Messianic Perspectives," and in a paper read by Yitzhak Greenberg at a dialogue sponsored by the Kibbutz Hadati at Kibbutz Lavi in January 1975, entitled *Medinat Yisrael and Geulat Yisrael* (The State of Israel and the Redemption of Israel).

[25] We have, of course, a religious obligation to recognize the agency of God in historic events. It is remarkable how some of our religious leaders, who are so insistent that we view every tragic event as the punishing hand of God (so as to remain innocent of the attitude of *Keri*, of viewing history as merely "chance" (see Lev. 26:23), refuse to apply the same perception to the "good" things that have happened in connection with Israel.

Chapter Eighteen. The Religious Meaning of the State of Israel

achieve it is unnecessary and does not constitute a unique implication of messianic designation.

In reply, it should first of all be stressed that in light of the threatening events of the past few years, the factor of *aliyah* assumes a most crucial importance affecting the entire future of the Jewish State. Almost every vital problem confronting Israel today, be it security, economics, settling the barren areas, or keeping the proper demographic balance between Arabs and Jews, depends for its proper solution upon bringing another two million Jews to Israel as rapidly as possible. Furthermore, the conditions for *aliyah* are changing such that Israel is becoming increasingly dependent upon ideologically-motivated *olim*. The decision to go on *aliyah* is becoming more and more a function of one's total understanding of what it is to be a Jew. This is borne out by the alarming increase of *yordim* (emigrants) after the Yom Kippur War, the steady "brain drain" of some of our finest academics, and the general decline in *aliyah* from North America.

Aliyah today is certainly not a *milta zutrata*, a small matter! It is of the utmost importance for the future of the State in general and for its religious character in particular, that religious Jews in their thousands see it as their religious obligation to move now to Israel. Unless they so perceive it, it is doubtful that a significant movement can be gotten underway at all. Historically, extrication from the *galut* has been a most difficult and painful process for Jews. Although we have proven to be rather mobile once the push of persecution and discrimination reaches a certain pressure point, our response to the pull of Israel once we have struck roots has been rather desultory, whether we are coming from Babylon or more recently from the "lands of affluence." As Rashi at one point comments, "So great is the day of the gathering of the exiles and so difficult that it would seem as though God Himself must literally take hold of each man with His hand to take him out of his place, as it is stated in Isaiah (27:12) "And ye shall be gathered one by one, O ye children of Israel."[26]

Most discussions of this issue have overlooked a crucial distinction. There is a vast difference between *aliyah* considered as a halakhic obligation stemming from the fact that it is a *mitzvah* which devolves on the individual and *aliyah* seen as an obligation created by certain

---

[26] Deut. 30:3.

historic events which devolve upon the people as a whole.[27] The *mitzvah* of *Yishuv Eretz Yisrael*, settling in the land, has been with us for a long time, possessing halakhic force in certain well-defined situations[28] and sometimes inspiring pious individuals to go on *aliyah*, but on the whole it is ineffective by itself in motivating any massive movement to Israel. The reason for this is that as a *mitzvah* functioning within the halakhic framework, it is subject to the halakhic process of qualification and exception. Thus, each individual has a right to question whether the *mitzvah* of *aliyah* obligates him in his particular concrete situation, considering the hazards of the journey, the dangers of living in Israel, and the effect of the dislocation upon his own and his family's religious life. In the event that every Jew, reasoning in like manner, finds himself a *heter*, permission not to fulfill the obligation, then nobody goes on aliyah! But that is a perfectly acceptable consequence, given the purely halakhic nature of the obligation.

However, the Jewish people sometimes faces divine obligations and demands which arise out of certain historic situations in response to which qualifications and exceptions acceptable in a normal halakha context become totally inappropriate. Thus, the hesitations and demurals

---

[27] A somewhat analogous distinction was made by Rabbi Joseph B. Soloveitchik in comparing the controversy between biblical Joseph and his brothers (how to prepare for the *galut* ahead) to the controversy within Orthodoxy at the turn of the century regarding whether to join with the Zionists in building a Jewish community in the land of Israel. Regarding the resolution of the controversy, Rabbi Soloveitchik states that while in halakhic matters the decision-making power was given to the rabbinic sages of every generation, in historic issues which touch upon the destiny of the Jewish people God himself decides the question through the movement of history. Thus the halakhic decision—the *psak*—of history was in favor of those who understood the need to prepare early a future home for the Jewish people in Israel. (See Joseph B. Soloveitchik, *Chamesh Derashot* [Five Sermons], trans. David Telzner [Jerusalem: Tal Orot, 1974], 23).

[28] According to the halakha, the refusal of a woman to accompany her husband to Israel, or vice versa, is grounds for divorce (Maimonides, *Mishneh Torah, Hilkhot Ishut,* chap. 13). Certain rabbinic restrictions on the Sabbath were waived if the act being performed on the Sabbath involved acquiring property in Israel (Maimonides, *Mishneh Torah, Hilkhot Shabbat* 6:11). See also the interesting variation of the law on how much time is required before a *mezuzah* has to be affixed to an entrance if the house where it will be affixed is in Israel.

Chapter Eighteen. The Religious Meaning of the State of Israel

of the Jewish people as they were poised to enter the promised land, two years after the exodus, which constituted the "Sin of the Spies," were entirely out of place. Although at another time and at another place the arguments of the people were perfectly reasonable (the military odds really were overwhelmingly against them, and they really were religiously better off in the wilderness), if the historic hour had truly struck, as Moshe reported in the name of God that it had, then what was required was a positive action on the part of the people, as a whole, now! Anything less than that, whatever reason was given, was the equivalent of a rejection of the call of the hour.

Thus, the *aliyah* obligation which originates in historic events seen as revelatory differs in two respects from the halakha of *Yishuv Eretz Yisrael*:

1) Since the former is the creation of a historic situation, the response to it depends upon a time factor.[29] Should the response be unduly delayed, the opportunity may pass and be lost.

2) The *aliyah* call implicit in certain revelatory events is satisfied by positive actions only. A case in point is the lack of response on the part of Babylonian Jewry when it had an opportunity to go up en masse to Israel in the days of Ezra.[30] There is no question here of finding halakhic justification for Babylonian Jewry. The only relevant and unfortunate fact is that they did not respond—which resulted in a lost messianic opportunity.

In our own situation, therefore, it makes all the difference in the world whether we point to the ongoing halakhic *mitzvah* of *aliyah* or whether our theology enables us to speak of the dynamic, history-charged call

---

[29] This concept has been used to explain why the Almighty punished the generation that was frightened by the adverse report of the spies, and refused to follow Moshe into the land of Israel, by requiring them to wander in the wilderness for 40 years. This number, according to the Torah, was based on the formula "For a day, a year" (Num. 14:34). That is to say, for every day spent by the spies on their journey, the Jewish people would wander for a year. Their punishment took this unusual form because their sin consisted of being blind to the demands of the hour. They sinned against the "times." Hence, their punishment was given in terms of "time": A year of wandering for each day spent in distorted perception of the land. (Heard from Rabbi I. Stollman, author of *Minchat Yitzchak*, 3 vols.).

[30] See *Berakhot* 4a; *Yoma*, 9b; *Sanhedrin* 94a.

for *aliyah* emanating from the revelational events of our time, to which the only appropriate response is positive action.

Several thinkers have shown apprehension over the application of messianic categories to the events centering about Israel's rebirth. Some have been frightened by the positions taken by some of the "Gush Emunim" people[31] on the retention of Judah and Samaria.[32] The latter seem to argue that since this is a period of *atchalta di' geula,* conventional political considerations can be disregarded and come what may, not one inch of the territories should be relinquished. However, it should be clear that neither the designation of the rebirth of Israel as messianic nor the teachings of Rabbi A. I. Kook support such dare-devil political brinkmanship. (Although these doctrines may well encourage the judgement that the policy of the Israeli government, in prohibiting settlement of the West Bank territories, is timid, shortsighted, and contrary to the interests of the Jewish people.)

Other writers with recollections of the aftermath of the Sabbatai Zvi movement and the profound disillusionment it created caution us against using messianic categories which excite and arouse unrealistic expectations.[33] One is tempted to apply here the observation of Franz Rosenzweig that perhaps our differences on the messianic question reflect the difference between those "whose faith is strong enough to give themselves up to an illusion and those whose hope is so strong that they do not allow themselves to be deluded. The former are the better, the latter the stronger."[34]

However, the answer to all those who would trot out against us the worn and tired strictures used traditionally against followers of "false messiahs," "forcers of the end," and "calculators of the end" is that the challenge we face today is decisively different from any messianic issues faced by earlier generations.

---

[31] Gush Emunim was a religious youth movement started by Chanan Porath after the Six Day War to settle the territories.

[32] See the article by Moshe Una in *Hatzofeh*, September 16, 1974, the article by Zvi Yaron in *Yediot Acharonot*, August 28, 1975, and the exchange between the present writer and Robert Gordis in the periodical *Sh'ma*, appearing in the issues published in May 1982, May 1986, and May, 1992.

[33] See the exchange between the present writer and Norman Lamm in the periodical *Sh'ma*, appearing in the issues published in April 1961 and April 1973.

[34] Quoted in Nahum Glatzer, *Franz Rosenzweig* (New York: Schocken, 1953), 350.

Chapter Eighteen. The Religious Meaning of the State of Israel

Consider the situation of those Jews who confronted a Bar Kochba, a David Alroy, a Sabbatai Zvi. The determination they had to make was whether to credit the messianic pretensions of these individuals and believe that they would be able to transform the miserable conditions of the dispersed of Israel.

Consider the conditions which prompted some of the truly great of our people to "calculate the end," to proclaim the "birth pangs of the messiah" and attempt to pierce the veil of the future by wresting a messianic date from our sacred texts. They were invariably active during times of great upheaval and catastrophe for the Jewish people and for the world: the crusades, the collapse of the Byzantine empire, the Napoleonic wars, the Holocaust. They were quite correct in intuiting that when the foundations begin to crumble and new political constellations form there arise new opportunities for Jewish redemption. But here again, it was all hope, flying in the face of a dismal reality.

We, today, are in a different situation. We are not being asked to consider whether something can come of the Zionist effort. The fact is that for the past 65 years, before our very eyes, a sovereign Jewish State has been in existence in the land of Israel. The task before us is not to dream dreams or to do scriptural mathematics but to interpret a historical reality. Our failure to perceive in a real historic achievement a partial messianic fulfillment cannot be justified as a case of guarding against hope being stronger than faith. If we do, we run the grave risk of having our failure construed as colossal ingratitude and self-induced blindness by the God of history. If our messianic tradition cannot be put to work in a time such as ours, then serious doubts arise as to whether it has any relationship to the real world. Of course, we must remain sensitive to the "inevitable tension between contingent historical present and absolute messianic future."[35] However, those who in the name of the messianic ideal persist in a life lived in perpetual deferment and who hurl at every current era the phrase, "You are not yet the right one," are coming dangerously close to projecting the messianic vision into an irrelevant infinity.[36]

---

[35] Emil Fackenheim, "The Holocaust and the State of Israel," 153.
[36] See Gershom Scholem, *The Messianic Idea in Judaism*, 358, and N. Glatzer, *Franz Rosenzweig*, 358.

The risks are undoubtedly great and the dangers, both physical and theological, of urging with messianic fervor large numbers of religious Jews to Israel abound. However, the example of Rabbi Akiva teaches us that as Jews, we cannot adopt a wait-and-see attitude toward messianic opportunities. Rabbi Akiva himself did not. Instead, he threw his support and his life behind the messianic effort of Bar Kochba, who was not a "false messiah." The reasons for Bar Kochba's failure must be sought elsewhere, and are outside the scope of this volume. His failure does not invalidate Rabbi Akiva's response.

The risk we are called upon to take are much less than those assumed by Akiva ben Joseph. However, what is at stake is no less momentous. We are asked to follow the leading God as He has revealed Himself through His fulfilled promise of a restored State of Israel. We must act thus, because it just may be that readiness of our generation to respond in this manner constitutes the crucial factor necessary to truly actualize the next phase of our messianic opportunity.

Chapter Nineteen
Religious Zionism: What is It?

A Zionist, presumably, is one who believes in the centrality of the land of Israel for the Jewish people and acts to actualize that belief. A religious Zionist would be one who is personally committed to Judaism, whose Zionist beliefs emanate from his Judaism, and who would like to see in the land of Israel a Jewish people committed to Judaism. There are many who believe that there is nothing in the above definitions that has not been an integral part of the belief system of every traditional Jew since at least the rabbinic period until the modern era. So what new information other than that he is a traditional Jew are we being given when we designate someone a Religious Zionist?

In discussing the ideological posture of religious Zionism, a balance must be maintained between what are perceived to be its problems and weaknesses and what are seen as its strengths. For it is precisely its strength that has shone forth most brightly in recent years, particularly when we compare religious Zionism with secular Zionism ("secular" from the point of view of secular Zionists, though from the point of view of religious Zionists all Zionism is "religious"). There seems to be a consensus among serious students of the Jewish scene that the Zionist movement generally in its ideological mode finds itself today in a deep crisis.[1] This is in sharp contrast to the practical aspect of the Zionist movement, which as a national liberation movement has miraculously achieved its goal of a sovereign Jewish State in *Eretz Yisrael*, which has demonstrated its viability for 65 years now. But paradoxically, this is precisely the problem. When an individual or a group strives for certain goals and these goals are achieved, there is an understandable let-down after the victory celebrations are over. Slogans have become fact. Hopes have become reality. We are an *am hofshi bearzenu*. But what has hap-

---

[1] Eliezer Schweid, *Israel at the Cross Roads* (Philadelphia: Jewish Publication Society, 1973); E. Urbach, "The Essence of Zionism," *Forum* 30/31 (1978); S. Ettinger, "Zionism and its Significance Today," *Forum* 28/29 (1978).

pened to the *Zionist vision?* It was particularly sad to read in a Time magazine article of April 4, 1988, that Israel has become a nation "with no sense of destiny; no vision."

In addition to this "crisis of success," Zionism has been experiencing a crisis of theory. Classical Zionism presented itself as a solution to the Jewish problem, which in essence is the double-edged threat to Jewish survival faced by Jews living in the Diaspora. In friendly lands, the threat is assimilation and spiritual destruction, and in unfriendly lands, the danger is persecution and physical destruction. All of this is a consequence of the abnormality of a Jewish nation living in exile from its land. Restore the Jewish nation to its homeland,; give the Jew back his national pride, remove the stigma of "eternal minority," and with normalcy, anti-Semitism will disappear.

These predictions of Zionist theory have unfortunately not come about. The analysis was evidently faulty. What actually did happen?

1) With the establishment of the State, new forms of hatred of the Jew have arisen. The Jewish People are more isolated than ever, more threatened than ever. True, the fact that the Jewish State can now defend itself is no small matter. However, the hatred is now directed against the State, which is used by our enemies to legitimize their anti-Semitism. They claim to be anti-Zionist but not anti-Jewish, because, they say, Zionism is racism.

2) While it is true that secular Zionism has given many Jews in the Diaspora a new and proud sense of Jewish identity and thus saved them from assimilation, it has on the other hand fostered new worries about assimilation regarding the State itself. If the State will not strengthen its Jewish character, then the State itself stands in danger of assimilation. Moreover, if all we aspire to is statehood, is it worth the price of continued strife?

Most critical of all aspects of the ideological crises for secular Zionism is the fact that it has failed as a solution to the problem of Judaism. Zionism offered itself as an optional definition of Jewish identity, as a total philosophy of what Jewishness is all about, as a nationalistic alternative to the classic religious definition of Jewishness, arguing "that one could be a good Jew outside the framework of Judaism." But this too has turned out to be inadequate. The dismal phenomena of increasing *yerida* and confusion among Israeli-born youth brought up on classical Zionist ideology support the contention that just as secular Zionism was not an

Chapter Nineteen. Religious Zionism: What is It?

answer to the Jewish problem so is it not an answer to the problem of Judaism.

Contrast these problems with the position of religious Zionism, and immediately we perceive the cogency, the completeness and the effectiveness of the approach.

1) In terms of the future, our vision has lost none of its lustre. Religious Zionism never said that a Jewish State was its ultimate goal. The re-establishment of *malkhut yisrael* was sought so that it may be governed *al pi torat yisrael*. The vision and dream of religious Zionism is still intact; is still ahead of us. The struggle has only begun. The partial successes—the establishment of the State, the return to Jerusalem, Judea, and Samaria, the economic development, the growth of a defense capability, the impressive gains in Torah education on all levels—are all taken as encouragement and inspiration to continue working to complete the task.

2) Religious Zionism never sought "normalcy" in the sense that it believed the Jewish People to be "like all the nations." Religious Zionism never predicted. the elimination of anti-Semitism, because our understanding of this virulent phenomenon comes from our sages, who traced it to its original roots. There will always be those who cannot tolerate the "stranger" be an individual or a nation.

3) Religious Zionism, noting the studied ambiguity with which our sages viewed the *galut*, could never negate the *galut* completely as did some early secular Zionists.

4) Finally, religious Zionism from the very beginning warned our other Zionist colleagues that nationalism is not a substitute for Judaism. It is not a total explication of Jewishness. Nationalism is but one component of a complex notion of Jewish identity whose essential core feature is a covenantal relationship between this people and the *boreh olam*. For religious Zionism, *yishuv Eretz Yisrael* is not a solution to a problem but a divine challenge to forge a higher reality.

As a religious Zionist, I do not say all this in a spirit of triumphalism, nor in a spirit of "we told you so!," but simply so that we might remind ourselves of our basic ideological strength, which recent history seems to vindicate.

But does this mean that we are ideologically untroubled? Does this mean that in the realm of theory, religious Zionism has nothing more to do?

We *have* an ideological problem and it has to do with our fellow religious Jews, our brothers in Torah and *mitzvot*. The sad fact is that we have not been able effectively to convey our theory, our *hashkafa*, our program, to many of our religious brothers. We have not articulated clearly and persuasively the outlook of religious Zionism as it confronts the reality of Israel today in terms that might at least challenge other religious Jews.

Involvement with *Eretz Yisrael* is, of course, the most obvious component of the program of religious Zionism, but it is only what may be termed the "middle section." Religious Zionism may be thought of as a missile with its freight section labeled "philanthropic involvement with Israel," its rockets consisting of the "primary ideas," and its war-head representing "*aliyah*."

It has been suggested that the primary ideas which make the appeal of religious Zionism possible and provide its motivational force are the following:[2]

1) That Jews both as individuals and as a group must no longer permit themselves to be victimized, nor must they remain passive in the face of physical danger, nor rely totally on the established forces of law and order (locally, nationally, or internationally) for protection. There is nothing more demeaning to human dignity and more debilitating to human personality than to be constantly exposed to violence without the means of self-defense. For the Jews as a nation this means nothing less than the political instrumentalities of statehood with defense forces of our own, adequate to defend our people, if necessary as far as Entebbe. Once this is grasped it becomes easier to understand, for example, the importance of the *Yeshivot Hesder*, whose students serve in the Israel Defense Forces as part of their study program. *Yeshiva* students who devote time to train to defend their people and their land embody the classic ideals of Torah Judaism and constitute the most authentic type of *yeshiva* in the world today. Commitment to this principle does not necessarily imply commitment to religious Zionism but the reverse does hold.

2) The principle that "all Jews are responsible one for another" has a corollary in terms of the collective called *Klal Yisrael*, the community of Israel. Religious Jewish leadership has a responsibility for all Israel, for their physical as well as spiritual well-being. The constant temptation of the religious Jew is to set himself apart in order to safeguard

---

[2] M. Rosenak, "Three Zionist Revolutions," *Forum* 34, 1979.

Chapter Nineteen. Religious Zionism: What is It?

his own spiritual welfare, but separatist policies, although legitimate in their original motivations, tend to proliferate out of control. The Zionist enterprise is important to the religious Jew not only because it involves *Eretz Yisrael*, but because it is open to all Jews; it provides physical and spiritual benefits to all Jews. To be a religious Zionist, therefore, gives us the opportunity to fulfill our obligation toward *Klal Yisrael*.

3) Religious Zionists believe that while Torah is, of course, the supreme value in Judaism, the other cultural creations of the Jewish People are also of value. To use the talents with which we have been endowed as a people to bring into the world things that are useful, beneficial, and beautiful, as individuals and as a nation, is a religious duty. Advances in the fields of language and literature, social and economic institutions, science and technology, which benefit all mankind, reflecting Jewish values which are truly possible only in a Jewish State, are sources of Jewish pride and Jewish inspiration. General cultural pursuits engaged in by Jews in the Diaspora rarely endure as Jewish contributions, and tend to draw the Jew away from his Jewishness.[3] A Jewish State gives us the opportunity to live life in its totality and fullness so that everything we do is in a sense a *mitzvah* because it is a part of *Yishuv Eretz Yisrael*: it is Jewish because it is the result of our own creative labor and it is Torah because it reflects Jewish values.

A religious Zionist is one whose work on behalf of *Eretz Yisrael*, whose appreciation of the importance of *Eretz Yisrael*, and whose commitment to *Eretz Yisrael* are based in part upon his understanding and acceptance of these three root principles. One of the weaknesses of our ideological posture in the past has been that we have not sufficiently concentrated on propounding these primary ideas. We have not made it clear that these principles are implicit in the ideology and program of religious Zionism. Nor have we systematically attempted to convince our religious brothers of their truth and validity.

But if we have ignored the primary ideas which are behind that portion of our ideology which can be called philanthropic Zionism, then we have, in my judgment, not been clear enough in explaining that vital "cutting edge" of the Zionist program which carries the "pay dirt," as it were, and that is the call for *personal Zionism,* the call for *aliyah*. Is this

---

[3] Consider Mendelssohn and Mahler in music, Pisarro in painting, and the Jewish Hollywood producers in the early years of the motion picture industry.

indeed a problem of theory, or is it more a practical problem depending upon proper *shlichim,* glossy brochures, and better tax incentives? I suggest that the problem is primarily one of ideology, particularly in regard to religious Jews. There is a steady trickle of religious Jews going on *aliya,* but we are far from having ignited a flame of religious enthusiasm.

In our literature we are still fighting the battle for religious Zionism on the basis of the question of whether *Yishuv Eretz Yisrael* is a *mitzvah* and what kind of *mitzvah* is it? What makes this type of scholarship irrelevant to the concrete question of going on *aliyah* is the fact that these questions are asked within the framework of halakhah, which is always open to qualifications and exemptions because of special circumstances. In the Middle Ages, when the *mitzvah* of *Yishuv Eretz Yisrael* had meaning only within the framework of the *halakhah*, Nachmanides, by walking four *amot* in Israel and settling in Jerusalem, fulfilled the *mitzvah*. The source of the *mitzvah* was the Torah, the focus of the *mitzvah* was the individual, and the conditions under which the individual fulfilled the *mitzvah* or was exempt from it could be spelled out.

With the establishment of the Jewish State and the liberation of Jerusalem, our sense of obligation received reinforcement from a new source. It is no longer the authoritative but defeasible voice of halakhah alone which commands *Yishuv Eretz Yisrael*, but the not-always-clear yet electrifying voice of history which is now heard.[4] It is always a *mitzvah* for the individual Jew to live in *Eretz Yisrael* if he can, but the pattern of events by which the God of history leads the people as a group into the land and then out of the land and then into the land again operates on a different level. These special momentous events are made known to us either by the explicit word of the Prophet or by the implied meaning of the events themselves. Moshe revealed to Israel that the intent of the Exodus was to bring the Jewish people into the land. Jeremiah announced that the Babylonian invasion meant expulsion and exile. Ezra and Nehemiah, Hagai and Zecharia interpreted the Persian victory to mean that God was now leading the Jewish People back to the land. When the Second Temple was destroyed, we had no prophet to tell us that "the King had once again driven His son from out of His presence." After the failure of the Bar Kochba rebellion, we read the "writing on the wall" of history: It was the will of God that we go into exile. We learned this not from a prophet but from the brutal facts of historic events.

---

[4] See discussion in Chapter 18 beginning p. 351.

Chapter Nineteen. Religious Zionism: What Is It?

Today once again we stand before special momentous events. The question of whether we are witnessing the "beginning of Redemption" is precisely the question of whether the re-establishment of the Jewish State and the liberation of Jerusalem are indeed "signs and wonders" which carry a meaning and a message. Religious Zionism believes that God is once again speaking to His people through history. Just as we did not require a prophet to tell us that God wants us to go into exile, so we do not need a prophet today to make it clear that God wishes us to return to our land: He has opened the gates. He has given us Jerusalem. He has made the land fruitful. He has given us a defense capability. He has gathered us nearly six million strong, and may that number continue to increase.

To experience in Israel the "beginning of Redemption" is to endow these events with revelatory significance which says to the Jews all over the world: "Enough sitting in the vale of tears—Go up and take possession!"

While this new *aliyah* obligation still devolves upon the individual, there is a respect in which the essence of the call goes out to the nation as a whole. That is to say, there can be no fulfillment of this aspect of the call until the overwhelming majority of the Jewish People return to the land. In this sense, the obligation today upon *Klal Yisrael* for *aliyah* is absolute. Should most of the people not go, although as individuals they might each have a *heter*, it would nevertheless be considered a betrayal, as it was in the days of the *meraglim* and in the period of the *Olei Bavel*. For then as now, it would appear that God wants nothing less than *biat kulkhem*, the coming of all to Eretz Yisrael.

Perceiving Zion today as the "beginning of Redemption" also adds a temporal dimension to our *aliyah* obligation, for it means that we must now view *aliyah* as a *mitzvat aseh shehazman grama*—a positive duty which is brought into validity by the demands of the historic hour against which all individual *cheshbonot* are irrelevant. It has been suggested in this regard that the reason why the sin of the *meraglim* was punished with a factor of time (a year of wandering for each day spent on that disastrous mission [Num. 14:34]) was because the Jews' essential sin was a blindness to the demands of the hour. The Jews then had excellent reasons for wanting to continue to live around the oasis of Kadesh Barnea and not get involved in the materialistic concerns of state-building, but their historic destiny at that time required otherwise. Therefore, *mida keneged mida*—the punishment is fitted to the transgression—and they wandered in the desert.[5]

Perceiving the State of Israel as the "beginning of Redemption" is not an empty semantic issue; it is in fact the dynamic element that can galvanize *aliyah*. How can we get our religious brothers to see Israel this way? This is not primarily a matter of logic, of deducing a conclusion from certain premises, but is a matter of perception, of vision, of seeing something "as."

We read in the first chapter of Jeremiah that God causes the prophet to see a vision and then asks him, "What do you see?" When Jeremiah answers, "I see a boiling pot which faces north," God remarks, "You have seen well." How shall we understand this approval of Jeremiah's vision by the Almighty? Do you really have to be an expert to recognize a boiling pot? The answer is that to be a prophetic seer, one must be able to select from a particular scene those elements, those particulars, that are relevant and significant to the Divine pattern. Jeremiah could have described the material from which the pot was made, or on what it was resting, but these particulars, while true, were irrelevant. Jeremiah "saw well" because he focused precisely on those elements which fitted into the Lord's metaphor: the pot *is boiling* and it is facing *north*!

Different people may view the same state of Israel and come away with different perceptions, as they can when confronted with any visual image. What can we do to help people see the present reality of Israel as the "beginning of Redemption? Perhaps we can borrow an insight from the philosophy of art.[6] It has been suggested that in describing, for example, a painting, one can refer to aesthetic properties and non-aesthetic properties. Aesthetic properties are referred to by words like "graceful," "dainty," "balanced," or "garish," and to use these terms one must possess a certain taste or aesthetic sensitivity. Non-aesthetic terms are those such as "curved," "red," or "angular," which can be perceived by anyone with normal eyesight. The interesting relationship between the two sets of terms is that, (1) aesthetic qualities are dependent upon non-aesthetic qualities for their existence, and (2) the non-aesthetic qualities of a work determine its aesthetic qualities. The practical insight

---

[5] Heard from the late Rabbi Isaac Stollman of Detroit and Jerusalem.

[6] Frank Sibley, "A Contemporary Theory of Aesthetic Qualities" in *Aesthetics*, ed. G. Dickie and R. D. Scanlon (New York: St. Martins Press, 1977).

Chapter Nineteen. Religious Zionism: What is It?

that this analysis yields is that if you wish to help people to see and judge for themselves that certain works of art have particular aesthetic qualities it is useless to concentrate on the aesthetic property and keep repeating, "But don't you see that the painting has a restless quality!" In order to bring people with a weak aesthetic taste to perceive a particular aesthetic quality, you must point out the non-aesthetic qualities upon which they depend.

Thus, you can say, "Notice how these jagged, wavy lines give the painting a restless character." Anyone can notice jagged lines. Concentrating on these easily observed elements may enable the individual to "see" how they produce the aesthetic quality in question.

The religious quality of "beginning of Redemption" is in some respects similar to an aesthetic quality. It doesn't do any good to get people to accept on authority that Israel is the "beginning of Redemption," just as it would not be meaningful for them to accept on authority that this music is serene or that play is moving. But to see it for oneself requires a certain religious and historical sensitivity which not everyone possesses. Therefore, the way we religious Zionists can be helpful is not simply by quoting more proof-texts which refer to the redemption or by researching more rabbinic endorsements, but by pointing to the non-religious properties of the reality of Israel upon which the religious judgment rests. Thus, for example, we might focus on the ways in which Israel today constitutes an "ingathering of Exiles" to an extent that is unprecedented in all of Jewish history. We must gather statistics, make comparative studies, design movies, portray the more than 100 different countries from which the people of Israel originated, draw maps, and then only as a brief final move make the connection to the biblical promise of an "ingathering," Or again, we might point to the fruitfulness of the land, which is clearly held forth by the rabbis as a "sign" of Redemption. But then we must cite figures, show pictures of what the land looked like in the early part of the nineteenth century. Then, utilizing all of the power of audio-visual media, we must show the explosion in living color of the trees, the fruits, the vegetables, the grains, the cotton, the flowers that are being exported, even the fish ponds that this "desirable, goodly, and broad land"[7] is generously giving forth under the loving care of the Jewish people. In short, the key to winning the battle for the heads and

---

[7] "*Eretz Chemda Tovah U'Rechava*," from the Grace After Meals.

hearts of religious Jews on the question of Israel as the "beginning of Redemption" is to help them appreciate the purely factual and physical aspects of Israel on which the religious perception is dependent.

A sense of obligation usually grows out of a relationship. Assuming that I perceive the State of Israel as "beginning of Redemption," and assuming I hear it to be saying—*alu raish* (go up and inherit), why should I think it is addressing *me?* The answer, of course, is: my self-image as a Jew. The relationship between the Jew and the Lord of history is such that once I perceive Israel as the "beginning of Redemption," my duty and responsibility are clear. But there is an added factor which the Jews of America and Western Europe ought to ponder which may strengthen their response to *aliya*.

How shall religious Jews view these last two thousand years of exile? How shall we regard migrations and movements of the Jewish People, spreading out from the eastern Mediterranean basin with one wave going across North Africa up to Spain, another going across Asia Minor to Russia, and still another following Rome all the way to Gaul? Was the ultimate outcome of these movements fortuitous and merely the result of the push of persecution and the pull of better opportunities, or can we discern an overall Divine plan to these seemingly haphazard wanderings?

We find ourselves today over 6 million strong on the North American continent, in a post-industrial democracy, heir to the best of the science, technology, and freedom of the West. Is there an element of destiny in all of this? Can we think of ourselves as having been "led" there? After all, we could have ended up stagnating in some culturally backward area in Asia Minor! Never in all of our history has there been under one government a larger, more affluent, more knowledgeable (in general culture), and freer Jewish community than there is in the U.S.A. today. We have indeed reached "royal estate." But for what historic purpose has Providence assembled and developed such an unprecedented Diaspora? As Mordechai said to Queen Esther, "Who knows but that you have attained royal estate for a time like this!"[8]—a time at which we must populate with superb human material the Jewish State; a time of "beginning of Redemption" in which Zion is once again able "to rejoice in her sons."

The Jews of America must respond to the vision of a Zion restored not merely as Jews but as Jews conscious of their unique place, which

---

[8] Esther 4:14.

Chapter Nineteen. Religious Zionism: What is It?

imposes a special responsibility upon them. Truly, He has spared us and sustained us and endowed us with wealth and skills so that we may be ready for the *aliyah* demanded by this historic moment. At one point, God says to Abraham: "Raise up your eyes and look out *from the place where you are at.*"[9]

Thinking about the significance of the *place you are* at—the United States in the modern era— will reveal the destiny for which we have been groomed.

While the need of the hour is for the *nation* to return, the responsibility will continue to fall upon the individual. We have no leaders with the requisite authority to "lead" the nation back to our land. However, all who exert any degree of leadership share in the responsibility of helping our people to see Israel in its true light. *Aliyah* has become the existential question of our time for Jews everywhere. It is an issue which tests our very Jewishness and calls into question the seriousness of our religious commitment. Once again, an act which for the rest of the world is quite mundane and pedestrian, moving from one place to another, which millions of people do each year all over the world for all sorts of reasons, becomes for the Jew a religious act of the highest significance.

It is going forth which is "for your good" in achieving self-fulfillment as Jew and therefore it must be "by your own free choice."[10]

It is perhaps for this reason that our sages tell us that the final stage of the ingathering of the exiles will be as "difficult as if God Himself will have to pluck each individual Jew out of the Diaspora!" This last stage of the ingathering will not take place in "waves" or by complete communities, but will be carried out by individuals, one by one, who will act not in response to material inducements but in response to the perception that God Himself is calling us back to Zion.

A "new light" is already shining forth over Zion, a light in which Zion appears as the *reshit tzmichat geulatenu*, the first blossoming of our redemption.

Now we must pray: "Open our eyes so that we might see these wondrous things."[11]

---

[9] Gen. 13:14.
[10] See Rashi on Genesis 12:1.
[11] Psalm 119:18.

Chapter Twenty

Does Messianism Imply Inevitability?

One of the great fears in Israel is that a growing number of people with strongly-held messianic beliefs are seeking to play an active role in contemporary politics. Historians are surprised, because in the past, belief in the Jewish Messiah has been associated with passivism and political quietism. On the other hand, readers of Gershom Scholem are panic-stricken because they recall how messianism has been described as a historical force of powerful and dangerous magnitude that gave us the disasters of Bar Kochba and Shabbetai Zvi, and the apocalyptic elements of which were with difficulty "liquidated" by Maimonides on behalf of tradition, "neutralized" by the early Hasidim, and undermined by modern skepticism of religion in general.[1] Could it be that this pitiful giant has been roused from its stupor, has somehow regained its strength and relevance, and once again threatens to unsettle the Jewish people?

Politically active messianists are seen as endangering the rational and orderly working-out of Israel's foreign policy and as impeding the search for regional peace. This perception, which is held by most of the liberal Labor-academic establishment with increasing apprehension and bitterness, lumps together in its nightmarish vision an unholy alliance of the followers of Meir Kahane with the members of *Gush Emunim* (a movement started by Chanan Porath after the Six-Day War to settle territories), most of the settlers, the Guardians of the Temple Mount, believers in a Greater Israel and elements of the Likud and smaller right-wing parties.

I wish to suggest that, like most perceptions driven by fear, this sense that "Messianists are upon thee, O Israel!" can be shown to lack coherence and to possess a poor grounding in reality. Let us bypass the crude sensation-mongers of the media, whose sole intention is to discredit

---

[1] Gershom Scholem, *The Messianic Idea in Judaism* (New York: Allen and Unwin, 1971), 26, 276.

Chapter Twenty. Does Messianism Imply Inevitability?

certain policies by association, and examine the view of the respected scholar Professor Jacob Katz as to how messianic beliefs work to endanger the Israeli future. "There are," Katz writes,

> men and women of political action who are impelled by the belief that the determination of Israel's geographical boundaries is a matter of messianic significance. Given this belief, it is considered unnecessary by them to weigh all the possible consequences of actions taken to further their goals, since those goals have in any event been ratified by the force of divine will.[2]

What we have before us in general terms are the complex questions of the relationship between certain beliefs and certain lines of conduct and regarding the effect that particular beliefs will tend to have on the believer's behavior. In specific terms, the question becomes: is it true to say that believers in traditional Jewish messianism will tend to make political decisions in a manner which lacks a full sense of responsibility?

Let us proceed to examine Katz's statement. What does it mean to say that certain "goals have been ratified by the force of divine will"? Does it simply mean that the divine will endorses or sanctions certain goals or does it mean that the realizations of certain goals are inevitable because they have been predetermined by divine will? I submit that in either case the statement is incoherent. If the former interpretation is intended then it is not at all true to say that this will cause those who hold this belief to consider it unnecessary to weigh the consequences of actions taken to further these goals. In his daily life a religious Jew is constantly faced by goals which he believes to be "ratified by the force of divine will" in this sense. These are the "commandments" which involve all sorts of activities from studying the Torah to exhorting one's fellow, from helping the needy to educating one's children. Certainly in regard to these "goals" there is no question but that the believer considers it quite necessary to weigh carefully the consequences of actions taken in order to further them. Only in rare and carefully defined cases does the Jewish believer consider the "divinely ratified goals" to be absolute in the sense that he must act on their behalf regardless of cost or consequences. In many situations, inattention to the consequences of

---

[2] Jacob Katz, "Is Messianism Good for the Jews?," *Commentary* 83, no. 4 (April 1987): 35.

well-intended actions may result in damage to other "divinely ratified goals" and actually be counterproductive.

Similarly, messianists who believe that God "ratifies" Israel's retention of territories won in 1967 are not thereby obliged to take actions designed to keep them in Israel's possession regardless of consequences. Some of the most authoritative religious leaders have repeatedly pronounced that the safety of the Jewish community in Israel stands higher than the sanctity of the land. The disagreements that exist involve the question of the precise conditions which might constitute a mortal danger to the State of Israel. But such disagreements are to be found even among non-messianic politicians. We must therefore reject this interpretation of the Katz statement.

The latter interpretation, on the other hand, fares no better. Here we assume that those who perceive in the establishment and expansion of the State of Israel the unfolding of a messianic process are committed to the belief that what has happened was inevitable and that the goals not yet achieved are likewise inevitable. Moreover, the entire process is considered irreversible. Therefore, claims Katz, such messianists are prone to initiate all sorts of actions in furtherance of the goals without weighing the consequences, since the outcome is assured in advance.

We shall later question this assumption regarding whether Jewish messianism does indeed include such an element of determinism. However, assuming that it does, why should the believer take any action at all if the goal is assured in advance? In another article, Katz puts it this way:

> Any action taken under the rubric of messianic determinism is necessarily limited in its rationality. It is based on the assumption that the individual is responsible only for the preliminary steps: their completion is assigned to the messianic power or in secular terms, to hidden historical forces.[3]

But if we examine the historical context in which traditional messianism moved from an insistence on political quietism to discovering a role for political activism, we note that this was done precisely to warrant *rational* actions which could not be construed as "forcing the

---

[3] Jacob Katz, "Israel and the Messiah," *Commentary* 73, no. 1 (January 1982): 40.

end." The "preliminary steps" advanced by post-Kalischer[4] messianism could be termed "of limited rationality" only in the sense that they were not designed to achieve the entire goal. However, judged as an entity by itself, this action most certainly had to pass the ordinary canons of rationality and not have consequences which could only make the task of Providence more difficult. Thus, as a proper "preliminary step" toward the messianic goal, Kalischer could advocate practical colonization of Palestine. In no way could a call to Jews to gather on their rooftops to await a messianic "magic carpet" to transport them to Jerusalem be considered a "preliminary step" under this messianic rubric.

Katz's disapproval of messianic determinism because of its effect on practical politics is reminiscent of the severe criticism leveled by Karl Popper against what has been called "historicism": "the doctrine that history is controlled by specific historical or evolutionary laws whose discovery would enable us to prophecy the destiny of man."[5] Popper includes in this doctrine the theistic form which simply says that the law of historical development is laid down by the will of God.[6] Of course, on purely philosophical grounds, Popper maintains that this doctrine in all its variations is simply false, that people who hold such beliefs are indulging in prophecy rather than social science. However, the question of truth or falsity is not our present concern. Katz is opposed to *Gush Emunim* not because of the truth or falsity of their views but because of the alleged harmful effects that their involvement in politics may have. But this also forms part of Popper's criticism. He claims that historicist doctrines are "harmful and dangerous."[7] Let us see why.

The examples of historicism that Popper treats at length are the historical theories of Plato, Hegel, and Marx. His main criticism is that these theories tend to favor totalitarianism and are opposed to the "open society." However, in terms of their psychological effect, Popper says that by resorting to pseudo-scientific arguments to claim that totalitarianism is the "wave of the future" and its universal adoption inevitable,

---

[4] Zvi Hirsch Kalischer (1795-1874), rabbi of Thorn, Germany, was considered the harbinger of modern Zionism. He was the author of *Derishat Zion*.
[5] Karl R. Popper, *The Open Society and its Enemies* (Princeton: Princeton University Press, 1950), 11.
[6] Ibid., 12.
[7] Ibid., 5.

they tend to discourage those who believe in the viability of democratic social engineering and who are prepared to oppose totalitarianism and the methods of violent revolution.[8] It is noteworthy that Popper sees the primary social danger of a theistic (messianic) interpretation of history to be that it has a psychologically suppressive effect on the human initiative of both its supporters and opponents.

In light of this, it is difficult to agree with Katz that "determinism" is the conceptual culprit whose effect is to be feared in the political activism of the messianists. If the *Gush Emunim* people believe that the present boundaries of Israel constitute the commencement of a redemptive process whose unilateral realization is inevitable, one would expect them to sit back and relax and leave the rest to God. The disasters of the Second Temple period associated with the first war against Rome and the Bar Kochba rebellion could hardly be counted as examples of the negative effects of messianic determinism. First, because it is extremely difficult to determine the precise nature of the messianic views of the Jews who initiated and fought these wars. While there is considerable evidence that the rabbis thought of Bar Kochba in messianic, though not deterministic, terms, the messianic beliefs of those who fought the first war against Rome are not at all clear, and neither is it apparent how both of these national struggles differed from the successful Macabbean revolt, concerning which there seems to have been a total lack of messianic pretension. There seems to be little evidence of any significant correlation between messianic belief and the rationality of the national policies it generates, let alone evidence of the separate effects of the deterministic component. Who is to say from this distance that the Macabbean undertaking was rational, while the Bar Kochba enterprise was not?[9]

Indeed, Katz explicitly points to the paradoxical side effects of traditional messianism. While it projected a radical change in the future, in terms of the present messianism "secured the status quo" and "served to enforce an extreme quietism and political passivity."[10] For Jews had in ef-

---

[8] Ibid., 6, 7.

[9] See the discussion in Yehoshafat Harkabi, *The Bar Kokhba Syndrome* (New York: Rossel Books, 1983), and Yisrael Eldad, *Disputation: The Destruction and its Lessons* (Jerusalem, 1982).

[10] J. Katz, "Is Messianism Good for the Jews?," 33.

fect "ceded their fate to the unfathomable wisdom of Divine Providence to determine the time of the redemption." Whatever human initiative was countenanced was restricted to "spiritual or ritualistic devices."[11]

What change was introduced into the concept of traditional messianism by the "rethinking" of Rabbis Y. Alkalay and Z. H. Kalischer in the 1860s? What they did was essentially to "integrate the historical experience of their age" into the traditional schema of messianic fulfillment.[12] First, they looked upon the political emancipation of the Jews in Western countries as a providential act, and as constituting the initial phase in the process of redemption. Aside from being "good" in itself in that it raised the social status of the Jew, opening possibilities for education and economic growth in their lands of domicile, political emancipation rendered feasible the next stage in the redemption process: the peaceful return to and colonization of *Eretz Yisrael*. In truth the ideas of human initiative bringing about aspects of the messianic process were neither new nor heretical. The Bar Kochba revolt, supported by the foremost rabbinic authority of its time, while a failure, testifies nevertheless to its being at least in conception a proper messianic enterprise. However, with the Jews no longer the majority of those cultivating the land in *Eretz Yisrael* as a result of the Muslim invasions and the Crusades, and the growing distance of elements of the Diaspora from the center of Jewish life as Jews moved deeper into religiously hostile societies, the sheer impossibility of an ingathering of the dispersed of Israel by natural means became a glaring, indisputable fact. Hence it was relegated to the Divine sphere as one of the items the Messiah would have to bring about.

The achievement of Alkalay and Kalischer was to perceive that after about 1800 years of exile, the entire international picture,. the situation of the Jews included, had undergone a radical change. It was like Noah looking out of his Ark and realizing that the flood waters had receded, making it possible for him and the animals to disembark.[13] What had

---

[11] J. Katz, "Israel and the Messiah," 35.
[12] Ibid., 36.
[13] See *Yalkut Shimoni* on Gen. 8:16, which records a significant difference of opinion among rabbis as to whether Noah should have left the Ark on his own after the waters began to recede or whether he should have waited for explicit permission from God.

been impossible before now became possible, feasible, and doable, and was therefore a challenge: return to *Eretz Yisrael* with the approval of the nations. Kalischer was able to demonstrate from the tradition that human initiative was not only permitted, i.e., that under the proper circumstances the Jewish people *may* employ their own resources in organizing a return to the land of Israel, but that Providence may even *demand* human involvement as a test of the people's readiness and desire for redemption.

It can be shown that a warrant for this sort of "rethinking" had been available since the middle ages in the writings of Maimonides.[14] Although retaining the centrality of the personal Messiah, Maimonides had made it clear that the precise sequence of the particular phases that make up the messianic process was not a religious principle. Thus it is entirely conceivable that prior to the appearance of any messianic candidate there could begin the ingathering of the dispersed by natural means as well as through other combinations of the various messianic components.[15] Maimonides had also carefully cultivated a thoroughgoing skepticism in regard to possible messianic pretenders. Since in his naturalistic approach the Messiah is not required to perform miracles, the ultimate test of his authenticity will be his complete success on the historical level. Thus, even a messianic candidate who has all of the required qualifications and has considerable initial success would only have the status of a *presumed* Messiah. This means that even under such favorable circumstances, the believer in traditional messianism would not have the right to assume that this particular messianic candidate or this particular messianic enterprise, no matter how many positive "signs" had been received, was the "awaited" one or was predestined to succeed. Traditional messianism is indeed deterministic in the sense that believers may proclaim, "I believe in perfect faith in the coming of the Messiah and although he tarries I wait for him every day, for surely he will come." The Messiah will, of Divine necessity, come some day. Universal redemption is a necessary component of the Divine scheme. However, until it has actually happened in its many-sided totality, not

---

[14] Maimonides, *Mishneh Torah, Hilkhot Melachim* 11:12.
[15] These are: religious revival, wars involving Jews and the land of Israel, the upbuilding of the city of Jerusalem, and, according to Maimonides, the re-establishment of the Sanhedrin.

even the most fervent believer with the most "perfect faith" may say in regard to any particular presumed messianic events that they will *necessarily* succeed or *inevitably* come to completion.

The only "fundamentalistic" element that lingered long in the concept of traditional messianism was its "political quietism" which was the offspring of historical circumstances and never really an integral part of its core concept. However, the element of "determinism" or "necessity" had never been a part of traditional messianism in the sense feared by Katz.

What bears further scrutiny is Katz's understanding of the role messianism played in the development of Zionism, which he sees as having been "good for the Jews." In an earlier treatment, Katz makes it quite clear that the Jewish National idea itself found its most dramatic and dynamic expression in the concept of traditional messianism: "the historical consciousness of being a son of a nation, ill fated in the present, divinely endowed in the past with splendid prospects for the future."[16] This future included the ingathering of the dispersed of Israel to *Eretz Yisrael*, which would be a sovereign Jewish state. Of course, in its traditional form Jewish messianism appeared as a religious belief. Under the impact of secularism and rationalism and the attendant weakening of religious belief, the power of traditional messianism was in turn weakened. In non-religious circles its influence survived primarily as emotional attachments to its symbols or appeared when, under secular versions of historicism, belief in Providence was replaced by alleged insight into "iron laws" of history. While here as well Katz concludes that "the force of the Jewish National idea derives its strength from the deeper sources of messianism," one is struck by certain different emphases that arise from this article.[17] First, he makes no mention at all of messianic determinism being the dynamic, motive element in the messianic belief. Secondly, Katz makes it quite clear that until the 1870s, the forerunners of Modern Zionism (read: "transformed messianism") had very little practical impact. The idea of Jewish Nationalism (which can also be described as "transformed messianism") "proved itself unable to up-

---

[16] Jacob Katz, "The Jewish National Movement," in *Jewish Society Through the Ages,* ed. H. H. Ben Sasson and S. Ettinger (New York: Vallentine Mitchell, 1971), 269.
[17] Ibid., 283.

root people en masse out of a well balanced social setting."[18] Only in the 1880s, when other forces such as political and economic upheavals were linked with the National idea, was there a beginning of the realization of the national goal of ingathering. One is therefore left with the impression that the power of the transformed messianic idea to move either believers or secularists was rather limited at least in the early period.

In his 1982 article, Katz makes a much stronger and explicit claim for the role of what he calls "messianic determinism."[19] He no longer speaks of traditional messianism as being merely the source for the Jewish National idea, claiming instead that messianism in its religious and secular versions was the operative force. Furthermore, he is able to pinpoint that element within messianism that comprises its dynamic component, namely "determinism": belief in the predetermined destiny that ties the Jewish people to the Holy Land, a destiny which guaranteed the success of the enterprise. "For the religious Zionists the guarantee was faith in the divine promise. For the secularist pioneers it was the action of historical inevitability."

Aside from the Zionists' copious use of messianic symbols, figures of speech, and biblical verses in their rhetoric, Katz gives the following examples of the effects of belief in messianic determinism upon the Zionist movement: (1) The decision to settle in Palestine rather than in some other place, which by all ordinary considerations must be considered "irrational." (2) Belief that the Zionist enterprise must inevitably culminate in a Jewish commonwealth imparted energy and a willingness for sacrifice.[20] However, in both of these cases what actually transpired could just as well be attributed to the effects of a deep emotional attachment to the land of Israel or a strong desire to have an independent country of one's own. To be sure, traditional messianism can be said to have played an important secondary role in preserving the historical memory and keeping alive an attachment to Palestine. However, the "irrational" preference for Palestine and the "willingness to sacrifice" does not necessarily imply a belief in messianic determinism. They could just as effectively be explained as the results of a kind of romanticism which dulls one's sense of realism.

---

[18] Ibid., 280, 289.
[19] J. Katz, "Israel and the Messiah," 38.
[20] Ibid., 40.

Chapter Twenty. Does Messianism Imply Inevitability?

Eliezer Schweid makes an important distinction in his discussion of the deterministic components found in Zionist ideology.[21] He points out that almost all of the major Zionist thinkers were as one in claiming to be able to know scientifically that historical forces economic, political, and cultural were making impossible the continuation of any organized viable Jewish life in the Diaspora. On the one hand, they pointed to the inevitable increase of anti-Semitism and the ejection of Jews from the economic life of countries in the West. On the other hand, there were clear and inexorable social forces which were pushing the Jew in the direction of assimilation. The disastrous end to Jewish life in the Diaspora was fore-ordained by the operation of unchangeable historical laws, and thus the Zionist solution was clearly indicated. However, at this point, the "scientific" or "deterministic" nature of Zionist ideology breaks down, for in the classical Marxist approach, the same historical forces and dialectic which are inevitably moving toward the dissolution and destruction of the old forms are those which will guarantee the emergence of the new shape and form of society. However, in the case of Zionism there opens up an obvious gap. It may indeed have been possible to demonstrate "scientifically" the bleak prospects of a Jewish future in the Diaspora and to show that the Zionist solution was "necessary" in the sense that without it the Jewish people could not hope to survive. However, the Zionist thinkers, including B. Borochov, the most Marxist among them, could not show that the same historical forces that were destroying Jewish life in the Diaspora were those what would inevitably bring about the realization of the Zionist plan. In this respect Zionist ideology lacked a deterministic component.

Schweid therefore claims that alongside a component of historical inevitability there is to be found in all shades of Zionist thought an element of free choice which aims in the direction of goals which are not indicated by the historical process. Thus Borochov in attempting to explain the anomalous case of the Jewish people is required to introduce the notion of a "therapeutic" national movement which must first provide a territorial and economic base before the people can rejoin the "natural" process of history. But this in itself is a moral decision based upon love, justice, and national pride.

---

[21] Eliezer Schweid, *From Judaism to Zionism: From Zionism to Judaism* (Jerusalem, 1983), 110.

There is another non-deterministic way in which messianism may be said to be a factor in the realization of the Zionist program. In a 1987 article, Paul Johnson points out how each of the four men who made possible the creation of the State of Israel, Theodore Herzl, Chaim Weizmann, David Ben Gurion, and Vladimir Jabotinsky, were "outsized characters" with a strong consciousness of special destiny who were possessed of tremendous will-power and perseverance. Says Johnson of the four: "Fervent secularists though they were, they seemed at times unable to drive the power of the spirit from their minds. It was as though somewhere in the background, the messiah was lurking, never quite making his appearance."[22]

It is instructive to see how this notion of "special destiny" differs from the concept of messianic or historic determinism. The latter is the belief that a certain event will inevitably occur, with the element of necessity coming from some source external to the believer. However, the notion of special destiny is a consciousness internal to the believer. He feels himself to be the chosen instrument through which something significant is to take place. Here there is no sense of inevitability, since there is no awareness of any force that is guaranteeing the outcome. How then does this consciousness of a special destiny build up in the persons of these four founders of the Jewish State?

As we review their biographies, certain elements are common to all of them. There is the early appearance of special talents recognized and applauded by family and friends, which give the individual self confidence and an appreciation of his own worth. Then there is some initial success which suggests that his program is realizable. Finally, there is the ability to attract coworkers and followers, which tends to confirm the growing conviction that he may indeed be the proper person for the historic task! These elements then go on to feed on each other.

Since the program we are talking about is Zionism, with its inextricable association with traditional messianism, the consciousness of a "special destiny," no matter how secular in origin, takes on a messianic tinge. Witness how Herzl's impressive personal appearance evoked emotional shouts of "David the King" when he appeared before audiences of East European Jews. Johnson concludes, "Together they give the

---

[22] Paul Johnson, "Israel's Providential Men," *Commentary* 84, no. 4 (October 1987): 60.

Chapter Twenty. Does Messianism Imply Inevitability?

lie emphatically to the claims of determinists that history is made by impersonal forces rather than great individuals. Israel like most other nations was built by inspired egoism."[23]

Rather than "historic inevitability," what Zionist ideology emphasized was a notion of "historical continuity."[24] Hiatory, instead of being regarded as some external force which affects the lives of nations in accordance with certain implacable universal laws, was now seen as the crucible of the distinctive spiritual forces which constitute the very essence of the nation. While Zionism was perceived as a revolutionary program, it was believed that the spiritual forces needed to effectuate the revolution must be marshaled by the people from its own history.[25] Thus, in deciding that the Jewish National Home could be only in Palestine, the Zionists were in effect saying that only the emotional attachment to the land of Israel which the Jewish people drew from their traditions and collective memory could prove sufficiently strong to achieve this revolution. Only a return to *Eretz Yisrael* could actualize this notion of historical continuity.

If we are correct that there is no reason to link belief in messianic determinism to a disregard for consequences, we may conclude that messianists will be no more prone than any segment of the population to support hawkish political policies. But what are we to say of the phenomenon of the *machteret* or Jewish Underground, a settlers' movement several of whose members were found guilty of criminal acts against Arabs in the territories?[26]

I wish to suggest that these unfortunate actions were not a function of their messianism. Undoubtedly, their religious Zionist orientation encouraged their belief that they had every right to be living undisturbed in their ancestral home—Judea and Samaria. However, their mistaken and regrettable actions arose out of a deep anxiety and

---

[23] Ibid., 63.
[24] Schweid, *From Judaism to Zionism*, 112.
[25] See S. Almog, *Zionism and History* (Jerusalem,: Historical Society of Israel, 1987), 58-80.
[26] Menachem Livni, Shaul Nir, and Uzi Sharlev, members of the Underground, were found guilty of a 1983 attack on the Islamic College of Hevron, which killed three and wounded many more. They were sentenced to life imprisonment. Their sentence was commuted by President Chaim Herzog and they were released in 1990.

frustration based on their feeling that their own government was not doing enough to protect the lives of the settlers and their families. Those who argue that the actions of the *machteret* were a direct outgrowth of their messianic determinism, in which they clearly evinced a disregard for consequences, must consider the following question: how was it that prior to the Six Day War of 1967, although many people who believe that the establishment of the State of Israel was the "commencement of the Redemption" were alive and well and living in Israel, there did not develop any program to liberate the old city of Jerusalem and the other Holy Places? There is no evidence of any such organized messianic effort between the years 1948 and 1967. Yet if the thesis that belief in messianic determinism leads to the taking of "preliminary steps of limited rationality" is correct, why were such steps neither advocated not taken during those years?

I submit that the above discussion supports the following conclusions:

1) It is not the case that belief in messianic determinism warrants taking actions whose consequences are not fully explored.

2) Traditional messianism even in its transformed version did not include this element of "determinism."

Are we therefore to conclude that being a messianist (viewing the State of Israel as the commencement of the Redemption) carries no consequences at all for our political decision-making?

We have argued elsewhere that belief in messianism would appear to have a most practical implication for Jews living outside of Israel.[27] If I perceive the ingathering for Jews to a sovereign Jewish State in *Eretz Yisrael* as a "goal ratified by the force of divine will" and I believe in human activism as playing a role, then I should feel a personal obligation to go on *aliyah*. The "ordinary," Zionist even if he is religious, can easily rationalize his continued living in the Diaspora. For the messianist, however, it is almost impossible to do so without loss of consistency and intellectual integrity.

What political policies are indicated for the Israeli messianist? The situation after the Six-Day War presented messianists with a breathtaking challenge. From the establishment of the State in 1948 and for

---

[27] See Chapter 19 in this volume.

Chapter Twenty. Does Messianism Imply Inevitability?

19 years thereafter, messianists had perceived in the situation the "commencement of the Redemption." They were able to do so by focusing on the positive elements: ingathering of the dispersed, establishment of Jewish sovereignty, reclamation of the land, and economic growth of the country. With the passage of time, as the novelty of these historic achievements began to fade, the incomplete nature of the situation began to loom larger in their consciousness: the vulnerable nature of the boundaries, which were mere armistice lines unfixed by formal treaty, the slow-down in *aliyah*, and the fact that the most holy places, such as the Temple Mount, the Tomb of the Patriarchs, and Rachel's Tomb were not included in the Jewish State.

In June 1967, after six days of defensive military action, Israel found not only that a terrible threat to its very survival had been eliminated, but that it was now in possession of its entire historic patrimony. For messianists, this was a striking confirmation of their earlier perceptions. Establishment of the State had indeed been the "commencement of the redemption," and now a short 19 years later a further and most dramatic stage had been reached. A pattern was beginning to emerge.

At this juncture it was perfectly clear to messianists and non-messianists alike that the new situation, both glorious and troublesome, with Jews in possession of a Greater Israel which included a large restive Arab population, had not come about as the result of messianic politics or by the irredentist agitation of religious zealots. It was the indirect consequence of the decision of a rational, secular, socialist, Jewish community to defend its population against the threats of the Arab neighbors, many times more numerous, who surrounded them. Even for messianists, the Six-Day War and its consequences were not "miraculous" but Providential, i.e., caused by a higher power acting through a concatenation of political events and rational human decisions to bring about desired goals.

Actually, this was the same type of experience that had occurred in 1948. The original declaration of the Jewish State, which was a freely chosen, daring action by the Jewish people, was also a rational response to an immediate situation which had been built up by historic events, many of which Jews had nothing to do with: Great Britain relinquished the Mandate and left Palestine, and the Arab States rejected partition and attacked the *Yishuv*. Responsible Jewish leaders were thus confronted by a very narrow range of choices. One might almost say they were nudged by events into founding the Jewish State. This too was seen by messianists as Providential.

Thus, if messianists take the events of 1948 and 1967 as paradigms of the redemptive process as it is unfolding in our time, a picture emerges in which Providence in the guise of political and social forces does all the "heavy" work to which Jews are obliged to respond at certain critical junctures with crucial decisions. However, the grounds for the decisions are never recognizably messianic but are rather conventional moral and utilitarian considerations and simple concern for the welfare of the Jewish people.

If this has been the process through which Providence has brought about such unprecedented redemptive progress, there is little reason to believe that messianists will feel constrained from using means which are no less moral or rational to bring about further steps in the redemptive process.

In the aftermath of the Six-Day War, while the government of Israel was still in a state of political shock and the Arabs had responded with the "Three Nos of Khartoum," messianists felt obliged to respond to the Providential gift of Judea and Samaria by launching a movement for Jewish settlement of these areas. In their drive to gain popular support and government approval, messianists employed conventional methods of political pressure and persuasion and went no further in their zealousness than occasional civil disobedience in the forms generally accepted today in democratic countries. Fears that the "settlers" would start a civil war if arrangements were made with the Palestinians to trade "territories for peace," in which settlements would have to be uprooted were never realized. Ultimately all Jews were removed from the Gaza strip in implementing the Sharon government policy of disengagement without undue violence.

In my judgment messianists, and I count myself as one, will continue to work toward the growth and development of the Jewish State in accordance with the same principles of rationality and morality (non-violence) that have been observed until now. Messianists assume that the pattern of Divine-human partnership of opportunity and response continues as before. We are not privy to the sequence of events in advance. We can recognize patterns only *de facto*. We did not bring about a sovereign Jewish State by ourselves: Providence created a situation in which a vote for Jewish statehood made sense morally and rationally.

Chapter Twenty. Does Messianism Imply Inevitability?

We did not bring about a united Jerusalem, a Jewish Kiryat Arba, or a Jewish Karnei Shomron by ourselves. Providence created a situation in which a preemptive strike against our neighbors was moral and rational. If it is now claimed that a situation has arisen in which Israel, for the sake of its very survival, must surrender portions of Judea and Samaria, then that claim must be examined very realistically, without any reference to messianic beliefs or religious convictions. Security and political considerations must be scrutinized, options weighed, consequences projected, possible outcomes charted, and gains and losses calculated and balanced out. We have said that the historic situation is the contribution of Providence. It is therefore of the most vital importance that we truly understand the situation and gauge our options realistically.

But if latter-day messianists place such a premium on realism and rationality, how do they differ from non-messianists in their political decision-making? True, in the decisions made in 1948 and 1967, the situations were so unequivocal that most messianists and non-messianists reasoned alike and came to the same conclusions. However, the situation seems, as of now, to be much more complex and equivocal.

Yet we must understand that the referendum to the Jewish people, if and when it comes, will not be an abstract, requiring a decision to be made between territories and peace. It will propose a particular plan with concrete terms undertaken with specific political partners with suitable guarantees. We will have to decide what is best for the Jews: to remain as we were or to accept a new plan. What will the new plan give us, and at what price? Can the partners to the new plan deliver the goods as promised? This will involve a process of weighing various factors, advantages and disadvantages, pluses and minuses, gains and losses. But the crucial methodological problem will be how much weight to assign each factor. Here there may arise a difference between messianist and non-messianists. The messianist can be expected to give more weight to the positive factor of retaining all of *Eretz Yisrael* as well as the negative factor of a legitimate Jewish government in Israel officially renouncing all claims to portions of historic *Eretz Yisrael*.

The messianist does not maintain that the territories must be retained at all costs. The messianist does not hold that his messianic beliefs entitle him to act without thought to consequences. But the messianist does have an obligation to act on his convictions that the present boundaries of Israel constitute an opportunity and challenge to the

Jewish people to settle thereupon. Therefore, should the security and political factors, pluses and minuses, more or less balance out with serious risks accompanying each option, the messianist in such a context might give greater weight to the policy that permits Israel to carry out its historic responsibility and retain the territories.

The messianist in Israel today has a religious and moral obligation to be politically active. His messianism may indeed endow him with more energy, staying power, and confidence which he may wish to use to convince the government and the citizenry of the cogency of his views, but he is not entitled to employ means that may be coercive or not completely rational in natural terms. Should his dream collapse and his efforts fail, the messianist in the final analysis will be bound by the will of the majority of the Jewish people living in Israel. The messianist can do no other and remain true to his beliefs.

We must understand and respect the workings of Providence in our time. According to Maimonides, God does not change the nature of humankind by miracles. It has never been His will to do so and it never will be.[28] The purpose of history is that human beings may come to God voluntarily out of their own free will. As the ultimate pedagogue, God exerts just the right amount of pressure, creates the right kind of historical situations so as to help human beings "see" their proper course to that they can make their "free" decisions. This is how we achieved a Jewish State. This is how we achieved a united Jerusalem. This is how we achieved a formal peace with Egypt. We strongly believe, though we are not certain, that when confronted by the next crucial historical situation, the people of Israel, and the messianists among them, will respond properly.

---

[28] Moses Maimonides, *Guide for the Perplexed*, trans. M. Friedlander (New York: E. P. Dutton & Co., 1942), III:32.

Acknowledgements

Nineteen of the twenty chapters in this volume have appeared over the years (1959-2008) as peer-reviewed articles in prominent journals. Although each deals with a different issue in Jewish thought, they have been grouped here in accordance with the type of philosophical approach they illustrate, as outlined in the Introduction. The articles are reprinted here with the kind permission of the following journals:

Tradition
Judaism
Modern Judaism
BDD Journal of Torah and Culture, Bar Ilan University
Torah Umada Journal
Perspective
Morasha
Forum

Index

A

Aaron, 120, 127–28, 140–41, 151–53
Abarbanel, Isaac, 79, 102, 147, 159, 215, 338
Abraham, 47, 68, 75–76, 80, 92, 122–25, 154–55, 168, 181, 214, 304–5, 309, 317, 343, 347, 367
acceptance, 24, 32, 52, 71, 78, 149, 319, 325–28, 333–34, 336, 361
Adam, 84, 98, 101, 103, 106–7, 113, 230, 269, 283
aesthetics, 19, 275–77; *see also* beauty
    aesthetic experience, 276–78, 280–81, 284–87, 290, 292, 294, 297–98
    aesthetic qualities, 286, 291, 294–95, 364–65
    aesthetic value, 50, 190, 279, 285–86
agent, 170, 172, 176, 199–201, 244, 254, 263
Akiva, Rabbi, 26, 51, 223, 230–32, 257–58, 356
Albo, Joseph, 27, 38, 66–67, 183, 209, 236–38
aliyah, 345, 350–54, 360–63, 367, 380–81
Alkalay, Y., 373
Alroy, David, 355
Amital, Yehuda, 307
analogical predication, 173, 179
animals, 18, 93, 106, 163, 223–24, 288
    domestication of, 94–95, 309
Anthropic Principle, 299, 301–2
Aquinas, Thomas, 173, 179
art, 42, 46, 69, 82, 192–93, 221, 275–78, 281, 285–88, 365
artist, 82, 193, 275–79, 281, 283, 287–88, 292, 294
Aviezer, Nathan, 90, 299
Azzai, Ben, 230–32

B

Bachya, 30, 209–10, 233
Balaam, 64, 129–32, 142, 151
Balak, 122, 131, 142, 147, 151
Bar Kochba, 56, 303, 355–56, 362, 368, 372–73
Barrett, William, 235
Barrow, John D., 301, 332
Barth, Karl, 74
beauty, 19, 39, 128, 192, 242, 278, 283, 288–90, 298; *see also* aesthetics
belief, 31–32, 35, 38–39, 52, 79, 83, 122, 131, 166, 180, 237, 245, 265–66, 273, 320–28, 331, 368–70, 376, 378–80, 384
    degrees of, 319, 334–35
    Jewish, 10–11, 24–25, 357
    rational/reasoned, 161, 206–7, 318, 322–24, 327, 333
    religious, 9, 18–19, 28, 31, 52, 163, 195, 199, 244, 275n, 311, 316–18, 321–23, 325–27, 335, 375
    traditional, 135, 274, 322
believers, 9, 21, 91, 96, 166, 368–70, 374, 376, 378
Berkovits, Eliezer, 33, 172, 346
Bethuel, 122, 124–25
Bible, 24, 26–27, 29, 37, 74, 76, 79, 91, 121, 133, 142, 154–55, 163–64n65, 167, 169, 194, 214–15, 222–30, 232–33, 241–42, 267, 306, 316, 339; *see also* Torah
Big Bang, 86–87, 90, 164, 309; *see also* creation
Black, Jeremy, 110
Borowitz, Eugene, 71, 73
Brahe, Tycho, 310
Bright, John, 155
Buber, Martin, 33, 157n52, 162–63, 342

C

Campbell, Norman, 329
Canaan, 12, 83, 85, 91, 123, 162
Chomsky, Noam, 202
Clarke, W. Norris, 178
codes, 18, 138, 140–41, 185, 187, 189, 191–92, 275
  moral, 49, 220–22
command, 66, 75, 103–4, 113, 118, 145, 182–83, 188, 210, 294, 297, 336
commandments, 16–18, 49–51, 62, 78, 83, 91, 99, 119, 134, 140–44, 147, 152–53, 157, 159–60, 184, 190–92, 213, 217, 225–28, 230, 235–39, 268, 272, 319, 324, 328, 369
  negative, 45, 236, 238
  ritual, 226, 229–30
command of God, 50, 103, 147, 149
consciousness, 66, 100, 102, 106–7, 112, 191, 199, 231, 236, 245, 251n18, 254–55, 260, 274, 378, 381
  historical, 311, 375
  human, 50, 52–53, 223, 244
  Jewish, 49, 54
  religious, 12, 15, 54, 60, 230, 235, 289
cosmology, 86, 88, 96, 299–301, 313
covenant, 47, 62, 128, 146, 154–59, 162, 225, 227–28, 269, 286, 297–98, 304, 339
  book of the, 157–58
creation, 10, 61, 63, 89–90, 116–18, 155, 190, 193, 198, 216, 222, 234, 240–41, 268, 283–86, 288, 293–95, 325n19
  seventh day, 292, 294–95, 298n82
  story of, 86-87, 92, 96, 98, 100, 115, 143, 223
creator, 13, 16, 31, 38, 103, 111, 117, 162, 171, 206, 223n10, 240–41, 292, 297, 336
Crescas, Chasdai, 38, 209, 234, 236–37, 240
Crombie, I. M., 177

D

death, 55, 57–58, 63, 65, 67, 70, 75, 101, 182, 217, 252, 262, 265–67, 304, 309, 331
deeds, 26, 61, 116–17, 133, 182, 191–92, 207, 224, 237, 252, 313, 323
demut (likeness), 109, 195, 226, 258
derech eretz, 44–45, 47, 50, 54
Deuteronomy, 83, 85, 119, 134, 141–42, 146–50, 158, 162
devar Hashem, 271–73
Dewey, John, 277, 291–93, 295
Diamond, Jared, 94–95
Diaspora, 307, 346, 348, 358, 361, 367, 373, 377, 380
doctrine, 32, 47, 66, 72, 133–34, 170, 181, 201–2, 229, 289, 354, 371
Documentary Hypothesis, 135–36

E

Eden, 28, 46, 78, 84–85, 96, 98–100, 103, 109, 111–13, 155, 224, 265, 286
Efros, Israel I., 253
Egypt, 91, 120, 125–29, 143n24, 145, 153, 155, 213–14, 304–5, 314, 342–44, 384; *see also* Exodus, exile
emunah, 316, 319–21, 323, 327–28
Eretz Yisrael, 22, 145, 307–8, 314, 346, 352, 357, 360–63, 373–75, 379–80, 383
essence, 16, 69, 168–73, 175, 209, 225, 246, 272, 289, 358
Esther, Queen, 366
Eternal Life, 84, 101
ethical theory, 18, 220–21, 224–25, 230, 241–42
Eve, 84, 98, 101, 107, 113, 269
evil, 47, 56–58, 66, 75, 78, 84, 101, 105, 110–12, 116, 203, 216–18, 221, 232, 248, 252, 259, 313, 349
  inclination; see *yetzer ha-ra*
  moral, 19, 222, 243
  problem of, 30, 77, 169, 180
  reality of, 72, 74–75

Index

evolution, 89, 93, 96, 301–2, 313
exile, 20, 43, 214, 265, 303, 308, 310, 340, 346, 348, 351, 358, 362–63, 366–67, 373; see also *galut*
existence, 31, 60, 67, 69, 85–89, 104–5, 177, 199–200, 240–41, 254–55, 266–67, 297–98
    fact of, 10, 14, 17, 24
    human, 59, 63, 68, 111, 190, 283, 290, 309n26
    of God, 10, 15-16, 35, 78, 168-69, 190, 199, 205, 208-9, 235, 300, 320, 334-35
Existential element, 73–74
Existentialism, 12, 69–78, 80
Exodus, the, 31–32, 51, 91, 128, 138, 150, 297, 304–5, 342–44, 346, 353, 362
Exodus (book), 48, 83, 119, 139, 143, 146, 150, 153, 155, 162, 170, 217, 293
experience
    human, 15, 86, 106, 110, 172, 176–78, 201
    moral, 111, 204, 223, 231, 256, 329, 331
    personal, 31, 321–22, 324
explanatory theory, 329–32, 336

F

Fackenheim, Emil, 343n8
faith, 24, 31–32, 53, 68, 76, 79, 111, 117, 125, 164, 208, 210, 218, 265, 319–22, 328n24, 354–55, 376
    facts of, 32, 36, 39
    "leap of faith," 78, 80, 115n26, 163, 207
    perfect, 334, 374–75
    reasoned, 318
    religious, 25, 163, 318, 334
family, 62–63, 68, 123–24, 251, 293, 304, 343, 352, 378, 380
fear, 27, 63, 65–68, 73–75, 236, 268, 272, 288, 340, 368
Ferdinand, King, 314
Fertile Crescent, 94–95, 97
finitude, 62–64, 78, 218

Flood, 92–93, 95–97, 109, 111, 113, 155
free choice, 104, 106, 113, 203, 264, 377
freedom, 50, 63, 70, 105, 111–12, 116, 121, 195, 201–4, 207, 214, 239, 244, 256, 258, 274, 313
    contracausal, 201–3, 262–63, 265
Freud, Sigmund, 58–59, 246–47

G

galut, 43, 338, 340, 344, 347–48, 350–52, 359; see also exile
Gamaliel, Rabbi, 196
garden, 45, 84, 92, 100–104, 108, 113, 286; see also Eden
Genesis, 37, 63, 86–87, 91, 96, 98, 101, 105–6, 113, 115, 139, 143, 153, 155–56, 158–59, 231–32, 239, 257, 297
Gerondi, Jonah, 65
geulah, 43, 340, 344, 348; see also redemption
God, 14–20, 27–31, 36–39, 50–53, 55–56, 61–68, 73–80, 84–89, 102–108, 111–117, 130-54, 157–59, 166–200, 203–18, 221–43, 251–55, 264–73, *see also* Creator, existence, unity, word
    image of, 36, 47, 104, 109–10, 223–24, 231, 239, 243, 251, 255, 257–58, 273
    knowledge of, 15, 31, 164, 166, 168, 170, 179, 187–88, 193, 196, 204, 228, 268, 282
    living, 34, 119, 131–32, 184, 188, 270
    love, 17, 62, 183, 185, 225, 257, 276, 282–285, 335
    nature of, 10, 43, 265
    service of, 72, 126–29, 162, 210, 213, 247–249, 304
    voice of, 19, 118–20, 144, 248, 290
    ways of, 88, 90-92, 96
Gordis, Robert, 354
Green, Anthony, 110

guilt, 61, 63, 65, 78, 106, 250–51
Guttmann, Julius, 175, 186, 189

H

Halakhah, 13, 18, 26–27, 34, 36–39, 42–44, 51, 54, 77, 119, 238, 295, 328, 362
   philosophy of, 37
Halevi, Yehuda, 29, 31, 73, 233, 317
Handelman, Susan A., 120
Hartmann, N., 193
Hebrew, 103, 110, 118, 125–26, 155–56, 215, 256, 259, 270, 320
Heilman, Samuel C., 41
HeMeiri, Menachem, 51
Herzl, Theodore, 378
Heschel, Abraham J., 32, 77–78, 271–72
Hirsch, Samuel, 32–33, 35, 38, 48–49, 52
historicism, 371, 375
history, 21, 36, 91–92, 94, 113–14, 116, 121, 161, 213, 215–16, 306, 308–9, 312–15, 329, 339, 342–43, 362–63, 371–72, 379
   dynamics of, 11, 311
   early, 48n18, 143, 155, 160
   human, 46, 91, 95, 156, 214, 218, 222, 232, 257, 272, 289, 324, 346
   Jewish, 7, 18, 135, 172, 299, 303–5, 306, 308, 310, 312–14, 318, 365
   Jewish concept of, 20, 212, 217, 346
   natural, 86, 88, 264
   philosophy of, 19-21, 26, 34, 37, 303
Holocaust, 314, 344, 346, 355
holy, 73, 119, 152, 157–58, 162, 196, 226–27, 235, 297
Hook, Sidney, 59
Hume, David, 53, 249, 254, 300

I

identity, personal, 240, 244, 255–56, 259
idolatry, 46, 122, 130, 222, 319

immortality, 99, 244, 265–67, 274
ingathering, 310, 348, 365, 367, 373–76, 380–81
intelligent life, 91, 301–2, 307, 332
interpretation, 13, 34, 52, 100, 110, 119–20, 268, 329, 347, 372
Isaac, 29, 75–76, 80, 122–23, 154–55, 168, 181, 347
Isaac of Corbiel, Rabbi, 213
Isabella, Queen, 314
Israel, 11, 33–34, 36, 65n29, 127, 157–59, 162, 216, 298, 303–4, 326, 328–29, 331–33, 342–47, 357, 360, 372–76, 379–84
   children of, 14, 134, 140, 145, 152-153, 298n82, 351
   people of, 20, 91, 119, 125–26, 128, 142, 213, 228, 235, 289, 297, 332, 365, 384
   rebirth of, 340, 342, 344, 354
   State of, 20–22, 30, 43, 48, 299, 307-312, 338–41, 343–51, 353–59, 364–70, 378, 380

J

James, William, 57–60, 69, 78, 338
Jeremiah, 10, 109, 117, 120, 139, 303, 362, 364
Jerusalem, 121, 305, 311, 345, 359, 362–63, 371
Jewish identity, 20, 155, 312, 324, 339n1, 358–59
Jewish life, 373, 377
Jewishness, 358–59, 361, 367
Jewish people, 21, 72, 91–92, 307–8, 311–12, 346–47, 352–55, 357–59, 361–66, 376–77, 379, 381–84
Jewish State; see Israel, state of
   sovereign, 355, 357, 375, 380, 382
Johnson, Paul, 378
Judaism, 7, 9–12, 19, 21–22, 26–28, 30–31, 33–35, 38–39, 50–52, 60–61, 67–68, 73–75, 114–15, 188, 220, 241–42, 244–45, 263, 265–66, 268–70, 289–90, 317-21, 327–32, 334–36, 357–61
   liberal, 55–57, 62, 71–72

morality, 7, 18, 180, 226, 231, 239, 275
  Orthodox, 31, 35–36, 39, 42–45, 48, 52, 54, 72–73
  practices of, 10–11, 24–25, 127, 133
  principles of, 29, 37, 74, 135, 182, 225
  traditional, 63, 66, 72, 209, 274, 318
justice, 30, 37, 48, 116–17, 194, 209, 213, 222, 224–26, 228–29, 237–41, 248, 250, 258, 266–67, 272, 342, 377
justification, 9, 28, 51–52, 64, 83, 237, 258
  rational, 237, 321–25, 332, 336

K

Kabbala, 75, 112–13, 318
Kadushin, Max, 119n6
Kahane, Meir, 368
Kalischer, Z. H., 371, 373–74
Kaplan, Mordechai, 46, 71
Katz, Jacob, 369–72, 375–76
Kaufmann, Yehezkel, 161, 163, 215
Kierkegaard, Soren, 63–64, 68, 71, 75-76
  Fear and Trembling, 76
Klal Yisrael, 54, 360–61, 363
knowledge, 11, 15, 22, 31, 43, 47, 51, 87–88, 99, 101, 104, 110, 155, 174–75, 180, 233, 235, 248–50, 320–21, 325–27, 334, 336
  human, 21, 67, 176, 184
  of good and evil, 84, 100-1, 252
  theoretical, 46, 50
kohanim, the, 151–53

L

Lamm, Norman, 354
language, 12–15, 82–87, 96, 118–19, 138, 148, 176–78, 180-81, 199, 223, 287, 319, 361
law, 9, 12–13, 18, 62, 83, 142, 152–53, 178, 221, 227, 230, 237, 242, 262, 360, 371
  Divine, 27, 50, 137, 143, 224

  meaning of, 133n2
  natural, 90-91, 329
  philosophy of, 37, 42
  scientific, 42, 121, 282, 301n7, 329n26
Leviticus, 139, 151–52, 162
Liebman, Charles S., 41
likeness, 115, 195, 230, 258
Livni, Menachem, 379n26
love, 43, 47, 117, 180, 211, 236, 242–43, 249, 267–68, 283, 285, 287–90, 297–98, 342
  as commandment, 16-17, 182-183, 187, 230-231, 238-39
  of God, 62, 183–91, 193, 234, 238, 243, 276, 282, 290, 322
loving-kindness, 116, 232, 234, 268, 272
Luzzatto, Moses Hayyim, 29, 39, 73, 78, 217

M

Maharal, 212, 239
Maimonides, 10, 29–30, 39, 133, 136, 233–35, 250n14, 282, 320, 349, 374, 384
  criticism and acceptance of, 25, 52-53, 167–68, 170, 174, 179-81, 184-186, 189-192, 197-199
  thirteen principles, 27, 135, 265
  views of, 14-17, 78, 166–75, 183, 186-88, 251
Mansel, Henry, 180
Maritain, Jacques, 290
martyr, 208–9, 218
Medieval Jewish Philosophy, 29, 236, 318, 325
megilla, 137–38, 150, 155
mercy, 30, 117, 170, 180, 225, 228–29, 240, 267, 342
Messiah, 29, 91, 266, 349–50, 373–74
messianic, 34, 56, 213, 217, 306, 347, 349–50, 354–55, 378, 382
  beliefs, 368, 372, 375, 383
  determinism, 370–72, 376, 379–80
  redemption, 293, 303

390

messianism, 21–22, 368, 371, 375–76, 378–80, 384
   traditional, 370, 372–76, 378, 380
Midian, 120, 129–30
midrash, 25, 36, 76, 83, 116, 120, 149, 156n51, 197, 201, 209–11, 229–30
miracles, 48, 93, 203, 264–65, 326, 342, 345, 347, 374, 384
mishkan, 143–44, 147, 151
Mishneh Torah, 187, 191, 352
mishpatim, 137, 139–41, 146, 150, 156, 227, 230, 237–38
mitzvah, 25, 27, 78–79, 137–39, 185, 187, 193, 202, 234, 292, 335, 340, 342, 350–52, 360–62
Moab, 129–30, 151
Moore, G. E., 193
morality, 7, 9, 42, 129, 194-95, 223–27, 229–36, 239, 241–43, 262, 382-84
   code, 18, 49, 220-22
   in Judaism, 18, 188-189, 220, 231, 239, 244, 275
   moral good and evil, 19, 110-11, 190, 192, 222, 241, 243, 256
moral rules, 46, 226, 231, 236
Moses/Moshe, 12–14, 34, 49n19, 76, 120, 122, 125–29, 133–63, 170, 214, 216–17, 227, 248, 273, 304–5, 316, 323–24, 344, 353
music, 19, 275, 279–80, 287, 361, 365

N

name, 101–2, 110, 169, 184, 187, 200, 210-12, 216–18, 255, 282, 286, 317, 320, 346-47
nature, 9, 34, 47, 58, 60, 79, 88–91, 97, 184–85, 190, 203–4, 244, 246–48, 261, 264, 278, 281–83, 287–89, 329, 332, 335, 339
   constants of, 301-2
   human, 52, 65-66, 70, 75, 84, 96, 100, 105, 112-13, 243, 250
   spiritual, 64, 118
nature of God, 10, 43, 154, 169, 194-95, 234–35, 265
negative theology, 167, 170, 173

neshamah, 245, 247, 251, 253–54, 258
Neumark, David, 317, 325
Noah, 92–93, 95, 111, 155, 214, 223–24, 269, 286, 373
Noahide Laws, 110, 224

O

optimism, 34, 56–58, 62, 68
Orthodoxy, 28, 43–45, 55, 72, 77, 80, 352

P

Palestine, 314, 371, 376, 379
Paley, William, 300–301
Panim, Hester, 344
Patriarchs, 74, 92, 125, 143, 145n24, 153, 155–56, 160, 222, 269, 309n26, 343, 347
Pentateuch, 114, 133, 135, 138, 147–48, 150–51, 161–62, 214, 216–17, 268, 303
perception, 21, 44, 98, 106, 171, 241, 254, 260, 285, 292, 350, 364, 367–68
   sense, 34, 277–78, 326
perfection, 175, 180, 215, 236–38, 241
   spiritual, 67, 237
perspective, 10–11, 22, 113, 122, 127, 285, 288, 313, 318
pessimism, 55–56, 58–61
Pharaoh, 122, 125–30, 146–47, 154, 156, 314, 343, 346
philosophers, 25, 31, 42, 166, 168, 181, 204, 208, 211, 265–66, 271, 273–74, 288
   medieval Jewish, 317, 320–21
philosophical analysis, 18, 33, 37–38, 168, 220, 287, 329
philosophy, 10–11, 18–19, 26, 38–39, 42, 52, 59–60, 70, 181, 199, 233, 244–45, 274, 317–19, 325, 327
   contemporary, 24, 29, 35, 201, 206, 259, 266
   Jewish, 20-21, 29, 33, 35, 37, 236, 318, 325, 358

of religion, 9, 25, 28, 44, 186
Pinker, Steven, 251n16
Plantinga, Alvin, 205–6
Plato, 19, 85, 245–47, 249–50, 275, 371
Popper, Karl R., 371–72
Prall, D. W., 277–80
privation, 174–75, 179
probability, 115, 300, 319, 333–36
process
   historical, 13, 16, 18, 339, 377
   prophetic, 12, 133, 136–37, 144, 150-51, 154, 156, 160
   reasoning, 79, 104, 106
   redemptive, 16, 315, 351, 372-73, 382
progress, 304–6, 346
   theory of, 299, 305–6, 308, 312
proofs, 17, 28, 64, 257, 300
prophecy, 12, 36, 118, 121, 136, 159, 227, 244, 262, 269–74, 332, 347–48, 371
prophets, 74, 131–32, 136, 148, 161n59, 202, 212, 228–29, 269–73, 281–82, 303, 316–17, 321, 347–48, 362–64
propositions, meta-halakhic, 38–39
Providence, 48, 61, 172, 198, 299, 308, 311, 340, 366, 371, 374–75, 382–84
Psalms, 66, 74, 153
punishment, 20, 37, 62, 91, 107, 230, 249, 252, 265–67, 342, 353, 364

R

Rabinovitch, Nachum, 345n14
Rabinowitz, Aaron, 245n1
Rackman, Emanuel, 7
Rashi, 26, 29, 103, 108, 137, 158, 212, 283, 296–97, 347, 351
rationality, 25, 52–53, 117, 163, 327, 335, 370–72, 382–83
Rawidowicz, Simon, 189
reason, 33, 50–51, 71, 78, 102, 104–8, 116, 204, 217, 235, 245–47, 316–19, 323, 335
   failings of, 70, 73–74, 80, 111

human, 52–55, 100, 249–50n14, 251n18, 266, 319
role of, 70, 265, 316, 326
Rebecca, 124–25
redemption, 16, 20–21, 26, 44, 54, 91, 213–17, 265, 304, 306, 308–10, 338, 340, 345–46, 350, 364–65, 367, 373–74, 380–81; see also *geulah*
   beginning of, 363–66
   ultimate, 213–14, 217
Reform, 43, 55, 70–72
religion, 12, 19, 25, 46, 57, 61, 72, 77, 79, 128, 134, 186, 188, 194, 199, 220, 227, 233, 270, 321–22, 325, 331, 368
religious beliefs; see beliefs, religious
religious experience, 19, 51, 73, 172, 181, 183, 276, 330, 340, 348
religious Jews, 52, 54, 202, 276, 281, 289, 295, 339–41, 346–48, 351, 356, 360–62, 366, 369
religious philosophy, 25, 28, 77
repentance, 64–65, 107, 213–14, 216
responsibility, 37, 47, 61, 63, 105, 107–8, 117, 256, 258, 308, 360, 366–67, 369
   moral, 201–2, 263, 331
revelation, 26, 31, 37, 51, 71–72, 79, 136, 138, 140, 148, 153–54, 158–59, 216, 225, 269, 273, 317, 319, 324, 326–28, 343
reward, 252, 265–66
righteousness, 30, 116, 194, 202, 222, 224–29, 231, 237–41, 243, 248, 250, 265–68, 342
ritual, 71, 133, 227, 229, 259
Roberts, David, 73
Russell, Bertrand, 24

S

Saadia Gaon, 10, 29–30, 66, 209, 234, 240, 246–47, 253, 325–26
Sabbatai Zvi, 354–55
Sabbath, 38, 49, 59, 119, 133, 290, 292–98, 352
sacrifices, 75–76, 126, 128–29, 228–29, 345, 376

sages, 12, 17–18, 36, 51, 98, 109–10, 117, 173, 237, 328, 359, 367
Salanter, Israel, 62, 252
Samuelson, Norbert, 166, 168
Santayana, George, 278
Schechter, Solomon, 26
Scheler, Max, 193
Scholem, Gershom, 112, 118, 368
Schonfeld, Moshe, 341n5
Schroeder, Gerald L., 309
science, 28, 30, 50, 70–72, 86, 199, 262, 277, 301–2, 307, 327, 329–32, 334, 344–45, 366
  development of, 310, 312, 319, 361
  Judaism and, 275, 299
  modern, 91, 94–95, 202, 327
scientific theories, 35–36, 329
sefer habrit, 158–59
Sefer ha-Mitzvot, 189–91
self, 17–19, 53, 63–64, 192, 194, 196, 198–99, 201–7, 231, 244–48, 251–57, 260–68, 271, 335
  knowledge of, 195–96, 204, 252, 254
  sense of, 100, 105, 112
  true, 63, 248, 252
self-consciousness, 106, 202, 223, 255, 267
self-identity, 18, 255–56, 258–59, 268, 274, 291, 293, 311
self-image, 106–7, 366
self-theory, 39, 244–46
serpent, 84, 101–2, 107–10, 112
service, 67, 72, 126–29, 131, 185, 232, 296
seudot, 293, 295–96
Shabbat, 100, 105, 113, 163, 292, 294–98
Shema, 29, 78, 208, 210–12, 218, 328
signs, 125, 159, 163–64, 286–87, 289, 298, 310, 316, 339–40, 346, 349, 365, 374
Sinai, 31, 48–49, 119, 139–40, 143, 156, 158, 224–25, 304, 316, 323, 329, 338, 342
singularity, 16, 21, 86, 96, 322–23

sins, 20–21, 61–62, 64, 66, 78, 103, 107, 143, 154, 248, 272, 353, 363
Six-Day War, 349, 368, 380–82
Solomon, King, 27, 56, 183, 305
Soloveitchik, Joseph B., 12, 27, 47, 73–74, 77, 164, 189, 235n37, 258, 276, 324, 339–40, 340n3, 352n27
Sommers, Fred, 167–68, 181
soul, 17–18, 68, 90, 185, 196–98, 200, 236–38, 244, 251–54, 259, 261–62, 267, 274, 320, 325, 330, 335
  additional, 296–97
  human, 203, 265–66
  longing for God, 66, 184, 188
Spain, 28, 314, 366
Spero, Shubert
  Morality, Halakha and the Jewish Tradition, 220n, 224n13, 313n28
spirit, 10, 28, 60, 111–12, 132, 149, 176–77, 199–201, 246, 253, 261, 264, 269, 312, 338, 344, 359, 378
spiritual substance, 261, 263, 265, 267, 271, 274
statutes, 46, 48, 83, 153, 162, 214, 226–27, 236
Stollman, Isaac, 353
subjectivity, 34, 176, 198, 200–201, 255
  pure, 253, 255

T

Tabernacle, 143, 145, 147, 150
Taylor, Charles, 255–56, 258
teleological argument, 190, 205–6, 300–301
theodicy, 10, 166–67, 313
theologians, 15, 17, 25, 32, 37, 78, 80
theology, 9, 14, 17, 19, 28–29, 35–36, 38–40, 80, 107, 178, 233, 244, 353
  depth, 32
  Jewish, 10–11, 20, 22, 25–27, 30, 32–34, 36–37, 40, 52, 64, 257

natural, 31, 205
Tillich, Paul, 63, 65, 78
Tipler, Frank J., 301, 332
Torah, 15–16, 19, 26, 33–34, 36, 42–49, 54, 79, 86–93, 99–100, 125, 133–42, 159–64, 170–71, 182, 189, 226–28, 230–32, 251–52, 256–57, 324–26, 360–62
   interpretation of, 50-52, 83-84, 284-87
   language, 12-14, 83, 100, 124, 188, 255, 269-70
   revelation of, 14, 38–39, 157
   written, 9, 12–13, 82, 109, 119, 121, 144, 146–49, 152-154, 273, 324
Torat Hashem, 14, 133, 159, 164, 273
Torat Moshe, 14, 133, 159, 257, 273
tradition, 16, 19, 27–28, 31, 36, 51, 79, 156, 251, 295–96, 308, 313–14, 317–19, 342, 368, 374, 379
   Jewish, 13, 59-60, 220, 248, 307, 321, 349
   oral, 144, 147, 150-51
   religious, 48, 326, 340
Tree of Knowledge, 28, 84, 87, 100–105, 107, 110–11, 284
Tree of Life, 101, 108
truth, 35, 37, 58, 70, 79, 98, 122, 128, 168, 186, 266, 327–28, 334, 348, 361
   and falsity, 50, 53, 371
   cognitive, 190, 192, 324
   seeking, 9, 166

U

unity, 15–16, 29, 141, 152, 162, 169, 171, 173, 181, 208–18, 275, 285, 291, 294, 305
   of God, 25, 56, 168, 209–12, 216
universe, 11, 19, 86–87, 89, 172, 175, 177–78, 197–99, 202–6, 276, 282, 289–90, 297–98, 319, 330–34
   creation of, 10, 16, 47, 87, 190, 206
   physical, 17, 198-99, 281, 301-2

V

value, 28, 43, 47, 60, 114-16, 152, 218, 221, 239–42, 259, 263, 302, 307, 310, 312, 336
   aesthetic, 50, 190, 279, 285–86
   apprehension of, 190, 193, 268, 283, 289
   intrinsic, 192, 229, 243, 289–90

W

wandering, 91, 344, 353, 363; *see also* exile
Weizmann, Chaim, 378
word of God, 13, 22, 118–23, 125, 129–31, 133, 135, 142, 144, 147, 149, 156-57, 159–60, 163-64, 251, 269-71, 273, 283, 319, 348
words, 12, 24–26, 32, 109–10, 140, 158–59, 176–77, 208–9, 228, 273, 328, 364
   meanings, 13, 121, 130, 179, 241, 284–85, 321
   use of, 83–84, 124-125, 147, 156, 199-200
Wouk, Herman, 72
Wurzburger, Walter S., 38–39
Wyschogrod, Michael, 35

Y

yetzer ha-ra, 18, 46, 110, 112, 248–49, 251–52
yetzer tov, 18, 248–49, 251–52
Yishuv Eretz Yisrael, 352–53, 359, 361–62

Z

Zion, 299, 345, 366–67
Zionism, 357–58, 375, 377–79
   religious, 357, 359–60, 362–63
   secular, 357–58
   ideology, 339, 377, 379
Zoma, Ben, 51